ADVENTURES

IN THE

WILDS OF THE UNITED STATES

AND

British American Provinces.

BY

CHARLES LANMAN,

AUTHOR OF "ESSAYS FOR SUMMER HOURS," "PRIVATE LIFE OF DANIEL WEBSTER," ETC., ETC.

ILLUSTRATED BY THE AUTHOR AND OSCAR BESSAU.

'Without registering these things by the pen they will slide away unprofitably —OWEN FELLTHAM.

WITH AN APPENDIX BY LIEUT. CAMPBELL HARDY.

IN TWO VOLUMES.

VOL. II.

PHILADELPHIA:

JOHN W. MOORE, No. 195 CHESTNUT STREET.

1856.

H. B. ASHMEAD, BOOK AND JOB PRINTER,

GEORGE STREET ABOVE ELEVENTH.

CONTENTS OF VOL. II.

A Tour to the River Restigouche:

	PAGE.
THE BAY OF FUNDY,	9
THE RIVERS ST. JOHN AND MIRAMICHI,	17
THE RIVER NIPISIGUIT,	24
THE BAY OF CHALEUR,	36
THE RIVER RESTIGOUCHE,	46
THE DISTRICT OF GASPE,	67
THE SOUTHERN SHORE OF THE ST. LAWRENCE,	81

A Winter in the South:

WASHINGTON TO SAVANNAH,	95
FLORIDA,	105
ST. AUGUSTINE,	114
BLACK CREEK AND TRAVELLING INCIDENTS,	125
THE SUWANEE RIVER AND WAKULLA FOUNTAIN,	133
THE CHATTAHOOCHEE RIVER,	146
HUNTSVILLE,	153
THE ALABAMA RIVER,	165
THE TOMBIGBEE AND BLACK WARRIOR RIVERS,	171
A JAUNT INTO MISSISSIPPI,	189
NEW ORLEANS,	199
THE LOWER MISSISSIPPI,	207
THE OHIO RIVER AND OVER THE MOUNTAINS,	213

Occasional Records:

THE SUGAR CAMP, - - - - - - - 221
ACCOMAC, - - - - - - - - 229
THE FUR TRAPPERS, - - - - - - - 238
ROCK CREEK, - - - - - - - - 245
A VIRGINIA BARBECUE, - - - - - - 256
RATTLESNAKES, - - - - - - - 260
A WESTERN PIONEER, - - - - - - 269
PLANTATION CUSTOMS, - - - - - - 273
DEATH IN THE WILDERNESS, - - - - - 280
THE CANADIAN RECLUSE, - - - - - - 284
TRIP TO WATCH HILL, - - - - - - 290
A WEEK IN A FISHING SMACK, - - - - - 300
A CHIP FROM BLOCK ISLAND, - - - - - 309
SALMON FISHING, - - - - - - - 316
TROUT FISHING, - - - - - - - 335
BASS FISHING, - - - - - - - - 345
ROCK FISHING, - - - - - - - 356
PIKE FISHING, - - - - - - - - 369
FISHING IN GENERAL, - - - - - - 387
INDIAN LEGENDS, - - - - - - - 394
APPENDIX, - - - - - - - - 481

ILLUSTRATIONS VOL. II.

THE PAPINEAU FALLS, - - - - - - - face page 27

ATHOL HOUSE, - - - - - - - - - " " 56

SPEARING SALMON, - - - - - - - - " " 65

VIEW ON THE ST. JOHN, FLORIDA, - - - - " " 109

GROUP OF GAME FISH, - - - - - - - " " 317

WINTER FISHING ON THE ST. LAWRENCE, - - " " 374

A TOUR

TO THE

RIVER RESTIGOUCHE.

ADVENTURES IN THE WILDS

OF THE

United States and British American Provinces.

THE BAY OF FUNDY.

ON the tenth day of June I left the city of Washington, accompanied by my wife, bound upon a summer tour to the River Restigouche, watering the provinces of New Brunswick and Lower Canada. I tarried in New York just long enough to run through the picture galleries, and replenish my stock of sketching materials and fishing tackle. On my way to Boston I was joined by a sister, whereby a party of three was formed, which being composed of an angler and two ladies was a capital arrangement; for while the former would have none to interfere with his sport, the two latter could so amuse themselves as to be quite independent of extra gentlemanly attentions.

To Portland we went by the Eastern railroad, the conductor of which, Mr. William Ackerman, an exceedingly polite and pleasant person, informed us that he had been stationed on this route, as stage-driver and conductor, for upwards of twenty-eight years. He also stated that the railroad had been in operation for thirteen years, and during this period not a single regular passenger had been killed by any accident to the cars. Mr. Ackerman spoke in a very pleasant manner of the many great men with whom he had become acquainted during his long-continued road business. He mentioned the names of Cass, Clay, and Calhoun; but of Webster, whom he knew better than all, he spoke in affectionate terms, and seemed to think it the prominent, and most mournful event of his life that he had been permitted to see his remains deposited in the tomb.

At Portland we took the steamer Admiral, for St. John. Passage made in twenty-four hours, and everything connected with our steamer was truly admirable, and with the Bay of Fundy exceedingly interesting. Shores and Islands bold and fantastic; rocks dark, gray and brown; waters deep blue; and the prospect seaward occasionally enlivened by the spouting of a whale, and always covered with a fleet of ships or fishing vessels. We had a favorable view of the island of Grand Manan, at the entrance to the Bay of Fundy, which is twenty miles long, five wide, well cultivated, and whose rock-bound shores are in some places six hundred feet high. To the Geologist, this island, and its more unpretending neighbors, present a most interesting field of observation; and, in some instances, for example, he will discover no less than a dozen distinct layers of different kinds of rock, each presenting the appearance of having been cut off by a sharp instrument, and these eccentric developments will astonish him, and puzzle his philosophy. The ornithologist also, as did our great Audubon, will find much here to delight him in his studies; for here the herring gull is found building its nests in the top of trees, and not upon the ground, whereby it abandons its ancient habit and resorts to an unusual instinct to preserve its eggs from the grasp of the greedy hunters; and, here too, will be found the breeding places of those famous little birds, the stormy petrels, which, during the breeding season, burrow into the soft ground or hide themselves in hollow rotten logs.

The lofty trap cliffs of Nova Scotia which loomed above the southern horizon were too remote to be appreciated, but we felt a little covetous as we thought of the splendid agates, cornelians, and amethysts which abound among them, some of which were picked up by the early French voyagers, and are at this day among the crown jewels of France.

I spent an hour or so on the forward deck of our goodly steamer, and had a pleasant chat with a party of Bay of Fundy skippers or fishermen, who had been to Boston upon a visit and were then returning to St. John to prepare for a new cruize. One of them, was, beyond all question, the very man Mr. Lorenzo Sabine honored with an introduction, some weeks ago, to the Secretary of the Treasury as a specimen of the race. Bred to the use of boats from his earliest youth, as Mr. Sabine has pleasantly written, he displays astonishing skill in their management, and great boldness in his adventures. He will cross, the stormiest weather, from island to island, and go from passage to passage through frightful whirls of tides which meet and part with a loud roar; and he will dive headlong, as it were, upon rocks and bars, merely to show how easily he can shun them, or how readily and certainly he can "go about" and stand off on the "other tack." He is neither landsmen nor seaman, a soldier nor a marine; but you would think by his talk that he could appear to advantage in either of these characters. He is neither a merchant nor a mechanic, and yet he can buy and sell, mend and make, as expertly as either. In the healing art he is wise above all others, and fancies that he possesses a sovereign specific for every aliment which all the world beside considers as incurable. He holds nautical instruments in high derision; for the state of the moon and the weather, predictions of the almanac, the peculiar sound of the sea when it "moans," and the particular size or shape of a "cat's paw" or "glin" in the sky, lead him to far surer results. He will undertake nothing of consequence upon a Friday, and can prove by a hundred incidents how infallible are the signs and omens which he believes in. He thinks to die in his bed. True it is that he has been overset; that his boat, loaded with fish to the "gunnel," has sunk under him, and that a vessel has run over him; but he is still alive and "was not born to be drowned." His "fish stories" are without end. In politics, he goes for the largest liberty. He has never heard of easements and prescriptive rights; but he occupies at will both beach and upland, without any claim to either, and will browbeat the actual proprietor who has the temerity to remind him of their relative positions. Against speculators he wages perpetual war; why should he not? since it is they who put up the price of his favorite "flat-hooped, fine middlings flour," and put down the price of fish and "ile!" And who shall do justice to his dress and to his professional gear? The garments which cover his upper and nether man he calls *ile sute.* The queer-shaped thing worn upon his crown is a *sou'-wester;* or, if the humor takes him, *north-easter.* He wears neither mittens nor gloves, but has a substitute which he has named *nippers.* When he talks about *brush,* he means to speak of the matted and tangled mass which grows upon his head; or the long, red hair under his chin, which serves the purpose of a neck-cloth; or of that in front of his ears, which renders him impervious to the dun of his merchant. His boots are *stampers.* Lest he should lose the moveables about his person, he has them fastened to his pockets by *lanyards.* One of his knives is a *cut-throat,* and another is a *splitter.* His apron, of leather or canvas, is a *barvel.* The compartment of his boat into which he throws his fish as he catches them is a *kid.* The state of the moon favorable for "driving herring," he calls *darks.* The bent-up iron hook which he uses to carry his burning torch on the herring ground, is a *dragon.* The small net with an iron bow and wooden handle, is a *dip-net,* because it is with that that he dips out of the water the fish which his light attracts to the surface. His *set-net* is differently hung, and much larger; it has leads on its lower edge to sink it in the water, and corks upon its upper edge, at regular intervals, to buoy it up and preserve it nearly in a perpendicular direction, so that the herrings may strike it and become entangled in its meshes. Nor ends his dialect here. Chebacco-boats and small schooners are known to him as *pinkies, pogies, jiggers.* He knows but little about the hours of the day and night; everything with him is reckoned by the tide. Thus, if you ask him what time he was married, he will answer, "On the young flood last night," and he will tell you that he saw a man this morning about "low-water slack;" or, as the case may be, "just at half-flood," "as the tide turned," or "two hours to low water." If he speaks of the length of line required on the different fishing-ground, he will compute by "shots;" he means thirty fathoms. If he have fish to sell and is questioned as to their size, he will reply that they are "*two quintal*" fish, by which he means that fifty will weigh one hundred and twelve pounds. He is kind and hospitable in his way; and the visitor who is treated to fresh smother, duff, and *jo-floggers*, may regard himself as a decided favorite. He believes in witches and in dreams. The famous pirate Kyd buried gold and treasure in Money Cove and Grand Manan, he is sure; and he has dug for it many a time. *His* "woman" is the "best;" the harbor *he* lives in is "the safest;" and *his* boat is "the fastest, and will carry sail the longest." When determined upon going home, whether he is upon the land or the sea, he says, "Well, I'll up killock and be off."

Among our fellow passengers were a husband and wife, who very deservedly excited general interest. The former had both eyes shot out of his head while on a hunting expedition, and subsequently, by another accident, had lost one of his legs. While in this condition, a beautiful and accomplished woman fell in love with him, and the twain, in the happiest mood, were now upon a pleasant tour.

We found St. John an uncommonly picturesque and romantic city, and its business greatly on the increase. At high water its harbor is one of the handsomest, and at low water, one of the most uninteresting on the Atlantic coast, and what is more, it is never frozen. St. John is built upon a rock and has some handsome buildings both public and private. Fifty years ago its site was covered with trees, and only a few straggling huts existed within its harbor, and it was first settled principally by American loyalists who came thither from Nantucket, after our Independence had been established. As is naturally the case in all the Colonial cities of England, European goods are much cheaper here than in the United States, and the supply of rich and beautiful fabrics is most abundant. The chief articles of exportation are lumber and fish, and the present population is nearly thirty-five thousand. The spacious harbor is filled with shipping, and, like all respectable cities each man seems to mind none other than his own business, while the society is excellent, polite and highly intelligent.

Since my arrival here I have learned with pleasure that the government of New Brunswick have concluded to make extensive scientific investigations, having for their object the elucidation of the remarkable tides of the Bay of Fundy. Able reports on this subject, on account of the fogs and winds which prevail here, are very much needed. On coming up the Bay, I noticed that at Eastport the tide rose some twenty-five feet, while at St. John it rises thirty; and I am informed that at the eastern extremities of the bay it rises some sixty-five feet. To the foregoing, during the spring tides, may be added the numbers five, ten and fifteen feet. By intelligent men who have witnessed its feats, I am told the coming of the tidal wave in some of the eastern estuaries is truly astonishing. It forms a perfect wall of blue waves, skirted with snowy foam, and travels with a rapidity far outstripping the fleetest horse. The beaches or shingles of sand which the receding water have exposed, extend at times a distance of several miles from the main land, and as these abound in various kinds of shell fish, it is customary for the swine of the neighboring farms to resort thither for the purpose of feasting upon the treasures of the deep, and it is a singular fact that long before the human eye and ear can detect the coming of the tidal wave, the acute senses of these brutes warn them of danger, and they flee to the shore for safety, and in spite of their fleetness it is frequently the case that they are overtaken and drowned. To the people of St. John the peerless salmon is a source of considerable profit. The fisheries of the harbor belong to the citizens of the city, and the fishing grounds or stations, are lotted out, or sold at auction, every year, for their benefit. The practical fishermen are the purchasers. The number of salmon taken in the last few years, has averaged about thirty-five thousand, which sold for as many dollars, to be packed in ice and sent to Boston. The fish are chiefly taken with drift nets and weirs.

A noble salmon, now being carried on the back of a boy under the window where I am writing, (one, by the way, of twenty caught by a single fisherman in the harbor of St. John this morning where the nets are staked out to within a few feet of the anchored ships,) reminds me of that great oceanic "kettle of fish" over which the two leading nations of the earth are at present holding a pow-wow. I am convinced that the tone of public opinion in this region on the political question at issue, is rapidly changing. The British provinces having recently become animated with a genuine spirit of enterprise; they are resolved to work out their own fortune, and the concessions they were willing to make to Brother Jonathan a year ago will never, I fear, be heard of more. We of the States have in this matter been too thoughtless and slow for our own good.

But if I cannot communicate to my reader any interesting information on the subject of the fisheries at large, I can give him a little gossip respecting the most distinguished angler and naturalist of this region. I allude to Moses H. Perley, Esq., Her Majesty's emigration officer at this port, whose pardon I hereby crave for mentioning his name. His family is one of the oldest in the province and although his grandfather and father were both honorably identified with its early history, neither of them accomplished as much as he, in adding to its fame and developing its resources. His taste for angling early led him to acquaint himself with the entire region formerly known as Acadia, but more especially with its finny tribes, and his various reports made officially to the colonial government, are exceedingly complete and valuable. Mr. Perley tells me that he performs an annual pilgrimage to remote parts of the country, that he has caught fish in every stream of any note which empties either into the Gulf of St. Lawrence or the Bay of Fundy. Many valuable collections of the rarer fishes and reptiles, as well as other natural curiosities, has he thus been enabled to make, and these he has presented to public institutions in which he felt an interest. The collection he is now forming is intended for the cabinet of his distinguished friend Professor Agassiz.

It may be well imagined that a person possessing the tastes of Mr. Perley would have an interesting depot for implements of sporting, and the spoils of forest and flood. His library is indeed just such a place. It is filled to overflowing with rare and curious books, rods of every style, (including one by Kelly, which has killed eight thousand trout,) guns of all kinds, busts, statuettes and pictures, unnumbered Indian curiosities, while moose and cariboo horns, ornament the walls, and stuffed animals every unoccupied shelf or bracket. In the centre of this charming room stands a large table, covered with the latest English periodicals and papers, upon which were written the several reports on the sea and river fisheries of New Brunswick and Nova Scotia already mentioned. On questioning Mr. Perley as to the number of fishes which he had catalogued and described in these reports, he informed me that they consisted of eighteen families, comprising forty genera and sixty-two species. With a very few exceptions all these fish are found in the waters of the United States. Mr. Perley has also done more than any other individual to perpetuate the history of the Indian tribes of New Brunswick, and in return for his kindness to one of the leading tribes, the Micmacs, he has been elected their Head Chief, and when decked out in his official dress his appearance is well nigh magnificent.

THE RIVERS ST. JOHN AND MIRAMICHI.

The distance from St. John to Bathurst is two hundred and forty miles, and I hardly know in what other direction one would travel to enjoy the same variety of charming scenery. I knew, from personal observation, that the upper portion of the river St. John, was remarkable for its beauty; but a summer-day's sail from its mouth to Fredericton, a distance of ninety miles, convinces me that it cannot be surpassed by any other stream in respect either to beauty or utility. This lower portion of the river which the Micmacs called *Looshtook* or Handsome River and which I have elsewhere touched upon, runs through a rich interval land, and is navigable for steamboats and small schooners, which do a thriving business. Just before entering the Bay of Fundy, however, the entire volume of its waters is forced through a limestone gorge, only one hundred and fifty yards wide, and running, as a matter of course, with great rapidity; and what is remarkable, when the tide of the Bay is high, a strong current sets inward from the sea. The result is, that a double fall of water is thus formed, the fresh water at one time descending twenty feet, and at another the salt water also descending, *up stream*, about fifteen feet. The time allotted to vessels for passing through this gorge is limited to perhaps one hour. For fifteen miles from its mouth the banks of the river are quite hilly, and as extensive bays or inlets come into it, both from the east and west, the expanse of water is occasionally very broad, and when dotted with sails and other evidences of civilized life, presents a most cheerful aspect. Extensive and picturesque meadows, with pleasant farm houses and drooping elms without number, attract the attention of the observer; and when these are connected with the singing of the birds, the tinkling of bells, the low murmurs of the dark and rapid stream, the immense floating rafts of lumber and logs, with their boarded cabins and red-shirted lumbermen, and also with an occasional Indian in his canoe, the impression left upon the mind is delightful in the extreme. The interval lands, which are highly cultivated, are of course annually covered with water, and it is the novel boast of some of the inhabitants that they gather two crops from the same land in one year—in the spring an abundance of herring, and in the autumn a crop of potatoes or grain. The hills lying remote from the river are also cultivated, evidently by a tasteful and industrious population. The steamers running on the river are small but comfortable, and like the people of New Brunswick generally, their officers are communicative and polite to all strangers. The total length of the river St. John is four hundred and fifty miles, and it waters a country comprising seventeen million square acres, nine millions of which are in New Brunswick, two in Canada and six in the United States.

The city of Fredericton, above which the larger vessels of the river do not ascend, occupies a perfectly level piece of interval land, flanked with hills on the western bank, and is one of the sunniest and most agreeable inland towns imaginable. Since it derives its chief importance from being the seat of government, it is an appropriate place of residence for retired gentlemen, who have congregated there to a considerable extent. It contains a number of handsome buildings, among which are the residence of the governor of the province, Sir Edmund Head, a college, the legislative buildings, with a small but good library, and a most polite librarian, and the barracks, which however, are only distinguished for occupying the pleasantest part of the town. In two particulars the town is far ahead of many more ambitious places; for it has a first-rate hotel, and a very elegant and substantial cathedral, built at a cost of $80,000, belonging to the established church of England, and in which a Lord Bishop preaches regularly.

From Fredericton we travelled in an open wagon; and after crossing the St. John, our course lay to the northeast, directly along the banks of the Nashwaak river. This is a stream to fall in love with, for it is rapid, clear, and wayward in its windings: but as it is crossed by one or two dams, its glory as a salmon stream is forever departed. At the mouth of it, however, capital bass-fishing may be enjoyed nearly all the summer. On leaving the Nashwaak about twenty miles from its mouth, we entered upon what was formerly an Indian portage, the crown of which is a ridge separating the streams emptying into the Gulf of St. Lawrence from those emptying into the Bay of Fundy. We struck the southwest and principal branch of the Miramichi at Bolestown, founded by an American, formerly a thriving place, but now a miserable hamlet, made up of the tottering remains of wooden houses, barns, mills, and mill-dams. At this point may always be found rare trout-fishing, and a dozen miles or more further up the stream a goodly number of salmon are annually taken with the fly. When I reached there, a couple of anglers from the States were already on the ground and others were expected.

We travelled down the Miramichi to where it is navigable for ships of the largest class, and were delighted with everything we saw and heard. This river derives its most appropriate name from the Micmac Indians, the meaning of which is the *Happy Retreat*. That it was a lovely and happy region in days of yore is quite evident, even from its present attractions. It is one of the largest rivers in the Province; its total length being two hundred and twenty miles, and its mouth nine miles in width, the tide flowing forty miles from the gulf. The lands on either side are fertile, the scenery rather tame but charming, and the farm houses scattered along its entire length have a cheerful and comfortable appearance. The inhabitants of the valley are of Scotch, Irish and English descent, and as a class, are intelligent, obliging, and industrious. In former times the traffic of the valley was extensive, for the forest afforded almost every variety of animals, yielding valuable furs, and then followed an extensive lumbering business, which at the present time only partially prospers, while ship-building and the exportation of fish are getting to be the chief sources of money-making. The attention devoted to agriculture thus far has been limited; but since all the crops growing in the Northern States, excepting corn, grow exceedingly well in this section of country, a decided change seems to be taking place, and the inhabitants are yearly tilling more soil. The four principal villages of the lower river are Nelson, Newcastle, Douglass and Chatham, the first occupying the junction of the northwest and southwest branches of the Miramichi, and the others, which are farther down, lying on both sides of the Bay of Miramichi. In the immediate vicinity of these busy little towns, which ought to have been concentrated into one, I counted at anchor no less than twenty large ships, and on the stocks some seven or eight, all bound to Great Britain, and thence to the remotest corners of the earth, as fortune might determine. The first ship that entered the mouth of the Miramichi was the frigate which took the remains of General Wolfe from Quebec to England in 1759, a storm having driven her in for safety.

Among the pleasant objects which attracted my attention while descending the Miramichi were the pretty churches, which occasionally loomed above the trees. Of these, five attracted my particular attention by their tasteful, gothic beauty; and on making inquiries about them, I learned the following facts: They are scattered over a space of fifty or sixty miles, and were built by *one* person, who, besides having accomplished this truly remarkable undertaking, is in the habit of supplying all his pulpits in person. Not only did he raise and expend the money for his churches, but they were built after his own designs, whereby he has proven himself quite an accomplished architect. He is an Episcopalian of the *higher order*, a native of Dublin, about forty years of age, and a bachelor. While superintending the erection of his churches, he usually occupied a room in the immediate vicinity of each, where he slept between his own sheets and on his own iron bedstead, to avoid the insect assassins of the country, and cooked his own victuals. All his thoughts have ever been, and still are, directed to the interests of mother church, and the only money he has recently expended for an entirely selfish purpose was invested in five iron bedsteads, which are the sleeping attachments of his several churches. As a preacher, I am told that the gentleman in question is really eloquent. As his self-established circuit is extensive, he is constantly on the move, travelling in a small one-horse wagon, and preaching as often as he possibly can in each of the churches, and all this without receiving a single farthing in the way of salary. And so much concerning the Rev. James Hudson.

But the deepest impression, in spite of the beauty everywhere seen, which a journey down the Miramichi is calculated to make, arises from the contrast presented by the rich lands of the country and the dwarfish or rather youthful appearance of the forest trees. In accounting for this, the older inhabitants will enter upon the oft repeated story of the great fire which in the year 1825 reduced to ashes some six thousand square miles of the fairest portion of New Brunswick, and fell particularly heavy upon the valley of the Miramichi. An eye-witness who resided on the river at the time, has furnished me with the following particulars respecting the calamity. The summer of 1825 was unusually warm and dry, and between July and October the smoke of burning forests arose in many portions of the upper province. These fires were not unusual, and for a time excited no apprehensions. But on the first of October an unnatural heat began to be felt all along the valley of the river, and on the sixth of the same month, the inhabitants were alarmed by the fitful appearance of immense sheets of flame in their immediate vicinity, while to their ears came the sound of falling trees, and a hoarse, rumbling sound, resembling distant thunder. On the seventh day the prevailing heat was oppressive and suffocating; and while in the morning a pale, sickly mist seemed to canopy the land, in the afternoon it was succeeded by an immense pall of vapor. Immediately on the river a gloomy silence prevailed, while the surrounding woods were in the greatest commotion. As night came on, a fiery zone seemed to encircle the land, and the air became filled with flaming brands and leaves, and as the roar of conflicting elements increased—for now a hurricane swept the hissing forests and lashed the river into fury—the horrors of the scene were increased by the crying and wailing of the inhabitants. The suffering and misery which followed can be better imagined than described. The fearful element accomplished its mission, and the entire country was one wide scene of blackened desolation. The number of persons who lost their lives by fire and water during the calamity was one hundred and sixty; buildings destroyed, about six hundred; cattle, nine hundred; and the total loss of personal property amounted to some two hundred and twenty-eight thousand pounds, including several entire villages. The destruction of timber was irreparable, and the effect upon the forest animals is felt at the present day in their great scarcity throughout the entire region. The sympathies of the humane, both in England and the United States, were excited in behalf of the sufferers in the Province, and a large amount of provisions and clothing was promptly forwarded to their relief. The cash subscriptions, as officially made known at the time, amounted to twenty-two thousand pounds, of which sum, about eighteen thousand pounds came from the United States.

The road from Miramichi to this place, (as it did all the way from Fredericton to Miramichi,) runs for the most part through what is known as the Burnt District, but is, nevertheless, quite agreeable. It is crossed by a number of beautiful streams, abounding in three to five-pound trout as well as salmon, where the angler can tire himself out with fly-fishing in a single day. The only one of these I had an opportunity of trying was the *Tabasintac*, and as I here threw my first fly for the season, the luck I enjoyed excited me beyond measure. I only fished for a single hour,—while our horses were being fed and watered,—and caught about a dozen *common* trout—not sea trout—the four largest weighing three and a half, three, two and a half, and two pounds each. I took them with the common red hackle, and in one pool, in the presence of my lady companions, and within twenty yards of the cabin where our horses where feeding. The scenery of the road in question is monotonous, but interesting on account of its primitive character; but as we approached the great basin of the Bay of Chaleur the prospect suddenly expanded into a wilderness of mountains, flanked by a marine view, which, when it first burst upon us as the sun was setting, was truly magnificent.

Before closing this letter, I ought to mention the fact that those who fancy stage-coach travelling will find the land route from St. John to the Miramichi, by way of the Bend, full of interest and quite comfortable. The time required to perform it is three days, and the first day's drive reveals to view a country abounding in arcadian charms called Sussex Vale; while the second day will bring the traveller to the small town but fine harbor of Shediac, where oyster-beds are inexhaustible; and the third day will take him through the flourishing ship-building port of Richibucto, in the vicinity of which it is asserted, Sebastian Cabot landed, on the main shore of this continent, in 1495.

THE RIVER NIPISIGUIT.

A PLEASANT and novel town, indeed, is this out-of-the-way Bathurst, whereof I am now to give a brief description. It is built upon two points of land, at the mouth of four rivers, the Nipisiguit, the Middle, the Little, and the Tootoogoose rivers, and at the head of a handsome but shallow bay. This sheet of water, from many points of view, resembles an inland lake, and is spanned by a well-constructed bridge half a mile in length. The harbor of Bathurst is secure for the smaller vessels of the coast, while those drawing more than twelve feet of water find a safe anchorage outside a bar which lies at the mouth of the bay. The town contains some six hundred inhabitants, and four churches, whose spires help to give it an attractive appearance. It has three ship-yards, from which are annually launched from five to ten handsome square-rigged vessels, and a very extensive lumbering establishment, belonging to Messrs. John and Francis Ferguson. The neighboring lands are well cultivated, and the scenery, in every direction, is exceedingly interesting. Next to lumber, its chief exportations are fish and a species of valuable grind-stone, as well as a good quality of slate; and I should imagine that its resources, in all these particulars, would give profitable employment to a large amount of capital. Its more influential inhabitants are English and Scotch; and I can say of them, that they are polite, intelligent, and accomplished to an uncommon degree, and a warm-hearted hospitality seems to be a part of their religion. It is also well supplied (and what North American town is not) with the sons and daughters of Erin, while the choppers of wood and the people of the water are Acadian French. The first white man who is said to have set his foot upon its soil was a French fisherman or walrus hunter, named Jean Jacques Enaud, and this he did as early as the year 1638. It is said he was married here to a Mohawk woman of distinction, and that, in consequence of some private pique, he was murdered by one of her brothers. At that period, the spot which it now occupies was the headquarters of the Micmac Indians, by whom their village was named Winkkapiguwick, which subsequently degenerated into Nipisiguit, or the place of troubled waters. During the dominion of the French it was known as St. Peter, and the name which it now glories in is that of one of the most honored of the Colonial Secretaries of Great Britain. Its hotel accommodations might be improved, and ought to be without any delay (for the home of the stranger in a foreign land ought always, for the sake of that land, to be comfortable and agreeable;) but, on account of its scenery, its healthfulness, excellent society, and especially its manifold piscatorial attractions, it is a place deserving a world-wide reputation.

As before intimated, the entire region of country lying on the Atlantic Coast of New Brunswick was originally inhabited by the Micmac Indians, and the people whose hunting-grounds joined theirs at the Bay of Chaleur were the Mohawks. These two nations were originally, and for many years, upon the most friendly terms with each other. On the very spot where I am now writing they often smoked the pipe of peace together; but in process of time, as the local tradition runs, a quarrel took place between them, which the shedding of much blood could not reconcile. It originated in the fact that two boys, a Micmac and a Mohawk, fell out with each other while shooting at a target with a bow and arrow, and had a severe fight. The fathers of the boys took up the quarrel, and as they could not settle it, the two nations took it up, when a severe conflict transpired. The Mohawks were beaten, and retreated to the Restigouche, some sixty miles further north. Another battle took place on that river, and the Mohawks were again vanquished. They retreated into the interior and again concentrated their forces, but at midnight the Micmacs fell unexpectedly upon them, and the small remnant left to relate the story of their extinction as a nation made their way to Canada, and the Micmacs were the sole masters of their immense hunting-grounds.

Of the four rivers which help to make Bathurst an attractive place, the Little and Middle rivers are chiefly interesting for their wildness and good trout-fishing, but the Tootoogoose—which in the Indian tongue, means the river of the fairies—is exceedingly beautiful. It is twenty-five miles long, winding in its course, and runs over a rocky bottom; it has also two or three picturesque rapids and falls, and affords first-rate trout and tolerably good salmon-fishing. And then again along its banks is to be found in abundance the curious plant called *Myrica Cerifera*, which yields a whitish wax, out of which the Acadians make a very good candle.

But the Nipisiguit is by far the most splendid river in this region, and for salmon-fishing, with the fly, I suppose it has not its superior in the world. It rises in the same Alpine wilderness which gives birth to the Tobique, (a tributary of the St. John, and most successful rival in point of beauty,) and its length is one hundred miles. It is marvelously clear, and runs with great rapidity—for the first half of its length over a granite bed, and thence to the sea, with two or three granite exceptions, over a calcareous formation. It may be well imagined, therefore, that it is by no means a monotonous stream. Aside from the gloom and grandeur of the mountain scenery at its source, and from its many lovely tributaries, it boasts of falls and rapids which are interesting in the extreme, and it is from these that it derives its name of *Nipisiguit* or Foamy River.

Twenty miles from Bathurst are the Great Falls, which it would seem Nature had deemed so beautiful that she encased them in flint and granite. For miles, above and below the "jumping-off place," the river is very much contracted, and the banks rocky and perpendicular. The total height of these falls is one hundred and forty feet, the leaps consisting of four,

VAN-INGEN—SNYDER.

THE PAPINEAU FALLS.

the last two only being visible from below; at the foot of each are deep basins, and below them for about a mile, a number of pools and rapids, whose gloomy but fascinating features are greatly enhanced by the prevailing roar, and by the blending together in some places of the black water with the white foam. The cliffs on either side are crowned with dense foliage, kept particularly green by the spray immediately at the falls, and affording a delightful retreat for the birds. But, while the Great Falls can never fail to delight the artist and poet, they are a great bug-bear to the lumbermen, whose logs and neatly-hewn timber they frequently curtail of their proportions, and not unfrequently wholly destroy, while passing through the chasm. After escaping from the gorge below the Grand Falls, the Nipisiguit pursues a quiet course between low banks for a little more than three miles, when it tumbles over a succession of ridges called the Chain of Rocks; and three or four miles still further down, is another charming spot known as the Middle Landing. Just below this spot there is a splendid pool with a charming rocky island in it, called *Betaboc* or Rock Island in the Long Pool, and a pleasanter camping-ground could hardly be imagined. The scenery at these several localities is by no means imposing, but it is full of interest to those who love the wayward and fantastic play of the purest waters, and all those indescribable charms peculiar to the lone wilderness.

And then again some seven miles from Bathurst we have what are called the Papineau, or Cranberry Falls, which consist of a series of schutes and small falls, declining perhaps within the space of half a mile, at an angle of thirty degrees. The rocks, which are a gray granite, frequently present the appearance of massive masonry, so square and regular are they in form, while some isolated blocks look as if they had just been prepared for the corner stones of a stupendous edifice. Although located in a dense forest, the rocks slope so gently and conveniently, and yet so boldly, to the very margin of the rapids and pools, that you can enjoy the various prospects, both up and down the river, with great ease and comfort.

Midway between the Papineau Falls and the mouth of the

Nipisiguit, there is a long reach of the river known as the Rough Waters, where a number of huge rocky barriers have been thrown across the stream by a convulsion of nature, whereby a gloomy and desolate impression would be produced upon the mind, were it not for the superb pools of deep and dark water which now and then take the fancy captive, and magnetize the nerves of the angler.

And now, after a long "beating of the bush," I come to speak of the Nipisiguit as a fly-fishing stream for salmon. In this particular it bears the bell beyond all question, so far as the easily accessible rivers of North America are concerned. In June the mouth of it abounds in the white or sea trout, and the whole river throughout all the year in the common trout, varying from eight ounces to three pounds in weight, which afford first-rate sport in their way; but when the angler is informed that the salmon are running, it is hard to think of anything but salmon fishing exclusively.

These fish are taken in the bay of Bathurst with nets as early as the month of May, but they do not ascend the Nipisiguit in any numbers until about the 20th of June; and from that time to the 20th of August the angler may, with an occasional rain, enjoy uninterrupted sport; but his harvest time is from the 20th of July to the 10th of August. The first run of fish usually consists of females alone; after which they are accompanied by the males, and in August come the grilse or salmon weighing under five pounds. They are sometimes so abundant, I am informed, that in the resting pools just below the swift waters or falls, they have been hooked up with the common gaff—indeed, I have myself had opportunities of killing the salmon in this manner; and the older fishermen on the river concur in mentioning the fact that the salmon run up the river in schools; that the larger fish always swim together, and the smaller ones by themselves also. Although netted to a considerable extent along the bay of Bathurst and the lower part of the river, there is but little done in the way of exporting them, excepting by the house of Wm. Underwood & Co., of Boston, who have an establishment here for the purpose of hermetically sealing them in tin cans, whereby they are exported to the four quarters of the globe. Thanks to the newly-awakened authorities of the Province, some little attention is beginning to be paid to the fishing laws, for on the rapid portions of the river the netting and spearing of salmon are well nigh prevented, though not quite, excepting by the few Indians located in the vicinity; and so much has been said and written about taking them out of season on their spawning beds, that this villainous practice is going out of repute. As an economist, and especially as an angler, I am bound to condemn the mode of taking salmon with the spear; but as an artist, or rather when in an artistic mood, I could forget to be rigid, and perhaps recommend the practice; for, indeed, there are few scenes more interesting to witness than the mouth of the Nipisiguit on a quiet night, when there are perhaps a dozen birch canoes floating over the quiet waters, manned by fantastically-dressed Indians, and each one led, it would appear, from place to place, by a brilliant birch-bark flambeau. The light canoes, the picturesque attitude of the spearmen, the gloom of the night and the silence of the surrounding wilderness, seem all to be in complete keeping, and inspire thoughts and feelings of a peculiar but agreeable nature.

The salmon of the Nipisiguit ascend no higher up the stream than the Grand Falls, where during the better part of the season, by those disposed to live in their own camp, and be ever prepared to fight the bears and wolves, the very best sport may be enjoyed. The uppermost pool which the salmon reach is quite large, but from the perpendicular nature of the rocky walls on either side, it is a most difficult place to throw the fly. Indeed it does not afford more than one good cast, but owing to the abundance of fish, three, or even four, *gentlemanly* anglers can occupy it within the same hour, by "taking turns," with decided satisfaction. The tail of this pool, just above where it tumbles over a rocky ledge, is supposed never to be without a salmon, and I know that from one point of view, I have seen more of the magnificent creatures than I could count, basking gloriously in their bed of amber. As the lands in this vicinity all belong to government, the only acknowledged right to a fishing cast is that of occupation, and I am happy to say that among the few anglers who habitually visit the Nipisiguit, there is a spirit of honest civility prevailing quite novel and gratifying. Not more than half a dozen persons have yet done much in the way of angling at the Grand Falls, and the most successful and persevering one of all, by far, comes all the way from England to throw the fly at this very spot, and during the season of 1850 captured no less than three hundred and twenty salmon and grilse within the space of two months. The angler who would do a good business at the Grand Falls, must be well prepared. His first business, after reaching Bathurst, will be to secure a canoe, manned by two men, into which he must transfer his luggage, and ascend the river. On arriving at the Falls he will pitch a water-proof tent, or be content with a bark one, and have everything so snugly arranged that he may sleep in a hammock, eat on a rude table, and, with the assistance of a good cook and an abundance of liquid luxuries, he and his companion, if he takes one with him, cannot fail to have a decidedly comfortable time. When the men are not needed to help him in his fishing, they may go forth and trap a bear or shoot a stray cariboo for the purpose of adding to his larder. After this manner he may not only live for a few weeks in a novel and healthful manner, but be always ready to profit by the early morning, and the dusk of evening, in throwing the fly. Better sport, I am confident, than may be and has been enjoyed at the Grand Falls, is never experienced in any country—not even by the anglers in the Namsen in Norway, the Findhorn or Tweed in Scotland, or the Godabout on the coast of Labrador. Although the Grand Falls afford the best sport on this river, the man who could not enjoy himself for a week or fortnight at the pools below the Falls, at the Chain of Rocks, and the Middle Landing, must indeed be hard to please. In fishing at all these places, canoes and good men, and camping out are requisite.

But a more accessible spot to kill salmon than the above places is at the Papineau Falls. There is a passable road leading to them from Bathurst, and those who only propose to devote a few days to salmon fishing can easily sleep at Bathurst, and by rising quite early, can ride to the fishing-ground in good season. The best companion for the stranger to take with him on these expeditions is Richard Henderson, an intelligent and kind-hearted old Scotchman, who lives in a log-cabin directly on the road leading to the Falls. A camp built of logs, and having a bark roof, is the domicil in vogue at this point; and my preference for this mode of making one comfortable while in the woods has been manifested by my having one built for my especial use at the four fishing grounds already mentioned. My first camp at the Grand Falls was at the foot of a cliff and within a few feet of the water, but I had a second one erected on the summit of the same cliff, while that at the Papineau Falls occupies an elevated and romantic position, directly in the midst of a sweet smelling grove of pine and spruce trees and commands a view of the entire series of falls. Directly at the foot of it is a schute, across which a fly can be easily thrown which is to my mind the most captivating cast on the river, but second best in regard to the number of fish taken, and just above and below it, are a couple of the prettiest landings places imaginable. But there are at least a dozen good casts for salmon in the immediate vicinity of said camp, and there is an abundance of room for half a dozen anglers, which is about the number who habitually visit the Papineau Falls; and I can only say that when the season is at its height a good angler expects to take daily half a dozen salmon and a dozen grilse.

On my arrival at Bathurst I was informed that the two Acadians who had built my first and most spacious camp, according to a letter that preceded me, had been much annoyed by a person named William Gillmore, who pretended to possess the exclusive privilege of fishing at the Falls, where he had kept a camp for years. I learned further, that when he discovered my men building a new camp, he threatened to shoot them, whereupon they had him arrested and put in prison. I arrived in Bathurst the day after he had been liberated on bail. He was represented to me as a desperate man, and I was told to look out for my life when I visited the Falls. I was of course, provoked and troubled at all this; but when further informed that Gillmore was the best angler who had ever fished in the Nipisiguit, that he made a capital fly, that he was a native of Dublin, came of a good family, had once been in affluence and an officer in the British army, that Gillmore was probably not his real name, that important points in his history were involved in mystery, that he had received a thorough education, and was now a schoolmaster, teaching only in the winter, however, and fishing at the Falls all summer, and that he had latterly been addicted to intemperance, my feelings were entirely changed, and I at once felt a peculiar interest in his welfare. I immediately visited his camp, and found him lying on a bed of spruce boughs and rags. I mentioned my name, and spoke kindly to him. He gave me the whole history of his troubles with the Frenchmen; and stated that he was intoxicated at the time, and that he only intended to frighten them, and thereby prevent them from illegally spearing salmon by torch-light.

He spoke of his imprisonment, for even two days, in the most humiliating manner, and added that if the court which was to try him should send him to jail again, he could never come out alive. I found him the mere wreck of a large and handsome man, and noticed with anxiety that he was constantly pressing his left side with his hands, and conversed with difficulty. In spite of this, he spoke to me in the kindest manner, using the very best of language; and when I told him I would intercede with the authorities in Bathurst to have him released from bail, and would assist him in other particulars, his eyes brightened to an unnatural brilliancy, and he said he had six dozen flies, and though they were all the property he possessed in the world, I should have them all; and that in a day or two he expected to be quite well, and would introduce me to the best pools in the river, and devote himself exclusively to my interests. I complied with my promise to interfere in his behalf; and having succeeded, went up to his cabin to give him the good news; but on opening the door I found him dead. He lay upon the ground, on a bed of rags, and a half-famished, sickly little girl, with an angelic countenance, was the sole watcher beside his corse. She was the daughter of a poor but kind-hearted neighbor, who had gone to Bathurst to obtain a coffin for the dead angler and schoolmaster: and this worthy man* informed me that among the very last words which the departed man had uttered in his ear were these: "Don't forget to give my flies to the stranger, for he is my friend; and tell him to remember the flat rock." The spot alluded to was the schute already mentioned, and it ought hereafter to be known as Gillmore's Cast. At the expense and by the hands of strangers was the dead angler buried.

On visiting his camp, (which is built of logs and bark, and on the most picturesque spot at the falls,) the day after his burial, I found the rude fire-place black and comfortless, and on the ground, carelessly lying, a small bag of meal, a pair of wading boots, a rude fishing-rod, and a bag of tackle, two or three rags spread on spruce boughs for a bed, a tin cup and pan, and a common jug half filled with molasses. And this was the death-place of one who was born to a handsome inheritance, had a superior intellect, had been the favorite of more jolly messes than Charles Lever himself, and died in the most abject poverty. The last place where he taught school was on Heron Island, in the Bay of Chaleur, and his income therefrom had been twenty-five pounds currency per annum, which was paid him by the government of the Province. And now in his own forest sanctuary lies the unmarked grave of the poor angler, and the stream that he so fondly loved will murmur his requiem for evermore.

From the Papineau Falls to the head of the tide, a distance of four miles, the Nipisiguit is quite rapid, and affords a great number of good salmon casts. The chances for sport at the rough waters are quite as good at times as any on the river. But the best sport is only to be had by employing a birch canoe and two men, Frenchmen or Indians. Although these canoes

* This man has since been drowned while crossing the Nipisiguit on the ice, which broke from under him while leading a horse across the river.

are exceedingly light and frail, the men who manage them are expert, and with their poles will hold a canoe perfectly still, even at the head or middle of the swiftest schutes. Excellent opportunities are thus afforded for dropping the fly into exactly the proper places; and as you thus have the pleasure of seeing many fish that you do not capture, have an extensive range, take the largest fish, and generally in greater numbers, than those who fish from the shore, the interest and excitement of canoe fishing are peculiarly agreeable. Although generally resorted to by those who have been disappointed in finding the best pools at the upper and rapid Falls pre-occupied, the greatest number of salmon caught in the Nipisiguit in one day by one person were taken last summer between the Rough Waters and the Papineau Falls.

The men expect to receive one dollar per day each for their services, and when the labor they have to perform is remembered, and the additional fact that the most unlucky angler can count upon at least a brace of fish in a day, the terms cannot be deemed extravagant. The best sport I have enjoyed on this river was at the Grand Falls, where I killed three twelve-pounders within one hour, and that before breakfast, landing them all at the same spot, which I designated beforehand. The truth is, that he from the States who visits the Nipisiguit for fly-fishing, must supply himself with a pretty long purse, and an extra allowance of patience, on account of the black flies and musquitoes. The travelling expenses are not unreasonable; but then the distance from New York or Boston is considerable, and long before reaching his *ultima thule* the angler will in fancy have captured quite as many of the peerless beauties of the deep as will in reality be afforded to him by the Nipisiguit, with all its superior advantages. This remark, I freely confess, is the result of personal experience. I did not, for want of time, kill as many salmon as I expected to kill, and I can only say that a couple of barrels, containing about thirty specimens, will soon be on its way to the States, there to be enjoyed by those of my friends who habitually enjoy my fish, if they do not believe my stories.

Before closing this letter, it is proper that I should say a single word about the flies, which do the best execution on the Nipisiguit. They are quite small, with red or yellow bodies, and brown or gray wings, and, from the fact that they were originally introduced by William Gillmore, they are known in this region by his name. And how a single one of these, which had killed its dozen salmon, was lost and strangely found, remains to be told. The angler was his Excellency Sir Edmund Head (a gentleman who sketches and angles with the same ability that he governs the province of New Brunswick,) who, on one occasion, while at the Papineau Falls, struck a very large fish, which carried away, with a part of his rod, the entire length of a capital line, including leader and fly. About a week subsequent to this event, and after his Excellency had returned home, William Gillmore caught a salmon, in whose mouth was fastened the Governor's fly, and to which was still hanging a considerable portion of the lost line. The fish was, of course, packed in ice, with the fly in his mouth, and transmitted to Frederickton, to remind Sir Edmund of his misfortune, and to testify to the attractive qualities of the Gillmore fly.

THE BAY OF CHALEUR.

THE road from Bathurst to the mouth of the Restigouche, where I am now writing, runs for fifty-two miles directly along the southern shore of La Baide Chaleurs, or, as the English maps have it, the Bay of Chaleur. Of all the good roads I have yet travelled in New Brunswick, this is by far the most excellent, and reflects great credit upon the government which first built it, and keeps it in complete repair; and I cannot help mentioning the fact here, that although a very large proportion of the province is still in a wild and uncultivated condition, the aggregate length of its highways, maintained out of the provincial chest, is about fifteen hundred miles. When we reflect that the lands are everywhere of the best quality, and the climate healthy, it is surprising that the immigration hither should not be ten-fold greater than it is.

In complimenting the road, however, over which I have just travelled with so much pleasure, I must not forget the people who have settled upon it. They are composed of French, Irish, and Scotch, and I have not talked with a single individual of the latter and most thriving class, whose eyes did not quickly brighten at the mere mention of the Highlands of his beloved Scotland. They are rough in their manners, but kind-hearted, honest, religious, and intelligent to an uncommon degree. They work hard, eat their favorite oat-cake, and delight in the music of the bagpipe, an instrument which may be found in almost every cabin. As we were storm-bound soon after leaving Bathurst, we had occasion to spend a night in a Scotchman's cabin, which happened to be located very near the shore of the beautiful bay. A cold wind blew fresh from the north, and the trampling of the surf was truly grand and impressive. Our supper consisted of fresh salmon, brown bread, rich milk, and maple syrup—all of which sufficiently enjoyable; but then the hour that we subsequently spent, talking with the family in the kitchen, was something to be remembered with peculiar pleasure. The fire-place was at least eight feet broad and five high, and was filled with blazing and hissing wood, whereby the room was illumined with a glowing light that made the fireside group particularly interesting. Here in one corner sat the stalwart farming inn-keeper, with his coat off, quietly smoking his pipe and talking with three or four hired men, who were occupying a bench in the shadow of the chimney; and in the opposite corner his wife was holding in her lap a pair of bright-eyed children, while the tidy and happy looking grandmother was amusing some of the older children with a story of the Covenanters. Rude, as the world would say, was the cabin and its scanty furniture, but then the words of the Bible and the voice of sincere prayer nightly echoed among its brown rafters; and on the night in question, to my mind, those sounds rendered agreeable even the moaning of the wind and the washing of the waves upon the neighboring shore.

As a general thing, however, the habitations along the Bay of Chaleur are exceedingly rude and comfortless; and yet it was pleasant to observe the first advances of civilized man upon the borders of this great forest world. One after another did we pass solitary log cabins or shanties standing in the centre of a small *clearing*, so called, but covered with whole regiments of blackened stumps, between which you could almost count the scattered spires of the growing grain; and close beside each cabin was usually standing the shed of a poor, unhappy-looking horse and cow, a sty for a melancholy pig, and a pine box for the accommodation of a few harmonizing chickens and ducks, while here and there might be seen the implements that were to make the wilderness blossom like the rose—the plough, the scythe, the shovel, and the hoe.

Few, and far between, were the travellers that we met on our way up the Bay of Chaleur. The only two that attracted our attention were a pedler of quack medicines, and a victim of New Brunswick leprosy. The first was from Maine, and possessed all the impudence and cunning of his tribe; and though decidedly a smart man, he was not sufficiently so to shield from even the casual observer the darker shades of his character. When informed (at the inn where we stopped) that I was from the States, he immediately introduced himself to me, became very officious, and talked very knowingly about a thousand things and men. He told me that he dealt in nothing but quack medicines, and professed to have made a fortune out of the isolated and illiterate people of this region, whom he mentioned with a sneer, because of their confidence in his promises and despicable merchandise. His equipage consisted of a very large and handsomely painted box-wagon, with a most luxurious seat, and drawn by a span of superior black horses. I felt provoked with the people for harboring in their midst such a miserable tradesman; but when I remember that some of the wealthiest men in our large cities were persons of the same kidney, I ceased to wonder that the poor Acadians, and Irish of this region should become the dupes of designing quackery.

The other traveller alluded to was a sick Acadian, who, in a one-horse cart, driven by his son, was on his way to Bathurst, and thence to a singular hospital for the cure of a species of leprosy, located on the Tracadie river, further to the eastward. My first thought on meeting him was, that he had fallen into the clutches of the Yankee already mentioned; but I soon discovered that he was the victim of a veritable disease, the exact character of which has never been decided upon, although the opinion prevails that it is closely allied to the leprosy of the ancients. The man in question was more frightened than hurt, although he pretended to have the usual symptoms of the disease, viz: a discolored skin, swollen features, with acute pain and stiffness in the extremities; but when informed that the effect of the disease was to cause the fingers and toes to drop off, and, before shattering the body to death, of making it exceedingly loathsome to the eye, I could not wonder that the supposed victim was alarmed. The hospital in question was established by the provincial government, upon the strength of a report made by a board of commissioners, who declared the disease incurable and contagious, but which conclusion has recently been combated by a Canadian physician, who is reported, beyond all doubt, to have relieved the sufferers, and repeatedly effected cures. In his opinion, I am informed, the disease is only the natural result of licentiousness, and therefore confined to families, who have none to blame for their misfortune but themselves. Is not this the same disease that we read of as existing in Greenland and Norway, and supposed to originate from the excessive use of fish diet.

The general healthfulness of New Brunswick is proverbial. Prudent people attain to a good old age; and although the winters are long, the air is usually dry, and the cold bracing —while the summers, though short, are delightful. And here by way of illustrating the salutary influences of the Chaleur sea-breezes, and also the *go-ahead activeness* of the American character, I must mention the following circumstance. In every cabin where we stopped, I was attracted by the large number of children; for in one Scotchman's dwelling we found ten, in another eleven, in another thirteen, and in another fourteen children. But how was our surprise subsequently enhanced by learning, from the lips of a most charming French lady, that she had been married nine years and gloried in nine beautiful children; and from another person of the same blood, that she was the mother of nineteen children. Here was a startling development, indeed; but when we stumbled upon a log cabin where dwelt a native of the United States, whose wife was an Irish woman, and learned that the happy pair were the parents of twenty-five children, (fourteen of whom with the father, had recently been baptized at one time,) we became most deeply impressed with the healthfulness of New Brunswick, and convinced, that by all means, and at every hazard, the fisheries of the province, as well as all other varieties of food, ought to be protected with the most jealous care.

On my way up the Bay of Chaleur, I had an opportunity of purchasing of a French hunter the skins of a cariboo and a bear, and from the same hunter I also obtained the following particulars respecting the game of this portion of New Brunswick. The Moose is the largest and most valuable among the quadrupeds, attaining sometimes the weight of fifteen hundred pounds. He obtains his name from the Milicete word *Moosu*, although the Micmac's call him *teeam*. By the native hunters he is killed after the following fashions:—in the winter by means of "creeping" upon him when in deep snow,—in the autumn and at night, by "calling," and then again with the assistance of dogs. He attains his full vigor in the autumn, and it is then that his massive antlers sometimes weigh as much as sixty pounds. At the present time they are found in the greatest numbers on the head waters of the St. John and Restigouche, in heavily timbered land. The Cariboo or Reindeer of America are also found in considerable numbers, though not so abundant as formerly. Their favorite haunts during the winter are the plains or mossy bogs which here and there slope down to the sea, and where they form their "yards," and feed upon the bay berry, or laurel, and the tender twigs and bark of young trees. In summer they congregate along the water-courses and around the lakes of the interior, where they have an abundance of their favorite food, and during the hottest weather, when the flies are troublesome, and their horns are tender, they spend a large proportion of their time in the water, which is also true of the moose. The flesh of the cariboo is excellent, sweeter and more tender than that of the moose; but the lip of the moose is considered a great delicacy. Fallow deer have been known to the hunters of the province for only about thirty years, and it is thought that they were driven and followed to the eastward from Maine by the wolves, which have since at times been numerous and destructive to the husbandman's cattle. At the present time the black bear is the most annoying animal in the region, and from five to eight hundred are annually killed throughout the province, the principal motive for hunting them, next to their skins, being a bounty of three dollars for every "bear's nose." In the more remote parts of the country beavers are still trapped to a limited extent, but all the rivers abound in the otter, whose depredations upon the salmon are occasionally extensive. The lynx, black cat, and all the smaller fur animals peculiar to the latitude, are still unlimited and trapped with profit; but the lumbering business is gradually diminishing their numbers. Of game land-birds, the partridge is the most abundant, while the quail is uncommon, and the woodcock and snipe are entirely new comers, and as yet found only in the cultivated districts of the lower province. In the way of valuable water-birds, such as the wild goose, the brant, the teal, the coot, and several varieties of the duck, the entire coast of New Brunswick is exceedingly fruitful. Their habits have been described to me as very much alike, and exceedingly interesting. In flying along the coast, whether going to the south in autumn or returning in the spring, they invariably fly from headland, and with such precision that to kill them from an ambush is a very easy matter. So abundant are some of these birds in the Bay of Chaleur, that an active man can at times fill his canoe in a few hours. And I may mention in this connection, that one of the famous hunters in this region, both for birds and quadrupeds, is a Micmac Indian, named *Poulois*, who is both deaf and dumb, but whose exploits are often narrated with wonder even in the cabins and the camps of his native wilderness.

But the great charm of the ride between Bathurst and this place is the superb Bay of Chaleur, whose waters and surrounding mountains are constantly in view. As we did not happen to see a single vessel on the wing during a leisurely journey of two days, the idea of loneliness which the broad expanse suggested was impressive, but on account of its novelty, really delightful. On the shore the quiet of the wilderness was only disturbed by the singing of the birds, and from the sea, when the wind was blowing, came no sound but the murmur of the waves, and, when a calm prevailed, the occasional shrieking of a gull. The aboriginal name of the Bay of Chaleur was *Ecketam Nemaachi*, or the Sea of Fish. Its entire length is about ninety, and its width from twenty to thirty miles, and with the river Restigouche, which comes into it from the west, it forms the dividing line between Lower Canada and New Brunswick. A wild, rugged and picturesque mountain land, known only to hunters and lumbermen, bounds it on the north; while on the south side the interior of the country is rather low and almost as little known although the immediate shore is sparsely settled, somewhat elevated, and occasionally iron bound. The whole bay may be considered one immense harbor, without shoals or rocky reefs, secure from the more stormy winds, abounding in fish to a marvelous extent, and receiving into its bosom at least a dozen rivers, which run through extensive tracts of superior and well wooded lands, where limestone, granite, coal, gypsum, ochreous earths and many valuable metals may be found to an unlimited extent. To particularize the undeveloped wealth of this northern land would require volumes; and it does seem to me that the governments of Great Britain and the United States are in duty bound to work together like brothers, and by their peculiar instrumentalities make this wilderness the garden-spot which the God of Nature originally designed it to be.

The islands in the Bay of Chaleur, and at the mouth of it, number not more than half a dozen in all. Shippegan, the largest, is twelve miles long, and from three to seven wide. It is flat and boggy, and a famous resting place for wild geese, which are sometimes slaughtered to such an extent as to be salted down for winter use. On the western part there is a long sandy beach, in which are imbedded innumerable granite boulders, which are said to have been brought by the ice from the north shore of the bay, a distance of at least twenty miles. The island of Miscou is nine miles long and four miles wide, and is also of a swampy character. The above two, with a smaller island called Pocksoudia, form a cluster on the southern side of the bay, among which are several superb harbors, and in the immediate vicinity of which are the most productive fisheries of the bay. Near the north shore, but in the Gulf of St. Lawrence, there is an isolated island of solid rock, called the Percé

Rock, with perpendicular sides, two hundred feet high, narrow, zigzag in shape, and twelve hundred feet long, in which two regular archways have been formed, sufficiently high to admit the passage through of a good sized fishing-smack; and also in its immediate vicinity is the small and picturesque island of Bonaventure, with inaccessible cliffs on three of its four sides, which is a famous rendezvous for the fishermen of the region. The only remaining island worth mentioning is Heron Island, near the head of the bay, and is chiefly interesting for having been the winter home of William Gillmore, the angling school-master.

With regard to the fishy treasures of the Bay of Chaleur, I can only say that they are astonishingly abundant. The houses designating the localities where they are chiefly taken are called "rooms," and the business done by a very few companies is very extensive. One of them, located on the south shore, has been engaged in the business for fifty years, and besides employing about a thousand men, has been in the habit of annually building a ship to send to Europe, during all this time, as a kind of memento of its success. As early as the year 1635, there was established at the mouth of the bay the "Royal Company of Miscou," at the head of which was the king of France. It was intended to carry on the fur trade and fisheries, but the principal animal it captured was the walrus—then very abundant, but now extinct—which was valuable on account of its oil, skin, and ivory tusks. And it is said that some of the finest palaces in France were built with funds realized from the capture of this animal by the early French fishermen; the remains of the buildings erected by this company may still be seen on the island of Miscou. The harvest time for the fishermen of the Bay of Chaleur is from March to September, and the great majority of those who fish in those waters are of course birds of passage, so that the fleets of ships and brigantines which come with the opening springs are certain to disappear before the blasts of autumn. To give an idea of the wealth of these northern waters, it may be mentioned that the black whale, white porpoise, black seal, the salmon, cod, sea-trout, haddock, herring, halibut, shad, bass, mackerel, capelin, ling, and lobster are all found here in immense quantities. But while some of these treasures of the sea are seldom or never captured, others are only occasionally taken, and those which chiefly support the several fisheries are not rendered one-twentieth part as profitable as they might be. The varieties which monopolize the present business, are the herring, cod, mackerel, and salmon; and the three principal markets to which they are now sent are Ireland, the Italian States, and Brazil. The modes employed in catching all these are of course various, but all behind the present progressive age; and that will be a happy day for this region of the world when the capital and the smartness of the Yankee race shall be permitted to develop themselves here. The proverbial dryness of the air in this region, and the absence of fogs in the Gulf of St. Lawrence, are particularly favorable to the curing of fish, in the best manner for distant voyages.

The first European who visited the Bay of Chaleur was Jacques Cartier, who entered it in 1534, just before discovering the St. Lawrence; and on account of the oppressively hot weather which he experienced on the occasion, (for it was midsummer,) he gave it the name, which, when correctly written, it now bears. During the dominion of the French, which continued until 1692, the surrounding country remained a perfect wilderness; so that the limited cultivation which now adorns its shores is the result of British labor and enterprise. The first man who visited, in a regular systematic business capacity, was a lieutenant in the British navy, named Walker, a Scotchman by birth, and a man of great enterprise. He came over about ten years after the capture of Quebec by the British, and, after manifest misfortunes, died at Bathurst. Some further items with respect to the history of the Bay of Chaleur will be given when the writer comes to speak of the river Restigouche.

In closing this letter, I must pay a passing compliment to the rivers which empty into the Bay of Chaleur between the Nipisiguit and the Restigouche. They are quite numerous, generally clear as crystal and cold as ice. They all abound in the common and white trout, and some of them afford very good salmon fishing. The two largest are the Jacquet and the Eel rivers. The first is fifty miles long, rich in lumber, and has a very good harbor at its mouth. The Eel is about the same length, runs through a heavily wooded country, is rather sluggish, abounds in the fish which has given it a name, and at the mouth of it, on a peculiar sand-bar, is located a small Indian village. Between this and the Restigouche are some picturesque cliffs of a red conglomerate, and a cluster of isolated rocks, which when seen from several points of view, and in connection with the expanse of three miles across the mouth of the Restigouche, the dreamy alpine land beyond, and the broad plain of the Bay of Chaleur, present one of the most splendid and fascinating panoramic prospects to be found on the continent of America, and has alone rewarded us for the pilgrimage we have made.

THE RIVER RESTIGOUCHE.

I HAVE at last reached the River Restigouche. I anticipated much, but so beautiful a river, and such a superb mountain land, I did not expect to behold in this out-of-the-way corner of the world. When I think of the confused and noisy hum of business from which I have so recently escaped, and fix my mind upon what I see and hear, in this region, I am almost inclined to believe myself in a land of dreams. Hardly could this be otherwise, since there is above me a rosy sky, around me, far as the eye can reach, blue mountains without number, and at my feet a flood of purest emerald; while the human voices which fall upon my ear in kindly and pleasant words, from stranger lips, as well as the caroling of multitudinous birds, seem attuned to the surrounding loveliness. I am indeed delighted; and so, too, are my companions, who have already quite forgotten, in their newly-awakened feelings, the fatigue of our long journey.

At its entrance into the Bay of Chaleur, between Point Magashua on the north, and the Bon Amie Rocks on the south, the Restigouche, or river like a hand, (so called from having five leading tributaries,) is three miles wide, and from that point to the head of the tide, a distance of twenty miles, it maintains a breadth, in general terms, of two miles, thereby affording one immense haven where the frigates of the world might sail in perfect security. From the head of the tide to its extreme source, near Lake Timiscouta, the distance is two hundred miles, and the main river, with its tributaries, is said to drain about six thousand square miles of territory. The five leading branches, which give it its name, vary from fifty to seventy miles in length, and are known by the novel names of Matapediac, or *Musical river;* Upsalquitch, or *Blanket river;* Wetomkegewick, or *Large river;* Mistouche, or *Little river;* and Waagan, or *Knife river;* and it is a remarkable circumstance that not one of these extensive water-courses, though all rocky and rapid, can boast of a single water-fall worth mentioning. The only thing approaching to a fall is an extensive Rapid on the Upsalquitch, where, by the way, rare salmon fishing may be enjoyed. The great valley thus formed, is hemmed in throughout its entire length and breadth with lofty mountains, which are covered to their summits with dense forests of pine, spruce, elm, birch, and maple, springing out of a rich soil, and for the most part still untouched by the grasping and mutilating hand of man, while here and there are extensive plains of table and interval land of rarest fertility. The scenery is everywhere both grand and beautiful, but a grandeur derived less from cliffs and chasms, than from long sweeps of outline and multitudinous domes mingling with the clouds. Sand-stone, conglomerate granite, or limestone formations occasionally spring up, however, to delight the eye, and their charms are usually enhanced by being surrounded with luxuriant foliage or mirrored in the purest water.

But as my design is to describe the local character of the Restigouche, it will be pleasanter, both for writer and reader, that I should turn from generalities to particulars; and I therefore begin with the charming little town of Dalhousie. It is on the south side of the river, two miles from its mouth, and though occupying a kind of inclined plane, moderately elevated above the water, commands to the eastward an extensive and unobstructive view of the Bay of Chaleur. The prospect westward and northward, is that of a large lake surrounded with mountains, while directly in front of it, and only a few hundred yards from the shore, are three rocky islands lying on a line, which resemble at first view a trio of huge whales on their way up the river. Immediately in the rear of the town is a high ridge of trap rock, called Challefour's Hill, from which the two water views already mentioned are seen to the greatest possible advantage, blended together in one magnificent whole, above which, far away to the north, loom high into the sky, the airy-like cones of the Tracadegash and other mountains of the district of Gaspe. Twenty-five years ago, the spot where Dalhousie now stands was occupied by two solitary log cabins, while at the present moment it contains at least one hundred and fifty comfortable houses; and claims a population of one thousand souls, the more wealthy and enterprising of whom are from the island of Arran. The place derives its chief support from the exportation of timber and fish; and as its principal market is Great Britain, its intimacy with the continent to which it belongs is quite limited, and hence its isolated and romantic character. Indeed, this very state of things holds good in regard to the entire Restigouche valley; so that certain objects or facts, which in the United States would be hardly worth mentioning, are here invested with a peculiar interest. A ship, for example, is by no means a very extraordinary affair in any country; but when we came suddenly upon the little town of Dalhousie, located in alpine wilderness, and discovered in its harbor from forty to sixty square-rigged vessels, we were somewhat surprised. We soon learned, however, that the object of such a fleet was quite plausible, and that every vessel would recross the Atlantic laden to the brim with substantial wealth. But why this apparent rush of business at the present time? Stern winter is the great ruler of this land, and the winged messengers from over the sea know too well that their harvest time is of short duration, so they come in flocks, and in flocks depart. As a matter of course, therefore, the population of Dalhousie at midsummer resembles that of the hive of the honey bee, and both alike spend a quiet winter, and live comfortably upon the fruit of their labors. But the foreign ships which visit the harbor of Dalhousie are not all which plough the waters. Many splendid specimens are built and equipped, as well as freighted here; and I can only say that the men, whose enterprise is thus exemplified, are as intelligent, high-minded and kind-hearted to strangers as they are liberal and industrious. And then again, the attractions of Dalhousie in a geological point of view are worth mentioning. Its original name was Sickadomeque, or *the place of bright stones and many shells*, and is itself a capital description of the place; for on the little islands already mentioned, agates and cornelians of great beauty abound, and everywhere along the neighboring shores, shells, various and rare, as well as many fossil remains, may be gathered by the student of Nature, who loves and can appreciate their mute but suggestive language.

On ascending the Restigouche from Dalhousie, whether by land or water, the traveller will be everywhere impressed with the manifold charms of its scenery; and among the more prominent objects of interest which will attract his attention, at the respective distances above the town, of eight, twelve, and fourteen miles, will be the several points named Aninnipk, Le Garde and Battery Point. Upon all these, as may be gathered from the older inhabitants of the region, there once stood warlike fortifications, but so long ago that their remains are almost obliterated by a dense growth of forest trees. The story which they recall is this:—When, in the autumn of 1760, the French were driven from Acadia, or Nova Scotia, the ships in which they sailed were hotly pursued by the British; and instead of making their "desired haven" which was the river St. Lawrence, they accidentally entered the Bay of Chaleur. The British pursued them as far as the mouth of the Restigouche; but as winter was nigh at hand, the pursuers abandoned the chase and went to England, while the pursued ascended the river, and built themselves cabins upon the shore, as well as the three fortifications already mentioned. Early in the following spring the British fleet, commanded by Capt. John Byron, of Louisbourg memory, returned from England, sailed up the Restigouche, and with one blow totally destroyed the habitations, batteries and vessels of the unfortunate French. Seven skeletons of the destroyed vessels—which numbered some twenty-two in all—may be seen in the bed of the Restigouche at the present day; and other memorials of this "great victory," in the shape of French cannon and swords, pistols, cutlasses, military buttons, spurs, gun barrels, bayonets, iron pans and spoons, may be seen in the possession of the older inhabitants; but the most curious articles recently discovered are a bottle of molasses, a small cask of wine, and a number of iron balls, found incased in the trunks of certain trees growing on the banks of the river. As the tide of good fortune was decidedly against France at the time in question—for with her defeat on the Restigouche terminated her dominion in Acadia and Canada —and as England unquestionably had the advantage in the affair, the result was not to be wondered at; and yet the victory was rendered more complete by the heroism of a British sailor. His name has not come down to us, but the deed he performed was this:—He was a prisoner on board of a French ship, and while yet the British fleet were at the mouth of the Restigouche meditating a plan of attack, he made his escape at night, and, with the assistance of a plank, swam a distance of sixteen miles, and having boarded one of the ships of his country, marked out the exact position of the enemy, and the victory immediately followed.

The next spot of interest that I would mention is the little town of Campbellton. It is sixteen miles from Dalhousie, and, like that place, is on the New Brunswick side of the river. Indeed, the two places are astonishingly alike in many particulars; for they do the same business, and contain about the same number of inhabitants, of the same character. Campbellton has an extensive saw mill which its rival has not; and it also builds the greatest number of ships, and does more business with the lumbermen of the interior, while Dalhousie takes the lead in the exportation of fish and timber, and in being surrounded with more magnificent scenery. The scenery around Campbellton, however, is quite novel and beautiful. Immediately in its rear, for example, is a mountain glorying in the very original name of *Sugar Loaf*, which though only about a thousand feet high, yet from its isolated position is quite imposing. It is rocky and destitute of trees, and so steep as to be inaccessible excepting from one quarter, and dangerous in that; and the view which it commands is exceedingly fine, for it embraces the very heart of the Restigouche valley. The summit of the mountain was formerly covered with huge boulders, weighing several tons each, some of which have been put in motion by mischievous hands, and committed sad havoc in the valley below, while a sufficient number remain to excite the imagination of the geologist, and the wonder of common travellers.

At the foot of this mountain, and claimed as the leading *curiosity* of Campbellton, is the residence of one Thomas Dodd, who, for his regal style of living, deserves to be treated with marked respect. The said residence, though only about *eight feet high* and *thirty long*, has the precise form of a Norman castle, with two wings and manifold turrets; the suite of halls or rooms, consist of three, in one of which is a stove, in another a bed, while the third is used as a reception room. Mr. Dodd is an Englishman, about fifty years of age, and a bachelor; he lives entirely alone, feasting perpetually upon the fat of the land cooked by his own hand, and having the most uncommon fondness for plum-puddings and superior wines, of which he keeps a bountiful supply. He is a thorough-going politician, feeding this delightful appetite with some half dozen partizan journals, and employing the lucid intervals of his intellectual life by reading the Edinburgh and Quarterly Reviews. His every day business, however, is that of *chair making* and *portrait painting* during the winter, and *painting the houses* of his fellow citizens during the summer. And then, as if to put the finishing touch upon this most harmonious character, he cherishes an insatiable hatred for the Micmac Indians; which, however, by those who have the honor of his acquaintance, is attributed to the following circumstance: On a certain Christmas night, a few years ago, while wending his solitary way over a deep snow to his turreted castle, from the village inn, where he had probably talked himself into a state of temporary forgetfulness, he unfortunately fell into a hole; and on coming to his senses, he found himself among the kettles of an Indian camp, having descended by the channel ordinarily used for the purpose of giving freedom to the smoke of the wigwam. Ever since that event Mr. Dodd has disliked the companionship of the Micmac Indians.

Just above Campbellton, but on the Canadian side of the river, is located the largest settlement of Micmac Indians now remaining in the province of New Brunswick. The reservation which they occupy is called Mission Point, and comprises about twelve hundred acres of the best land in the Restigouche valley, and the owners thereof number three hundred souls. Their houses are built of logs, covered with shingles or boards, and are usually provided with chimneys or stoves, and, to a limited extent with chairs, and bedsteads. Fishing and hunting are the chief employments of the men, although some of the more industrious among them pick up a little money by lumbering, while the women take pleasure in tilling a garden spot, and keeping a cow. Some few of the men, however, cultivate small farms, containing from ten to thirty acres, raising potatoes, green corn and a little wheat. They are expert managers of the birch canoe, and are almost invariably employed by those who visit the interior of the country for business or pleasure. They are a fine looking race and some of the women are beautiful, having remarkably small feet and hands. They are devoted followers of the Roman Catholic Church, having in the centre of their village quite a respectable chapel, with steeple and bell, whose patron is St. Anne. At the expense of the Canadian government they are supplied with a priest; but as he cannot speak their language, and they know nothing about French, the intercourse between them is chiefly carried on by means of an interpreter. The name of this person is Sam Sucke, and, aside from being a conspicuous member of the community on account of his learning, he is remarkable for being by birth a cross between the negro and the Indian, as well as the chief judge and lawyer in all legal proceedings occurring in the village, bell ringer to the chapel, a faithful temperance man, a strong wrestler, a good lumberman, a capital story teller, and a most expert salmon fisher with the spear. But Mr. Sucke is also acknowledged to be extensively informed on the subject of the present condition of the Indian race in New Brunswick and Lower Canada. He says that there are only two tribes now remaining in this region, the Micmacs and the Melicites, numbering in all about fifteen hundred souls.

The former speak a dialect of the ancient Iroquois, from whom they claim to be descended, and inhabit, as a general thing, the sea coast of the provinces; while the latter speak a dialect of the ancient Delawares, from whom they are descended, and occupy reservations on the interior rivers. The colonial governments have made many efforts to ameliorate the condition of these people, and, besides, appointing commissioners to guard their interest, have occasionally given them money, and granted the use of valuable lands. But upon them, as a matter of course, and as the titles are not in the Indians, the whites have trespassed, cutting down their valuable timber, and occupying their most fertile grounds. What wonder, then, that they should still retain their idle and wandering habits, and frequently become familiar with suffering and wretchedness. To this, however, there are exceptions; and some of them occasionally enjoy a little civilized comfort. Excepting when addicted to intemperance, they are inoffensive and kind, and on account of their expertness in the mysteries of woodcraft are really a very serviceable class of people. The original names of these tribes were *Mickmakis* and *Maricheets*, and though formerly dependent on the Government of Cape Breton, they were the aboriginal owners of the whole of Acadia or what is now known as New Brunswick and Nova Scotia.

Notwithstanding the fact that the two tribes of Indians above mentioned profess to be on the most friendly terms, and should be so in reality, it is quite evident to the careful observer that they are somewhat jealous of each other, and a curious incident apparently illustrating this has but recently occurred. Business or pleasure had brought a small party of Melicite Indians from the valley of St. John to the Restigouche, and the meeting which took place between the visitors and the Micmacs was managed as follows: The former pulled up their canoes just before reaching the outskirts of Mission Point, and, as it happened, while in full view of a small party of Micmac citizens, and as the latter walked slowly forth to extend a friendly hand, the visitors treated them with apparent indifference, and simply looked around upon the beautiful scenery, and upwards at the sky. Both parties then performed a circle in single file and approached a few yards nearer each other, and all took another quiet look at the scenery and the sky. This movement was repeated three several times, until the parties had approached within speaking distance, when they mutually came to a halt, and looked earnestly into each other's countenances as if to read the intentions depicted there. Another circle was performed, but now only by the visitors, and a smile of recognition was exchanged; another circle, and kindly words were spoken; another still, when there followed a general and hearty shaking of hands, with much talking and laughing, and the climax was capped by a miscellaneous display in the way of embracing, and kissing, and so the ceremony ended.

To expatiate scientifically upon the native language of the New Brunswick Indians is neither to my taste nor in my power, but as they have a decidedly original method of speaking the English language, I will play the part of a reporter, and transcribe the narrative of a snuff-taking personage touching his encounter with a bear, which is as follows: "One time I go hunting moose, night come dark, rain and snow come fast; no axe for makum wigwam; gun vet, no get um fire; me tired, me crawl into hollow tree; me find plenty room, almost begin sleep. By and by me feelum hot wind blow on my face; me know hot bear's breath. He crawl into log too, me takum gun, she no go; me think me all same gone, all eat up. Then me takum snuff and throw um in bear's face, and he run out; not very much like um, me guess. Me lay still all night, he no come again. Every leetle while hear cough; every time bear he cough um sneezum, over and over a great many times. Morning come, me fix um gun, and shoot um dead; he no more cough um sneezum."

And now, having crossed the Restigouche from Mission Point, (at the very spot, by the way, where only a few weeks ago, five out of seven poor Indians, including two women, lost their lives while crossing in a rotten canoe,) the reader will allow me the pleasure of introducing him to Athol House, a place most worthy to be loved and long remembered. The spot in question is three miles from Campbellton, and directly on the river, and consists of a large and commodious house, furnished with every possible comfort, flanked by at least two dozen outhouses, behind which is spread out a level tract of more than one thousand acres of rich and well cultivated land; while the surrounding panorama, with the several exceptions of the lake-like looking river, Mission Point, and the point occupied by Campbellton, is composed of one vast brotherhood of wild but very beautiful mountains. So far as remoteness is concerned, Athol House is to New Brunswick what the North Cape is to Norway. Here, however, there is an Arcadian atmosphere; instead of howling storm winds and the roar of waves, we have the tinkling of cow bells, and the quiet singing of lovely streams stealing along under a canopy of reeds and sedge to the peaceful bosom of their parent river. An estate like this would attract attention in any land; but strangely, and most agreeably, indeed, does it strike the tourist when he finds it in the very heart, as it were, of a wilderness, erroneously associated in most minds with nothing but savage animals and uncouth men.

As the Athol House estate was the very first one permanently established on the Restigouche, it may be well imagined that its founder must have been a remarkable man. He was a native of the district of Athol, in Scotland, and hence the name which he gave to his estate. His own name was Robert Ferguson, and he was one of the earliest explorers and pioneers of this region, having settled here in the year 1796. He died in 1851, at the good old age of eighty-three years, leaving behind him, beside some ten children, his wife, Mrs. Mary Adam Ferguson, who was the first white person born in the county of Restigouche, and whose strong mind—for she is still living—is fully stored with historical and legendary lore. Mr. Ferguson came to the Restigouche country in the capacity of a fisherman, and was soon sailing his own vessel across the ocean, through the Gulf of St. Lawrence, and along the Bay of Chaleur; but having lost a couple of vessels with their cargoes, during the war of 1812, and been carried as a prisoner to Salem, Mass., by an American privateer, and fortunately released, he changed the character of his business, and spent the remainder of his days building ships, exporting lumber, and cultivating his extensive property. The artificial materials for building his house were brought all the way from Halifax, and for many years after his first settlement here, his nearest post office was the one at Frederickton, to which place, as well as to St. John and Halifax, he was in the habit of making a winter pilgrimage on snow shoes. His last journey to Frederickton was performed in this manner, and in obedience to a call which the government had made upon him for military services; but as they did not happen to be required at the time, he was feasted by those who admired his exalted heroism, and again, through the pathless woods and over the snow, alone and fearless, he sought his distant wilderness home.

Athol House and its estate are still in the possession of the Ferguson family, and the master-spirit of the place at the present time is the eldest son, Adam Ferguson, Esq., who, in the companionship of a most intelligent, amiable, and hospitable family, consisting of his mother, a sister, and two brothers, leads here a life that even Rasselas, would have envied. His chief attention is devoted to farming, and I do not remember to have seen in any part of the United States, nor even at Marshfield, a greater variety of fine cattle than those which flourish under the fostering care of Mr. Ferguson.

But as the Restigouche is a famous river for salmon, and as many of the best fishing stations belong to the Athol House estate, a considerable revenue is derived from this business. The fish are taken in set nets, and at every ebb tide during the summer, are conveyed to the shore in canoes, and by experienced men, are salted and subsequently shipped to Great Britain, or, as has of late years been the case, sold on the spot t American vessels, which have visited Campbellton for the special purpose. Mr. Ferguson informs me that in the early part of this century, his father was in the habit of capturing and exporting nearly two thousand barrels of salmon annually; but that the character of the Restigouche, in this particular, is rapidly changing, since he is now quite contented if he can, with

ATHOL HOUSE.

the assistance of a dozen men, manage to export three hundred barrels per annum. He attributes the great falling off in their numbers, to the spearing and netting them by the Indians and other barbarians while on their spawning beds, far beyond the settlements. And then, again, the gradual extermination of the salmon is also attributed to another cause. At the close of autumn, as I am informed, large quantities of provisions and other supplies, intended for the various lumbering parties are sent up the Restigouche, a distance of eighty miles or more, in large tow-boats or scows, drawn by horses; and as the upper part of the river is much impeded by broad, sandy shallows, which are the favorite spawning places of the salmon, the dragging of the scows over these shallows, washes away in immense quantities the precious embryo deposites of the poor fish. As a general thing, the salmon of the Restigouche are much larger than those of the Nipisiguit and Miramichi; and the fish which frequent the various tributaries are as distinctly marked by some peculiarity of form or color as are the streams themselves. In former times it took about eleven salmon, upon an average, to make a barrel of two hundred pounds; but fifteen and seventeen are now required to reach the same bulk and weight. Odd specimens, weighing from forty to sixty pounds, are alluded to by all the fishermen, but I have it from the lips of Mrs. Ferguson herself, that she has seen a salmon caught within a stone's throw of Athol House, which weighed fifty-three pounds, and was actually blind, as she supposed, merely from old age. The first run of salmon in the Restigouche, as is also the case in the Nipisiguit, consists invariably of females, and fish of a large size; and it is said, that before entering the Restigouche, they go roving for a week or two along the Bay of Chaleur, and are taken in set-nets everywhere on its coasts. The facilities for taking salmon with the hook in the immediate vicinity of Athol House are not worth mentioning; but farther up the main river, and especially in the tributaries, by employing the canoe and expert Indians, the industrious and fearless angler may capture them by the hundred; and with regard to trout, both the white and the common trout, he can take them in all weathers, at all times, and almost without any lures but the glistening hook. For salmon fishing, I found the small Gillmore fly of the Nipisiguit the most killing in the Restigouche.

But I must return to my excellent friend Mr. Ferguson. He tells me that he occasionally relieves the apparent monotony of his life by making a pleasure tour to England and Scotland, but that he always returns a more contented man, for he finds nothing, even in father-land, which fills his heart with such a peaceful joy as the lonely valley and the beautiful mountains of his native Restigouche. I doubt not, that, as a mere lover of nature, he would prefer to see no change in the present aspect of this region, but as a patriot, if not as a business man, I am confident that he feels a decided interest in prospect of the change about to be effected by the great Halifax and Quebec railway. This work has already been commenced, and I am told, will be prosecuted with zeal. The distance from Halifax to Quebec by the proposed line is six hundred and thirty-five miles; of these, one hundred and twenty-four are in Nova Scotia, two hundred and thirty-four in New Brunswick, and two hundred and seventy-seven in Canada. It avoids the broken and lofty chain of highlands in New Brunswick, by following the level shores of the Bay of Chaleur, crosses the Restigouche near Athol House, and ascends the range of highlands north of the Restigouche by the valley of the Matapediac river and the lakes at its head waters, by easy grades, attaining its summit level seven hundred and sixty feet above high water, at a point six miles north of the great Matapediac lake, from which it then descends along the valleys of different tributaries of the St. Lawrence to the Metis river, which it crosses above its mouth, and then it has a level course along the south shore of the St. Lawrence to Quebec. Of immense importance in a national point of view will be this railway to the mother country; and it cannot but do wonders in the way of developing the resources, and therefore increasing the wealth, of the several provinces through which it is to run. No lovelier or more substantial district will it pass through than that watered by the Restigouche, where fish and lumber abound to an unlimited extent; where the more important grains yield from thirty to sixty, and the invaluable potatoe, from twenty to forty fold, and where the people are uncommonly moral, loyal, intelligent, high-minded, and industrious. And then if the said railway should be preceded by some amicable commercial arrangement between the North American Provinces of England and the United States, (for which Mr. Crampton, the British Minister at Washington, has so long and so ably been striving,) and such an one ought speedily to be made, for we are the children of one brood; then will the world, and especially the United States, enjoy the advantages to the fullest extent, of what is now a comparative wilderness. The great objection to this region, prevailing in most minds, is the climate, but facts without number prove this to be one of its many recommendations. According to one of the older inhabitants, Mr. Robert Cooney, the climate is healthy and temperate; local diseases are unknown, and instances of surprising longevity very common. The snow commences, generally, about the latter end of December, but rarely becomes permanent till early in January, from which time, until the end of March, intermittent frosts and snow storms prevail. These, however, though in an eminent degree essential to the manufacturing interest and trade of the country, are neither so frequent, nor so severe as formerly. It is a remarkable fact, that during the last thirty years, the climate of this portion of the provinces has wonderfully improved; a change, ascribable to the growing influence of agriculture, tempering the keen northerly winds. Indeed, although the winter is still cold, it is remarkably pleasant. The frost, by providing the people with excellent highways, only facilitates intercourse; the air is clear and bracing; the sky generally cloudless, and illuminated by a fervent sun. And although the spring comes round rather slowly, no inconvenience results from its tardiness, for nature kindly obviates the embarrassment, by favoring the country with a surprisingly rapid vegetation, ending in an early and an abundant harvest. To vindicate the fruitfulness of the soil, and to show the rapidity of vegetation, it need only be stated that seed-time commences about the middle of May, that the harvest is generally collected in September, and that potatoes, planted early in July, often yield a luxuriant crop at the same time in October. The summer season, though for a while very warm, is neither dangerous nor distressing. May and June are invigorating and salubrious months; and the intense heat of July and August is fanned by refreshing sea breezes that ventilate the atmosphere and qualify its fervor, while the evening dews protect the earth from the parching influence of the sun; at the same time, the dews themselves are deprived of their sting, by light westerly winds that seem to kiss away their venom. September and October are delightful months; and November and December, though cold, are very pleasant, and regularly distinguished by a brief interval of the pleasant Indian Summer.

But the attractions and agreeable associations of Athol House are not yet half told. Located as it is, upon the outskirts of civilization, its doors are not often opened by the hands of travellers; but when such do happen to call, they are invariably welcomed in the most hospitable manner. Fortunately for myself and party, the letters of introduction which we brought were from Sir Edmund Head, and other valued friends, and the great kindness with which we have consequently been treated by Mr. Ferguson and the lady members of his household, can never be forgotten. Not only have we been feasted in a princely manner, but every thing has been done that could be done to have us see every object of interest peculiar to the place. As time and chance determined, we have glided to and fro, in a beautiful sail boat, over the bosom of the Restigouche—now visiting the Indians at Mission Point, and then the wrecks and other objects of historic interest, as well as the romantic and charming place called *Bordeaux* on the Canadian side, where reside some of Mr. Ferguson's kindred—a most hospitable and agreeable family—and which is a kind of duplicate of Athol House; we rambled along the gravelly shores of the river, gathering pebbles and shells, and curious plants, mounted good horses and threaded mountain paths to enjoy the most charming scenery; and attended woodland festivals, to which neighbors and friends were invited to meet us, and among whom were some of the most agreeable ladies and gentlemen we have ever known. But with regard to my individual movements, however, they have had for their object the picking up of local information, and of course I have spent the greater part of my time with Mr. Ferguson.

In speaking of the Arran settlers on the Restigouche he told me that they were not only the most numerous, but also the most industrious, frugal, and religious portion of the community, and that the love of country, which had once bound their hearts to their island home, had been to some degree transferred to their adopted mountain land. Indeed a very large proportion of the present population have only a traditionary idea of fatherland; but though remarkable for high toned morality, they are not quite as scrupulous as was the first pair who settled here, and of whom the following circumstance is related. They crossed the ocean as lovers; and when the time appointed for their marriage arrived, they looked about for a clergyman of their own persuasion to perform the ceremony, but no such indispensible individual could be found. A justice of the peace and a Roman Catholic missionary were at hand, but neither of these would answer. The only alternative that suggested itself, was to cross the wilderness to the mouth of the Miramichi where the right kind of clergyman was known to be located. The distance was two hundred miles, and it was mid-winter. Their minds were made up, however, and they could brook no delay. Whereupon they secured the services of a friend who was to accompany them, and on snow-shoes, performed the necessary journey. It took them fourteen days, and their only food was that which they carried with them, and their only sleeping places hollows made in the deep snow. And the descendants of that courageous pair now number one hundred souls. But stumbling blocks to a matrimonial life are not peculiar to the times of old. I am informed that many months have not elapsed since another Arran couple, who wished to become united in the happy bands, but could not decide in which of the two provinces they ought to be married, New Brunswick or Canada, entered a canoe, accompanied by a minister, and sailing to the centre of the Restigouche, which they considered a neutral ground, were there made husband and wife, according to law, and their ideas of propriety.

But I have been particularly interested in some incidents mentioned by Mr. Ferguson, touching the natural history of this locality, and which I believe are new. The fish, for example, which ascend the Restigouche during their proper seasons, are very numerous; and to illustrate this fact the oldest inhabitants will tell you that small black whales have been stranded in full view of Athol House; and that during the most severe winters, even the cod-fish will sometimes leave the deep waters of the Bay of Chaleur, and ascend the Restigouche to a point where it is so shallow that the Indians spear them through the ice; which by the way, until covered with snow, is usually so clear that the fish may be seen swimming about near the bottom. Now, when we remember the natural antipathy of the above-mentioned fish to fresh water, the why and wherefore of their journeying up the Restigouche are questions for the naturalist to settle. If we could imagine them lovers of fine scenery and of pleasant people, we should not then be surprised at their wayward wanderings. In the way of birds, especially the larger kinds, which are undoubtedly drawn hither by the numerous fish, there are to be found here a very great variety. Among them is that most mysterious and poetical creature, the Great Northern Diver, whose mournful and wolfish wailing is so closely identified with dark and tranquil waters, and grand old hills, with silence and solitude, whose supposed spirit is feared and venerated by the red men, and whose matted feathers accomplish so much good in keeping warm the hunters of the North. The eagle, too, and the fish-hawk, are also abundant; but more numerous than all are the crows, which build their nests on almost every rocky watch-tower on the river. But Mr. Ferguson tells me that at mid-winter they have one particular congregating-place, which is on the ice, about a mile from Athol House. What brings them together has never been discovered; but that they meet at stated times, and by appointment, seems perfectly apparent. Thousands upon thousands will assemble in the course of one hour, and when standing along in rows, or walking about, and keeping their mouths closed, they positively appear to be transacting business of the highest importance. Who among men can question the possibility of their being the transformed spirits of the poor French people who perished here by fire and sword in the olden-time, and who are now preparing to revenge their wrongs by flocking to the standard of the *modern Bourbon* and mastering the world? A "wild-goose chase" indeed they might have of it, but that would not prevent me from mentioning a singular fact or two respecting the wild geese of the Restigouche. For three or four weeks during the spring and autumn they visit this locality in immense numbers, and instead of conducting themselves like silly birds, they habitually display a great deal of sagacity. For example, they can discover, long before any human eye, the approach of a storm, which they always herald by a peculiar mode of flying, accompanied by a scream. While on their journeys they are always seen formed into a wedge-like phalanx, the larger and more powerful birds invariably take the lead, while the duty of thus cleaving the air is divided among the noble fellows, and the ceremony of changing places is said to be exceedingly beautiful and graceful, and then it is, "that the leader, ambitious of his temporary station, utters the cheering and reiterated cry; his loud but simple clarion, answered by the yielding ranks, dispels the gloom of solitude through which they laboriously wander to uncertain and perhaps hostile lands." But, alas! as among men, the shining marks are too often the first to suffer; for in shooting them the Indians always first fix their arrows or guns upon the leader. To this we cannot perhaps object, but the habit of killing these poor creatures by torch-light is indeed abominable. The French hunters as well as the Indians, are generally the depredators in this business. They seek the lonely haunts of the geese in their canoes, and with the blinding torch in one hand, and a club in the other, sometimes kill more birds than their canoes will hold; and it is a singular fact that on the spot where such a slaughter has once occurred not a single member of the family or the race, has ever been subsequently seen. Although the Restigouche is only a periodical resting-place for the birds in question, there is one reedy and sedgy island, not far from Athol House, where a small colony, some twenty years ago, were in the habit of building their nests and rearing their young. When discovered, however, their nests were wantonly robbed of their eggs and then destroyed. For ten years thereafter not a single bird of the kind was seen in that locality, when a Scotchman, who was fishing in the vicinity, was startled by a hissing noise, which seemed to come from the tops of a few dry trees. He investigated the matter, and to his astonishment, found that the said trees contained about a dozen nests, and that in each nest was seated a matronly goose. Now, the deductions to be drawn from this fact are also left to the naturalist. But the manner in which wild geese take their departure for the South, after a sojourn of a few weeks, has also been described to me as very interesting. For several days before their departure they are seen flying about in immense circles, calling to each other in loud tones, while the larger birds are not only the most active, but also shout louder than their fellows, like generals marshaling and encouraging their forces for a great battle; and so, indeed they do, for the long way which they must soon travel, will resound at times with the artillery of the air, and be found to be beset with many a storm of wind and rain.—And now, the departure of the birds brings up the thought that I am myself, only a sojourner at Athol House, and must be again on the wing.

One or two words more in passing, however, the first of which shall be about one of my favorite lovers of the wilderness. His name is Peter Campbell, and his parents reside in the immediate neighborhood of Athol House. He was born in Prince Edward's Island, and is twenty-five years of age. He was brought up in a counting-house; but becoming tired of that confining employment, and having a passion for the arts of the chase, he went alone upon a hunting expedition to the Island

SPEARING SALMON.

of Anticosta, in the Gulf of St. Lawrence. He was successful in killing game, and the furs he collected were sent to Quebec, and brought him a handsome sum of money. With this he purchased a schooner, filled it with supplies from Quebec, engaged the services of four Indians, and returned to his island hunting-grounds. He made more money, and with it purchased the pleasant home which his parents now occupy, and which he annually visits to make them happy, and fortify his energies for the fatiguing but most romantic life of a hunter, which he still continues to lead. According to his account, the island of Anticosta is one hundred miles long, twenty wide, skirted with rocks, upon which are annually wrecked many vessels; is covered with woods, of a stunted growth, and so dense that they can only be penetrated by following the paths of the moose, while the smaller animals are in the habit, in some places, of travelling on the top of the matted cedars; contains not more than half a dozen small log cabins, and one light house, one hundred feet high, and lighted from March to December; has a cold but pleasant and healthful climate, and abounds in the bear, the martin, the sable, the beaver, the otter, the black cat, the black fox, the wolf, and the moose, and, better far than all, in the peerless salmon. It is under the jurisdiction, I believe, of Lower Canada, but is the private property of a family in Quebec.

The tide-waters of the Restigouche terminate about two miles above Athol House, at which point the river narrows considerably, and is filled with about fifty very beautiful islands, covered with a luxuriant growth of maple and elm, and interspersed with poplar and other trees, which, during the summer, fill the air for miles around with a delightful fragrance. These islands afford a fine pasturage for the cattle of the neighboring settlers, while at night, a novel and spirit-like effect is often produced among their shady nooks by the torches of the Indians, who habitually spear salmon among them, on every night that the air is calm; and from the maple trees which predominate among them, the Indians obtain their chief supplies of wholesome sugar. That portion of the Restigouche, extending from the above-mentioned islands to its fountain-head, waters a tract of country eminently rich in timber, mineral wealth, and charming scenery. Narrow strips of flat land occasionally appear, along which are scattered a few industrious settlers, chiefly employed in the lumbering business, whose doors are ever opened to the traveller, and whose humble boards are ever spread with the best of potatoes and game. For the most part, however, the valley is uninhabited, and its natural solitude seems only to be enhanced by the echo of the axe during the winter, and during the summer by the occasional shouting of the lumbermen, while driving their timber and logs along the windings of the river, and down its impetuous rapids. In a picturesque point of view, however, that portion of the river is the most interesting, where it forces its way through the mountain lands which gives birth to the great streams of New Brunswick, and those of the United States emptying into the Atlantic. Here the eagle, unmolested, builds its nest upon high cliffs, the bear and black cat secrete themselves in caves and rocky fissures, the moose and the cariboo "brouse" upon their favorite food, and the salmon, fearless and free, reflects the sunshine in the deepest and darkest of pools.

THE DISTRICT OF GASPE.

I HAVE at last reached the shore of the St. Lawrence, which, at Metis, is one hundred miles from the Restigouche. Of all my wilderness expeditions, this has been by far the most fatiguing, and its anxieties have, by no means, been alleviated by the companionship of women. Albeit, my fellow-travellers have borne their trials bravely, and with uncommon fortitude. But, before proceeding with my narrative, I must record what I have picked up respecting the great and remote peninsular of Gaspé, which I have just crossed and partially explored.

Although this district belongs by nature to New Brunswick, it is the property, and under the jurisdiction of the government of Lower Canada. From what circumstances it derives its name, I cannot tell, but I know that the old French authors called it *Sachepe*, and a tradition is extant to the effect that the original inhabitants, the Gaspesians, were remarkable for their civilization, that they were acquainted with the points of the compass and the position of the stars, and were at the same time worshippers of the sun.

As stated before, the distance directly across the peninsular is one hundred miles, while its sea coast, extending from the head of the Bay of Chaleur to this point on the St. Lawrence, is estimated at more than five hundred miles. The interior country is still in a wild and uncultivated condition; but, so far as it is known, the Northern shores are generally low, while through the interior and along the Southern shore are two ridges of high mountains, which are beyond all question the most northern spurs of the Alleghany range, whose extremest southern peaks look down upon the Gulf of Mexico. The district is well wooded, but while the interior is exclusively covered with the pine and kindred trees, I am informed that the entire district is skirted with a belt from eight to ten miles wide, composed chiefly of maple, elm, birch, and other hard wood trees. Here and there are elevated valleys, where the soil is rich, and, when properly cultivated, yields the common fruits of the earth abundantly, and it is well watered with beautiful lakes and rivers. For about four months in the year, the climate is delightful. The inhabitants are chiefly French Acadians, whose habitations are sparingly scattered all along the southern coast, from the Restigouche to the eastern extremity of the Cape. Though simple in their manners, they always treat strangers with kindness, and are quite content with their lot, provided the cod and herring do not fail to make them an annual visit, and their small fields are not monopolized by the snow more than eight months out of twelve. At those points where something like a town makes its appearance, especially at a place called Carlisle, the population is composed of a class of Americans and British more notorious for their bad rather than their good principles and habits. The only road, worthy of the name, runs through the extended settlement already mentioned; and many portions of this lie directly upon the beach; but the great highway of the sea is theirs, and here, in small vessels of their own building, they are quite at home. The oldest, largest, and most picturesque settlement is that of Perce, which derives its name from the rocky island heretofore mentioned, and which looms out of the sea in its vicinity. The hamlet of Perce is entirely supported by the fishery business; and directly in its rear rises a very high granite mountain or cape, which is considered the most northern limit of the Alleghany mountains. The character of the scenery here is wild and terrific, especially so in the autumn and winter, and associated with some of the cliffs looking down upon the sea, are several stories of dreadful shipwrecks, where the more superstitious Acadians fancy they at times hear the wailing of those who have been long drowned. The principal harbor, and one of the best in the world, is that of Gaspe, named after the district itself, and here the shores are very rocky and perpendicular. It is thinly populated, and, in addition to the more common kinds of fish, its inhabitants do a small but thriving business in the way of capturing whales, which are of the *hump-back* species, yield from three to eight tons of oil, are hunted in schooners, and harpooned after a fashion which the local fishermen obtained from the whalemen of Nantucket. So much for the district of Gaspe—in a general way.

On reaching the Restigouche, and there declaring my intention of crossing over to the St. Lawrence, I was informed that, attended as I was by ladies, the journey was impracticable and even hazardous. The road was represented to me as no better than a forest trail, that the distance could not be accomplished in less than five days; and that there were no accommodations whatsoever. I was also told that nearly parallel with this land route, and touching it at several points, was a water communication by the Matapediac river, and I was advised, if determined to proceed, to travel in canoes. My fondness for this mode of travelling settled the matter in my own mind, and its novelty to my companions made them anxious to try the experiment, and we determined to take to the water. Two small birch bark canoes, manned each by two Micmac Indians, were secured, into one of which was placed our baggage, and into the other when ready, we embarked ourselves. The men were to receive one dollar a day each and found for their services, and one dollar per day was to be allowed for the two canoes. They were to take us only about sixty miles, to the head of Matapediac lake, and to accomplish the trip in four days. As we would have to spend three night in camp, all the necessary requirements in the way of blankets, extra clothing, and provisions, were kindly furnished for the occasion by the Fergusons. A large party of friends came to see us off, and we pushed from shore on one of the loveliest of mornings. We ascended the Restigouche about seven miles, alternately by means of the paddle and the pole, and enjoyed to perfection the islands which studded the river, the deep black pools, and the mountains on either side. On approaching the Matapediac we found that it had three mouths or outlets, and on entering the principal one of these we were met by several logs and pieces of timber which came booming down on the bosom of a flood, and the paddles gave place to the spiked poles. The chief canoe-man shook his head, and I began to feel sick at heart. The river was full of salmon, and they were leaping out of the water in all directions, as if delighted at the fullness of the river. The wind began to blow, and presently a shower of rain and hail passed over us. The rapids in the stream, which were usually surmounted with ease, demanded the straining of every nerve; and now one of the poles of the passenger canoe was broken, resulting in its being thrown upon a rock, and rendered unsafe on account of a hole knocked through its bottom, whereat we scrambled ashore as best we could, and then unitedly fell into a profound contemplation on the pleasures of travelling. As a matter of course, we determined to return to the place whence we had departed in such fine spirits only a few hours before; and while the canoe was being repaired, I quieted the nerves of the ladies with a cup of tea, and satisfied our several appetites with a bit of bread and the shoulders of a salmon trout, baked in the Indian fashion, which had been speared by one of the Indians as we first turned into the Matapediac; and just as the sun was setting, while yet the unruffled Restigouche, and the surrounding mountains, were bathed in a soft purple atmosphere, we landed on the pleasant beach in front of Athol house, and were warmly welcomed by the hospitable inmates, whose jokes and laughter were a good deal subdued, as they freely confessed, by the thought that we had barely escaped the dangers of the flood.

The night which followed the day of excitement was beautiful enough to banish every feeling of regret; for in the confined valley of the Matapediac, and especially under a canopy of spruce boughs, it could not have been enjoyed at all. But the case was far different, as I sat alone at one of the front windows of Athol House, (after every arrangement had been made for continuing our journey on the morrow,) and mused upon the lake-like Restigouche, with all its mountains, and a cloudless northern sky completely mirrored in its tranquil waters. I happened to be in just the mood to appreciate the more poetical influences of nature, and I know not that I ever before enjoyed so many objects of peculiar interest in such a happy combination. The water, the mountains, and the sky were enough in themselves to fill me with delight; but then the blandness of the night, and the deep silence, in striking contrast with the perils of the day, greatly enhanced their marvelous beauty. At one time, from a neighboring grove, an owl sent forth a note or two of its dismal hooting, which was presently answered by the long low wail of a loon, floating a mile away upon the water, and then the sudden splash of a leaping salmon was heard so near, and so distinctly visible in the starlight, that the wavelets which he made were seen to melt upon the shore. But the great event of that night was an aurora, which commenced its evolutions in the northern sky about midnight. Its first display was in the form of a multitude of small white clouds, and as they increased in size, and moved from point to point with great rapidity, I was forcibly reminded of the Indian tradition, which accounts for the northern lights, by seeing in them merely the shadows upon the sky of immense herds of reindeer, fleeing before the hunters over the snowy plains of the Arctic Sea. And now a sudden change took place, and it seemed like a grand review of celestial soldiery—a sort of manœuvre of celestial battalions. Now they would advance in line of battle, stretching entirely across the north from east to west, and then they would march and countermarch, break up, divide, rush together, and commingle in a sort of general contest. All this was continually attended with the most extraordinary vividness of motion—here flashing, there trembling, now darting, then standing still. Once, in the very zenith, it resembled an immense eye, in which were blended all the colors of the spectrum, opening and shutting with lightning rapidity. At another time it took the shape of a crown of vast diameter, and then it began to dissolve, slowly and fitfully, until it was hidden behind a newly-risen cloud, when it reappeared in slender spires, and moved still further to the eastward, looking like silent troops, sent away with their long silvery lances to keep sentinel on the bounds of heaven; and then the gloom of common night settled upon the world.

The land across the peninsula of Gaspe was formerly known to the Indians and French as the Metis portage, but is now called the Kempt road, after the colonial governor, through whose instrumentality it was opened about twenty years ago. The objects of this road were to afford facilities for carrying the English mail between Halifax and Quebec, and to facilitate the settlement of the Restigouche and its tributaries. It was laid out and built after the turnpike fashion, but having been for some unaccountable reason entirely neglected by the government of Canada ever since the day of its completion until the present time, it is now entirely overgrown with a new generation of trees, and is but little better than a common Indian trail. It crosses some three or four spurs of high mountains and several beautiful rivers, all in a state of nature; also here and there a peat bog and a tamarack swamp runs along the entire length of the several Matapediac lakes, and is enlivened by three log cabins—houses of entertainment.

On looking about, after our unsuccessful voyage up the Matapediac for a suitable person to pilot us across the portage, I was referred to George Dickson as the only person who could, and probably would, convey us to the St. Lawrence. I found that he lived on the road, about eight miles from the Restigouche, and kept the first of the three public houses already mentioned. We journeyed to this point with little difficulty, passing two or three clearings, and a small river that was fearfully clear, and full of small trout. We found Mr. Dickson glad to see us, and willing to help us. He informed us that our first stage beyond his house must be performed in one day, or we be subjected to camp out; and that we must spend that night with him, and he would get all things ready for an early start on the following morning.

To this proposition we, of course, assented, and then, with our minds at ease, we proceeded to ascertain where we were, and who were our new friends. We found that our stopping place was a double log cabin, with a good barn near it, located in the centre of five or six highly cultivated fields, on the summit of a mountain. On looking abroad, we could not see a single vestige of civilization, but only wild mountains upon mountains, propping the circle of the sky, and no signs of water, excepting a very narrow but charming view of the distant Restigouche, which resembled a lonely mountain lake. All the green crops of the neighboring valley were on this mountain farm, in a flourishing condition, and a better, neater, or more enjoyable supper was never eaten, than that with which we terminated the rambles of the afternoon.

But a good supper, an hour's conversation in front of a wilderness fire-place with a tidy and intelligent family, and a refreshing sleep, were not the only things which the travellers to Metis enjoyed in the Dickson cabin. Of more permanent value was the information I picked up respecting our host and the *highway*—literally speaking—of which he is the overseer. Mr. Dickson is a Scotchman, and as plain, honest, hard-working, intelligent, and kind-hearted a man as ever crossed the ocean. He was chain carrier to the surveying party that laid out the Kempt road, and when the mail route was established, he was appointed the chief and only manager of all its affairs, and has continued in the position ever since, for which duty he receives some two hundred and fifty pounds currency per annum, and to which he has naturally added that of carrying over the road the few passengers who annually seek the St. Lawrence by this route. In former times he was himself the post-man, but that arduous duty is now performed by his deputy or assistant, a handsome and smart Acadian, named Noble. And this forest mail carrier very well deserves the name in which he glories, for his powers of endurance, which I am told, are certainly of a high order. Twice in every week, from the beginning to the end of the year, does he pass on foot over the route from Dickson's house to Metis, fearing neither the heat of summer nor the snow of winter, and always unattended excepting by the three dogs which, in tandem fashion, drag the mail bag behind him, lashed in a tiny cart, or upon runners.

For about one half the year he performs the journey upon snow-shoes, and at certain places along the route he has his *caches* where necessary food is periodically deposited, bread and pork for himself, and when obtainable *horse* flesh for his dogs, which they devour in enormous quantities. For seventeen years has the royal mail of England been thus conveyed across this wilderness under the superintendence of Mr. Dickson; and if I remember rightly, he told me that it had never been robbed, or failed in being promptly conveyed to its destination. He stated that the dangers which the postmen sometimes experienced from wild beasts and winter storms were truly alarming, and that the wear and tear of so much toil upon their constitution were so great that very few of them could endure more than a siege of two years. And he further informed me that during the coldest weather his men were usually far more anxious about their snow-shoes than about their clothing, and that all such shoes were condemned as utterly useless by them when not made of yellow birch wood and moose hide, and did not measure just exactly four feet and two inches in length. The snow in this region usually falls about six feet on a level, but sometimes drifts to the height of fify feet, and it is in travelling over this foundation that the snow-shoes are so serviceable, and in fact indispensable; and the speed usually accomplished by an expert man is six miles an hour. The natural speed of the dogs would take them on with a mail bag weighing from sixty to eighty pounds, three times as rapidly, and this is the reason why the postman always precedes the animals; and Mr. Dickson tells me, that the very best dog for winter travelling now in his possession, is one that has been upon the road for eight years and is totally *blind.* The sagacity of these dogs is also represented as remarkable. Seeming to know the value of the mail entrusted to them, when once attached to the sledge or cart, they never allow a stranger to touch the bag or conveyance, and would tear to pieces any man or wild beast that should assault their master. And what is more, these dogs seem to enjoy this business of carrying the mail as if it were only a kind of sporting.

But the day is breaking, and Mr. Dickson has summoned us to an early breakfast. This is speedily dispatched, when the ladies are packed and partially strapped in a small but stout cart, drawn by two well-trained, sure footed horses, one before the other, which are to be led by Mr. Dickson, while our luggage is placed in a similar cart, but without any seat, so that the manager of the cart and the deponent, like Mr. Dickson, have the privilege of travelling on foot. Our heads are all enveloped in thick veils to keep off the black flies and musquitoes, which promise to be particularly tormenting, which precaution will be rendered more serviceable by sprinkling upon said veils occasionally a few drops of turpentine from a small vial which Mr. Dickson carries in his vest pocket. A hearty "good morning and a pleasant journey," came to us from the members of the household, and we are on our winding way.

Down into a little vale, and nothing is to be seen on every side but a dense forest. Slowly and steadily we now begin to climb a mountain side. Our pathway is not visible, but we know that if the leading horse attached to the baggage cart can find a foot-hold, we can follow on with confidence. Over our heads the trees come together and form a most refreshing canopy. The ladies, delighted with the novelty of their situation, are plucking blossoms and the twigs of curious bushes, which seem to lean forward as if happy to be handled by stranger hands, although thickly gloved; while I, ahead, or in the rear, drive dull care away with an uncouth song, or tramp along by the side of our Commodore, asking him questions and listening to stories of the woods. Higher and higher, when, lo! our eyes take in at a single glance a boundless sea of mountains, those of the far off Tobique and St. John lording it over their fellows in the South, and the Shackshock range looming ambitiously into the northern sky. Down, down, and we halt upon a bridge to water our horses, drink a cup of liquid amber deepened only a shade or two by artificial means, and to light a cigar, while one of the party takes a hasty sketch of the torrent beneath, which soon rushes out of our sight on its way through an unknown land. Another hill do we climb, another valley cross, and others upon others do we compass at the same slow pace, until we halt at noon upon a bridge spanning a strange but beautiful stream called *Aswaquegan*, where we tarry to feed our horses and enjoy the substantial contents of our portable larder. Two lofty hills rise almost perpendicular within a few hundred yards of us, down one of which an avalanche has made a perfectly smooth pathway, and between which blows a fresh breeze, whereby the flies are driven away, and for a brief time we enjoy the luxury of breathing with unveiled faces. A clean white cloth is spread over the flooring of the bridge, and when covered with tongue and ham, and other Athol House substantials, presents a most tempting picture to a hungry man, but not sufficiently so to prevent the angler of the expedition from first throwing a fly in a neighboring pool and capturing a dozen or so of the spotted beauties, when his dinner is eaten with a clear conscience; for surely it would never do for a true angler to turn a deaf ear to the singing of a stream like the Aswaquegan.

But who are these coming down the pathway of the avalanche, resembling an aged Indian with a pack of furs upon his back, and accompanied by a boy, who would fain break bread with us upon the bridge? Surely, as music hath power to soothe the *savage* breast, it is an *Italian organ grinder* accompanied by his son! Five months ago, he left his boyhood's home in the shadow of the Appenines; three months ago he was playing and singing "There's no place like Home," in the rotunda of the Astor House, New York; and three weeks ago, from the lower portion of the city of Quebec, was echoing, with his machine, "God save the Queen," as it pealed sweetly on the evening air from the plains of Abraham. Our foreign friend seems somewhat bewildered at his present position, and his state of mind is by no means quieted when we inform him that he must yet travel some twenty miles before coming to a house. Our hearts are moved with pity, and we cheer him and his companion with a good thick slice of bacon and a cup of wine, leaving him to journey on, through a land of wolves and bears, with music on his back, if not in his heart. Another long, tedious, hilly, lonely, and now somewhat monotonous ride; and while watching the clouds gathering around the setting sun, we descend into the valley of the Matapediac, and at the junction of that stream with the Carzepshell, (which we cross,) thirty-six miles from our morning starting place, we pull up before the cabin of one Jonathan Noble, the father of our friend the postman.

A queer, queer place, indeed, is this to spend the night in, (the house of Jonathan Noble,) after a journey of nearly twelve hundred miles in pursuit of pleasure. It is called the half-way house between the Restigouche and St. Lawrence, but one might fancy it to be the half-way house between the outskirts of civilization and oblivion. It is a mere log-cabin, containing two divisions upon the first floor with a pair of closets honored with the name of bed-rooms, and one spacious garret, the usual herding place at night of Sir Matapediac Noble and his extensive family; mellowed to a rich vandyke brown by the smoke of untold years, are all its rafters and rough walls, and so feeble is the whole building from the effects of the storm winds of this northern land, that it has to be propped up with massive timbers to prevent it from tumbling into the neighboring stream. A small but poorish farm surrounds this cabin, bespeaking a kindred poverty in the proprietor, and we learn with pleasure therefore, that he receives a pension of some twenty-five pounds (for he could not otherwise survive) from the provincial government to keep open house for strangers, and to facilitate the weekly progress of the post. We attempt a twilight reconnoitre of our location, but are soon driven into the house by the black flies, or, as the Indians call them "Bite-um-no-see-um," as well as by the smoke from burning chips, intended to keep them off, but even harder to endure. We ask for water wherewith to refresh our faces, and receive it in a dish which is yet warm from performing very recent duty upon the table; we ask for a towel, and receive a dingy pillow case; we ask for a little supper, but so dubiously is it placed before us that the salmon goes untasted, and even the eggs and potatoes are looked upon with many doubts, and we rejoice with extreme joy that we still have left a portion of our Athol House supplies: we ask for beds, and do receive them, but with accessories, numerous, gigantic, minute, and venomous beyond the power of common language to describe; and then, as if to increase the pleasures of our condition, our ears are all night long saluted with the wolf-like howling of two dogs, and the natural emanations of a midnight brawl between our hostess and her lord.

But now the day is breaking, and our broken slumbers are at an end. The ladies rush forth, and, in something like a frantic mood, inquire how soon we can possibly resume our journey, to which I very coolly reply—just as soon as I can make ten casts of a fly in a deep pool, just below the cabin, at the junction of the two streams. I expect only to kill a few trout, but nevertheless take my biggest Conroy rod, and put on a Gillmore fly. My companions follow me, and also one of the Noble boys. I stand upon a gravelly point, and in a very few minutes seven one and two-pound trout are skipping upon the green sward. The ladies have wet their feet; are also tired, and have started on their return to the cabin, when they are summoned back again by a pretty nervous shout, accompanied with the word *salmon*. Just where the waters of the two streams come together I have hooked a splendid fellow. With one single rush he carries off two hundred feet of line—one, two, and three leaps high into the air, and another rush of fifty feet or more—now he is quite docile, and allows me to reel him almost to my feet—another rush and he has sought the bottom, and is trying apparently to break my hook upon the rocks; he fails—another rush, and then he comes gently to the shore; my attendant obeys instructions, wades into the stream, makes one good sweep with the gaff, and the vanquished salmon reaches a bank of luxuriant clover—a fit place to breathe his last—just in time to receive upon his side the first kiss of the uprisen sun. Weight, a fraction over *twenty-six* pounds; length, forty-two inches; and the Matapediac lives in my memory as the paragon of streams.

The miseries of the night are partially forgotten; we breakfast upon trout, pack away our salmon, and continue our journey,—slowly as before,—up hill and down, but over a rocky uneven road. I question friend Dickson about the Matapediac half-way house. He tells me he has done all in his power to make it a respectable and comfortable place, but without success. He has threatened to report the inn-keeper to the government, and frightened him into the propriety of keeping on on hand a ham, a little flour, and some white sugar and tea, for the benefit of travellers; but the travellers have not come, and in self-defence the poor man and his family have eaten up the dainty fare—the last assortment, probably, while entertaining for a holiday week the organ player and his boy. We now pass in review three or four most lonely little lakes, through which the Matapediac runs, and where it is said the salmon come to spawn in immense numbers. Anon, we come to a cabin, only about four feet high, where a courageous young lady named Ritchie, accompanied by her father and Mr. Dickson, once spent a night at mid-winter, while journeying on a sledge drawn by dogs from Metis to the Restigouche; and then a wooden cross surmounting a grave attracts our attention, and we are told that here repose the ashes of the man who led on the party which first surveyed the route for the Kempt road, and who was drowned in a deep pool only a few paces from his resting-place. The day is nearly spent; twenty-nine miles have been accomplished, we are all fatigued, and of course, arrive with joyful hearts at the upper end of the larger Matapediac Lake, and in a cabin, kept by one Bruchet, and located on a pleasant, grassy point, we spend the night in a comparatively comfortable manner. The lake in question is about two miles wide, and a dozen long; near its centre is a single island, said to be a fine breeding place for loons; its immediate shores are flat, but receding into highlands, and entirely uncultivated, abounding in blocks of limestone resting upon a sandstone formation, and containing fossils of many varieties; and the principal fish which it yields are the common trout, tuladi or great gray trout, and a small species of white fish. Like his neighbor Noble, Bruchet is a pensioner upon the government, but fulfils his obligations in a more creditable manner. Another dawn is welcomed; we breakfast upon a portion of our royal salmon, and onward do we journey. The same rough, and now exceedingly monotonous road continues, for no new plants can now be discovered, and the eye becomes weary with the excess of deep green foliage, and we compass the remaining distance of twenty-seven miles to Metis without meeting more than two human beings—the famous postman, Noble, with his mail, and three dogs, who tells us that he had just seen a bear upon the road, and a French hunter coming out of the woods, who joins our party, carrying upon his back a small assortment of peltries and a few common birds. And here, by a strain now ringing in our ears, we are reminded of the fact that the quaint sweet whistling of the *Peabody-bird*, has accompanied us on our journey, all the way from the far off Potomac, and it has at one time so forcibly reminded us of home, that we have felt like clapping our hands with delight. In this region it glories in the ambitious name of the *non-commisioned officer*, as its note is like that of one calling "pen and ink, pen and ink, pen and ink, quickly come, quickly come," and while it seems to love the presence of man, its favorite haunts are the leafy solitudes of the wilderness, as if its mission was to cheer the woodman and traveller in their loneliness. The summit of our last hill is attained, and we come in full view of the great St. Lawrence, with ships gliding over its bosom like the spectres of a dream, and the far off Alpine land of Labrador, and the ocean-like gulf of the St. Lawrence blending with the blue of the sky, while the foreground of the picture is composed of the parish of Metis, with its cultivated fields, and white houses reposing quietly at the foot of the declivity, down which, to a comfortable inn, we rapidly descend, sincerely thankful that we have escaped the dangers of the Great Portage, and are once more permitted to enjoy the blessings of civilization.

THE SOUTHERN SHORE OF THE ST. LAWRENCE.

THE distance from Metis to Quebec is two hundred miles, and the country intervening, is the home, more completely than any other section of Canada, of its French population. On several occasions have I had a passing view of this southern shore of the St. Lawrence while sailing up and down the river, but never, until the past week, have I travelled directly through the country and made myself personally acquainted with its physical aspect and the character of its inhabitants. It took six days to accomplish what need not have required more than three, my two companions and myself occupying the everlasting caleche of the country, while our luggage was conveyed in a cart, each vehicle drawn by a tough pony and the driver of the cart officiating as pilot. But the result of my observations I will record in a more systematic manner than a consecutive account of our adventures will allow.

To speak in general terms, the entire Southern shore of the St. Lawrence, between Metis and Quebec, is traversed by no less than three most excellent roads, running parallel with the river, crossed at right angles by other roads from two to four miles apart, the squares thus formed being cut up into very regular and narrow slips of land, upon which are located the comfortable dwellings and accompanying out-houses of a farming community. This peculiar division of property had its origin in the naturally social disposition of the Canadian French, and the result has been that the entire section of country in question presents the appearance of a continuous village. And yet, in spite of this circumstance, a remark made by Mr. John

McGregor is quite true, that the counties of Gaspe, Rimouski, and Kamorouski are less known in the mother country than Kamschatka. All the roads are good, but that running more immediately along the shore is the best, the most agreeably diversified, and thickly settled; and it is with this that the others converge whenever a considerable stream is to be crossed, whereby one bridge answers for the three. On the river road are also located all the parish churches, whose glittering twin spires loom into the sky in sight of each other throughout the entire distance, and many of which are quite beautiful outwardly; filled with pictures—generally of questionable merit, and they are always admirably situated. The farms in question are all in a high state of cultivation, and the pastures are covered with well-fed flocks, although the gardens attached to the houses seem to be the main dependencies of the proprietors, for they are quite extensive, and, next to the rye or barley fields, yield the two principal articles of consumption, potatoes and peas. The habitations are almost exclusively built of wood, and, though generally alike, I did not see any two that precisely resembled each other. They seem to have been built by men who had a decided taste for the picturesque in form, if not superior ideas in regard to comfort and utility.

They are usually one story high, with steep, curved, and overhanging roofs, dormer windows in abundance, porches and piazzas of manifold varieties, and are painted after every imaginable fashion. A large iron stove occupies a conspicuous position in every house, being placed in the partition of the two rooms, into which the houses are generally divided; and in this is all the winter cooking done. In the summer it is done outside, in the open air, whilst the bread is invariably baked in a clay oven, and occasionally kneaded by the road-side on the ground, at the foot of the oven, into which it is subsequently placed. The barns belonging to them, and to which is always attached a wind-machine for grinding grain, are large, similar in style to, and oftentimes more beautiful and comfortable than the dwellings themselves; and were it not for the almost total absence of domestic trees, the rural beauty of these settlements could hardly be surpassed. A few fruit trees do occasionally ornament a garden spot, but we see nothing in the way of cheerful shade trees; and if you wish to enjoy a forest walk, you must retire to the highlands, which are from one to two miles in the interior. At the mouths of the principal rivers are located extensive saw-mills, chiefly owned by William Price, Esq., of Quebec, whose astonishing enterprise has done so much to develop the resources of the Lower St. Lawrence and the famous Saguenay river; and in their vicinity is generally found a ship-yard, with two or three vessels on the stocks, intended for the Quebec and European trade. In truth, the region in question cannot be visited without affording the traveller much pleasure, for everywhere are to be seen the abodes of simplicity, virtue, and happiness.

The scenery that you witness in travelling up the southern shore of the St. Lawrence, is everywhere spread out on a grand scale, and quite as beautiful as it is imposing; for the great Alpine region of the northern shore is never out of sight, and you continually have the watery plain at your feet, dotted here and there with the most luxuriant islands, occasionally surmounted with a lighthouse, and, like butterflies upon a mirror, huge ships, without number, sailing in safety and peace. Such is the general aspect of the country at midsummer; but on the approach of winter, an immense change takes place: the scenery becomes wild and desolate; the storms terrific; the dangers of navigation formidable; the river and gulf are choked up with broken fields of ice; and the entire country is covered with snow to the depth of many feet.

The people inhabiting this romantic region are almost exclusively descendants of the French, who have at different times emigrated to Canada. Indeed, I do not remember to have seen on the entire road between Metis and Quebec, except at one or two of the watering-places, a single individual who was not of French extraction. The provincial word *habitan* is said to be more strictly applicable to the inhabitants of this section of country than to any other in Canada; from which circumstance I am led to believe that its proper interpretation is, *the people who cultivate small farms*, or the peasantry of the country, although its original meaning, as understood by the old French voyagers who first used it, was the legitimate one of inhabitant. All this, however, is of little consequence when compared with the interesting character of the people. The great majority of them are tillers of the soil, and are quite content, and even happy, if they can but have an abundance of the simple food which their lands yield, albeit a few of the more ambitious and enterprising do a considerable business in the way of fishing. They are, however, quite as illiterate as if in a state of barbarism. School-houses may indeed be known among them, but they are few and far between. They pay but little attention to the raising of domestic animals, and yet their little cows are said to be good milkers. From their sheep is obtained the material out of which, in domestic looms, they manufacture their clothing and (with the assistance of their geese and the useful flax) their bedding. But their favorite and most indispensable animal is the horse, the smallest, homeliest, smartest, and toughest creature imaginable. Like the quadrupeds, the people are generally small in stature, with dark complexions, caused by the admixture of Indian with French blood; the men common-place, but the women almost invariably handsome. Both sexes dress with taste, the men in their homespun woollens, and the women in bright calico gowns, set off in summer with white aprons, neckkerchief, and broad-brimmed straw hats. They are civil and polite to an uncommon degree, men, women and children always bowing to strangers as they pass, with a careless grace and ease truly captivating. They are warm-hearted, maintaining their own poor and generously relieving the wants of the distressed, and so hospitable that regularly-established inns are almost unknown among them, and the best accommodations can be obtained at the majority of dwellings, by merely soliciting the favor. They are strictly honest in their every-day dealings, and the *civilized* custom of bolting and locking doors at night, is practised to a limited extent. They are cheerful and sociable in their dispositions, frolicsome, but temperate; fond of visiting each other, playing on the violin, and getting up dances, and in going from place to place employ their only vehicles, the two-wheeled caleche, or cabriolet, and a common cart. They are withal a most cleanly race of people, not only in their persons, but their houses and farms. But their ruling passion is the church—the Roman Catholic Church, with its thousand and one ceremonies, customs, and commands. They respect and love their priests, spend their money freely for all ecclesiastical purposes, filling their houses with crucifixes, statuettes, and pictures of the Virgin, and the innumerable saints; and on spots by the roadside, to which trifling legends are attached, they have erected large wooden crosses, while in some places the eye is pained with the sight of large plaster casts of the crucifixion, standing under wooden canopies supported by tall pillars.

Upon the whole, the traveller through this region would at all times be impressed with the spirit of contentment and peace which reigns among the people, if not with their superior intelligence. But as the Sabbath is their most devotional as well as their principal gala-day, it is the one best calculated to witness their excessive happiness by mingling with them, whether upon the roads, crowded with vehicles, and talking and laughing groups of gayly-dressed women and children, or around the churches, where they congregate before and after morning service in immense multitudes. With all their virtues, the habitans are by no means an enterprising people, and it would seem to have been impossible to wean them from the customs and habits of their ancestors.

In regard to all domestic ties and duties, the *habitans* are quite as circumspect as any class in more refined communities. Husband and wives live in commendable harmony, and parents usually treat their children with great kindness. Early marriages are common; and this fact, together with the healthfulness of the climate, accounts for the annual increase of the French population of Canada at the rate of five per cent., while that of England only increases at the rate of three per cent. When a father dies his property is divided equally among his children, so that the evils necessarily attendant upon the original narrow shape of the farms are greatly increased; but the father's farm proper usually descends to the oldest son, with whom the mother domiciliates for the rest of her days. But by far the most interesting and touching custom peculiar to the *habitans* is that of *second marriage*, so called. Whenever a venerable couple have trod the path of life together for fifty years, they summon to a banquet under their roof, from every quarter of the land, all their children and grand-children, in whose presence is re-performed the ceremony that made them man and wife half a century before, when the feasting and the dancing, which continue for two or three nights together, bespeak a most heartfelt happiness as well as gratitude; and at the expiration of every five years from that period until separated by death, the aged pair continue to repeat the ceremony of publicly pledging their vows of fidelity and truth.

It may well be imagined from the foregoing description that our journey from Metis to this city was both novel and agreeable; but there were two or three places which made a particular impression upon my mind, and to these I will now allude. And first as to the parish of Rimouski. It is more populous than its neighbors, contains an unusually large number of handsome houses and a small inn, kept by a Frenchman named Martin, which is first-rate in every particular, and of course made a deep impression upon us who had just escaped from the woods. Those who have a taste for business would like Rimouski on account of its extensive saw-mills and ship-yards, which give it a thriving character; but the lover of scenery and angling could not remain quiet until he had explored the valley of the river Rimouski. It is partially settled throughout its whole length by an industrious and happy class of small farmers, and the mountains which hem it in are covered with thick woods and belong to that range which here boldly swoops down to the St. Lawrence and forms a headland resembling the beak of an eagle, and known by the name of Le Bic. But as a stream for trout it is unapproachable. From personal experience, however, I can only speak of one of its tributaries, which is without a name, and comes into it about twenty miles from its mouth, and runs almost near enough to the parish of *Trois Pistoles* to answer as its southern boundary. It is not more than a dozen miles long, and runs through some four or five beautiful little lakes, upon which, standing in the bow of a canoe managed by a Frenchman, it was my privilege to spend an entire day throwing the fly, and from whose crystal waters I took *two hundred and thirty trout.* Very many of them exceeded two pounds in weight, and it was frequently the case that half a dozen trout would dart after my fly at the same instant, and, in experimenting with three flies, I caught a trout with each fly. It was the greatest day's sport that I ever enjoyed, and I remember with pleasure that about a dozen poor families, besides myself and party, feasted upon the results of my good fortune.

The parish of *Trois Pistoles* is another place to which I must pay my compliments in passing, not so much on account of its charming location and the pretty river which gives it its name, but because of its chief inhabitant, in regard to age and wealth, all church matters and judicial proceedings, general character and influence—FELIX TETU, Esq. I first became acquainted with this gentleman while upon my last summer's tour to the Saguenay river and the coast of Labrador, where he has an extensive lumbering establishment, whence he took me and my party at that time to Trois Pistoles, and where we spent a most delightful week. To revisit him and his most accomplished and excellent wife was indeed one of the chief incentives to our recent journey across the Metis portage. But, alas! we were most sadly disappointed, for our worthy friends were both absent on a tour; and yet we made ourselves perfectly at home in their mansion, where every attention was paid to us by their household. It would take a long time to relate the story of our former visit there. During that visit, as one of the party has since very happily expressed it, we rambled, rode, and saw the lions of the parish, fished for trout in lake and brook, and came home to bounteous dinners. We had bounteous breakfasts, too, and generous suppers. And what was more, nay most, we had Felix Tetu both at and between them all. Though full of business, he seemed to have leisure to be full of pleasure.

Between them both he was certainly the most industrious of men. When he slept we had to guess. Wake up at the dead of night, there was the light of Felix Tetu, writing letters or reading the news; get up at daybreak, there again was Felix Tetu, writing letters or looking at the papers. When he came in he always came with a festive spirit; when he went out he seemed to be going to a bridal. Breakfast, dinner, supper were all festive; full of fun, speeches, theatric gesture, anecdote, and song. Evenings were merriment itself. Madame played the piano and Monsieur sang or danced his noiseless hornpipes, and filled the house and hearts of his guests with joy. I remember certain gleams of sunshine across the meadows of my childhood; so I shall forever remember the glowing smiles of Monsieur Tetu. Happy, happy Felix Tetu! sparkling with the wine of youth and blooming with its very roses, the odorous freshness of childhood hand in hand with the powers of manhood, and walking gaily down to old age, flowery with virtues and musical with genial words and feelings.

The river scenery opposite Trois Pistoles is particularly interesting, for in the distance we have a view of the mouth of the famous Saguenay, and in the foreground a number of picturesque islands. The principal object of wonderment, however, is a rocky islet, a couple of miles from the shore, upon which is a wooden cross, and with which, to use the language of the friend already quoted, is associated the following incident: During the Christmas holidays some twelve years ago, the St. Lawrence froze in a night off against Trois Pistoles to the width of six miles. In the morning, which was calm and bright, this extent of ice was seen to be spotted with hundreds of seals basking in the sunshine. As soon as the news could fly, people from all parts of the parish hastened to enjoy the promised sport. The seals nearest to the land were first killed and drawn off bodily on sleds. Those further out were skinned on the spot where they were slaughtered. In the course of a few hours the massacre of the poor creatures became general, and extended to the outer edge of the ice; heaps of reeking hides and blubber multiplying in every direction; pools and paths of blood all around—a field of carnage as shocking as it was novel. But the wild excitement attending the killing of the seals was presently to be followed by an excitement of a different kind. It seems as if the genius of the deep, offended by the effusion of blood, silently determined to turn the sudden good fortune of the people of Notre Dame des Anges into a deadly snare. A southerly wind sprung up, which, working with the ebbing tide, broke the main field of ice from the shore and floated it off into the stream. This was happily discovered in time to secure, though with the loss of large portions of their booty, the escape of all except a few parties of the more ardent and adventurous, who were too distant to be seasonably warned of their peril. When at length they became apprised of it there was half a mile's space of blue water between them and the land. The distance was rapidly increasing, the wind freshening, the tide swiftening, and the short December day speedily drawing to a close. At this crisis there was made evident an appalling fact: there was not a boat available along the shore, all were under cover at home. By no possibility could the ice stand the swell through the lengthy night. All were given up for lost. They gave themselves up to inevitable death, and lay down several of them, in an agony of grief and terror, flat upon the bloody surface. There were forty men of them. Poor fellows! They went wandering, little parties of them, up and down the landward edge of their dreadful float, which seemed to be bearing them from their homes and families, who also were running back and forth along the beach, shrieking and distracted at the horrible position of friends whom the approaching darkness would shut from their view forever. Heightening the solemnity and tenderness of the awful parting was the giving of absolution by the priests; now to one company from the church, then to another from the chamber-windows of M. Tetu's house, to another from a point below. During these solemnities all, both upon the ice and upon the shore, knelt or prostrated themselves, with their heads bare and their hands stretched towards Heaven, pouring forth floods of tears and volumes of cries and supplications. In the midst of this thrilling, painful scene a bold fellow launched a little skiff and darted over the roughening water to the rescue. With this frail barque, only capable of taking three or four at a time, he succeeded, almost miraculously under the circumstances, in landing every one of those forty men upon a rocky islet past which they were drifting. The last one was taken off late at night when the ice was in a state of rapid dissolution. From the crag upon which they were saved they walked over solid ice to the mainland, and were received with frantic joy by crowds of friends who regarded them as good as raised from the dead. In the morning there was not in sight a vestige of the field upon which the people had been so busy the day before. In remembrance of their happy deliverance there was erected upon the rock of Rosade, the islet of their escape, a large cross, with a memorial in French, under a glass cover. This cross is visible from M. Tetu's residence, and stands to the parishioners of Notre Dame des Anges a silent witness of God's mercy in the hour of peril, and of his rebuke of the spirit that prompts men to rush thoughtlessly into danger for the sake of gain.

On our way from Metis we tarried for a short time at the several watering places of Canada—Cocona, River du Loup, and Kamarouski. They are all thriving little places, abounding in fish and good bathing houses, have each a comfortable inn or two, with good accommodations, but only patronised to a limited extent. Between these places and Quebec, during the summer, there is a steamboat communication, and the pleasures of a sail to either of them are manifold.

Another place worth mentioning is the hamlet at the mouth of the river Ouelle, where a very superior oil and a capital leather are manufactured from the blubber and hide of the white porpoise. The proprietors of the establishment are Charles H. and Vital Tétu, Esqrs., of Quebec, who are cousins to our friend Felix Tétu, and, like him, are among the most enterprising citizens of the province. Our next stopping place was at St. Anne, where is very beautifully located a handsome college or seminary, managed by a Roman Catholic faculty, and accommodating one hundred and fifty students, the annual expense to each student being twenty pounds currency. The institution is said to enjoy a good reputation, and one of twenty established in Lower Canada, and many of its pupils come from Nova Scotia and New Brunswick. The largest *habitan* town through which we passed was St. Thomas; where seems to be transacted quite an extensive business of a miscellaneous character, and in the centre of which stands a church that would do honor, in point of architecture, to any city in the United States. Between that place and Quebec the scenery is exceedingly beautiful, comprehending among other things, the very best view of the Island of Orleans, and also the Falls of Montmorency, on the opposite shore, as well as the ancient looking town at Point Levi, through which we had to pass on our way to the ferry connecting it with the citadel city.

We were all deeply impressed with the view of Quebec, as it burst upon us from the southern shore of the St. Lawrence. We could take in at one view the monument to Wolfe and Montcalm, the slab marking the spot where Montgomery fell, and the plains of Abraham. The lower and upper city presented a singular contrast, one so high above the other. The river was crowded with numerous vessels of every form and size. On landing we were fortunate enough to secure the only four-wheeled vehicle upon the wharf, and were driven or whirled through the crooked streets of the lower city, and by the gateway guarded with cannon, into the more cheerful upper city, and thence to the Albion Hotel, where we took lodgings, and found a gentleman from the States for our landlord. After a good breakfast, which was superintended by a negro, who presided as head waiter over a dozen white men, we walked to the Roman Catholic Cathedral, and I was glad to find its interior arrangements somewhat improved from what they were when I paid my two previous visits to the city. We sauntered to the citadel with a *permit*, which gave us a guide through the curious and romantic place. We looked off from the immense height upon the shipping and busy city below, where men and horses looked, as usual, quite insignificant, and out upon the great St. Lawrence, which presented a grand and impressive prospect. In passing through the city I was more forcibly struck than ever before with the appearance of those singular vehicles called caleches, which reminded one of my companions of the old-fashioned vehicle by that name. They were to me more like an antique gig than any thing else I have seen. Quite as curious and laughable were the tiny milk carts drawn by dogs.

On returning to our lodgings we found an invitation to dine at half-past seven o'clock with the Governor-general of Canada, Lord Elgin, to whom we had brought letters of introduction. We left for his mansion, Spencer Wood, at seven o'clock, allowing just thirty minutes for a drive of three miles, crossing on our way the famous "Plains of Abraham," from which the most striking scene at that hour was a long line of flickering lights, extending far up the valley of the St. Charles. On arriving at the mansion, which is surrounded with woods and occupies the brow of a point overlooking the St. Lawrence, we were received at the door by servants in livery, and in a short time were ushered into the drawing room, where several gentlemen were already assembled, including one or two officers of the British army. Presently, Lord and Lady Elgin, with Lady Bruce, one of his household, entered and met us cordially. He is rather a short man, with white hair, piercing black eyes, self-possessed, and very polite and affable in his manners. Lady Elgin is a gentle and fairy-like personage, with dark hair and eyes, and an uncommonly intellectual and sweet countenance. Lady Bruce is handsome and jovial, with fair complexion, light hair and eyes, and rosy cheeks. The conversation at table was high-toned, and to me entertaining and instructive. Much was said connected with the political state of our country and our great men, and it rather surprised me to hear how familiar his excellency seemed to be with all that was transpiring in the States. Much was also said by Lord Elgin about the method of school education among *us*, and he seemed to think there was not sufficient discipline for the young. I also obtained from him an interesting account of the removal to the British Museum, by his father, of the famous Elgin marbles. We left the delightful company at eleven o'clock; and I can only add that this visit will long be remembered by myself and party as one of the happiest events of our summer pilgrimage.

A WINTER IN THE SOUTH.

WASHINGTON TO SAVANNAH.

I LEFT Washington on the 5th of December, 1853, bound upon a zig-zag journey through the more Southern United States; and I now send you my first sheaf of way-side gleanings. While passing down the beautiful Potomac, my thoughts, with my vision, naturally wandered to the peaceful resting-place of our great Patriot Hero, and the inheritance which we as a people have received from his deeds was strikingly typified by the graceful gulls that followed our steamer; for, as is the case with our country, power and freedom were the chief elements of their happiness. In recalling the railroad journey through Virginia and North Carolina, I can only say that it was to me as a twice-told tale. Of the three cities, Fredericksburg, Richmond, and Petersburgh, the second seems to be the only one that is keeping pace with the progress of the age. I was forcibly reminded of its importance as the legislative centre of a great State, by the fact that, among the familiar faces that I met, there was a member of the Legislature with whom I had hunted deer among the highlands of the Kanawha, and another with whom I had fished for sea trout off the sandy shores of Accomac, and whose residences are separated by no less than three hundred miles. The monotony of the scenery along the route in question was pleasantly relieved by a glance down the valley of Rappahannock, a stroll under the rickety bridges and among the Islands of James river at the head of tide water, and a view of the moss-enveloped trees which skirt the Roanoke; to which might be added an occasional turpentine distillery, a steam saw-mill, a cotton press and gin, and a negro corn-husking scene, in which toil and hilarity were most agreeably united. Our only fellow-passenger worthy of note was a blind missionary, who informed me that he was an Episcopalian, had lost his sight while preaching to the sable children of Africa, was travelling through the country in behalf of his favorite society, only attended by a colored servant, and whose gentle words and self-denying occupation convinced me that he was a true and noble Christian. I spent a night at Wilmington, and what I there experienced made me sigh for a camp-fire on the Upper Mississippi or the coast of Labrador, and wonder that so glorious a State as North Carolina should contain within its borders such wretched accommodations for the traveller, and such vindictive swarms of the insect race.

I crossed the eastern portion of South Carolina by a railroad of such excessive newness that some dozen miles of the route were necessarily past over in post coaches. A pleasanter drive, however, I never enjoyed in the wake of a locomotive: and as I remembered the peculiar characteristics of a sea voyage from Wilmington to Charleston, I doubt not that a feeling of security constituted one of the charms of the inland journey. But the train of cars in which I took my seat for the central portion of the State, was almost the very first that had taken any passengers, and, as many detentions occurred, and no cheerful station-houses had yet been erected where refreshments could be procured, the journey resembled a kind of exploration expedition into an unknown land. And the romantic illusion was by no means dispelled by the circumstance that, as we had brought no food with us, we were hard pressed by hunger, and that one of our passengers, an Arkansas gentleman, occasionally regaled us with mournful strains from a violin, which, with a gold watch, a huge cane, and a cloak, comprised his whole travelling equipment. In his way, this person was an oddity. He proclaimed himself a citizen of the world, and was travelling in search of a wife. He said he had been down East to see the Yankees, had caught a glimpse of Mr. Museum Barnum and Mrs. Harriet Stowe; that he had well nigh spent all his money, and must soon begin to borrow; and that if the cholera did not nab him in New Orleans, he hoped before long to be dancing the bran dance with the girls of Arkansas. To the music of this man's fiddle it was that we were ferried across the Great Pedee river, which is associated in the minds of all historical readers with the revolutionary exploits of Marion and his brave men, and upon the banks of which our general regaled a British officer with a mess of roasted sweet potatoes. As to the railway itself, when I found that it was as smooth and comfortable as any at the North, I was surprised to learn that it had been built exclusively by negro labor, and that an intelligent slave occupied the post of assistant superintendent.

The first *novelty* that attracted my attention after leaving Cape Fear river was a *continuation* of the long-leaved pine forests which cover the eastern portion of North Carolina. Here as well as there the very air had a piney smell, and pitch, tar, rosin, and turpentine were the prominent themes on every tongue. The sap of the pine tree is obtained by tapping, which operation is performed three or four times a year; and after doing good service for about five years the older trees are converted into lumber and the younger ones protected with care for future use. Cotton and corn fields came into view only at distant intervals; but then the cart-loads of sweet potatoes and ground or pea-nuts which were offered for sale at the cross roads, proved conclusively that there was no scarcity of the good things of life on the neighboring plantations.

But really the great charm of a journey through South Carolina consists in her cypress swamps. To a Northerner they are unique, and to the lover of the picturesque superb. Not only does the road already alluded to run through many of them, but the same is true of the continuation to Augusta, in Georgia. Though their general aspect is dismal in the extreme, the continuous cypress columns, with their tops reaching to an immense height, and heavily festooned with the drooping grey moss of this Southern land, are grand and beautiful to an uncommon degree. They remind one of the patriarchs of the olden times, and like them seem to link whole centuries into a single life. They rise out of a soil that is perpetually covered with water, and while this liquid is commonly tinged with a dark wine color by the roots of the juniper and aquatic plants, flowers without number, during the spring and summer, make a kind of twilight in the more shady recesses, and load the air with fragrance. The vines, which frequently climb the stupendous trunks, and then branch off to find a pillow of moss or resting place in the tops of other trees, are often larger than the heaviest cables of a frigate, and I have fancied that they looked down with pride upon the bay, the holly, and palmetto, the evergreen creepers and cypress cones which cluster below. The mind oppressed with gloom will find enough in these solitudes to feast its daintiest fancies upon; for the snake, the lizard, and wild beast may be every where seen, while the joyous and hopeful spirit will find music enough in these forest aisles to increase its happiness, and make it bless the birds for their sweet minstrelsy.

But a night view of one of these cypress swamps is a thing never to be forgotten, and, were it not for the moon and stars and a cloudless sky, I am persuaded few solitary travellers could endure their desolation without real pain. Fit places would they be for the admirers of Byron to read his night-mare poem of "Darkness." I looked upon them and into them, however, from the window of a comfortable car, and I remember that in one of them there was an encampment of negroes who had been working on the road, and who, on a dry spot and around an immense light-wood fire, were dancing away the midnight hours to the music of banjo and fiddle. The scene was as romantic as could well be imagined, and the effect of the hanging mosses, which received and reflected back the fire light, was like that of a hundred chandeliers hanging from the roof of a great Gothic temple. I remember, too, that whenever the train of cars came to a halt on the borders of these swamps, as was frequently the case, a number of negroes bearing bright torches would start suddenly into view, and though their real object was to see that all was right with the wheels before crossing the trellised causeways, yet they sometimes seemed like evil spirits gathering angrily around the locomotive monster which had dared to penetrate their forest home.

Just before quitting the western border of South Carolina, I cast a single thought upon the pleasant and prosperous city of Charleston, which I had before visited, and upon the many chivalrous and distinguished citizens, the great and good Calhoun, the admired Simms and learned Bachman, who have done so much for the fame of the Palmetto state. With the fine location, broad streets, and thriving aspect of Augusta I was of course well pleased; but the weather was cold and cheerless, and I soon took the cars, running upon another unfinished road, for Savannah. Along this route the country is undulating, sparsely settled, and although pine forests predominate, we here discovered a decided change in the character of the vegetation. The fan-like palmetto is more luxuriant than it is in the Carolinas, and the ever-green magnolia, with its gorgeous leaves, and bearing in its season a stupendous but most lovely and fragrant flower, and the live oak, also an evergreen, with shawl like mosses hanging from every bough, here rivet the attention at each turn, and speak more plainly than words to the traveller that he is approaching a climate of perpetual summer.

And now I am in the charming city of Savannah, whose situation, on a high bank of its parent river, proves the founder thereof, Oglethorpe, to have been a man of taste and judgment. The place is regularly laid out, abounds in substantial but not flashy buildings, is completely embowered in evergreen oaks and other picturesque trees, and contains a greater number of ventilators, in the shape of public squares, than any city in the Union. Although the centre of an extensive commercial business, and having a lively appearance, yet, from the fact that its streets are not paved, but sandy, it is as noiseless as a country village. Its public buildings are tasteful, and about its private residences, which are generally approached, even in winter, through beds of flowers, there is an air of home-like comfort which is quite refreshing; and its hotels are well kept, and not inelegant in their accommodations. The position of the city is just sufficiently elevated to overlook the shipping in the harbor, and from a promenade at the eastern extremity an interesting prospect is obtained, comprehending a long reach of the Savannah river, an extensive island of rice fields, and a broad expanse of level country, dotted with oaks and willows, and skirted in the extreme distance by a line of elevated forest, fading away to the ocean. The society of the town is refined, polite, and hospitable, and pride of family is a predominating characteristic of the inhabitants, who are in general sufficiently wealthy to support their position, and at the same time too sensible to make themselves unpopular by undue pretensions.

On taking an early walk through the market, I found it abundantly supplied with vegetables, game, and fish—sea-trout, whiting, and black sea-bass—and also with an occasional round of beef, all the way from New York. Negroes, men, women, and children, were the only dealers out of the good things of life, and a more jovial set of creatures is seldom met with anywhere; and while waiting for their customers, the principal employment of the market people seemed to be eating sugar-cane, of which they are very fond, and which is sold at the rate of two cents for a single cane. I wondered, as I took one in my hand, whether this was the same kind of "sweet cane from a far country," spoken of by the Prophet Jeremiah.

On attending the leading churches of the city, I was edified in each of them with a truly eloquent sermon, and especially so while listening to Bishop Elliott. I also enjoyed a most agreeable walk through the Savannah Park, which borders the city on the south. It is quite an extensive affair, surrounded with a handsome iron railing, completely filled with majestic pine trees, and is the favorite resort, on every pleasant afternoon, of the old who would forget their troubles, and the young who would meet and have a happy talk with their friends and companions.

The climate of Savannah is genial and salubrious; but, though the city itself is considered healthy, the surrounding country is subject to malarian diseases. But those who would defend it on this score have quite a serious stumbling-block to overcome. The number of people who die here is not a correct criterion of its healthfulness; for, occupying as it does the position of a half-way stopping-place between the Northern States and Florida, many invalids are overtaken at this point by death while fleeing from the blasts of the North, or returning home from a vain search for health in the South. As may be imagined, therefore, the cemeteries of Savannah are objects of special attention with its citizens and of interest to the stranger.

The first of these which I visited was Bonaventure; and though I know that the drive thereto was along a wooded avenue three or four miles in length, composed of the water oak, pride of India, cabbage palmetto, and magnolia, that overlooks one of the outlets of the Savannah river and a salt marsh or savannah landscape, and contains many tasteful monuments, yet, in my recollection of it, I can only see its majestic and venerable trees. I question whether a more superb forest of live oak can any where be found. Though evidently planted by the hand of man in regular order, they appear to be as old as the bed of the neighboring river. Their fantastic tops are everywhere woven, as it were, into a kind of stupendous net-work, surmounted with a canopy of deep green leaves, from which, as well as from the enormous serpent-like limbs stretched forth in every direction, hang a thousand festoons of the graceful gray moss, which ever clings to the live oak as if determined that in itself and the parent tree beauty and grandeur should be perpetually symbolized. At times, too, this moss falls from above and clings lovingly to the blackened trunks of the old trees, and then again steals down their huge branches, encircling them in its soft folds, and only ceasing its apparently sportive movements when coming in contact with luxuriant beds of green mosses and vines growing upon the horizontal portion of the limbs. And when the wind chanced to enter this forest sanctuary, charmingly indeed and with a kind of life-like grace would the tendril mosses sway to and fro, and nothing was wanting—since there were present an occasional glimpse of the blue sky, and the familiar voices of the jay, sparrow, wren, and blue-bird—to complete the strange and very lovely scene. There was something really glorious in the aspect of this retinue of giant trees, and, after divesting my mind of the disagreeable personal associations of their proprietorship, I could not help gazing upon them with affection, and I felt that their outstretched arms bespoke a kindred sentiment. As I walked among them, and now and then discovered a peerless magnolia casting its shadow upon a grave overgrown with the rose-bushes and creeping plants, while the twain were themselves enveloped in the neutral-tinted shade of the towering oaks, I felt that if aught on earth could make one in love with death, it would be a combination of natural objects such as I then beheld. I thought upon the dead, but before I could repeat the familar words, "peace to their ashes!" the oaken boughs and the swaying mosses seemed to take them from my lips and waft them in a hymn-like tone far upward to the sky.

In returning from Bonaventure I took a roundabout course for the purpose of visiting a model plantation, where I saw no less than one hundred negroes in a single field, which they were preparing to receive the spring planting of cotton and corn. Some two-thirds of them were able-bodied men, and the remainder buxom women; and as many of the former wore red flannel shirts, and the heads of the latter were crowned with fanciful handkerchiefs or turbans, and as an occasional mule and frequent bonfires were also visible, and nearly every individual was smoking a wooden pipe, the picture which they presented was decidedly interesting. That they were happy was quite apparent; and when I expressed surprise at their leisurely way of ploughing and hoeing, my companion informed me that each person had a limited task to perform, and that this was usually completed by three or four o'clock in the afternoon; by which arrangement the slaves had an opportunity of following their own inclinations. One side of the above field was skirted with a grove of luxuriant trees, through which lay our road, and in whose shadow were many negro children playing and frolicking, but whose ostensible employment was bringing a good dinner to their parents. In this vicinity it was, too, that I had my first good view of an extensive rice-field, which was so ditched, dammed up, and scientifically arranged that it might be flooded at pleasure by the salt water in its vicinity, which is indispensable to the growth and nourishment of the rice grain. And on a green fronting the plain but comfortable residence of the proprietor of this plantation I saw three or four magnificent specimens of the live-oak standing by themselves, the diameter of whose shadows measured from a hundred to a hundred and fifty feet.

But, notwithstanding Bonaventure, the most convenient and popular burial-place belonging to Savannah, is Laurel Cemetery. It has been recently laid out, and, occupying as it does a sunny position in the immediate vicinity of a virgin forest where thousands of birds have built their nests, it is, as all such places should be, distinguished for its cheerfulness. It abounds in handsome monuments; but the leading feature in this way is the memorial of a young husband to his young wife, representing a Gothic portal with a heart suspended over an open Bible, bearing appropriate inscriptions, and carved from the purest white marble.

Not far removed from Laurel Cemetery, is the burial-place of the black population. Here the monuments are brick with marble slabs, and frequently of wood. Some of the inscriptions I thought worth copying for their novelty. Over the grave of a child, for example, are these words:

"Sweet withered lily, farewell."

The fate of a man who had been drowned, is thus commemorated:

"Sacred to the memory of Robert Spencer, who came to his Death by a Boat, July 9th, 1840, aged 21 years.

"Reader, as you am now, so once I;
And as I am now so mus you be shortly. Amen."

On the monument of a woman are the following touching words:

"Go home, mother, dry up your weeping tears.
God's will be done."

On a slab, erected to the memory of a cooper who had been

killed in tightening the hoops of a keg of powder which exploded during the operation, is this curious sentence:

> "This stone was erected by the members of the Axe Company, Coopers, and Committee of the 2d African Church of Savannah, for the purpose of having a Herse for benevolent purposes, of which he was the first sexton."

From the above specimens, it cannot be questioned that *Horatian* philosophers would have a fine field for their genius in the negro grave-yard of Savannah.

In a long and pleasant conversation which I have had in this city with William B. Hodgson, Esq., many highly interesting particulars came to my knowledge respecting the extinct gigantic quadrupeds of the coast of Georgia, as developed by the discovery of their fossil remains in no less than three widely-separated localities. The names by which these animals are known are the megatherium, mastodom giganteum, mammoth, hippopotamus, and the horse. Their fossil remains consisted of teeth, vertebræ, tusks, and skulls, and they generally occurred in groups, and in some cases the greater part of the bones of the same skeleton were found in immediate juxtaposition. When first uncovered many of the specimens were quite perfect, but on being exposed to the air began to crumble, and all the specimens were found at nearly the same depth below the surface and embedded in the same formation, resting on yellow sand, and enveloped in recent clay alluvium. The testimony adduced to prove that these relics are really what they are alleged to be, consists in the united testimony of many eminent geologists both in this country and England. The most important of these fossils are now in the cabinet of the Academy of Natural Sciences of Philadelphia; and though to the casual observer they present only the appearance of a few uncouth and formless substances, yet to the Christian philosopher most eloquently do they proclaim the power and unsearchable wisdom of the Creator.

FLORIDA.

I CAME from Savannah to within twenty miles of St. Augustine in the good steamboat St. John, and by what is known as the inland route into the river St. John. The coast of Georgia along which we sailed possesses many features which were new to me; and as these, with few exceptions, are known to mark the Atlantic coast of the United States from Chesapeake Bay to the Mississippi, an allusion to them may not be uninteresting in this place. Along the Georgia section the prominent sea islands number no less than ten, and they are generally covered with a luxuriant growth of forest trees called hummocks. They are comprised within a belt of about twelve miles from the sea to the main land; and attached to all of them, on the inner side as well as to the main land, are very extensive salt marshes, which are usually cut up by tide-water streams, forming the natural outlets to the various rivers on the coast. The sea side of these islands is commonly a white sandy beach, interspersed with occasional spots of marine vegetation; and while the hummock land is held in high estimation for its good qualities in producing the long staple or Sea Island cotton, the interior marshes abound in sedges and rushes of several varieties. The basins of salt water or sounds which border the main land are generally so linked together as to form a continuous and secure navigation for the smaller class of vessels; but, instead of being covered with the white wings of commerce, by the acquiescence of Southern enterprise, they swarm with water fowl throughout the entire year. To the casual observer the appearances of this coast would seem to indicate that the land in ages past had trespassed upon the sea; but the students of geology affirm, upon the strength of phenomena presented by the tide-water marshes, that the sea itself has been the invader, and that where once the cypress, live oak, and magnolia bloomed in primeval luxuriance, the porpoise and devil fish now sport in undisturbed freedom.

And here, in passing, I would devote a short paragraph to the devil fish. This sea monster I am only acquainted with by reputation, having never seen one; but I know that there is a specimen of his satanic majesty in the Philadelphia museum; that he belongs to the *Cartilaginous* class of fishes and to the family of *Rays;* that he is an uncouth four-cornered creature, with a creditable tail, and varies in length from eight to eighteen feet; that he is very active, has a huge and frightful mouth but feeds upon small fish; also, that he is found in considerable numbers along the coasts of South Carolina and Georgia; that he is partial to the sounds, and is apparently of no use, unless it be to gratify the taste for sporting, and try the fortitude of its chief annihilator, Hon. William Elliott, of Beaufort Sound, South Carolina. This well-known planter and accomplished gentleman has for many years past devoted himself to the study as well as the harpooning of the devil fish, and, for private circulation, has written a small but highly interesting volume on the subject of Carolina sports in general. For him to be drawn about for hours at a time by this fish in a fairy-like boat and after a fairy-like fashion is by no means an uncommon occurrence; but, while the sport must be exciting in the extreme, it is quite venturesome, and requires an uncommon proportion of both nerve and sinew. The book referred to is, in its way, one of the best and most original in the language, and an edition for general circulation ought to be published, and would be well received by the sportsmen and lovers of natural history throughout the land.

Many of the passages through which our steamer had to make her way were very narrow, so that we were constantly getting aground, and, as the banks were muddy, it was a novel sight to see the negro sailors go ashore in mire up to their waists for the purpose of planting the stakes, by which and a stout hawser we were set afloat again. Upon the mud banks in question I noticed a small variety of the oyster which were scattered along the shore in immense quantities, sometimes in isolated clusters and then again in layers or beds of considerable extent. Though quite small, I found them well flavored. I heard them spoken of as the raccoon oyster, and was told that they are so called on account of their being the favorite food of the raccoon in this section of country. The feeding time with the four-legged animal is of course when the tide is low; and the same remark might almost be made in regard to the oyster itself, since it is not uncommon for this intelligent shell fish to seize with its pearly hands the foot of the eagle, the crow, or the crane, while these bipeds are sauntering along the muddy shores. As to the game found along this coast, I am told it is inexhaustible. In their proper seasons and their favorite haunts the deer and turkey, the woodcock and snipe, the partridge, quail, and curlew, as well as many kinds of the duck race, are slaughtered in marvelous numbers. The deer are hunted with dogs and horses; and one gentleman whom I met on the steamboat, and who showed to me a five-hundred dollar gun just received from England, informed me that, within a few weeks past, he and four companions had killed in three days no less than thirty nine. Cultivated fields along our route were few and far between; but I was told that all the islands contained highly cultivated plantations, where cotton and corn flourished almost spontaneously, upon which were employed from four to fourteen hundred slaves; and where the society, though comparatively isolated, is distinguished for its refinement and warm-hearted hospitality. The only towns that our steamer visited were Darien, at the mouth of the Altamaha, and St. Mary, at the mouth of the river so named. The first I saw by moonlight, and it looked imposing; the second on a bright sunny morning, and it was beautiful; but I imagine that the surrounding scenery, with the fragrance of orange groves in their midst or neighborhood, did more to make them attractive than the habitations.

The chief novelty in the vegetable kingdom that attracted my attention was the cabbage palmetto, which was sufficiently palm-like in its aspect to remind one of oriental scenery. The waters through which we passed are said to be filled in the summer time with alligators, but none of them were seen during our trip; and I was surprised to learn that, like the bear, they remain secreted and partially dormant during the winter in large holes, which they burrow into the muddy banks.

In a conversation that I had with our captain he related many affecting incidents resulting from the folly in invalids of seeking the South after their diseases have been pronounced incurable. Many persons with feeble gait, hollow cough, and the hectic flush upon their cheeks had he assisted to their state-rooms on his vessel at Savannah bound to Florida, who in a few months made the return trip in their coffins. But he gave it as his opinion that the great majority of those who hopelessly journeyed to the South for their health, were sent away from their homes by the physicians who desired to be spared the pain of witnessing the death of their patients. The idea struck me with astonishment; and yet two of my fellow passengers, who appeared too feeble to survive another day, and who told me they had been driven away by their physicians, convinced me of its truth. Incipient consumption may undoubtedly be banished for a time by seeking this genial climate; but it were better, far better, to die at an early day among one's kindred, and surrounded with the comforts of home, than to die a few weeks or months later in a strange place among strangers and subjected to all the privations of a sparsely-settled country.

But, after a short outside detour, our little steamer has crossed a surf-covered bar, passed into still water, between extensive beaches of white sand, covered with immense flocks of the white and gray pelican, and is quietly pursuing her romantic voyage up the river St. John or *Welaka*, as the Seminoles called it, the meaning of which is Lake River. This stream is justly the pride of Florida; and, what is remarkable, it is the only considerable one in the Union which runs in a northerly direction from its fountain-head. Its name indeed is the only unoriginal

VAN-INGEN-SNYDER.

RIVER ST. JOHN, FLORIDA.

thing about it; but this is quite appropriate, for, like its apostolic namesake, it performs its allotted duty in the wilderness, and where reeds without number are shaken in the wind. I ascended the river in the steamer, and when tired of sailing I left it at Picolata, and from that point crossed over to St. Augustine, on the sea-board, in a private carriage. The waters of the St. John are broad and lake-like, say from two to four miles wide, from ten to twenty feet deep, flowing without any perceptible current, of a dark wine color, but clear and somewhat sluggish. Its shores are generally low, scarcely ever attaining an elevation of fifteen feet, and, though commonly skirted with forests, composed of pine, cypress, live oak, magnolia, Spanish bayonet, and palmetto, yet the monotony of the scenery is often relieved by broad reaches of swamp or grass land. Islands and points of land having the aspect of islands are numerous, and, during the calm weather, their only mission would seem to be to rival the clouds in harmless vanity and admire their manifold charms reflected in the waters which surround them. They give sustenance, however, to a great variety of game, including deer and turkeys; their shores swarm with water-fowl, and in the shadow of almost every oak overhanging its sandy or reedy banks may be seen a sentinel crane or bittern. Generally speaking the shores of this noble river are as wild as they were centuries ago; and the loneliness of a sail upon its bosom is only enhanced by the solitary vessels stealing away as if among the trees the occasional rafts with their lazy navigators, and the few steam saw-mills which, to the poetic eye, appear to view, and depart more like visions than realities. But those engaged in the lumbering business here are chiefly Northerners, and they of course are thinking more of dollars than of nature and the picturesque. Within the last three years they have built some twenty steam mills at as many eligible points on the river, costing from six to twelve thousand dollars each; and their lumber finds a ready market not only in the Northern States, but in the West Indies. This new spirit of enterprise, coupled with the fact that the winter climate of Florida is getting to be considered a certain cure for many incipient diseases, is doing much to make this wilderness blossom into a blessing to the human family; and it is natural and right that watering places and small villages should spring up in every direction, as they undoubtedly will, albeit their presence may detract from the lonely beauty of its scenery.

The varieties of fish found in the St. John are quite limited; the only game fish being the black-bass of the west and northwest, but which is here universally and erroneously designated a *trout*. In these waters, however, it grows to a great size, sometimes attaining a weight of twenty pounds. By the natives it is taken with the minnow and a piece of flannel which they call a *bob;* and as I knew by intuition, before I saw it, that it was not a trout, and am ready to declare that the common trout is found nowhere in Florida, so am I disposed to assert; that the fish in question, if angled for with a fly, as they do in Lake George and the St. Lawrence, would be found to afford first-rate sport. And it is a singular coincidence, which I may mention here, that while the St. John and the St. Lawrence are the only rivers emptying into the Atlantic which contain the beautiful and delicious fresh water fish correctly called the black-bass, their waters are both unvisited by the invaluable shad. If I am correctly informed, this fish has never been found in the St. John, (although its cousin, the herring, run up the stream by thousands,) and, if ever taken in the St. Lawrence, they are there very scarce and very puny, and held in no better esteem than the herring. The red fish of Florida, which is a species of mullet, is a capital fish for the table. By the Indians they are killed with the bow and arrow, while the Spanish inhabitants have a mode peculiar to themselves. They have a circular net, ten feet in diameter, which they throw with dexterity, so that it opens while it flies, and having lead around it, all the fish that are under it are enclosed, and then the cord, which is retained in the hand, is drawn, and thus the fish are *bagged*.

In navigating the St. John the traveller may go as far as Pilatka in a steamboat of good dimensions, but when he is anxious, as he certainly will be, to go from fifty to a hundred miles through a chain of most beautiful lakes, he must ship himself on board of a steamboat just large enough, "and nothing more," to deserve the name. Throughout this region the vegetation is rank and summer-like during the whole year, and, though there is positively no end to the wilderness pictures which present themselves at every turn of the tiny vessel, the voyage soon becomes monotonous, and the heart of a Northerner sighs for the scenes and associations of home. I would rather read of the "land of the cypress and myrtle" than spend my days among its reptiles and in its enervating climate; and if I can only enjoy the orange and lemon, the banana, the pine-apple, and olive, under a roof mantled with snow, I will relinquish the pleasure of gathering them to the negroes, whose business it is to do so, in the valley of the St. John and other portions of Florida. As the sources of the river St. John have never been surveyed, it is impossible to give its exact length. Indeed some of its native explorers inform me that the canoes of the Indians have, in times past, undoubtedly traversed its basin even to the most southerly extremity of the State, thereby passing through *At-See-Nahoopa*, or Big Cyprus Swamp, the Lake called *Okee-Cho-bee* or Big Water, and *Pah-hay-o-kee* or Grass Water, commonly called the Everglades. During a rainy season this was undoubtedly possible; but, if future explorations should prove the existence of such a communication, it could then be said of the St. John that no less than three of the great wonders of the United States had conspired to form its cradle or fountain-head. The Big Swamp, now the home of the few Seminole Indians remaining in Florida, is said to be about one hundred and fifty miles in extent, and a thousand-fold more desolate than its dismal competitor in Virginia; and in regard to its varied and luxuriant vegetation, its large trees, heavy mosses, venomous reptiles, damp atmosphere, and primeval solitude and gloom, is probably not surpassed by any other spot of the green earth. From this swamp, on one way up the basin of the St. John, and yet in a southerly direction, we glide into the large and still more lonely lake called Big Water, which is some forty miles in diameter, and whose waters are only disturbed by tropical winds and myriads of the feathered race. Bordering this lake upon the south, and extending therefrom almost to the Keys of Florida, a distance of more than a hundred miles, are located the famous and wonderful Everglades. Here we have what appears to be an emerald ocean, filled with innumerable islands, varying in size from one acre to two thousand. The grass which gives the plain its brilliant color grows to the height of ten feet, and is remarkable for its triangular shape and saw-like edges, and springs from a bed of water, from one to four feet in depth, which is perfectly clear, and swayed to and fro after the fashion of a tide. The islands are circular in shape, high and dry, composed of a black and very rich soil, and always covered with a solid mass of the rankest vegetation, where the oak with its long beard lords it over the orange, where the magnolia vies with unnumbered nameless plants in filling the air with fragrance, and where the mocking-bird and the parrot build their nests in perpetual solitude.

And now, as the object of this letter was to conduct the reader to St. Augustine, it is high time that I should leave the St. John and cross the belt of country lying between the river and the ocean. In passing, however, I must pay my respects to Picolata, which, like many other Florida towns, figures largely on the maps, but consists only of one house and a long rickety wharf. At this point a grove of mossy oaks will be viewed with peculiar pleasure by every one; and while the antiquarian may turn aside to peer into the nooks and corners of an ancient Spanish fort, long since razed to the ground, as tradition says, by a party of savages, the lover of books and authors may visit the log cabin in the neighborhood of one Williams, who has published a very readable book about the history and natural productions of Florida, and here leads the life of a literary recluse. The drive from Picolata to this place is over a level sandy road, through a pine forest interspersed with swamps and hummocks, or islands of unusually rank vegetation, and across many charmingly clear streams. I made the journey on a quiet moonlight night, and, whilst my ear was pleased with the croaking of frogs, the singing of the wood cricket, and the hooting of owls, my eye wandered among the columns of the forest, in "intricate mazes lost," and watched with interest the glancing of the brilliant moonlight upon the leaves and grasses all drooping under a heavy dew, as well as upon the blossoms of the yellow jessamine which filled the air with fragrance. My coachman on this occasion was a negro, and possessed of sufficient intelligence to inform me, as we drove across two particular swamps, that in one of them, during the Indian troubles, the late amiable and accomplished Major Searle was wounded by a party of Seminoles, and that in the other, a number of play-actors, on their way to St. Augustine, were murdered by the notorious chief Wild Cat and his followers, and who, on a subsequent occasion, made his appearance in a pitched battle decked out in the costume of Richard the Third.

ST. AUGUSTINE.

As this Augustine is the oldest, so is it the oddest town in the United States. I propose not to go at all into its interesting and romantic history, although if I had time and opportunity to rummage among the archives of Spain and England, I would like nothing better than to write its history in full; for since the time that its site was usurped by Melendez from the Chief of the Yamassees, just two hundred and eighty-nine years ago, it has been the scene alike of Spanish rule and persecution, of Huguenot misfortune, of Buccaneer outrages, of British valor and conquest, and of savage revenge, until we find it, as it is now, the least thriving and in its aspect the most foreign city belonging to our Confederacy. We may indeed say of Florida in general that, as the scene of continued changes and violence, its history is more melancholy than that of any of its sister states. War and bloodshed have, from the earliest times, been its chief inheritance; and the Fountain of Perpetual Youth, with the gold mines that helped to give it a universal fame, have long since melted into air, and will only be remembered in future years, when connected with the names of De Leon and De Soto, as the fables of the land. But, as the sword and the spear have given place to the plough and the pruning-hook, and peace is resting in all her borders, we may now hope that what has heretofore been the arena of discord and carnage, will hereafter be the home of prosperity and contentment.

My object in this letter is simply to describe St. Augustine as it now appears. The position of the city is upon the extreme point of a tongue of low sandy land, formed by the junction of the St. Sebastian river and the small bay of North river, which affords a safe harbor for the smaller class of vessels; and while the country on the west is low, sandy, and covered with a pine forest, the prospect on the east comprehends the flat island of Anastatia, famous for a shell stone or coquina quarry, and surmounted by a lighthouse, originally a Spanish lookout, and beyond which sweeps the Atlantic ocean. The plan of the city, which is in the style of the ancient Spanish military towns, is a parallelogram, traversed longitudinally by two very narrow streets, intersected by equally narrow streets, all of them unpaved, whereby a number of squares are formed, around which are built of wood and occasionally of stone, the few hundred dwarfish, fantastic, ancient, dilapidated, and extensively-balconied and gable-roofed houses which characterize the town. You enter the place on the landward side by a common bridge spanning the marshy Sebastian; and it is protected from the incursions of the ocean by a massive sea-wall, which is the fashionable promenade, and from which projects the one solitary wharf of the port, whose commerce is represented by the occasional arrival of a steamboat from Savannah and some half-dozen fishing boats. In every direction are unmistakable evidences of the fact that fire and time have done their best to make this spot the home of desolation; and while the more ancient houses such as the residence of some old Governor or an old custom-house, proclaim the opulence and good taste of their builders, many others would lead one to suppose that their owners were cramped for room and very poor. Ruined mansions and ruined walls predominate, with not a few reduced families; and while the mere business man could hardly spend a day here without sighing to be away, there is an abundance of material to be found in the town and its vicinity to gratify for a long time the lovers of the picturesque and a kind-hearted population, of good living and fair sporting, and agreeable society, which may all be enjoyed under a sky where the rose-tints of summer are almost perpetual, and where roses, rich and rare, bloom throughout the winter, and the beautiful date tree, with the cabbage palmetto and orange, vie with the oleander and magnolia in lording it over the more unpretending but not less interesting plants which flourish everywhere in this latitude.

The population of St. Augustine is somewhere about twenty-five hundred; and, although it boasts of a small but highly intelligent class of American citizens, a large proportion are descendants of families who, as the story goes, were deceitfully lured to Florida, for selfish purposes, from the island of Minorca, by an Englishman named Turnbull. Though it has changed owners a number of times, having passed from the Spaniards to the English and back again to the Spaniards, and from them purchased by Uncle Sam, the character of its people has undergone but little change. The Minorcans are chiefly Roman Catholics, are a mild and inoffensive race, and in the small ways of fishing and shop keeping, industrious. They live on little, and their limited savings are mostly invested in slaves, whose services as hired servants yield them a small income. Their numerical superiority enables them to elect their own city rulers, and, by way of showing their regard for the doctrine of protection, they impose an annual tax upon their own slaves of fifteen cents, and upon those owned elsewhere, but employed here, a tax of ten dollars. As a community they are poor, and yet native paupers are unknown. They are small in stature, but delight in large families; and that they are honest is proven by the fact that they do not harbor in their midst such an affair as a jail. In their social intercourse the Minorcans are generally somewhat exclusive, for a very good reason, no doubt; and, as a matter of course, the more intelligent and refined portion of the community, among whom are several Minorcan families, occupy a sphere of their own. The little business of the place is carried on by the former class, but it may please future visitors to learn that the hotels and boarding-houses are all under the management of Southern individuals with "Northern principles" of domestic economy. From personal experience I can only speak of one of these establishments kept by Miss Fatio, a most estimable and popular lady; and if the others are as home-like and comfortable as this, the ancient city may well be proud of her houses for the accommodation of travellers and invalids. And thus much, in a general way, of the quaint, isolated, famous, and almost useless city of St. Augustine. That it abounds in curiosities may well be imagined, but the only two that can be understandingly described by the pen, are the Castle of St. Mark and the City Plaza.

St. Mark, though a castle by name, is really nothing more than a fortress of great strength, built by the Spanish Government according to the most approved principles of military science. By many intelligent people it might be correctly deemed a splendid affair; and yet, in some official document of our General Government, by whose mandate it is sometimes called Fort Marion, it has been pronounced merely a "good specimen of military architecture." It covers a number of acres at the northern extremity of the city, and is approached through a very picturesque gateway in ruins. It is built of coquina stone, with thick walls twenty-one feet high, and its four bastioned angles are surmounted with graceful watch-towers. The work, which slopes to the water on one side, is surrounded on the three others by a broad and deep ditch or moat, with perpendicular walls of masonry, over which is thrown a bridge to the entrance gate, which was formerly protected by a draw. The descent to this bridge is by two flights of winding stone steps, at the junction of which is placed a block of stone, with a round basin hollowed in the top of it, intended for holy water. Above the main entrance are cut in a block the Spanish coat of arms, and an inscription in Spanish, which may be translated as follows: "Don Ferdinand the Sixth, being the King of Spain, and the Field Marshal Don Alonzo Fernandos de Herida, being Governor and Captain-General of this place. St. Augustine of Florida and its province, hereby declare that this fortress was finished in the year 1756. The works were directed by the Capt. Engineer Don Pedro de Brazas y Garay." The cost of the fortress, which was more than fifty years in building, has been estimated at several millions of dollars. Whatever that may have been, it has been stated that when the builders petitioned the King for one of the later instalments to complete it, he replied, that they must either be building it high enough to look across the ocean, or of solid silver.

So much for the exterior; and now for a glance at the interior of this old fortress. My first and only visit of exploration was made in company with a small party of ladies and gentlemen, whose talking and laughing voices contrasted strangely with the feelings inspired by the gray storm-beaten walls which surrounded us, and the rank grasses and weeds, which not only covered the earth upon which we trod, but grew in wild profusion upon the ramparts and parapets of the war-worn ruin. I cannot attempt from recollection to give the number of rooms and cells that we visited. Among those which interested me particularly was the jail-room, whence the Seminole chief *Co-a-coo-che*, or Wild Cat, and twenty-three of his fellows, made their escape through a loop-hole, apparently too narrow to admit the smallest human head; and the story goes, that on the day preceding his escape, Wild-Cat informed his great fellow-prisoner, Oceola, of his intentions, to which hint the noble barbarian replied; "I will not go with you; you may go, and I should be glad to have my old father join you, but I cannot. They brought me here once, and they would bring me back again. Let me alone." The hero was even then broken-hearted, and so he died. The subsequent career of Wild-Cat has proven him a knave.

Another of the cavernous rooms of this old fortress contains an ancient Spanish money chest. So heavy and so huge it seemed, that nothing less than horse-power could ever turn the key or lift the lid, and resting against it were a pair of massive cannon wheels, made of solid mahogany. In another room there lay scattered upon the stony floor, in a sleep that could hardly experience another waking, a litter of great war-dogs in the shape of battered cannon; while members of the same family might be seen lying dismantled in every direction in the open spaces of the fort. Another and far more curious room was that which the builders had designed for a chapel, with niches in the solid walls for holy water, and a recess for the altar and the crucifix, and where many an old Spaniard must have knelt to count their beads and pray only a few moments, before their loyalty called upon them to apply the match that would send their civilized or savage enemies by hundreds into eternity.

But of all the half-hidden, low-arched rooms in this old fortress, the one denominated the dungeon is the most interesting. In an accidental manner was it discovered, by the falling in of a portion of the rampart attached to the sea wall, and in the deepest mystery is its history involved. It came to light soon after the fortress had been ceded to the United States, at which time, as our official guide informed us, there was found in one corner of it a human skeleton, the soles of a pair of shoes, and an earthen jug and cup. Not a single other object did its naked, slimy, arched walls cover, and these, even after a wall five feet in thickness had been broken through, could not be seen without a torch, so intense was the darkness. When we entered this dreadful prison-house the relics had been removed and scattered, but the same heavy darkness was there, and by the match that we lighted we could see nothing but the solemn walls and our foot-prints upon the dust-covered floor. Who, if the story be true, was the being that perished in this living grave? Of what nation? What his crime, if indeed he was a criminal? Was he a victim of religious bigotry? If so, he must have been a noted one. What a death was that to die! What a subject for thought, the fancied history of that poor mortal! And oh how cheerful and balmy was the pure air of heaven, the delicate fragrance of the flowers, and the sight of sweetly smiling faces, after we had escaped from this horrible place!

The city square of Augustine, to which I have alluded, occupies a central position in the town, and is quite a characteristic ornament. The promenading portion is only partially enclosed, and that too with what might be called a post and rail fence, and in the centre of it stands a monument some twenty feet high, which commemorates the giving of a constitutional basis to the Spanish Government. It is one of many which were erected in various portions of the Spanish dominions, and, with this single exception, the whole of them were demolished by order of Ferdinand the VII., on his accession to the throne.

It is quite a graceful affair, and its only inscription is "Plaza de la Constitution." Along the several streets which bound the square are situated the principal public buildings of the place. On the west is an old dilapidated mansion, which was the residence of a former Spanish Governor, but is now used as a hall of justice and for the public offices; on the north is a half-demolished Catholic church, interesting from its antiquity, with bare stone walls and a stone floor, several images, and a flat piece of mason work running up to a point in front, in which are cut four window-like holes, containing each a partly cracked bell; on the east is a small market-house, which is never occupied after sunrise, according to a peculiar custom of the place; and the bell which summons the Catholic population to mass, warns the market people to suspend their dealings in the things of life; and on the south side of the square is a small but neat and well-proportioned Episcopal church, in which, as well as in the Presbyterian church in another part of the town, may be enjoyed at the present time unusually good preaching, from the lips of two talented gentlemen. The prevailing religion of Augustine, however, is the Catholic, and, as Christmas is at hand, I have had an opportunity to witness the custom which in this town invariably precedes the Carnival. Masquerading parties are formed by the young men of Minorcan blood, and with bands of music they parade the streets until midnight, and, by virtue of the forbearance of the Protestant population, enter their dwellings without ceremony, and cut up their fantastic capers; after which, they retire to some rendezvous in their own quarter of the town, and spend the remainder of the night in dancing and festivity, to which they are universally addicted.

An amusing spectacle is also exhibited at the close of Carnival week, in honor of St. Peter, the fisherman of Galilee, by which his professional skill in the use of the net, is attempted to be illustrated. An eye-witness describes it as follows: "As I passed along one of the streets, my attention was arrested by a motley crowd of black and white people. I was at first at a loss to account for the rabble and the horrid noises they made.

On a nearer approach I perceived two half-grown men heading a company of maskers, who were clothed in a fisherman's dress. Over the shoulder of each was hung a common Spanish net. Whenever an unsuspicious person came within range of a cast, the net was suddenly thrown over his head, so as to enclose his person; and then, of course, followed a roar of boisterous laughter. Thus the streets were beset until the farce was ended."

In describing the objects of interest at St. Augustine, I must not forget to mention the United States Barracks, which occupy a spot where formerly stood a monastic retreat. The buildings are plain, but have a cheerful and comfortable appearance, and command a fine view of the country in the rear, as well as of the ocean. In the military graveyard adjoining, under appropriate memorials, repose the ashes of one hundred and seven American soldiers, who fell a sacrifice to the Seminoles in the Indian war, and who were the first fruits of the famous threat which Osceola made on closing his intercourse with the whites, after he had declared his intention never to leave the grave of his fathers, and had been refused the privilege of purchasing powder: "Am I a negro?" said he, "a slave? My skin is dark, but not black. I am an Indian, a Seminole. The white man shall not make me black. I will make the white man red with blood, and then blacken him in the sun and rain, where the wolf shall smell his bones, and the buzzard live upon his flesh."

But my pen is impatient to touch upon a more genial theme, and that shall be the climate of this region. That St. Augustine enjoys many advantages in this particular cannot be questioned, and the same may be said of the peninsula of Florida in general. If grey-haired men, who have passed the greater part of their lives here, are to be believed, a more equable and salubrious climate can hardly anywhere be found. It is, indeed, an evergreen land, whose breezes are ever soft, balmy, and exhilarating. While its short winters are usually so mild as to render fires unnecessary, its long summers are far from being irksome or depressing; and while whole volumes of testimony could be produced tc prove that nearly all, if not quite all, the pulmonary diseases, when taken in their incipient stages, may be eradicated under the influence of this climate. The average number of fair days in a year, and for a series of years, has been ascertained to be two hundred and fifty; while in the Northern States the average number of fair days per annum, has been fixed at one hundred and twenty. Once in a great while jack frost makes a flying visit to Northern Florida, but by the time that he covers the little pools with a film of ice, and nips with his fingers the more youthful orange trees, he hears the sighing of the trade winds, and departs for the north more suddenly than he came. It is not my province to speak at length upon the subject of this southern climate, with regard to its advantages or disadvantages in a medical point of view. The theories are so numerous, and so antagonistic, that those who flee to Florida, to escape their diseases, had better trust themselves to the Divine Physician, than to their medical advisers, or to the learned dissertations of the writing doctors, who are getting to be so very numerous throughout the land.

For those who would sing the praises of this climate no better plan could be devised than to catalogue the flowers which are now in full bloom here in the open air—the jonquil, the Spanish pink, the rose, the oleander, the datura, and geranium, and its chief productions in the way of fruit. It is indeed so genial that it nourishes with luxuriance in the open air nearly all the fruits peculiar to tropical climes. Among those which flourish within the limits of Florida, (though some of them do better in the more southern portion,) are the orange, pineapple, lemon, cocoanut, banana, date, citron, olive, and fig. Now, if these are not enough to make even a well man's mouth water, and suggest the idea that even his constitution might be benefited by Florida climate, then I hardly know what would. But, after all, even though it is but an hour since I had the pleasure of plucking with my own hand, and enjoying an orange and a few fine figs, I cannot forget the pulpy peach and the crisp apple of "my boyhood's home." The orange and pine-apple, however, are unquestionably the staple fruits of Florida, and consequently demand a more particular notice. Of the orange, there are three varieties—the sweet, bitter-sweet, and the sour. Previous to the year 1835, the groves of the former had, for a long time, been numerous and thrifty. Much attention was paid to their cultivation, and the average yield of good trees was five hundred oranges. The trade was brisk, and from St. Augustine alone were exported annually about three millions, yielding a revenue of $75,000. In February, 1835, however, a severe frost swept over this region and destroyed the entire species of the orange tribe, from which calamity the State is now only beginning to recover. The culture of the pine-apple has been found to be quite as successful and profitable as the orange, especially in the southern part of the State, where it is said to mature from cuttings in about eighteen months. An acre of land, which has to be of a peculiar quality, has been known to yield four thousand pines, and to be sold on the spot at five cents each. These few particulars indicate the superior advantages possessed by Florida for the cultivation of tropical fruits, and which, in future years, will undoubtedly do much towards enriching her more industrious inhabitants.

The foregoing allusion to the fruits of Florida naturally brings to mind the stately and magnificent live-oak. They usually grow in what are called "hummocks," and the approach to them, after a monotonous drive through the pine barrens, never fails to fill the traveller with delight. In their vicinity the air is cooler and more salubrious than elsewhere, the vegetation more luxuriant, the flowers larger and more fragrant, and the birds sing more sweetly. But their destruction, for the benefit of our navy, has kept pace with the gradual annihilation of the poor Indians, and the nobler specimens are few and far between. The men employed in cutting this oak are called "Live-Oakers;" they are generally citizens of New England, and spend only the winter in Florida, where the life they lead, toiling by day in the midst of so many beautiful and pleasant things to gratify the senses, and sleeping at night in rude log shantees, is full of romance. Occasionally, however, are to be found individuals, who have permanently abandoned their northern homes, and brought their families to Florida where they are happy and at peace in their possessions.

But the climate and soil of Florida are also well adapted to the growth of indigo. When the English had possession of the country, it was cultivated to a much greater extent than at present, and not even Caraccas could produce a better quality. It grows wild upon the barrens of nearly the whole peninsula of Florida. The seed of this plant is small and is sown, in March, in drill-rows. It blooms about the first of July, when the flowers and tender branches, which resemble white clover, are cut off with a sickle, and in a vat go through the process of steeping in water. The purple liquid thus formed, is then *churned*, whereby a blue *fecula* is formed, and this with the *sediment* form the solid indigo. The plant will yield three cuttings in a season, and one person can obtain two hundred pounds of the marketable article from three acres of land in a single season.

And now, by way of proving the authenticity of this letter, I must append to it an item or two in the sporting line. Within two or three miles of Augustine, with well-trained hounds, may be enjoyed the very best of deer-hunting; and in its immediate vicinity duck, turkey, and curlew-shooting to any extent. In the way of fish, the sheeps-head takes the lead, and a species of the salt-water trout follows it in popularity. The alligator is found here in great numbers. Though savage in their appearance, these monsters are afraid of man. They vary in length from three to twelve feet; live in dens, built of mud and weeds, after the manner of the beaver-houses; are very destructive to hogs; quite prolific, hatching from one to two hundred little wretches at a time; are supposed to attain a very great age, and, next to man, their greatest enemy, strange as it may seem, is the black porpoise, which frequently pursues them to their very dens. And speaking of porpoises, reminds me of the fact that only a few days ago one of these creatures was captured which was positively known to have been wounded in the upper fin by a rifle-ball over twenty years ago, and he was killed by an old fisherman, who has annually seen him feeding off the bar of St. Augustine ever since he was first wounded.

BLACK CREEK AND TRAVELLING INCIDENTS.

After leaving St. Augustine I retraced the land route to Picolata, crossed the St. John to the mouth of Black Creek, and in a small steamboat ascended that stream to Gerrey's Ferry, a distance of some twenty miles. From that point to Newnansville I was compelled to travel by private conveyance, and I managed to reach here in safety. The same feat, or something like it, has undoubtedly been performed by the officers of our army in former times, but their only enemies were the revengeful Seminoles; the dangers from which I have escaped were those of starvation and a rickety vehicle. But I have seen some curious places and people, and the first which I propose to mention is Black Creek.

This stream is forty miles long, some three hundred feet wide, and from fifteen to thirty feet deep. Although fed exclusively by springs, its waters are apparently as black as black can be, and its principal inhabitants are the alligator and the cat-fish. It is exceedingly winding in its course, and runs for the most part through an immensely dense cypress swamp, where silence and solitude reign supreme. Indeed, I do not suppose that more than a dozen human habitations could be counted immediately upon its banks in traversing its entire length, and these are so small and so dingy that they but add to the prevailing desolation. The vegetation is so rank and matted that you may travel for miles without catching even a glimpse of mother earth, and when you do you wonder if she is not getting to be amphibious, so very low and moist are her developments. While in summer the general aspect of the stream is that of a winding and beautiful black canal, walled in with green; its present appearance, now that the cypress trees are all leafless and gray, and completely covered with long hanging gray moss, is that of a stream hemmed in with a frieze-work of dark granite, at the foot of which is a line of green shrubbery, mixed up with reeds, while everywhere are floating upon the placid stream huge water-lilies without number, all golden in their attire. On peering more closely into this conglomerate mass of vegetation, however, the eyes of the traveller will ever find much to enjoy; for in just such a swamp does the magnolia attain its greatest perfection, and vines grow more luxuriantly and fantastically than in any other locality. And then, again, the hoary forest, as if jealous of its inner recesses, seems to have stationed its soldiery at every convenient spot, and as these huge giants extend their branches far over the stream, now holding high in air vines enough to rig a frigate, and then waving to the breeze their banners of moss, they proclaim their power and antiquity in a most impressive manner. Water-fowl of every variety and in immense numbers were gliding over the water and winnowing the air in every direction as we ascended the stream, and the one solitary camp-fire of a trio of negro raftman, which we saw at a late hour in the afternoon, tended but to increase the loneliness of the scenery.

Gerrey's Ferry, to which I have alluded, was the stopping place of our steamer, and a curious one in several particulars. The few buildings which compose it stand upon a desolate sand hill, with a pine barren on one side and on the other a cypress swamp. Among them is a store, owned by a person who is making a fortune by selling goods and shipping cotton; a grocery, where were assembled about twenty planters and teamsters, several of them intoxicated; a miserable tavern, where I occupied the same room and bed in which several individuals had recently died of consumption; one comfortable dwelling occupied by a very gentlemanly person, and a Methodist meeting house. The tavern accommodations were very poor, and the doleful aspect of the place was a good deal heightened by the circumstance that our ears were all night long saluted with the croaking of innumerable frogs in the neighboring swamp. Although large quantities of cotton are exported from this spot, as well as thousands of deer skins and horned cattle hides, whose original owners were wont to range in one common herd through the surrounding piney woods, yet, from all the information that I could gather, it is more famous for its alligators than any thing else. So abundant are these revolting creatures in this vicinity, that during the summer evenings their bellowing, which resembles distant thunder, is quite annoying even to the inhabitants, and it is a common occurrence for the more ambitious of these amphibious monsters to ascend and sun themselves in the road upon which the cabins of the embryo city are planted. On questioning an old hunter about this animal, he informed me that they were now quite as numerous as in former times, but smaller in size and more shy of their enemy, man. He had seen individuals sixteen feet in length, but a specimen nine feet long was now considered huge; and he further informed me that, on account of their peculiar organization, they had a habit of swallowing whole quarts of gravel and small stones by way of helping digestion.

In the way of incidents, I am indebted to Gerrey's Ferry for only two worth recording. I visited the encampment here of an emigrant family, consisting of an intelligent man and woman and fifteen children. They had built their watch-fire directly upon the bank of the stream, and as the woman was cooking their humble meal, children were playing with the dogs, the father cleaning his rifle, and the blue smoke ascended into the quiet air, to be lost among the neighboring cypress trees, the effect of the scene was picturesque in the extreme. The man informed me that he was a carpenter by trade, was born on the Atlantic coast, in one of the Carolinas; that he had lived some twenty-seven years in the interior of Western Florida, sighing annually for the breezes of the salt sea, and that he was now journeying to some pleasant place upon the Atlantic where he might spend the remainder of his days. He was a poor man, and yet the music of old ocean, which had lulled him to sleep in boyhood, had caused him to abandon a good business, and was luring him in his old age back to the shore of that same ocean. The other incident alluded to was not one that I witnessed, but I can vouch for its authenticity. A few weeks before my arrival, there had been a great drought throughout the country, and a venerable Methodist preacher happening to come along, who lived some sixty miles off, and who always looked out for the main chance, and bore no love to Baptists, was requested to pray for rain. He complied with the request, and when it is remembered that he was invited to plead for Black Creek especially, and that the towns alluded to were without any Baptists, but full of Methodists, the unselfish tone of his prayer was remarkable, and it ran in this wise:

"Let it rain, beginning at my plantation in Hamilton county, coming down the religious neighborhoods of Columbia and Nassau, where immersion is not practised, and reaching Black Creek—even Black Creek—and bringing forth in abundance—none of your little *nubbins*, however, but long ears—long as this good right arm."

From Gerrey's Ferry we drove to this place, a distance of forty-eight miles, the cost of which journey was twenty-four dollars, or just about half the value of the horse and buggy. We only experienced one break-down, but then the road was very good. Between the two places we noticed less than a dozen plantations, the owners of which occupied the most common cabins. The face of the country was perfectly level, and covered with a continuous pine forest, relieved at distant intervals by small cypress swamps or stagnant lakes, with here and there a very pretty stream. Corn and sweet potatoes appeared to be the main products upon which the inhabitants depended for a living, though a half-cultivated cotton-field was attached to each habitation, and I was informed that just enough sugar-cane was planted to supply the home demand. One of the natives informed me that he owned more than a thousand head of cattle, but when solicited for a cup of milk he was quite astonished, and told me that his family never used it; for, as the cows were always ranging through the woods, he had found it too troublesome to hunt them up and milk them. And when I found that venison and wild turkeys took the place of beef upon the tables of the inhabitants, it became apparent that horned-cattle were valued solely for their hides, and I was not surprised to perceive, therefore, that the poor, neglected, and naturally puny creatures were often compelled to resort to the Spanish moss for their daily sustenance.

The market value of a cow was reported to be about six dollars, while a county tax of three dollars per head was demanded from every proprietor. The opinion that I formed of the people generally who lived secluded in these piney woods, was that they were uniformly kind and obliging, moral as could be expected, but certainly not over-burthened with intelligence. Many of them had never seen a canal, a railroad, or a steamboat; and all they knew of the North was that the Northerners wanted to free all the slaves. During the day we passed a solitary "grocery," situated in the forest, where were assembled some fifty men and boys, from various unknown parts, who were in the full enjoyment of a horse-racing frolic.

But the most interesting event of our journey to this place, was the spending of a pleasant hour in the rude but comfortable cabin of one of the mothers of this Southern Israel. She was a widow, and her name Ann Munroe; seventy years of age, and a noble old soul. She was born in South Carolina, brought up in Georgia, and had lived in Florida ever since it was organized into a territory. We found her living in great seclusion, her only companions for months at a time being a servant woman and two children. We halted under her roof for the purpose of eating the cold dinner that we had brought with us, but to this she insisted upon adding a cup of excellent coffee, some delicious syrup, and oranges of her own raising. She told us that the last of her kindred, excepting one son, who was her only neighbor, had been long dead; and, in speaking of Florida, she called it "*Flurida,*" the "*Blossom of the United States,*" and the "*Garden of the Earth.*" She took it for granted that we were seeking a place in which to settle; we might travel hundreds of miles further, but we could find no region so desirable as Florida; people never came here once without coming back again. She was astonishingly active both in body and mind, and when seated at the corner of a fire-place that was near ten feet in breadth, with a cat lying at her feet, she presented a charming picture of domestic comfort and repose. She gave us her views upon religion; avowed herself a Baptist in belief, but had never joined any church; all churches were *ambitious*, and always getting into trouble; she loved her Bible and read it constantly, indeed it was her only reading. In speaking of her schooling, she said she had been to school for sixty years; not a school of books, but of the natural world. She knew that we had been to schools, to academies, and colleges, but in regard to her kind of school we were yet in our A B C's, and said that when we were as old as she, we would remember her words and pronounce them true. She told us to remember one thing wherever we went, and that was, "to do unto others as we would have others do unto us;" that was what she tried to do. We were welcome to her fire-side, and her fare was poor, yet there was a good deal of happiness in her rude home. On our expressing a preference to live among our friends at the North, in Maryland, rather than in Florida, with all its attractions, she said we were mere *babies*, and not yet weaned; *she* had to leave *her* friends, and thought it hard, but she soon felt contented, and found that she had friends everywhere; and her parting words were that she was our friend, and that we might throw ourselves upon the world, and if honest and industrious we should always have many good friends, and God would be our friend. We left the good old woman with reluctance, feeling that she

———"Had been kind to such
As needed kindness, for this single cause,
That we have all of us one human heart."

On reaching Newnansville we found the entire population, masters and slaves, in the full enjoyment of Christmas tide, or Christmas week, as it is here called. Indeed, every thing, as well as every body, seemed to be at loose ends, and it was with the utmost difficulty that we could secure any hotel accommodations. The houses were numerous enough, since they numbered about twenty, but then they were built of logs, very old, and few of them could bear the native test of a comfortable dwelling, which is to have the logs so near together as to prevent the slinging of a cat between them without injuring the animal.

Another peculiarity of these Florida houses is that they are always built upon blocks or sunken posts, and though the objects are to escape dampness and secure the greatest circulation of air during the warm weather, these open spaces beneath the floor are invariably occupied by all the dogs and poultry belonging to the establishment. The idea of thus building was obtained from the aborigines, who built their wigwams on this plan using pine sticks for flooring, grey moss for bedding, and palmetto leaves for a canopy.

We were deemed fortunate in obtaining lodgings, and I am now writing in the best apartment in the house. It is just large enough to hold a plank bedstead and admit one person at a time. It has two windows, but neither of them with a pane of glass; the roof is allied to those which make people wonder when they enter a modern New York church, and the space between the floor and the ground is inhabited by a sow and thirteen beautiful pigs. Hog, hominy, and sweet potatoe are our staples in the way of food, and, if not over delicate, are substantial, sweet, and good; they must at least be very fattening; but the negro servants who serve them up are very dirty.

But, with all its discomforts, I shall ever remember Newnansville with great distinctness and not without pleasure for having presented me with a comprehensive picture of southern life. Indoors and outdoors I have been perpetually reminded of an engraving which I have seen of *Vanity Fair*, by Cruikshanks. High and low, rich and poor, good and bad, the sober and intemperate, white and black, the wise and the foolish have come together, from village and from country cabins, to enjoy the most ancient festival of Christmas with the most boisterous hilarity. I have witnessed groups and scenes that were perhaps more peculiar than beautiful, and more exciting than interesting. The exercises of Christmas holiday usually commence with a casual meeting of the blacks by twos and threes at the corners of the streets, and, by the time all things are ready for a foot race, out step upon the sward as if by magic a bevy of sable damsels, dressed in white, with fancy turbans and huge pantalets and scarlet sashes around their waists; and then follow the scrub races, upon which the planters bet their dollars and the darkies their shillings; then the drinking and the merriment proceed after the most approved manner of the South. In the mean time a very nice young man, whom everybody praises, but who will have his "spree," has jumped into his buggy, and is racing his horse through the streets for his own private gratification, whereby he proves to the satisfaction of all who see him that his spirits are as abundant as they are good. Now the banjo and the fiddle are taken up, and two negroes are placed each upon a dry-goods box for the purpose of ascertaining which of the twain can dance the longest time without stopping to breathe; and then the negro children try their skill, and the patting of Juba seems to become universal. Anon we have a systematic street fight between a couple of rowdies; and then the motley crowd gather around an old hunter, who has just entered the village, riding upon a gaunt horse, and bringing to market the hams of his one hundred and fortieth deer of the season. At the approach of night the pastimes and noises of the day gradually subside, and give place on the part of the negroes to the break-down dance and religious services; and while the more jovial make the night hideous by their animal hilarity, those who are serious accomplish the same end by their moanings and wailings and wild singing. Indeed the perfect freedom which the negroes here enjoy during Christmas week struck me with surprise, and I am inclined to believe that if we have any tears to shed they should be shed for the master rather than for the slave.

THE SUWANEE RIVER AND WAKULLA FOUNTAIN.

The general characteristics of the country lying between Newnansville and Tallahassee, are similar to the portions of the State already described. It was only while approaching the capital that the monotony of pine woods and uncomfortable log cabins, was relieved by an occasional belt of hard wood forest and a respectable farm house. We travelled hither in dilapidated stage wagons, and experienced all the botherations of a new country. The only places that tempted us to tarry in them longer than a single night, were the village of Alligator and the banks of the Suwannee river; and these, with an account of Wakulla Fountain, shall be the subject of this epistle.

The place called Alligator consists of a collection of log cabins, occupying a cheerless sandy clearing in the midst of the pine woods. Its leading families are intelligent and respectable, but it harbors a set of tavern and grocery-keepers who are a disgrace to Florida. What supports the hamlet I can hardly imagine, unless it be the fact that it is a sort of resting place for the teamsters and travellers, who have occasion to pass from Jacksonville to Middle Florida. It derives its poetical name from a famous Indian, who was the head chief of the ancient Seminoles. It obtained its first mite of reputation from the circumstance, that when a party of Government surveyors once entered its limits for the purpose of defining its boundaries, for the benefit of a person who had purchased it as wild land, under a Spanish grant, the hundred inhabitants who occupied it made war upon the public officers, and drove them away. Its only attractions in the way of scenery are a couple of small lakes in its immediate vicinity, where alligators and cranes abound. And those of its inhabitants who have a taste for historic lore claim for it the honor of having been trodden by De Soto and his mad followers. It was this intelligence, indeed, that tempted me to tarry an extra day in the village, and as I was the guest of a very intelligent and pleasant gentleman, who felt a special interest in its history, my opportunities were all that could be wished.

As no two authorities had ever yet told the same story, in regard to the explorations of De Soto in this region, it is not to be wondered at that every village and plantation in Florida, Alabama, and Mississippi, should claim to have been one of his stopping places. That he landed at Tampa Bay, and struck the Mississippi river near Helena, is undoubtedly true; and that he was three years in performing the strange wild pilgrimage is equally certain. His force, according to Vega, was one thousand men; while Prescott alleges that Cortez entered Mexico with only five hundred, and Pizzaro entered Peru with one hundred and eighty-five men. When De Soto entered Florida he told the Indians he was descended from the Sun, that he came from the land of the Sun, and had come to visit the wealthiest lord of the new country. He moreover led his cavalcade mounted upon a horse of giant proportions, and as the poor barbarians had never seen such an animal, no wonder they were stricken with fear, and hastened to obey the orders of the Spanish chief. When a stranger, they treated him with kindness, but when they found out his real character they met him as an enemy. His scheme of conquest was conceived an iniquity, and met its legitimate fate; he was proud and cruel, died in the dreary wilderness, and to this day his burial place is unknown. The evidences that De Soto ever called a halt on the site of Alligator are by no means convincing. A local tradition is related, however, to the effect that a great battle was fonght on this spot between a multitude of Indians and an army of white men; and this is corroborated by the existence in the vicinity of the remains of a systematic earthen fortification and a number of mounds. One of these was opened for my especial benefit, but all the wonders it revealed were a few decayed bones and some bits of charcoal. It is said also that mounds and fortifications, like those at Alligator, are to be found all along the best authenticated route travelled by the famous Spaniard. In some of the mounds lying between Tampa Bay and Alligator, there have been found human bones nearly twice as large as the present race of men. In one of them seven bodies were found, seated in a circle, and facing the centre of the mound; in another a skull, with a hole just above the eye, and on the inside a flattened bullet; and in another, with such Indian relics as pipes, hatchets, arrow-heads and earthen pots, was found a steel and silver spur, marked with a Spanish coat of arms.

But the personal history of my Alligator host interested me far more than the De Soto traditions. He was born in Tennessee, the son of a worthy man, who was one of the best scholars of his day, and traced his ancestry to the landing at Jamestown. He first visited Florida about twenty years ago as a volunteer against the Seminoles; and, after quitting the army, he studied theology, graduated at a Western college, and was a preacher in the Methodist Church for ten years. The result of this campaign was that he impoverished himself, and, looking at his wife and children, he determined to do something else for their support. His last service as a preacher was to travel through the Southern States and obtain money enough to establish a religious institution. He then read law, was admitted to the bar of Tennessee, and, remembering the pleasant days he had passed in Florida, emigrated to this State. He pitched his tent in Alligator, and on the day that he opened his office his debts amounted to five thousand dollars. He was successful from the start, and as time progressed he became a free man, paid for the education of two brothers, both of whom are wealthy, and one a member of Congress, and through his influence was established a regular line of steamers between Charleston and Jacksonville, which has been of immense advantage to his adopted State; and at the present moment he is not only the wealthiest man in Alligator, but one of the most talented and influential lawyers in Florida.

After leaving Alligator, our route still continued through pine woods and over a level sandy road. As before, log cabins were few and far between, and the only objects that helped to relieve the monotony of the journey, by way of suggesting thought, were the Gophar and Salamander hillocks, which are from one to three feet high and cover the whole country, and the lime-sinks, which are also very numerous. The gophar is a species of hard-shelled turtle, considered, by those accustomed to them, good eating; they are said to live wholly on the land, feeding on grass in the night-time and chewing the cud like the cow. The salamander is a variety of the burrowing or pouched rat, which derives its name from the circumstance that it is in the habit of running over the ground while still warm after a recent burning of the woods. The lime-sinks alluded to, are among the more striking natural wonders of Florida. They occur in the dense woods, in groups, and isolated localities, and consist of perfectly circular basins, gathering to a point as they sink below the surface, and some of them are so deep as to bring the tops of large trees on a level with the eye of the spectator. They usually contain a small quantity of lime-stone water, and are affected by the freshets in the neighboring rivers. Living in their vicinity is considered unhealthy, and they are accounted for upon the supposition that they are a mere sinking of the earth, caused by the porous quality of the earthy formations in this region. It is, indeed, believed by some that immense subterranean passages underlie the whole of Florida. The sinks in question would seem to prove this theory, and a more striking proof is derived from the fact that there are many localities in the State where the jumping of a single man will cause the earth to sway or undulate like the surface of a thinly frozen lake. The person who acted as our coachman from Alligator to the Suwannee river was quite intelligent, and some of his conversation proved him to be well acquainted with men and things in Florida. He congratulated us upon our escape from Eastern Florida, the land of "hog and hominy," and upon our speedy entrance into Middle Florida, which he denominated the land of "sowins and chickens." The term *sowins* we found to be an abbreviation of *sourings*, which is a dish of pounded corn made sour by baking in the sun, and usually served up with a *gophar-steak*, than which nothing but India-rubber can be more tough and elastic. By way of illustrating the sometime effect of this food upon strangers, he mentioned the following circumstance: A solitary horseman, as Mr. James would say, was on his way through the pine country of this region. Having spent a night in a cabin, where he could procure nothing for his horse but corn husks, and been himself regaled at breakfast by some sourings and gophar-steak, the former dish turned his stomach and made him sick, while the latter resisted all his masticating efforts to the very last, and so he continued his journey. He travelled some thirty miles further, and at night-fall pulled up before another cabin. He asked if he could get a night's lodging and something to eat; to which the good woman replied, "Yes, if you can put up with 'sich as it is.'" Sowins and gophar were again placed before him; but he slept soundly and was off before day-light the next morning. As night came on again, he made another appeal for food, and "sich as it is" rang again in his ear; upon which he frantically mounted his half-famished steed, exclaiming, "It won't do; I tried 'sich as it is' at the last house and couldn't eat it no how." And thus, by the dim light of a new moon, and looking the picture of famine, he changed his course of travel to the nearest boundary line of the State, and was never more seen in these parts. As to the "*chickens*" of Florida, I know not that they differ materially from the chickens of other lands; but the rapidity with which they are here placed upon the table is truly astonishing; for the same individual which may have awakened you at dawn with his crowing will not unlikely be placed before you at break of day, floating in the fat of his old companion the pig. As in New England a broiled chicken is looked upon as a thing to be talked of, both before and after its enjoyment, so in some parts of Florida is a fried chicken considered appropriate food for only the more neatly dressed of travellers, and they are therefore generally reserved for the preachers. And it is said that when a genteel-looking person approaches the house the "chickens break for the woods," having so often seen the necks of their fellows wrung off after such an arrival. Would not, therefore, a Florida chicken, on account of its intelligence, if properly introduced, be considered as great a curiosity as the uncouth Shanghai or Chittagong, which now bear the palm in our Northern heneries?

The Suwanee river, which separates Eastern from Middle Florida, is a rapid stream, very dark, but clear, emptying into the Gulf of Mexico, running a directly opposite course from the St. John, thereby presenting another of the many singularities of this country. It runs over a bed occasionally of the purest white sand, and again over limestone ledges, where interesting fossils are found in the greatest abundance and perfection, and its bold and fantastically formed banks, with their wealth of vegetation, afford for the artist choice studies without number. Though watering a comparative wilderness, it boasts of two large white sulphur springs, which are twelve miles apart, and pour their medicated treasures immediately into the river. The accommodation for invalids at both of them are quite good, and they are annually visited by a large number of the Southern gentry. They gush from rocky fissures in a most copious stream, maintain an even temperature of sixty-seven degrees, and the sulphur pictures of every possible hue, with which their bottoms and sides are encrusted, struck me as among the most perfectly beautiful objects I had ever beheld. At one of these springs I had my first view of a sugar mill in operation. It was a small affair, consisting of two sheds or roofs, under one of which were the huge wooden screws between which the sugar-cane was pressed or ground, while under the other were ranged, over a brick furnace, three huge iron kettles used for boiling the juice. Negro children fed the fires and negro women watched the boiling; by whom also the very delicate task was performed of pouring, at precisely the proper moment for crystallization, into large wooden troughs, the hot and fragrant syrup. As I witnessed the operation of boiling or sugaring off on a very dark night, when torches were abundantly employed, the effect of the scene was exceedingly picturesque, and reminded me of an Indian sugar camp in the wilds of Michigan. On my arrival at the spot the head woman knocked one of the ebon boys heels over head for poking a long stick into one of the kettles for his own pleasure, and then presented me with a nice little pine stick with which to perform the very operation which had been vetoed in the urchin; and when about to take my departure another woman paid me the usual compliment of handing me half a dozen stocks of the sugar cane to luxuriate upon while traveling. In a conversation that I had with my landlord at this place I learned the fact that, by burying it in the earth, sugar cane may be kept in a fresh state for a whole season; and furthermore, that it requires the very best of land to bring it to perfection, and that in planting it all that is to be done is simply to lay stocks in the furrow and cover them slightly, as you would corn. I picked up at the same time the following particulars respecting the natural history of this region:

I was told, for example, that the beaver, which I had supposed was mainly to be found in cold and temperate climates, was not only a native of Florida, but were found here in considerable numbers, and that many of their dams and wonderful houses were to be seen in the valley of the Suwanee river. I have already mentioned the fact that the common red deer are very abundant in this State, and in Middle Florida they are particularly so. The more expert hunters kill from two to three hundred in a single season, and while the sportsmen usually employ the hound, those who kill for gain resort to fire-hunting. This latter custom is cruel in the extreme; for, owing to the blinding effect of the torches and the unsuspicious character of the animal, it is sometimes the case that a herd of half a dozen are killed from one position. Wolves, which were once very numerous in this State, are now seldom met with; but bears, wild-cats, and panthers are still to be found in considerable numbers. Of the smaller wild animals the opossum, raccoon, hare, squirrel and fox are very abundant; and wild ducks, brandt, snipe and curlew frequent all the ponds and marshes, and the common quail is found in every field. Turkeys are so plentiful as to be considered an important item in provisioning a family; they are commonly taken in traps, and when pursued with the gun, the old hunters think they are doing a small business if they kill less than half a dozen at a single shot.

But in the way of mere wanton sport there is nothing in this region to compare with alligator shooting by torchlight. The eyes of these monsters are large and brilliant, and when you go to the banks of a lonely lake or river at night and make a noise, it is a custom with them to rise to the surface by the dozen, and it is when stealing stealthily along to see what kind of meat they can get hold of, that they are shot with the rifle. When wounded they commonly climb on the shore, there to remain until they die. When instantly killed their bodies sink to the bottom, but rise again in a few hours. By some people the alligator's liver, if they have such a thing, is considered good eating; but the only use that I could ever find for them was to extract their teeth, which make very pretty whistles. The climate of the extreme Southern States seems perfectly adapted to the growth of alligators, and when undisturbed in their native haunts, their happiness seems to be complete. Delighting as they do in the smell of rankest vegetation and foul miasma, and in the companionship as well as flesh of fish, snakes, lizards and toads, they find here an abundance of these luxuries. Though not distinguished for their beauty, they are so for their affection and intelligence. In protecting their young they will brave every danger, and their manner of turning their jaws into traps for the capture of mosquitos and birds is most interesting to contemplate. A portion of their tails is considered by the negroes a luxury of no common order. Their teeth, which are eighty in number, have a cone-like shape and are shed every year. Their tongues are so small as to be almost imperceptible to the casual observer, and though their jaws are terrible to contemplate, they are by no means as destructive to animal life as their long scaly tails. As on the seaboard of Florida their most formidable enemy is the porpoise, so in the interior swamps is the black bear, between which the combats are sometimes terrific. As their history as a family, is classical and romantic, so are their habits strange and incomprehensible. They hunt and devour food with the greatest voracity, and yet have been known to fast for many months at a time. Their eggs, which number from one to two hundred are little larger than those of a hen, and are deposited in the sand, and the young when pursued flee for safety, down the throat of the female parent. They relish equally the sunshine or the sandbank and the gloom of their damp subterranean abodes under the grassy banks of the streams. They seldom attack man and as seldom are disturbed by his presence. They are horrible creatures to look upon, and yet there is a fascination about their wary movements. Though naturally quiet creatures, their love song resembles the bellowing of bulls; and while their eyes are thought to resemble those of the Chinese, like the Chinese too, if Charles Lamb is to be believed, they have a peculiar partiality for little pigs.

The great drawback, however, to all kinds of sporting or rambling in this otherwise goodly land are the rattlesnakes which abound here. They are perfect mammoths in their way, some of them measuring nine feet in length, four or five inches in diameter, and carrying fangs nearly an inch long; and it was only a few weeks ago, as my landlord informed me, that a negro child, while pursuing a chicken under a barn, scrambled over one of these horrible reptiles, but was not bitten, by the unheard of compassion of the snake; which, however, produced such an effect upon the child as to make him sick.

At the second spring to which I have alluded I stumbled upon and was much pleased to examine two portraits painted by ALLSTON when quite a young man. They were good in color, but defective in drawing, and had the stiffness which it seems to me characterizes the majority of this distinguished man's productions.

And now, before leaving the banks of the charming stream, associated in so many minds with a famous negro melody, I will allude to the freshets, of which it is sometimes the victim. The water has been known to rise some thirty or forty feet above low-water mark, which, for a river that comes out of a swamp and runs through a level country, is remarkable. At such times the forest and plantations are of course all inundated and much damage done. After one of these freshets, the surrounding country remains boggy for a long time, so that cattle and even men frequently break through the sod; and it is said that at such times the springs which empty into the Suwanee river eject from the bowels of the earth tufts of grass and bunches of dry leaves, thereby proving a connection between them and some neighboring marsh or lake. It is sometimes the case, however, that the traveller in this region is compelled to exclaim, with the ancient mariner,

> "Water, water, everywhere,
> But not a drop to drink;"

for good drinking water is scarce, and little dependence can be placed on wells, for they dry up and fill up in proportion to the quantity of rain; and one instance has occurred where the *bottom* of a well, forty-seven feet deep, to the astonishment of the digger, actually fell through a distance of eight or ten feet.

The country, as we travelled westwardly from the Suwanee river, gradually improved in fertility, the pine woods giving place to sturdy hard-wood forests, and the sight of an occasional church steeple, with a few white houses, had a very refreshing influence upon our spirits. Our stage-driver on this portion of the route was a worthy but poor man, and his friends gloried for him over the circumstance that he was the nephew of an ex-President; but the man himself had never received any political favors, and evidently felt himself happy in his humble position. The most curious thing I saw on the road was a pretty bonnet, made out of the fibrous portion of a native squash; and the best thing that we had to eat was another kind of squash, which was roasted in its shell, after a fashion of the ancient Seminoles.

With this Tallahassee, the capital of Florida, I am well pleased. It is a pretty town in location, capping as it does a high hill, contains some cheerful houses, with intelligent and hospitable inmates; and fashionable ideas in dress and equipages are quite prevalent. It is the centre of a productive cotton-growing region, and is connected with its seaport of St. Marks, by a *mule* railroad. As a place of residence, it is already desirable, and all it needs to make it a more prosperous town, is a sprinkling of Yankee enterprise, and the establishment of modern travelling facilities. The State-house is a handsome edifice, and by the gentlemanly officials connected with it, I was politely treated. The drives about the country are pleasant; but one, about fifteen miles in length, to Wakulla Fountain, eclipses all the rest; and with an account of this most perfectly beautiful and enchanting natural curiosity, I will conclude my present letter.

The springs of Florida are indeed among its most peculiar and attractive features. The Orange and the Silver Springs, in the eastern part of the State, one of them surrounded with an orange forest, and the other possessing the magic property of giving a white coating to the turtles and alligators that live in it, would repay the lover of nature for a long pilgrimage; but Wakulla Fountain surpasses them in every particular, and will hereafter live in my memory with the Saguenay River, Niagara Falls, the Mammoth Cave, and Tallulah Chasm. An adequate idea of this mammoth spring could never be given by pen or pencil; but when once seen, on a bright calm day, it must ever after be a thing to dream about and love. It is the fountain-head of a river which is twenty miles long, empties into the Gulf of Mexico, and is of sufficient volume to float a steamboat, if such an affair had yet dared to penetrate this solemn wilderness. When first I looked upon it, I was forcibly reminded of the old ballad description, which says,

"On the lakelet blue the water coot
Oared forth with her sable young,
While from its edge, 'mid the bordering sedge,
The fisher hern upsprung."

It wells up in the very heart of a dense cypress swamp, is nearly round in shape, measures some four hundred feet in diameter, and is in depth about one hundred and fifty feet, having at its bottom an immense horizontal chasm, with a dark portal, from one side of which looms up a limestone cliff, the summit of which is itself nearly fifty feet beneath the spectator, who gazes upon it from the sides of a tiny boat. The water thereof is so astonishingly clear that even a pin can be seen on the bottom in the deepest places, and of course every animate and inanimate object which it contains is fully exposed to view. The apparent color of the water from the shore is greenish, but as you look perpendicularly into it, it is colorless as air, and the sensation of floating upon it is that of being suspended in a balloon; and the water is so refractive, that when the sun shines brilliantly every object you see is enveloped in the most fascinating prismatic hues. It contains a great variety of serpent-like plants, and its mossy-looking bottom resembles the finest carpet, with white ground and fantastic figures of every possible color. It abounds in fish, both large and small, among which I recognised the black bass, the sea-mullet, and red fish, the bream, the sucker, the chub, and the shiner; and it seems to me that I can now recall every individual to mind as a personal acquaintance. They at times made the surface of the water alive with their gambols; they swam about their beautiful home in schools and singly, some of them watching our boat with curious looks, and others perfectly indifferent to our presence or movements. On dropping a sixpence into the water, a couple of them followed it in its zig-zag course to the bottom, pushed it with their snouts, and then scornfully turned tail upon it; and it was a most novel and interesting sight to see an occasional fellow floating gently up the sides of the cliff, from the deep chasm below, as if himself astonished that such fine scenery should exist so far under the surface of his native element. It was also very strange to witness the shadow which our little boat cast upon the bottom, which seemed to be refreshing to some of the fish that floated into it, but was not liked apparently by the alligators and huge turtles that went crawling along the sub-marine highway. A rim of rankest grasses and lilies surrounds the entire fountain, and at the foot of the numerous and gigantic cypress trees, all hoary with moss and heavily laden with vines which hang over the water, were the nests of innumerable water birds, such as the crane, the duck, and the bittern, whose screaming voices conspired to give a most wild and desolate aspect to the scene. Were it not a desecration to do so in such a fairy-like place, fishing with a fly in Wakulla Fountain for black bass and bream, would be superb; and were it not for the developments of science, we might imagine that the mammoth bones which were found in the spring in 1850, were the remains of some primeval angler who had been killed for daring to disturb its beautiful inhabitants. It has been discovered, however, that the relics in question were the fossil bones of the great mastodon, and those who have a tase for such matters, can be gratified with a sight of the remains of the Wakulla monster, by visiting the museum of Philadelphia, where they were deposited by George S. King, Esq., of Florida.

That the ancient Seminoles should have attached a legend to this brightest spot in their domain, was quite natural. Old men told it to their children at the twilight hour, under their broad palmetto trees. At night, said they in substance, may be seen around the shores and on the bottom of the fountain, tiny fairy creatures, sporting and bathing in noiseless glee; but at midnight, when the moon is at its full, there appears upon the water a gigantic warrior, sitting in a stone canoe with a copper paddle in his hand, from whose presence the fairies affrighted flee away, leaving, as the last object seen in the darkness of a cloud, the spectre warrior alone in his canoe, which seems anchored and immovable.

THE CHATTAHOOCHEE RIVER.

On leaving Tallahassee I took the coach to the Chattahoochee river, passed up that stream in a steamer, *rail-roaded* it through western Georgia, and came down the Tennessee river in a steamboat. That portion of Florida whence I made my exit appeared to be, and in reality is the most highly cultivated in the State. Broad and handsome plantations are numerous, and here reigns the very pretty little village of Quincy, where reside many of the more aristocratic families in the State, and which, as a matter of course, has a fashionable reputation. Our road as we approached the Chattahoochee, was much blocked up with fallen trees which had been blown down by a hurricane. It might indeed be said that the whole forest had been prostrated, for as far as the eye could reach, in every direction were to be seen the mammoth roots holding aloft their banners of greensward, memorials of the destroying winds. On the borders of this scene of desolation and towering high above the Chattahoochee, stands the State Arsenal of Florida, a handsome building, with pleasant residences beside it, but from its isolated position presenting an imposing appearance; all the materials for its erection, like those of many other buildings of like character in the South, having been brought from the Northern States. From this point we began to descend into the neighboring valley, and on emerging from the gloom of a circuitous and thickly-canopied road we found ourselves on the margin of the Chattahoochee river, and at the threshold of a lonely but most comfortable hotel, which we were told occupied the summit of an Indian mound. We reached this spot just as the sun was setting, and the gloom of the hour was in strict keeping with the tranquil stream, in whose depths, on every side, was mirrored a dense forest; and it was while dreaming, after a good supper, of this scene, and of the skeleton in Spanish armor which is said to have been found in these waters, that I was suddenly awakened by the shout of "*boat coming*," and had to finish my dream in a state room on board the *South Carolina.*

The Indian word Chattahoochee means muddy water, and the river is appropriately named. At the mention thereof my fancy wings its flight to the mountain land where this stream springs into existence, where Trail mountain and Tallulah chasm are the grand features of the land where I spent one of the pleasantest summers of my life, and which owes much of its reputation to the brothers Richards, who, with the pencil and the pen have lovingly described its interesting scenery. The navigable portion of the Chattahoochee extends to Columbus, Georgia, which is called two hundred miles from the Bay of Apalachicola, into which it empties. It is a lonely stream, with alluvial banks ranging from ten to forty, but averaging some fifteen feet in height, and covered with a dense vegetation, where the magnolia flourishes and tangled clusters of vines abound continuously. The adjoining country is sparsely settled, but the Georgia side is more populous and thriving than that of Alabama, and the monotony of the scenery was pleasantly relieved by an occasional cotton-shed immediately on the bank, in the rear of which were invariably to be seen a cotton-gin and a cluster of dingy cabins occupied by the planter and his slaves. The only incidents worth recording that we met with were the swimming of a hunted deer across the river, the flying across our bows of an occasional flock of turkeys, and the attempts of incipient sportsmen to shoot the wild ducks that everywhere winnowed the air. But the gradual fading away of the verdure of the more remote South into the wintry aspect of a colder climate was full of interest, even to the casual observer; and I noticed that north of what might be called the dividing line the magnolia and long gray mosses did not appear.

The steamboat in which I came up the Chattahooche was the

best upon the river, quite comfortable, and, like the great majority of those in Southern waters, was built at Pittsburgh. She was of the high-pressure genus, had a stern wheel, drew only two or three feet of water, and in making the dangerous passage from New Orleans to Pensacola had narrowly escaped being swamped. Her captain was all that could be desired in such an officer, and was assisted in his responsible duties by a couple of men who deserve particular mention. His engineer was Thomas Stubblefield, the inventor of an *alarm water-gauge* for which he had received a gold medal from the State of Pennsylvania, and which has been of immense service in preventing explosions by steam on the Western waters. His pilot was an intelligent slave, but a man who had frequently refused his freedom. His name is Peter Porter, and the amount of money which he was then earning for his master was one hundred and fifty dollars per month, one-half of which was regularly paid to the slave himself for his own use. Besides being the best pilot on the river, and scorning the idea of being a free man, he was the best swimmer in the country. He had been on a number of cotton boats at the time they were sunk or consumed, and had saved the lives, at different times, of no less than seven persons—one colored girl, two ladies, two boys, and two young children. The last person whom he rescued was a lady who knew him, and had such confidence in his skill that, when standing on the burning boat and told by our sable hero to jump into the stream, she promptly obeyed; when he plunged in and brought her safely to the shore. Indeed, all the subordinates on board the South Carolina were slaves, and not one of them but was abundantly able to instruct the free negroes on our Nothern steamers in the art of politeness. Most of these men were hired from their owners, and our captain informed me that it was customary everywhere in the South for the steamboat men to pay their hands from five to eight dollars per month more than their regular wages, which additional sum is called "Sunday wages," and is for the exclusive use of the slave. Such facts as these need no comment from my pen, and ought to put to the blush the ignorant fanatics of the North.

Among the passengers who ascended the Chattahoochee when I did, was a poor German taking to the State asylum of Georgia his only two children, who were deaf mutes and motherless. One of them was a boy of seven years, and the other a sweet little girl of ten, and their expressions of wonder at everything they saw and their strange efforts to be playful were painful to behold; and never can I forget the picture which they presented on a moonlight evening as they stood upon the upper-deck gazing in blank astonishment upon the sky, while their fond parent was pointing to the bright stars, and by signs attempting to explain their wonderful mission. The lonely river and the gloomy forest on either side were in keeping with the sadness which seemed to rest like a mantle upon the poor orphans and their sorrowful parent. Although this man resided in Alabama his children were born in Georgia, and for that reason and the man's poverty, the State had promised to give the boy a profession or trade, and to instruct the little girl that she might become a useful and happy member of society. A noble deed, and worthy of that most noble, intelligent, and prosperous State!

But I must not forget to mention the cheerful aspect which our steamboat presented as she came in sight of Columbus and paddled her way up to the levee. While the captain invited the passengers to assemble on the upper-deck the mate treated his negro boatmen to a drink of whiskey, which was a signal for them to march to the bow of the boat for the purpose of singing a song. There were twenty of them, and the ceremony was commenced by one of the fellows mounting the capstan and pretending to read the words to be sung from a newspaper, which he held upside down. Their voices were exceedingly good, but, instead of a regular song, the music was more of an incoherent chant, wild and mournful, and breathing forth such impromptu words as these:

"We's up the Chattahoochee,
On de good old South Calina,
Going to see my true love,
How is you my darlin?
Now de work is over
We's all coming home!"

To my unsophisticated ear there was more melody and pure sentiment in this native chant as it echoed over the tranquil waters, than I ever enjoyed in a fashionable concert room.

From the Chattahoochee to the Tennessee river we travelled by railroad, taking the cars at Columbus, which is a thriving place, with four or five cotton factories; spending a night at Macon, another business place, with a capital hotel; passing through Atlanta, which was quite a wilderness only a few years ago, but is now a kind of whirlpool of railroads; and after a ride of over three hundred miles arriving at the growing town of Chattanooga, on the Tennessee. Western Georgia, in a picturesque point of view, is somewhat tame, but the soil is fertile, and the people industrious to an uncommon degree. Indeed, the present very prosperous condition of the whole State would seem to prove that, though a slave State, it can hold its own when compared with the more enterprising ones of the North.

That portion of the Tennessee river extending from Chattanooga to Whitesburg (which is the port of Huntsville) is estimated at more than one hundred and fifty miles, and is by far the most picturesque and interesting on the river. The former place is surrounded with mountains which extend down the river for some twenty miles therefrom, hemming it in with jealous care, when they recede from the immediate banks and are only seen on either hand clothed in the enchantment of distance. In the immediate vicinity of Chattanooga rises a lofty peak, known as Look-out Mountain, from the summit of which the eyes may revel over all the mountain scenery of Georgia, North Carolina, Tennessee and Alabama. It obtained its appropriate name from the Cherokee Indians, who, in their time, were in the habit of looking out from this point far up the Tennessee, for the provision boats of the early emigrants that might be floating down, and which they often captured, murdering the poor whites who thus toiled for a support. But the grandest feature of the Tennessee is a mountain gorge called the Suck, through which the river passes, about fifteen miles from the Chattanooga. A travelled gentleman informed me that the scenery here reminded him of the Rhine; it reminded me, however, of the Upper Mississippi and the palisade portion of the Hudson. For a dozen miles or so, limestone bluffs rise to a great height on either side, a little back of the river; and while the immediate shores are covered with the most luxuriant vegetation, interspersed with gray rocks and an occasional log hut, the summits of the hills loom against the sky in a great variety of abrupt outlines. The waters of the river rush through this mountain gate-way with great velocity, and, though the small steamboats descend the stream without danger, it is with great difficulty that they can ascend, and during high freshets it is quite impossible. Whirlpools and eddies, as a matter of course, abound in the Suck, and the Georgia crackers or Tennessee trappers, who gave it that poetical name, have fastened upon certain localities such names as the Pot, the Pan, and the Skillet. That such a spot should have been the scene of many narrow escapes from drowning, as well as of cruel Indian outrages, is to be expected; and, among many others, the natives will tell you of Nancy Glover, who was the only survivor from an attack of Indians of a party of Royalists in 1780, and who, after seeing her father, shot down took the helm of their little boat and guided it through the entire length of the gorge, thereby escaping with her life. That portion of the Tennessee extending from the Suck to Whitesburg runs through a hilly country but not mountainous; and though the country is in reality well cultivated, yet the hard wood forests are sufficiently abundant to suggest ideas of the wilderness. Upon some of the bottom lands the trees and vines grow to immense size, and cotton and corn both attain their greatest perfection. Although the vegetation, when we came down was just beginning to assume its spring or summer garb, yet, it every where bore a most cheerful aspect, and the mistletoe hung from the trees in such great profusion as often to present a continuous wall of green along the banks of the stream. The red deer, I was informed, are very fond of this plant, and the hunters often decoy the poor creatures to death by plucking off bunches of the plant from the upper branches and hanging them upon the lower limbs, so that they can be reached by the browsing animals. The only drawback to the pleasures of a voyage down the Tennessee arises from the miserable steamboats, which are usually stern-wheelers and exceedingly filthy, and the hotel accommodations on the route. The road hitherward, however, is good, and so are the coaches. The country is rolling, soil very rich, plantations highly cultivated, negroes numerous and happy, and more than one-half of the real estate lying directly on the road is the property of a young, beautiful, and accomplished woman, who is justly celebrated for her qualities and wealth as the heroine of these parts.

HUNTSVILLE.

WITH the town of Huntsville, Ala., I am quite delighted, and do not wonder at its reputation. It occupies an elevated position, and is hemmed in with high hills, from the summit of which it presents an uncommonly picturesque appearance. The surrounding country is very fertile and highly cultivated, and the cotton interest has made it a place of considerable business. It claims a population of some twenty-five hundred souls, contains many handsome residences, with several neat churches, and is the seat of two institutions of learning, the Bascom Institute, and a Presbyterian College. It is supplied with the best of water by a mammoth spring which gushes from a rock in the centre of the town, and this, with the array of from one to two hundred saddle-horses which are daily collected around the county court-house square, ought to be mentioned as among the features of the place. But, on becoming acquainted with the people of Huntsville, (as it has been my privilege,) the stranger will find that *they* are the leading attraction. Owing to its pleasant and healthful location a large number of the more influential families of the South have congregated here; so that the society is all that could be expected from a happy union of intelligence, refinement, and wealth. Several of the fortunes which are enjoyed here were acquired in New Orleans; and, judging from the intimate intercourse existing between that city and this inland village, it might almost be imagined that the latter was the country cousin of the former. To this condition of things, therefore, may be attributed the fact that knowledge of the world and expansive ideas in regard to life are more a matter of course in this somewhat isolated place than in other Southern towns of the same size. To give an idea of the wealth of Huntsville it is only necessary to state that the aggregate fortunes of twenty well-known families, are said to amount to six millions of dollars. Some of the private hot-houses and gardens in the place would delight the most fastidious of horticulturists, albeit the mercury has fallen sixty-one degrees in the last ten hours. The lover of art will be surprised to find here a private gallery of paintings and statuary which is said to have cost seventy-five thousand dollars, and contains some productions of decided merit, which is a remark that many private galleries in the country cannot bear.

On the score of hospitality, the people of Huntsville are unsurpassed by any of their neighbors, if indeed they do not excel very many of them. I would not make any unjust comparisons, but I must judge from personal experience. I entered Huntsville a stranger, and took lodgings at its best hotel, which was comfortable, but by no means luxurious. Its reputation was not good, however, and this circumstance, in spite of my earnest excuses, caused me to become the guest of one of the leading families of the town, under whose roof I have been made to feel perfectly at home, and where I have been treated more like an old friend than a stranger. This is the way they treat pilgrims in Alabama, and no wonder, therefore, that the interpretation of its beautiful name should be *Here we rest;* and now I remember, moreover, that Huntsville lies within the bend of that portion of the Tennessee river which caused it to receive the name of *Spoon river*, thereby appropriately suggesting the idea that the good things of life are here most abundant. And thus much in a general way of this pleasant Southern town.

And now for a *sable* incident or two, which I think worth mentioning on account of the morals they inculcate. On Sunday last, in one of the leading churches of the town, and by an eloquent man, was preached a funeral sermon on the body of a negro child. There was a large attendance of rich planters and their wives, and much feeling was manifested by all present. The father of this child, though a slave, is an expert blacksmith, and earns annually one thousand dollars, three hundred of which are given to his *master*, while the remaining seven hundred are retained by the "down-trodden" victim for his own use and benefit. It would seem, therefore, that to hear the clanking of this man's chain the practical abolitionist would have to enter his workshop. I have also witnessed since my arrival here a public sale of slave property. The number of persons disposed of was some half-dozen; they belonged to the estate of a deceased planter, and were sold by his administrator for the benefit of his orphan children. The conditions of the sale were that no family-ties should be broken, and that deeds would be given only to those purchasers who would pledge themselves to be perfectly kind and humane. The prices ranged from one thousand to sixteen hundred dollars, and as much hilarity prevailed among the darkies when assembled in front of the court-house as if they were about to enter upon a frolic; and I was forcibly impressed with the manner in which the more high-priced jeered those of the party who had only brought a thousand dollars, calling them "cheap thousand dollar niggers." The effect of the sale upon the orphan children, however, was sad in the extreme, and I heard one of them exclaim, a young lady, that she was altogether "the greatest sufferer there." The same roof had sheltered them in other days, and I verily believe that if there had not been some legal impediment the orphans would have sacrificed their whole property before parting from their well-tried and devoted servants.

The vicinity of Huntsville, although rich in many more important things, is especially rich in odd characters, and one of my particular favorites of this genus is old John Evans, who must now make his bow to the public. He was born a vagabond, bred an overseer, and leads the life of a wayward and wandering hunter and fisherman. He is a middle-aged man, lank and brawny, amiable to the last degree, and a natural naturalist. It is said that he has made and been worth his fifty thousand dollars, but he sold himself to the Mephistophiles of

Monongahela, and now lives in a log-cabin on the banks of the Tennessee, the poorest and most independent man in his county. He has been a close observer of the creatures with which he chiefly spends his time, and his conversations upon their habits are always interesting. I give you a few items that I remember. He had killed a rattlesnake measuring six feet in length, in whose stomach was found, nearly in a perfect state, a young fox; and he has seen a water moccasin snake seize a small fish and hold it above the surface of the water, as if conscious of the fact that this was the quickest way to deprive it of life: and he also asserted, what seemed to me incredible, that the eyes of the common buzzard, after being pricked to blindness by a sharp knife, possessed the power of completely recovering themselves in the course of fifteen minutes, provided the head of the bird was placed under its wing during the time. In regard to this last assertion I proclaimed myself quite skeptical, and yet John Evans will declare upon oath that he tried the experiment on five different birds with complete success, and I may add that one of the most intelligent and honorable gentlemen in Huntsville testifies to the truthfulness of Evans's strange story. From time immemorial old women have declared that down, under a buzzard's wing was good for sore eyes, and if the marvellous story cannot be traced to this medicinal one, then must we see in the latter a proof of the former. But as John Evans's explorations in natural history are usually more amusing than useful, so are his hunting expeditions more frequent than profitable. He objects not to trapping an occasional beaver for the sake of the novelty, or to killing a deer, a few turkeys, or a score of ducks for the market, but he is a far happier man when he is lying in wait for the varmints of the country, as he calls them, such as the fox and the coon, the hedge-hog and the skunk, the mink and the corn-stealing crow. And in more than the figurative sense is our vagabond hunter a marked man, for the first glance at his countenance never fails to convince the stranger that he carries a double-face, since the right side has been blackened with bruises and rendered almost fleshless by the continual kickings of his rusty old gun, which he declares shoots to perfection when about half filled with powder and shot. So industrious is he withal that he has been known to spend an entire day in wading a muddy pond for a few ducks, and devoting a whole night to revenging himself upon some unfortunate dog that may have chanced to annoy him on a quiet road which he is wont to travel. In spite of all this, however, he has a lazy look and a languid air; and yet the most unaccountable of all his eccentric and contradictory traits is an overweening passion for wild horses. He dotes upon them, spends all his spare cash for good specimens, and the more vicious they are the better, and whether drunk or sober he is a superior horseman. Indeed, so many have been his narrow escapes from being killed that he is known the country round as "the man who never lets go;" and the last two stories related of him, by way of proving his chief characteristic, are as follows: On one occasion, while journeying to a neighboring town, he chanced to kill a rattlesnake, and, desiring to preserve its oil for the cure of rheumatism, he cut off the serpent's head and deposited the body for safe keeping under a bush until his return home. He was riding at the time a very wild but partially blind horse, and, when the moment arrived for picking up his plunder, he seized the snake in his left hand, and, holding it aloft, continued his journey. The horse became frightened, and with a loud snort started to run away. The tail of the snake occasionally touched his flank and increased his fear; he became unmanageable and flew like the wind, until the people of Huntsville were alarmed by the sudden appearance in their midst of the steed and rider, around whose head the snake was flapping at a terrible rate, and whose only exclamation was a grunt of defiance, while the reptile was perfectly secure in his convulsive grasp. On another occasion our friend John promised an acquaintance a mess of pickerel, (here erroneously called salmon,) and started upon a fishing expedition. He was successful, got drunk, and, mounting his horse, started for home. On his way thither he rolled from his saddle, caught his foot in a stirrup, and in this manner by the gentle and sagacious horse was dragged along the road, holding on like grim death to his string of fish, and muttering to himself "this is a devilish rough road, any how." As fortune would have it, the very man for whom the fish were intended happened to meet the fisherman in his unhappy plight, and rushing to his assistance asked him if he was hurt; whereupon John Evans exclaimed: "I told you so, Billy, by gum; I've caught the two biggest salmon you ever did see." Many a black bottle has our hero emptied since that time, and many times has he been thought a dying man; but he is still "holding on" to life, and is still pointed at as "the man who never lets go."

Since my arrival in Huntsville, about ten days ago, the rains have been unusually heavy, and the streams of the country are at present much higher than ever before known. All travelling by water as well as by land has been suspended, and the Tennessee river, which at Whitesburg (the port of Huntsville,) is usually half a mile wide, is at present nearly five miles in width, and a three-story house, standing on a high bank, where I took breakfast on my arrival, is only now discoverable by its chimneys. I revisited the place for the purpose of sketching it, and the man who drove me down descanted upon it as a "one-horse concern," which I found to be a sneering epithet indiscriminately applied here to a poor town, a small steamboat, or a mean man. At one of the only two cabins belonging to Whitesburg which were not submerged I witnessed a young and delicate white girl chopping up a huge log of wood, and was told that, as her father was seldom at home and her mother was sick, she was in the habit of doing all the wood-cutting for the family. This picture reminded me of the back settlements of New England, where were born some of the more notorious political declaimers against the slavery of the black race.

But of all the impressions made upon me during my visit here, the most agreeable by far was made by Miss Julia Pleasants, the young and accomplished poetess. She is as great a favorite in the entire South as she is in this her native town, and is destined to be wherever the thoughts of genius can be appreciated. She commenced her literary career by contributing an occasional poem to the Louisville Journal, whose distinguished editor, George D. Prentice, Esq., has done more by kindly words than any other man, to foster female talent and encourage the female writers of the country. Born and bred in the lap of luxury, it is a wonder that the intellect of Miss Pleasants should have been so well disciplined as its fruits, in spite of their unripeness, would lead one to suppose it had been; but death having recently made her an orphan, and taken from her side a much loved sister, she has been schooled in the ways of Providence as well as of the world, and now, when she strikes the lyre, it responds chiefly in those tones which find a resting-place in her sorrowing heart. That she has written and published too much is, perhaps, a matter of course. Her numerous admirers have been gratified, undoubtedly, but she has not been benefited thereby, any more than was Mrs. Hemans by her poetic repetitions. Like Mrs. Hemans, however, Miss Pleasants is a thinker and writer of a high order, and her mission upon earth cannot but be both beautiful and profitable. As she has not yet published a volume of her poems, it is hardly proper that I should view her with a "critic's eye;" but the carefully considered compliment that I would pay to her genius, is abundantly fortified by a manuscript volume of her better productions, which it has been my privilege to read and to enjoy. The most ambitious and most faultless poem which she has yet written, is called "*The Viewless Bride,*" and is a superb personification of the New Year. It is allied in spirit to Bryant's "Thanotopsis," quite as original in conception, and nearly as melodious and hymn-like a composition. And another poem, entitled "*The Lost,*" written in memory of her parents, can hardly be read without tearful emotions. That I am permitted to append these two poems to this letter, is simply an evidence of my importunity and the lady's kindness.

The Viewless Bride.

Sad, sad and low the Old Year's dying sigh,
Steals up the cloudy ramparts of the sky;
And gaily to the midnight's silvery chime,
The fair Young Year trips through the wintry rime.
The beautiful Young Year! all tears, all smiles,
Emerging from the future's shadowy aisles,
Her snowy garments flutter far and wide,
And vaporous mystery veils the Viewless Bride.
The night-winds warble as she wanders by;
The night-clouds flee the empyrean laguli,
And merry stars come, singing joyous rhyme,
To grace her bridal with primordial Time.
With time, that grand and high mysteriarch,
Who leads his rites through regious dim and dark,
And wins the vestal years, a lovely race,
To bloom and perish in his wild embrace.
And yet how bright and careless glistens now,
The cloudless radiance of the New Year's brow;
The gentlest twilight-fall not yet hath shed
Its dewy darkness on her youthful head;
Swift o'er the glacial sward she gaily flies,
And carols to the blue columnar skies.
She recks not of the cycles gone before,
That died like surges on a storm-beat shore,
But light and airy is her printless tread,
And joyous o'er the slumbers of the dead.

Ah! who can tell through what a wildering way—
Through what a wild her onward track shall stray?
How often will she view the night-stars pale,
And lordly forests totter to the gale,
The morning sky with weighty tempests bowed,
And tears descend from evening's lilac cloud;
What wrecks shall strew the stretching ocean sands,
When glory leads to strife the clashing bands;
What cities fall to rise not up again,
When earthquakes desolate the peopled plain.
Alas! it needs no prophet's trump to peal
The woes her future wanderings shall reveal;
We see her marching now—a victress chief,
In all the dark emblazonry of grief;

Around the bright Olympian sun she drags
A ruined star, and waves her flamy flags.
A myriad fluttering pulses cease to beat,
And crimson heart-drops stain her snowy feet.
Far down the star-lit vistas of the sky
Her pean wild-like muffled thunders fly—
They fly, alas! the saddest, saddest song,
In all the chorus of the astral throng.

The fair Young Year! her dowry is the tears
That stricken mortals fling on silent biers;
Her bridal garlands are the sorrowing rue,
The funeral cypress and the tristful yew.
She cannot shun the woe her touch imparts,
For each fresh footstep crushes human hearts;
And still where'er she turns through boundless space,
Death, death she finds the heir-loom of her race.
The bright New Year! What dark and fearful change
Her step will bring upon the mountain range—
Beside the silver stream—out on the sea,
And where the desert girds the lone palm-tree;
To many a tropic clime—where icebergs roll
In silent grandeur round the frigid pole—
Where lava-tongues fork through the crater's mouth,
And swift Siroccos sweep the lovely South—
Where iron battle leads his crested van—
Wherever roams the restless race of man.
Ah! yes, though now she carols but of glee,
To many a one her silvery song will be,
The honey-birds, that wiles with tuneful air,
The Eastern traveller to the wild beast's lair.

Such sorrows are, and oh! far more beside,
The pale attendants of the youthful bride;
And yet sometimes she circles, like the larks,
With music through the dawning grey and dark,
The fair young Year! pale trembling thing! She brings
Some blessings dripping from her dewy wings;
Not altogether is she crowned with tears,
But here and there a sunshine streak appears.
And who could not forgive a double face,
When half is wreathed with smiles and gilt with grace?
Aye! though she only boasts of terrene birth,
She'll make for some an Eden of this earth:

We see her now with angel wings unfurled,
In pitying guardage of a shipwrecked world.
She calls her children out by bright blue streams,
And gives to truthful spirits pleasant dreams.
She loads with song the night-bird's silver tongue,
And nurtures tulips for the gay and young;
While round the good man's wrinkling brow she weaves,
With tender hand, the snowy almond leaves.
She thrills with joy the artist's raptured soul,
When crimson twilights round the welkin roll;
And cheers the swain with thoughts of future ease,
When Autumn's fruitage bends the orchard trees.
To one she gives a proud and lustral name,
And circles genius with the wreath of fame,
Then where the bright hymeneal altar glows,
She crowns another with a blushing rose.
And some shall find a bright and shining hope,
That long had mocked the costliest telescope,
When they shall learn the joy of sins forgiven,
And tread the straight but starry path to Heaven.

The Lost.

How kind they are, to come in sleep,
When earth is robed in silence deep,
And soothe, with pressure soft and mild,
The weary temples of their child.

How good, to leave unswept the wires
Of gold, which grace their angel lyres;
And breathe such loving lays divine,
Across a heart so sad as mine.

It is no dream, I see them now—
Above my couch they gently bow,
As oft in childhood's morn they came
When illness touched my tender frame.

They look not old, (their veins are rife
With gushings from the fount of life,)
But young, as when they joined their lot
In love, which death divided not.

Their locks are thrown, as if to hide
The scarce-seen wings on either side,
For fear I might not recognize
Such shining wanderers from the skies.

But memory never could forget
Those white-arched feet so firmly set,
Which seemed to childhood's wondering mien,
Fit only for a fairy queen.

'Tis she! beneath its dark-brown hair
No other brow could shine so fair,
And with the soul's pure radiance grace
That soft divinely Grecian face.

That chiseled head—that clear profile—
That living intellectual smile—
Those soft blue eyes—that voice, which stirs
My very soul—they all are hers.

"My child"—what tones of love profound,
(Earth hath not now so sweet a sound;)
"Let grief no more corrode thy breast,
And break thy sainted mother's rest.

"My stricken darling, mourn her not,
But be contented with thy lot;
Let all thy life be good and pure,
And teach thy spirit to endure."

And who is he, with visage bland
Who holds in his her slender hand?
A mien so free—a heart so true,
This clouded earth sure never knew.

He speaks, and to each tender tone,
My soul returns impassioned moan;
While shades of bright but fleeting years
Are mirrored darkly in my tears.

"My daughter"—oh! that thrilling word—
My heart is quivering like a bird
Through which, while breasting stormy skies,
The archer's gilded arrow flies.

"My daughter"—ah! a thick'ning flight
Of sighs break through the bars of night,
And all its flood of tear-drops roll
Upheaving from my billowy soul.

They stain the loving hands, which now
Would calm the aching of my brow,
While fast their heavenly features grow
O'ershadowed with terrestrial wo.

They cannot brook so sad a sight,
On wavering wings, they take their flight;
They seek again the Eternal Throne,
And I am left alone,—alone.

THE ALABAMA RIVER.

In coming from Huntsville to Mobile I took a round-about course of no particular interest, to *Montgomery*, and came down the Alabama river by steamboat. The seat of government of this State is one of the most thriving towns in the South; and I can well believe what I have heard, that all its inhabitants have a business to follow, and are invariably true to their interests as business men. The city lies directly on the great United States mail-route from Washington to New Orleans, and is of course much visited by strangers; and it is the centre of one of the most productive and wealthy cotton-growing sections of the Southern States. It is pleasantly situated on an elevated bank of the Alabama, and commands two interesting views of the river, which bounds it on the north. The highest point within its limits is capped by the Capitol, from which the eye wanders down a broad street somewhat resembling Pennsylvania avenue. It boasts of a large and handsome hotel, which is kept in a manner to please the most fastidious. By virtue of its character as the law-making place for the whole State it is a fashionable city, and, as the fashions of the South are somewhat peculiar, I will touch upon a few of them in passing.

Everybody is highly dressed, and while the gentlemen confine themselves to black, wear massive gold chains, and always support their dignity with a cane, the ladies dress in the brightest colors obtainable. The size of the canes used by the former is graduated by the size of the gentleman, in an inverse ratio, and occasionally you may meet a small dandy with a club large enough to frighten Hercules. The use of tobacco is almost universal among the men, and not uncommon with the other sex; the former devoting themselves to it in the shape of cigars and fine-cut, and the women, hailing generally from the country, in the form of snuff. "Dipping for snuff," as they express it, is a prevailing practice with ladies in several of the Southern States, and is used ostensibly as a dentifrice. While travelling I have met at the hotels and in private houses females carrying in their hands a small bottle of snuff, and, instead of using it after the common mode, they apply it to their *teeth* by means of a soft pine stick, prepared for the purpose. That this habit affords an exhilarating pleasure to those who practice it, is undoubtedly true, but to the mere looker-on it caps the climax in the way of tobacco abominations. But the city ladies of the South, if they do not use tobacco after the forementioned fashion, often follow another fashion which is hardly less offensive to good taste—the fashion of powdering their faces and painting their cheeks and lips; and instances have occurred where a mother has actually ventured to paint the lips of her infant child. Let but such facts as these become notorious, and the proverb of "painting the lily" will become obsolete. The poet says, "a thing of beauty is a joy forever," and the remark is true; but I could never see any more beauty in a painted white woman than I could in a painted Indian man. Were it not for the practice alluded to, more beautiful women could nowhere be found than in the South; and it is to be hoped the day is not distant when all such unhandsome habits will be abolished.

Although Montgomery is considered at the head of navigation, steamboats occasionally ascend a few miles further to Wetumpka, on the Coosa river; and from that point to Mobile the distance is rated by the pilots at four hundred and forty miles. I came down the river in a leisurely manner, whereby I had an opportunity of trying all the better steamboats and of examining the towns and landings which line the river. Of the latter my note-book tells me that there are no less than two hundred, which simply means that this is the number of private individuals whose plantations are honored with the same attention which in the Northern States is only conferred upon villages and towns. In the time of high freshets, however, the *lowlanders*, who constitute the majority, are compelled to haul their cotton for shipment to the bluffs of their more fortunate neighbor, the *highlanders*. Upon these spots are generally erected spacious warehouses, some of which are shed-like in their appearance and a hundred yards long; while others built up from the ordinary water-mark, are many stories high. Long and steeply-inclined planes are necessary appendages to all these storehouses, down which the heavy bales are slidden with wonderful dexterity by the plantation negroes, and tiered up on the steamers by the negro boatmen to the number sometimes of two thousand bales. To the traveller who is in a hurry, this important business of taking on cotton is a great bore, but to those who can take pleasure in witnessing athletic feats, or have a taste for the picturesque, it is full of interest. The negroes, as individuals or in gangs, are always amusing to contemplate or talk with, and it needs but little sagacity to discover that, if they are low in intellect, they are often far from deficient in humanity and moral culture which cannot always be said of the plantation overseers and steamboat mates who superintend the loading of cotton. The whole aspect of an Alabama bluff when a steamer is shipping cotton at night is truly beautiful; for then it is that pitch-pine torches illuminate the entire scene; and, while the gay passengers are dancing and feasting in the gilded saloon of the steamer, the loud and plaintive singing of the negroes gives animation and cheerfulness to all whose lot it is to toil. In managing the heavy bales the negroes invariably work in pairs, and an iron hook, which each man always carries about his person, is the unmistakable badge of his profession. A hard time of it for a few weeks in the winter do these fellows have; but then they seem to be quite happy. Hardly ever, for even an hour are they permitted to sleep undisturbed upon their only beds, the cotton bales, and at all times are they summoned by the perpetually ringing bells to their severe labor. They are well fed, however; and I noticed that they were usually supplied with a moderate but comfortable quantity of grog. Their wages vary from thirty to thirty-five dollars per month, with one dollar and a half for Sunday wages. The freight upon a bale of cotton for any distance is one dollar.

Of the few towns or villages at which I tarried I have but little to write. Selma, which is flanked by a rich and well-cultivated country, is a place of schools, and is flourishing. But with this place is associated, in my mind, a picture which was quite touching. It consisted of four slaves, three women and one man, who were seated upon the upper forward deck of the steamer, while directly at their side stood two gentlemen, between whom a bargain had been completed in regard to the servants. When the boat was about to start and the parting moment came, the old master went up and spoke kindly to the slaves, shaking each one *twice* by the hand, and said, " Good-bye ; take good care of yourselves ; I was too poor to keep you but you are not separated." To which the slaves all replied, "Good-bye, good-bye, good old master ; God bless you !" Cahaba is another flourishing and cheerful little place, where I found comfortable hotel accommodations and witnessed the performances of an artesian well which is said to yield thirteen hundred gallons of water in a minute. Of Claiborne the next and only village on the Alabama worth mentioning, I have to say to you that it is chiefly remarkable for its elevation, since you have to ascend to it by an almost endless flight of steps, and for its bed of fossil tertiary shells. In this town it was, by the way, that Sir Charles Lyell was mistaken for a Methodist clergyman, and it is to be regretted that he did not doff the man of science for an hour and give the citizens a few ideas on the advantages of temperance, hospitality and common decency.

In describing the Alabama steamboats it is only necessary to say that they belong to the same high-pressure and boiler-bursting genus found on all the Southern and Western rivers. They are almost invariably built somewhere on the Ohio, and when above the mediocrity, are really splendid affairs. The fare from Montgomery to Mobile is ten dollars, and for this you are furnished with a state-room and as good eating as the country affords, the great drawback being the half French fashion in which the food is cooked and placed upon the table. Claret and white wines are also furnished without additional cost, and if you desire it you can have a cup of coffee served to you before leaving your berth. Even the negroes revel on all these so considered luxuries. As a general thing more attention is paid to the comfort of the lady passengers by the officers on board these Southern steamers than is usual in the Northern States, and the servants are universally polite and accommodating, if not particularly tidy. As an offset to the above-named advantages, however, must be mentioned the annoyances identified with bar-rooms and gaming tables. The habit of gambling is very common, and, excepting in a few of the better boats professional blacklegs, usually travelling in pairs, but always appearing as strangers, are allowed the freedom of the boats. Their regular business, as a matter of course, is to fleece the unwary, which they do by marked cards and other tricks; and I am informed that it is no uncommon circumstance for an innocent but silly planter to lose five thousand dollars in a single night. Once in a while, however, you may find a captain of a boat who has enough love for his kind to inform his marked passenger of his danger by warning him against certain meek looking gentlemen. The speed of the Alabama boats varies from ten to twenty miles an hour.

And now for a running account of the Alabama river. For about two hundred miles below Montgomery its characteristics are moderately-elevated banks and a vegetation peculiar to a temperate climate, where even in winter the forests have a greenish tinge on account of the great quantity of mistletoe. But, as you descend the stream, the banks gradually become almost level with the water, and a continuous forest of cypress and magnolia, of live oak and juniper, fades away to the sky in every direction; and their sombre effect upon the mind, with their never-ending festoons of gray moss, is by no means mitigated by the muddy, sluggish and lonely stream. Cultivated fields and comfortable mansions are nowhere to be seen from the river; but in their stead, linking the dark woods with the yellow water, are long lines of reedy jungles, all green and monotonous, with here and there the huts of wood-chôppers and hunters of the bear. Many of the trees which lie stranded on the shores or loom gloomily out of their watery beds are of enormous size. As I have seen specimens bending with the weight of their grape vines, huge and multitudinous, I have been reminded of an old monarch in chains; and when I have seen others holding aloft over the stream their great masses of moss they have almost seemed to breathe the words, "Beware, stranger! Come not here; death is here, death is here." From that point where it is joined by the Tombigbee to Mobile, the Alabama was formerly called after the city of Mobile, and as it widens into the bay of that name its long reaches are truly grand and imposing; and at the sunset hour, when in one direction the smoke of an unseen steamer in a bend of the river is rolling high into the air ánd in another you see an extensive marsh on fire, the effect is marvellously fine and imposing.

THE TOMBIGBEE AND BLACK WARRIOR RIVERS.

INTENDING to revisit Mobile, I only remained there long enough to secure a passage up the Tombigbee and Black Warrior rivers, and in this letter I propose to embody my experiences in regard to them. What has been said generally, in the preceding letter, of the scenery, towns, and steamboats of the Alabama river is quite applicable to the rival streams flowing through the westward section of the State. My first steamboat trip up the Tombigbee took me to the quiet and pleasant town of Columbus, in Mississippi, between which place and Mobile it was impossible for me to ascertain the distance, since no two of the natives told the same story, but I remember that the landing places numbered two hundred and seventy-three. Our boat was one of the best on the river, but, as there was a strife between her and her captain as to which would carry the highest head of steam, the sail was anything but soothing to the nerves; and moreover we were nightly beset with heavy fogs, so that the local vulgarism of "going it blind" was fully appreciated.

With the efforts of our steamboat hands to make the nightly darkness visible I was amused, for they accomplished their object by hanging out huge pinewood torches from either side of the boat, and whenever she got entangled among the trees, which was frequently the case, there was a display of fireworks among the mossy trees more novel than interesting.

Our supply of gamblers was unusually large, and the manner in which I saw a game of cards broken up was quite exciting. The hero of the incident was a rich planter, who had been swindled out of several hundred dollars by means of marked cards, and who, having had his suspicions roused, called for a fresh pack, and when the game commenced, very coolly laid a loaded pistol on the table, and remarked that he would shoot the very first man whom he even suspected of foul play. As a matter of course he lost no more money on that trip. On my way up the Tombigbee I was first made acquainted with the true version of the witty incident which has done more than any thing else to give this river its reputation. When William H. Crawford was Secretary of the Treasury he wrote to the collector at Mobile, Silas Dinsmore, to ascertain the length of this river, which request he worded to this effect: "How far does the Tombigbee run up?" To which the laconic Collector replied: "The Tombigbee does not run up at all; it runs down;" and was by the return mail dismissed from office. Mr. Dinsmore is universally mentioned as a man of ability. A favorite theory with him was that America was peopled by the Northmen, and, as a compliment for several articles that he wrote upon the subject, the King of Denmark presented him with a diploma. The original name of this river was Ich-tom-big-a-bee, which in the Choctaw tongue means Trunk River. It was so called because in very early times a man lived upon it who made boxes. Those who now live on its banks tell me that it is subject to high freshes and of course muddy, but that in summer it is picturesque and very clear. A single day was enough to exhaust the wonders of Columbus, as well as those of its more aristocratic neighbor and rival, the town of Aberdeen, beyond which steamboats seldom ascend; and a drive of two days, over a horrible road and an uninteresting country, brought me to Tuscaloosa, on the Black Warrior river.

And what shall I say of this famous Tuscaloosa, which derives its name from a noted Indian chief who had the honor of giving De Soto a thrashing in the times of old? It is a beautifully situated and tastefully laid out town, with broad streets and many pleasant residences, but at the present time sadly dilapidated. It was formerly the capital of the State, but everything like government patronage having been transferred to Montgomery, its people seem to have become disheartened and lost all their former enterprise. Nothing more forcibly reminded me of this fact than the appearance of the hotel where I lodged, which in its dimensions is quite imposing, for it measures in length three hundred and forty feet, and is three or four stories high. Many a time in other days has it been the home and congregating-place of three hundred and fifty persons, while its present list of boarders does not number more than ten persons. A walk through its deserted chambers reminded me of Moore's song about the halls of Tara. I felt a respect for the house for its apparent antiquity, and when informed that the landlord had been stationed here for nearly twenty years, I looked upon him as a curiosity, for such things are not generally permitted by the "fast" age in which we live.

Many objects that I stumbled upon reminded me of the gay life which was once led here by the aristocracy of the land, and as I reflected upon the cause of this great change which had taken place, and upon the intrinsic merits of the town, I felt provoked with its present race of inhabitants. They are a stagnant people, in a stagnant place, but the fault is their own. Not only is the town the centre of a fertile corn and cotton-growing region, but it is at the head of navigation on the Black Warrior river, and is flanked by a coal and iron region ninety miles long and from ten to thirty wide, with coal seams not less than ten feet in thickness. Its climate is all that could be desired for health and comfort, and it is interesting to naturalists as constituting the extreme southern limit to which the ancient carboniferous vegetation has been traced in the northern hemisphere. In addition to all this, its citizens are highly intelligent, and it is the seat of a flourishing institution of learning, the University of Alabama, whose officers consist of a president, eight professors, a secretary, and librarian. A more intelligent or refined body of literary and scientific gentlemen I have never seen anywhere.

One of them, Prof. Michael Toumey, an amiable and talented man, is the geologist of the State, and has published a number of able reports; and another, the Professor of ancient languages, Samuel M. Stafford, in a career of official duty extending through eighteen years, has only lost two days, and on these he was an invalid. The college buildings occupy a very pleasant spot in the vicinity of a romantic fall of water; and, while its general library of 8,000 volumes is particularly rich in rare and valuable works, its cabinets are also of superior excellence.

The present number of students is one hundred and eight, and I was informed that the expenses of obtaining an education there, with economy, and without room furniture, clothing, and travelling, need not amount to more than $200 per annum. There is also going up in Tuscaloosa an extensive building, intended for a State asylum for the insane. It is to be built of brick, is eight hundred feet long, and while the architect, Samuel Sloan, is from Philadelphia, all the masons and carpenters are slaves. A cotton factory and a paper mill have also been established here, and in the hands of Yankees are both doing well. What folly, therefore, is it in the people of Tuscaloosa to be forever sighing over the departure of their former glory, which was, after all, not much more than a fanciful idea? Tuscaloosa ought to be a gem of a place, and if its men of property would only boast less of their cotton bales and smart negroes, and do a little more with their own perpetually gloved hands, they would increase their own happiness and respectability as members of the body politic. Though a very slow one at the present time, it was in former days a very fast one; and, as an evidence of this fact, it may be stated that every lawyer glories in the title of judge, every sporting character in that of colonel, while the titles of general and captain and major are as plentiful as politicians.

From my agreeable landlord and other persons in Tuscaloosa, I obtained a number of items which I think worth recording, as illustrative of some of the peculiar phases of fortune and Southern life. The "Flush Times of Alabama," which have been so admirably described in the popular book bearing that title, occurred in the memorable year of 1837. One individual, whose credit was at that time so low that he could not obtain his grog upon credit, was nevertheless so great a favorite of fortune, that he went to New York and purchased goods upon credit to the extent of $50,000; and what surprised me a little was the recollection that my own hands had marked his numerous packages, when I was a Pearl street clerk. By way of depicting the peculiar business traits of the modern Tuscaloosians, it has been stated to me that while an extensive bed of coal is known to exist within a mile of the town, it is customary to order even from Philadelphia the needed supply; and that while the country affords a beautiful quality of marble, the tombstones of the place are all imported from Italy. To give their sons a liberal education is a paramount idea with the planters of this region, and where they can afford it no expenses are spared; but when you come to talk about acquiring a profession and practising it, that is altogether a different affair. With many persons the impression seems to be that the only elegant way in which to pass through life, is to have a plantation and do nothing at all. To such an extent is the idea of doing nothing sometimes carried, that this story is told of one individual: He had obtained a new book, and while he threw himself in his wife's chair to enjoy its contents, she went out to make some calls. On her return she found her husband in bed, and, on anxiously questioning him about his health, he very coolly replied that "the fire went out, and he had resorted to the bed to get warm," although at the same time there was a pile of wood in an adjoining room, and a dozen servants on the premises, but the trouble of ringing the bell was not to be undertaken. But I would not be censorious in my remarks; and, by way of illustrating the healthfulness of the public mind, (though I cannot say much of what the *hands* are doing,) I would state the fact, that the National Intelligencer and New York Observer are the journals which you most frequently find patronised by the reading men of this section of country. And this allusion to good papers reminds me of a circumstance connected with a good book, viz: Horse-Shoe Robinson, by Mr. Kennedy. Within an hour's ride of Tuscaloosa, and in a lonely forest, is the grave of the hero of that novel. He came from South Carolina into Alabama at an early day, and died here about ten years ago. Many people now living remember to have heard him recount the manifold adventures he had experienced in the campaigns, and his name is ever mentioned with respect and affection. His real name was Galbraith, but from the fact that he had been a blacksmith, he obtained the soubriquet of Horse-Shoe Robinson; and I am informed that to the description of his person by Mr. Kennedy, ought to be added the peculiarity of remarkably high cheek bones and deeply sunken eyes, both strikingly indicative of his true character. He has a grandson living in Tuscaloosa at the present time.

The character of the Black Warrior or Tuscaloosa river is precisely similar to that of the Tombigbee; and, as I came down it in a steamer that was overloaded with cotton and cattle, I will pass on to what I have to say of Demopolis. This town lies on the eastern bank of the Tombigbee, and differs from its neighbors in being flanked by a rich prairie country. It was settled by a colony of French families at the conclusion of the Napoleon wars, and among them were several of his officers. One of them, named Raoul, who was a genuine colonel in the French army, came to this country with a letter of introduction from Lafayette to Madison. During his sojourn at Demopolis, he obtained his living by keeping a *scow ferry*, but subsequently returned to France, was reinstated in the army, and died a general. A few of the old French residents are still left in Demopolis, and are a most interesting portion of the community, where all are intelligent, hospitable and polite.

One thing that I heard of, but unfortunately did not see in the vicinity of Demopolis, was a manuscript Bible of great antiquity. It is the property of Dr. John B. Witherspoon, who believes it, on the testimony of tradition and the title page, to have been written about the year 850. It has been described to me as being eight inches long, six inches broad, and five inches thick, and is written on parchment, richly illuminated, and bound in oak. The fortunate proprietor is a resident, I believe, of the village of Greensboro', in this State.

My voyage from Demopolis to this place was attended by no

remarkable incidents, but by many that were characteristic of the river. We stopped at scores of plantations, now taking on board a hundred and then only five bales of cotton, at one place a few horses and mules, and at another a lot of cattle, which the frolicsome negroes forced on board the boat by biting and twisting their tails. At nearly all the landing places we noticed the negroes at work in the fields, and the women had a trick of dropping their hoes and running to the steamboat, to receive from the boatmen presents of tobacco, which were always distributed with great liberality. The only dwellings that we saw were rude log-cabins, and it was difficult oftentimes to distinguish the planter's residence from the domicils of his slaves; and, while a cotton-gin was invariably attached to each plantation, there were occasionally to be seen forlorn and deserted cabins, which reminded me of a man walking on stilts, so high were the blocks or trunks of trees on which they stood. The owners of the plantations where we stopped were seldom or never seen, but the overseers always. All the parties that met each other seemed to be personally acquainted, and so free and easy were the "down-trodden" negroes, that I have frequently seen them go up to the captain of the boat, or to the overseer, and ask him for a bit of tobacco or a cigar. As in the works of Nature in this Southern land there is a free luxuriance, so among the people is there a freedom of intercourse, which gives the lie to nearly all the assertions of the political fanatics of the North.

And now for a "disjointed chat" about St. Stephen's, which is decidedly, to my mind, one of the most interesting places in Alabama, because not only of its history and its patriarch, but on account of the model plantation with which and with whose proprietor I have become acquainted. But I must particularize. The modern town of St. Stephen's consists only of a picturesque bluff overlooking the Tombigbee, a post office and land office, hidden in the piney woods some two or three miles from the river, four or five rude cabins within a rifle shot of each other, also in the woods, and one large plantation, extending from the river north of the bluff mentioned, to the public offices. The ancient town of St. Stephen's as it might be called, however, and which stood upon the bluff, was a very different affair ; for, about fifty years ago, it was the largest town and principal post in the Alabama valley, as well as the centre of an extensive Indian country. It numbered several thousand inhabitants, was protected by a Spanish fortress, under which was a natural cave which is still worth visiting. It transacted quite a large commercial business, and contained a theatre, a bank and an academy. All the better buildings in the town were of stone, and it is said, altogether presented a handsome appearance. But nature and fortune were against the place, and more rapidly than it arose did it degenerate into a hamlet of no importance, when the few remaining inhabitants posted off almost in a body to Mobile; and it is a singular circumstance that some two hundred of the picturesque edifices now to be found in that city once towered in beauty on the bluff of St. Stephen's.

But the glory of this old town is forever departed, and the Georgia Cracker spake truly when he said of it that it reminded him of what he had read in the Bible—*Babby Lion.* Rank weeds have taken sole possession of the abandoned cellars, while here and there may be seen the unmarked graves of men whose fortunes were identified with and who ended their days on this spot. One that I remember deserves to be mentioned with particular regard. His name was J. M. Thompson, and he was the first man who ever took a cargo of provisions from the Ohio river to the Alabama valley, and this he accomplished by means of a barge of thirty-five tons, propelled by fifteen oars and manned by as many Kentuckians, who were all "half-horse and half-alligator" fellows. They had an easy time of it floating down the Mississippi, rather a dangerous one in coasting the Gulf of Mexico, and when they came in sight of the then Spanish fort of Mobile, they hoisted the American flag and passed directly up the river without even condescending to ask permission. It was a daring and high-handed act, and the guns at the fort were got ready to fire upon the trespassers, when the commandant concluded that the men must be mad, positively crazy ; so they escaped unharmed. Thompson made money by his venture, became a citizen of St. Stephen's but died a few months after his arrival. The crew that accompanied him from the Ohio took to evil ways, and the majority of them were either killed in private fights or executed by the Spanish authorities for breaking the laws.

Another man formerly identified with St. Stephen's was one McGrew. He led the life of a hunter and man-of-all-work, and had a cabin in the pine woods just without the limits of the town. He hated the Spanish authorities with his whole heart, and the compliment was reciprocated. Difficulties were constantly occurring between the parties, and his Rob Royish exploits were frequent and desperate. But the great event of his life was in substance the following: An ox belonging to McGrew chanced to wander into the vicinity of the Spanish fort, and, being in a good condition, and having the hunter's *brand* upon him, was shot down, and ordered to be dressed for the commandant's larder. The hunter was of course very angry, and scrupled not to express his opinion of the outrage and its perpetrators. He was then arrested, imprisoned for a month, and sentenced to be publicly whipped at the flagstaff within the fort. The unhappy hour arrived, and he was on the spot; but before a lash was given he bolted suddenly out of the clutches of the turnkeys, and running to a wall that was eight feet high, scrambled over it, and, though twenty-five guns were fired at him he made his escape. A reward of one hundred dollars was offered for his body, dead or alive, and four Spanish soldiers went upon a hunt for the hunter. They got upon his trail; even caught sight of him; and his chances for life were slender enough. He was without a weapon, while his pursuers were well armed; but, as fortune would have it, the first soldier who came up to him was killed with a pine knot, the second with a stone, and the third had his shoulder blade broken with a club, whereupon the fourth Spaniard suddenly changed his course of travel, and poor McGrew was at leisure to meditate upon the loss of his favorite ox.

I come now to speak of the man whom I have designated as the Patriarch of St. Stephen's. Of just such a man was Shakspeare thinking when he wrote:

"His silver hairs
Will purchase him a good opinion,
And buy men's voices to commend his deeds."

James Magoffin is a man as modest as he is venerable, but I trust that he will not censure me for printing his name. Officially speaking, he is the register of the land office here, and as the St. Stephen's office is the oldest in the Southern States, so is Mr. Magoffin the oldest land office register. To add that he knows every thing about the landed interests of the South would be superfluous. He was born in Philadelphia and commercially educated in that city. When nineteen years old he was thought to be consumptive, and having been told that the only chance to prolong life would be to emigrate to Alabama, where the piney woods, an abundance of milk, and riding might do him good, he took the advice, and, though an old man, he is still in the enjoyment of good health. He came to the South about fifty years ago, and from the start he was taken in hand by the authorities of the general government. His first appointment after the country became ours was that of post-master, his second that of collector of the customs, and his third that of issuing commissary and sutler; and as he was a good penman and a map-maker, when the land office was established at St. Stephen's in 1809, he was invited to attend to that business, and for five years thereafter he was not away from his office, at one time, more than thirty minutes. He was a member of the Convention that formed the Constitution of Alabama, and has also done something in the way of mercantile pursuits and land speculation, and many a city lot in St. Stephen's that may now be bought for a dollar or two has he sold for a thousand in other days. He has been connected with the land office of St. Stephen's ever since its establishment, and the innumerable and massive books that he has filled with his penmanship would hardly display their neat and business-like pages, I ween, without his presence. He was never married, and has been as constant at his post as the old Dutch clock which clicks upon the mantel-piece of his log-house, office and home. He came to the South with letters from Gen. Jackson, who was his personal friend; and among his other intimate friends were such men as the late William R. King. He was the first man in the South who paid particular attention to the culture of grapes, and as long ago as 1809 he made his hundred gallons of wine. For thirty years has he been a correspondent of Mr. Longworth, of Cincinnati, who is now making a fortune by a business that was suggested to him by Mr. Magoffin. Horticulture is evidently Mr. Magoffin's hobby and while he boasts of the fact that he cultivates forty varieties of grape and annually makes some four hundred gallons of wine, which he distributes among his friends and neighbors with a most liberal hand, he is at the same time constantly trying experiments and making discoveries in regard to the culture of corn and other valuable grains. His life has been a useful one and it cannot be said of him that he knows not how to be old. With propriety may we turn from Shakspeare to Armstrong, and say of him—

"Though old, he still retains
His manly sense and energy of mind.
Virtuous and wise he is, but not severe;
His easy presence checks no decent joy.
Him even the dissolute admire; for he
A graceful looseness when he will puts on,
And, laughing, can instruct."

But I have obtained from Mr. Magoffin a variety of local facts and incidents which cannot but make an interesting paragraph or two; and these shall now be the burden of my song.

The first has reference to an interview that Mr. Magoffin had with Tecumseh, the celebrated Shawnee warrior, on the banks of the Alabama. The former had been arrested while journeying through the Creek Nation with Government despatches, and it was while domiciliated with his kind protector —who was a medal-chief, lived in a log cabin, and worked twenty negroes—that Tecumseh made his appearance on a friendly visit. As the oft-repeated question of "Who killed Tecumseh?" has never been answered, it may be gratifying to behold a physical and mental portrait of the warrior, sketched by a man of Mr. Magoffin's intelligence. He was five feet ten inches high, brawny and stout, had a Roman nose, and an eye that could not be looked into without emotion. He was attended by a suite of thirteen warriors, and in everything that he did conducted himself like a prince and a gentleman. Mr. Magoffin having asked and obtained permission to shake his hand, the Prophet remarked "that he was glad to see a white man from the father city, and that General Washington was a great warrior." He inquired as to the stature of Washington, and on being told "just about your height," he drew himself up and took a complacent glance at his own person. After asking many questions about the "big men" at Washington, he was invited to take something to eat; and, while daintily enjoying himself—for he was much of an epicure—he turned to Mr. Magoffin and said: "Your people are fond of good living, but they don't live right. I noticed in Missouri that they eat too much hog; that is not good. If they would eat more deer meat they would run faster. If they eat so much hog they will turn to hog." On being questioned about the Indian dish of *suckatash*, he remarked "that he knew all about it, that it came from the North, and that the western Indians got it from King Philip."

And here is an anecdote with a twofold bearing. When Lieut. Col. Richard Sparks was in command of Fort Stodart, in 1808, Mr. Magoffin was his clerk, and executed all his writing. The proclamation with which Sparks fell into the movement of Reuben Kemper to invade Florida was written by the aforesaid clerk, and the press on which it was printed was the first that ever appeared in what is now the State of Alabama, and that press was brought to Fort Stodart from Knoxville, Tennessee, by a man named Samuel Miller. Sparks was undoubtedly quite willing to act as he did without any urging, but he was unfortunately supported by the then Governor of Louisiana, Mr. Claiborne; and just before his arrest, and in time for the court-martial, he cunningly obtained a letter from Governor Claiborne sanctioning his course in the most explicit manner. This letter was kept secret until the trial was nearly ended, when Sparks, who had played many a game of cards with the presiding officer, but with whom he had quarreled, stepped up to that gentleman, and, handing him the Claiborne letter, very coolly remarked as follows: "I have all my life been in the habit of fighting savages; I have never been taken by ambush or surprise; and now, General, I will thank you to play to that card." Sparks was acquitted and Claiborne's integrity was seriously questioned; but I believe his conduct was subsequently satisfactorily explained.

Another local incident obtained from Mr. Magoffin was about Hal's Lake, a stagnant sheet of water lying between the Tombigbee and Alabama rivers, a short distance above their junction. The lake obtained its name from a negro who, about thirty years ago, ran away from his master, and in an extensive cane-brake swamp bordering the lake built himself a cabin, and subsequently established a kind of colony of runaway slaves. The spot was far more desolate than Cowper's "lodge in some wilderness," and almost the only creatures that ever penetrated into it, besides the darkies, were black bears and alligators. The business which supported that interesting clan was that of stealing, which they carried on principally in Mobile, which they visited furtively in their canoes, travelling at night and remaining in ambush by day. In process of time they hatched a foolish conspiracy to murder the people of Mobile, but a repentant fellow exposed the plot, whereupon the officers of justice ferreted out the outlaws; a desperate fight took place, many persons on both sides were killed, and so Hal's Lake returned to its former state of desolation. The stolen property which was discovered here was of considerable value, and among the prisoners taken were black children who had never seen a white man.

And still another, but more amusing incident touching a citizen of this region, happened in this wise. He was an old and wealthy, but inexperienced planter. Happening to be in Mobile on one occasion, he repeatedly expressed a desire to witness a fire, but as often as the bells rung, was disappointed. On one occasion, however, he was gratified, for the hotel where he lodged chanced to take fire at midnight. The excitement was of course great, but the consternation of the planter knew no bounds. In his fright he hurried from his room, and down into the street with breeches and coat in one hand and trunk in the other, shouting with might and main "Run, Tom, Dick, and Harry, run quick and help, for the d—d plantation is on fire!"—and meeting one of his most intimate friends in the street, he rushed up to him and exclaimed: "Stranger, help me to take my trunk to the boat; only help me, sir, I want to go home." This man has since sent his son to transact his business in Mobile.

The model plantation to which I have alluded is by no means what Southerners call an extensive one, but the productiveness and appendages thereof are precisely similar in character to those of all well-conducted plantations in Florida, Georgia, Alabama, and Mississippi. Exclusive of a huge domain of pine lands, the estate contains eight hundred acres, and lies in a bend of the Tombigbee river. Its negro force consists of one hundred men and women, with some fifty horses and mules, and its annual yield is about two hundred and fifty bales of cotton and six thousand bushels of corn, or perhaps fifteen thousand dollars. The very comfortable house of the overseer occupies the summit of a bluff which commands a view of the whole farm, a long reach of the river, both up and down, while the country on the opposite side of the river seems to be one vast cypress swamp, without a human habitation; while in the immediate vicinity of the house are the cabins, some twenty-five in number, occupied by the slaves, with the barns, cotton gin and press, and usually a pile beside them of cotton seeds, which when rotted, make a profitable manure. The residence of the planter himself—L. J. Wilson, Esq.—is pleasantly situated about two miles from the river, in a fragrant pine forest, and is in every particular an elegant establishment.

At the present time the crops of the plantation have been gathered, and are either sold or prepared for market, so that ploughing is now the chief employment of all hands, both men and women. The toils of the day begin at a stated hour, an hour and a half or two hours assigned to dinner, and the plough left in the furrow, or the "shovel and the hoe" thrown aside, long before the factory girls of Lowell have thought of leaving their looms. As many as four or six times in the day do the women who have young children leave the field where they may be working and march up in a line to nurse their children. When the negroes are at work in one body in a single field, as is usually the case, they present an interesting picture. Dressed as they commonly are in loosely made clothes, as dark as the soil they till, but frequently relieved by bits of red in the way of a cravat or turban, they are always picturesque; and the jibes and jokes, the loud laughter, and witty remarks which are constantly heard, prove that the slaves have quite as happy a time as the morose looking massa whose business it is to journey on horseback from one end of the plantation to the other, perpetually. When a young rascal has been caught stealing or will not do his duty, he is brought up to receive a *strapping*, and that literally; for the much-talked-of "*lash*" is nothing but a piece of leather, eighteen inches long and two and a half wide, which is attached to a wooden handle, and never could draw blood. But not more than one in ten of the slaves on this plantation were ever touched even by this harmless strap. As to the amount of labor which the faithful servants perform, three of their days would about balance one day of a Yankee yeoman; and it is a singular fact that, while the greatest amount of labor is occasionally performed by the women, they have a custom of boasting of their superior dexterity, industry, and strength. When the women become too old to do field-work, they are employed as nurses or cooks, and treated with kindness. Rude are the cabins which they all inhabit; but, when the warmth of the climate is considered, their homes, where every husband is master, are as comfortable as need be. Among the negroes of the plantation, every individual man, woman, and child is weekly supplied with the following articles: four pounds of bacon, one peck of corn meal, one pint of molasses, three salted fish, a supply of fresh meat when killed, together with all the vegetables they may desire; and this in addition to what each man is permitted to raise on his own account in the way of pigs, poultry, and grain. And it should be borne in mind, that at least one-quarter of the above rations are assigned to the youngest children. The rules of the plantation are strict, as they should be; and when obeyed there is no trouble. On the score of religion, the negroes are not without its privileges, for there are negro preachers in abundance, and they have regular Sabbath services. The people on an isolated plantation are necessarily removed from the "stated preaching" of cultivated men; and here, on these Southern plantations, I have thought, was a most appropriate sphere for the Northern missionary enterprise. Let the people of the North send to this region the Bible, with pious missionaries, both of which would be always gladly welcomed, and keep the fanatics and demagogues at home, and much good might be done. The overseer of a plantation is of course the great man upon it, and so accustomed to absolute rule that he is very apt to conduct himself before strangers in an authoritative manner; and in speaking of every thing on the farm he uses to excess the personal pronoun of the "first person singular." The house that he occupies is quite comfortable, and in the case before us is supplied with a few books, a medicine chest, and a stock of guns, with which he amuses himself during the game season.

And by the way. Just behind the overseer's house alluded to, and between two trees, is the grave of a former proprietor of this plantation, and of which the following curious circumstance is related. Shortly before his death the planter had sold a horse, to a neighbor residing eight miles distant. One day this horse made his appearance on the old plantation, poor and in a sickly condition, and on the following morning was found dead, lying across the grave of his master.

Let us now direct our steps to the present planter's residence. It is a large, cottage-shaped building, situated in the centre of a handsome lawn, besprinkled with fruit trees and clusters of flowers, flanked by comfortable negro-quarters and spacious stables, and surrounded with the tall columns of the pine forest. The spirit of genuine hospitality reigns supreme, and everything that a reasonable guest can desire is at his command.

If refined politeness and high-toned conversation are expected, they will be enjoyed to perfection; if the guest have a weakness for the pleasures of the palate, here he will find game in abundance, capitally cooked, wines of the most famous vintages, and, far above all, the famous gumbo, which, like the chowder of Yankee land and the pea-soup of Canada, is made of a score of ingredients; if books are his hobby, here is a well-selected library; if music, none can strike the keys of the piano with more grace than the accomplished hostess; if sporting is the order of the day, he has but to mount a horse, call for the darkey Nimrod and his dogs, and go forth either to kill a deer, a wild-cat, a wolf, an opossum, a coon, or perhaps a bear, merely by way of getting up an appetite for dinner; if blooded horses are to his taste, he will find the stables well supplied; if ornithology is his passion, here he may study the habits of the wild turkey, (which are killed by the hundred,) of the partridge and quail, of many varieties of the duck tribe, of the vulture and the crow, of the robin, (which becomes intoxicated by feeding on the buds of the China tree,) of the tropical paraquette, with its bright-green plumage, of the glorious mocking-bird, and of the whippoorwill, whose song to the superstitious negro, portends, in times of sickness, a death on the plantation. If the guest have a fondness for creatures of the reptile genus, the neighboring lakes will supply him with any number of huge alligators, and the swamps with rattle-snakes, the chicken, the ribbon, and the moccasin snakes; if a student of geology, the limestone bluff of St. Stephen's will exhibit to him a curious cave, with its floor covered with sea-shells, while other localities will supply him with petrified sharks' teeth and deer horns, and whole terrapins transformed into solid stone. And he who may have a relish for curious incidents will be told that upon this very plantation did a Dutchman, many years ago, sell himself into slavery to pay for his passage across the Atlantic, and is now one of the wealthiest planters in Alabama; and also that across a neighboring wilderness, one hundred miles in width, did a white woman, who had been deserted by her husband and was pursued by Indians, once travel on a pony with no companion but her dead infant, and that the same person was subsequently a leader in fashionable life in Washington. And now do I take my leave of St. Stephen's and the Tombigbee river, and that, too, with almost as much reluctance as was manifested by Mr. Wilson's body servant, a fine boy, who, when I pretended to be negotiating his purchase, wept as if his heart would break.

A JAUNT INTO MISSISSIPPI.

I LIKE Mobile much. It has a substantial as well as a dashing appearance, and the business habits and manners of the people remind me of old Gotham. Its "Battle" House would be the boast of any city, and, like most of the better hotels in the South, is kept by a Yankee. Mobile is an opulent place, and has been made so almost exclusively by the cotton interest. It is an extravagant, joyous, and free and easy town; so that sporting characters, thorough bred and fast horses, and lovely women are as "familiar as household words." Warm-hearted, it seems to me, are all its citizens; polite to strangers, and affectionate among themselves. Its position is convenient and pleasant, and, excepting when visited by the yellow fever, is considered healthy. On a bluff or high land in the vicinity of the city, and connected with it by a capital shell-road, the wealthy inhabitants have built themselves country residences, some of which are elegant, while all of them command a fine view of the city and bay of Mobile. With the market of this city I have been particularly pleased, and it is deservedly the centre of attraction to all strangers. The building itself is common-place, but as a depot for all the good things of this most bountiful land, and as a congregating-place for queer characters, it is worthy of a frequent visit. The butchers and hucksters are usually of French or Spanish extraction, and when you add to these, their wives and daughters, negroes of every age and shade of color, and an occasional group of Choctaw Indians, you have a sufficient variety. Fruit of every kind peculiar to the tropics, is found here in the greatest profusion;

so also is it with game, deer, wild turkeys, ducks, and birds of the partridge tribe being the staples in this line; and as to fish, the following are what I noted during a single walk through the market, viz., salt-water trout, rockfish or striped bass, black bass, bream, sunfish, pike, redfish or red horse, sheepshead, salt-water mullet, buffalo or drum, flounder and flatfish, the common sucker, and catfish of every imaginable size. The number of Indians who spend much of their time in Mobile, but who live in the neighboring pine woods, is estimated at one thousand. The men, some of whom are fine-looking, do a little hunting for the market, but their principal business is to deck themselves in bright colors and hang about the market or the hotels, very much after the manner of their brother snobs in our Northern cities, who loiter about the church doors on Sunday; but the Indian women are industrious, and manage to keep themselves quite comfortable by selling bundles of fat-pine for lighting fires, and beautiful willow baskets.

In my letter from St. Augustine I gave a slight account of a Minorcan masquerade, but, as the Mobilians evidently take the lead in this business, I must devote a paragraph to their fantastic doings. As these take place annually on the first of January, I did not see any of them, but from an intelligent eye-witness I have obtained the following particulars: It appears that there are here two regularly organized societies, which glory in the names of "*Cowbellions*," and "*Strikers*." They have each from sixty to a hundred members, who are of high respectability and wealthy. Their ostensible purpose is annually to dismiss the old year and welcome the new one, which they do by parading the streets at night, by the light of torches and colored lanterns, decked out in fantastic dresses and singing uncouth songs. This part of the programme is followed by a dance at the theatre, where a company of ladies have assembled to meet them, and the winding up is a sumptuous entertainment. Often the processions are very grotesque, and set the whole town a laughing; but of late years their customs seem to have been to personify the more noted characters of

Shakspeare and Sir Walter Scott or the ancient mythologies, and to reproduce the games of old England. With the origin of this custom I am not acquainted, but it is evidently allied to the more sedate and sensible custom which formerly prevailed among the Dutch inhabitants of Manhattan, when the last night of the year was wholly devoted by them to visiting from house to house and drinking hot toddies of Holland gin.

From Mobile I made a desperate journey into the interior of the State of Mississippi; and as I saw and heard a number of things during the jaunt, it is meet that I should make them the theme of a few paragraphs. My ostensible object was to visit the town of Augusta, which is eighty miles from Mobile, and I accomplished the trip with my companion in five days, paying for the services of a man and his "one-horse concern" the moderate price of fifty dollars. The road for the most part lay through a monotonous pine country, and, as the weather turned out to be inclement and the accommodations we met with very bad, we had any thing but a "good time." We went by one road and returned by another. We came in contact, however, with a few men, women, and things that were excessively characteristic of the wilderness, and for that reason they ought to be chronicled.

Our first night was spent in a cabin on Dog river. Our supper consisted of sweet potatoes, molasses, bacon, and diluted coffee; and our bed-room was ventilated on an entirely new principle; that is to say, by wide cracks in the floor, broad spaces between the logs that composed the walls, huge openings in the roof, and a window with a shutter that could not be closed. Our host was a man who, some twenty-five years ago, had left the *back settlements* of Mississippi for the purpose of finding a home in Alabama, but having reached Dog river during a freshet, he was compelled to encamp with his family for a few days. During this halt it struck him that he would erect a bridge over the river for the benefit of pilgrims like himself and also build himself a cabin and turn innkeeper. Both of these important things did he accomplish; and, as he had a son who was fond of hunting, and as the few people who travelled through the country were compelled to tarry with him at least a night, he has thus managed to obtain a living. In politics he was a Jackson man, because he had once fought the Indians under the old General; and in the way of religion he had been a Methodist and a Baptist, but left both of these denominations in disgust, as he said, but upon compulsion, as I afterwards learnt. He now avowed himself an "Independent Religionist." The only fruit of his religious opinions which I witnessed were that between supper and bed time he drank nearly a whole decanter of bad whiskey, and then insisted upon gathering his family and reading a prayer. His wife seemed a very worthy woman, and he had a daughter whose face struck me as beautiful, and verily seemed "like sunshine in a shady place."

Our second night was spent in another cabin in the pine woods, belonging to an industrious and obliging man. His estate numbered a thousand acres, but his main support was derived from the business of cutting spar timber, which he hauled to the Pascagoula, floated to the mouth of that stream, and sold to an agent of the French Government. Our host's family consisted of a wife and *eighteen* children, three of whom were girls, whose average weight we estimated at two hundred pounds, who could, and to our sorrow did, all play on the violin and accordeon, and who were so fond of dancing that whenever two or three spar-cutters happened along to join them they would "dance all night till broad day-light." It was evident that this family was well enough off to live in comfort, but, true to habits which prevail among a large class in the South, they did not seem to know the sensation of real comfort. Negroes of all ages were abundant in and about the dwelling, whose market value would not have been less than ten thousand dollars; and yet, with two or three exceptions, wooden benches were used in the place of chairs, one iron spoon answered for the whole family, and the mother added the sugar or "short sweetning" to the coffee with her fingers, and tasted each cup before sending it round to ascertain if it was right. Such things as andirons, tongs, and wash-basins were considered useless; and the bedstead upon which we slept was a mere board, yet the sheets were charmingly fringed with cotton lace, and in their freshness did not remind me of those once alluded to by Isaak Walton. All the family, excepting the parents and two sons, were barefooted, and yet the girls sported large finger rings in abundance, and wore basque dresses of calico. Only two of the eighteen children had ever travelled from home as far as Mobile, and the first crop knew not how to read; the second were more fortunate, for a school had lately been established in a settlement about five miles distant, which consisted of fifteen scholars, seven of whom were the children of our host. On the night in question the "schoolmaster was abroad," for he had come on a visit to the family of our host; and when he started for his lodgings, which were three miles distant, he went alone through the pathless woods, carrying a gun in one hand and a pine torch in the other.

On questioning our worthy host about the game in his region, he gave me some interesting particulars. Deer, he said, were very abundant, but were hunted chiefly by torchlight. He knew a small party who in a single week had killed one hundred; and, though he did not seem to think this mode of hunting cruel, he was very severe upon the hunters, because they sometimes killed his cattle instead of the game, by mistaking the shining eyes (the mark shot at,) of the one for the other. He stated that the deer always ranged through the pine woods at night for the purpose of feeding, remaining hidden in the swamps during the day; that a good hunter could always tell, by the noise which the deer made in leaping, after being shot, whether he was mortally wounded or not; and that many of them were also killed by still hunting and driving, but that fire hunting was the most profitable. In speaking of the habits of the deer, he told me that they were much more tame in summer than in the winter, and that he had often killed them wandering about his cleared fields in company with his cattle; that he has known them to feed upon green corn and upon various kinds of soft-shelled nuts, as well as tender buds and wild grass; that he had witnessed some terrible fights between the bucks, and that the fawns when kindly treated are easily tamed, but very mischievous.

Another denizen of the wilderness that my Mississippi friend has killed in great numbers is the wild turkey. He thinks them exceedingly cunning, but not sufficiently so to be aware of the danger lurking in the baits of corn that are laid for them, and which, with the gun or the trap, secure their destruction by scores. They are also deceived by the call which the hunters make by means of a whistle formed out of the wing bone of the same fowl. They spend their days in the enjoyment of the happiest freedom, and on returning to their roosts at night never fail to have at least one sentinel on duty. In every sphere of their brief lives, however, are they an interesting race, but in no condition are they more interesting to the lover of nature than when a flock of them are making an onslaught upon a decayed stump in whose heart are imbedded a colony of grubs or crickets. The average weight of the female turkeys in Mississippi is estimated at twelve pounds, and that of the male at twenty pounds. The deer and turkeys are the two most profitable kinds of game which are hunted on the upper waters of the Pascagoula; but to those who fancy them—and who does not?—the sport of quail shooting is inexhaustible. Those who enjoy the killing of ugly creatures can here amuse themselves by hunting wildcats, and those who have the good sense to appreciate a roasted opossum can here luxuriate on them to perfection.

The third night of our pilgrimage was spent at Augusta, which I must not attempt to describe, except as one of the worst specimens of a Mississippi village. We reached the place in a cold rain, found the first three houses that we came to deserted; that three grog shops usurped the business of a public house, and that shelter from the storm could only be obtained in one house, into which we begged our way, and the owner of which, excepting the officers of the land and post office, appeared to be the only gentleman in the place. But even this man was a probationer, for the business of *sparring* had brought him there and the scarcity of timber was about to drive him away. Though living in a log-cabin, he and his truly accomplished wife had gathered around them the luxuries of good beds, a cleanly and well-furnished table, and a piano. The latter article had been not only a source of intellectual gratification to the owners thereof, but of great wonderment to the denizens of the surrounding pine woods. One man, when he first saw it, thought it an ironing table; another took the pedals for pistols, and another mistook it for a fancy chest for keeping nice clothes; and whenever it was played upon, the villagers congregated around the house to hear the music, and on more than one occasion have the simple but kind-hearted people insisted upon giving the lady musician half a dollar for the treat they had enjoyed. Sweet indeed was the tone of this instrument, and the performances as well as voice of our hostess were admirable, but they had not the power to keep us in the village longer than a single night, as we started for home after an early breakfast.

Our fourth night was spent under the roof of a planter who is reputed to be worth a hundred thousand dollars in negroes, mills and cash. His residence was a log-cabin, and one of the worst of its kind, and its furniture in keeping with it. As he was a postmaster and had received a surplus of "Gleason's Pictorial" for distribution, he had faithfully distributed them, with the addition of a little paste, on the walls of his cabin by way of ornament. Two iron spoons here figured at the table, and our temporary wash-basin was in reality a pudding bowl. Little negroes and big were everywhere to be seen, staring wildly at our every movement and pushing themselves into exactly the most disagreeable places. The number of guns that I counted *hung* up along the rafters or stacked up in the only two rooms of the house were thirteen. Pigs, dogs, mules, and geese were also very numerous in the large yard where stood the negro cabins, but in the small room where we attempted to sleep there was a regular mass meeting of domestic insects. After doing all they could to annoy us, they congregated on the large hearthstone, where we kept up a blazing fire, and it required no great exertion of the fancy to see them running races and performing a variety of other gymnastic feats. On picking up my hat in the morning, into which I had placed my watch and other articles for safe keeping, I found it inhabited by a colony of the "same sort."

On continuing our journey, and just before reaching the Pascagoula, we came to a cluster of neat log-cabins, and were told that here was established a public school, with ninety scholars and two or three teachers, who receive each a salary of six hundred dollars and their board. Having once before crossed the Pascagoula in a scow, we now recrossed it in the same manner, the boat being managed by a half-witted negro, and we had a narrow escape from drowning. The scenery of the river was at this point most uninteresting, but our road soon took us across an extensive and very picturesque swamp. The trees here were many of them immense, and their trunks were often completely enveloped in deep green mosses and air plants, while from their limbs the gray moss hung in folds, reaching frequently to the ground, and the vines in their variety and profusion were truly wonderful; and among the flowers that we noticed in bloom were the daisy, the arbutus, the woodbine, and yellow jasmine. We saw no large game in this grand swamp, but we could readily believe what we were told, that it abounded in bears, wolves, and panthers; and lion-hearted must be the man who can hunt them in such a place, bivouacking, night after night, in the deep gloom formed by the cypress and cotton-wood trees.

Our fifth and last night was spent upon the eastern bank of the Dog river, which we recrossed at sunset, and which is here a very picturesque stream, with black water, white and yellow sandbanks, and skirted with rich vegetation. The cabin and supplies for the table were much poorer than any we had before met with. We slept upon some boards in a windowless and almost doorless room, and the only incident worth recording was that at dead of night we were suddenly awakened by the loud and dreadful howling of a dog, and, on ascertaining his whereabouts, we found him directly under our rude bed, which was his accustomed lair. We had seen Dog river, and heard the voice of one of its dogs, and long before the dawn we were on our way to Mobile, where we arrived, thankful and happy, in time to enjoy a good dinner with our host of the Battle House.

My last evening in Mobile, as fortune would have it, was spent with Ole Bull. I had met him before at Mr. Webster's table in Washington, and, as I have always been an enthusiastic admirer of him, the few hours that I passed in his company will be long remembered by me with peculiar pleasure. For mentioning the following particulars, gathered from his conversation, I hope he will forgive me. He was born in Bergen, a Norwegian town, and is about forty-five years old. He is tall and slender in person; his countenance is pale but full of thought, and, though wearing a melancholy cast in repose, there is something in his smile truly bewitching. He was educated in his charming art by Paginini, and he was first heard and fostered within the walls of Hamburgh. He said he had seen a great deal of the United States, and admired our people and Government, but he spoke of his misfortunes attending his various colonization schemes in a desponding tone; he had been so often deceived he could hardly trust any man in these latter days. He expressed his partiality for heart-music, and contempt for fashionable music; Mozart and Rosini seemed to be his favorites. He had just been delighting the people of Mobile with a concert, and the instrument that he used was one that he had *made with his own hands in four days*, immediately after his jewelled violin had been unjustly and cruelly taken from him in New York. He talked lovingly about the National Theatre of Norway, which it had been his privilege to establish. He delighted me with a long description of a valley in Norway which had been recently discovered. It was so hidden among rugged rocky mountains, that travellers could only reach it by means of rope ladders, and the inhabitants were very large, very kind, and very simple. He told me that when in summer they went from the valley to tend their flocks upon the mountains, they left their cabins unlocked, and supplied with food for all strangers, who were free to help themselves. He thought there was something wonderfully grand about the scenery of Norway. How often had he looked upon it and sobbed with overpowering feelings! Indeed, he always did so when he visited his native land. But he was now an exile and a wanderer, he had no home, and there were none to care for him. His devotion to his people seemed to be a chief element of his character, and a more unselfish and affectionate man, it seems to me, I never knew. That his musical powers are wonderful is the verdict of the world.

NEW ORLEANS.

I CAME from Mobile to New Orleans on a New York steamer, which was one of a trio belonging to James L. Day, Esq., of Connecticut, and forming what I consider the most comfortable and best managed line in the United States. The waters of Mobile Bay were muddy, and its low and uninteresting shores were completely covered with drift-wood, far as the eye could reach. At the extensive bar, where the muddy waters became merged into the pure green of the Gulf of Mexico, a fleet of ships was moored; and I was surprised to learn that they seldom or never actually visited the city, from which they obtain their cargoes of cotton. Among our more agreeable fellow travellers, was a large flock of gulls; they followed in our wake until sunset, and I remember noticing with interest the circumstance, when feeding them with biscuits, that the older birds not unfrequently picked up a bit of the bread, and flying aside, dropped it upon the water again, for the benefit of a young bird, which was supposed to be its offspring. What little we saw of the main land, proved the whole coast of Mississippi to be flat and swampy, the long-leaved pine and live-oak disputing with each other the right of possession, while the magnolia and date-palm, the orange and palmetto, are sufficiently abundant to deepen your first impressions as to the torridity of the climate. We had a distant view of the mouth of the Pascagoula river, and from what I had heard of the spot, I regretted my inability to visit it, although my recollections of the sources of the stream were not particularly agreeable. It is said that this river was one of the very first in the State of Mississippi inhabited by civilized people, having been settled by the French some twenty years before the founding of New Orleans. On its banks are yet to be seen the ruins of these ancient settlements. The picturesque charms of the Bay into which the stream empties, and the salubrity of the climate, have transformed a number of localities on its shores into watering places for the citizens of Mobile and New Orleans. At the eastern extremity of this Bay, are the ruins of a fortification, built of shell stone, and apparently centuries old, amid which have been discovered fragments of a peculiar kind of earthenware, together with some human bones of gigantic size. According to a local tradition, this fort was built by a tribe of Indians long since extinct, known as the Biloxies, and who, after an unsuccessful battle with a more powerful tribe, marched into the sea and perished as a nation. And at the present day it is asserted, strange music may be heard off this coast, on mid-summer evenings, and those who are not beyond the influence of superstition, believe it to be in some way connected with the extinction of the Biloxi Indians. Balmy was the air and misty the western sky, as we passed out of Pascagoula Bay; but by the "cold light of stars" we glided by a number of beautiful islands, and crossed the lonely and uninteresting Lake of Pont Chartrain, when a railway train, running through a marsh, rank with vegetation, and bright with flowers, took us in half an hour into the Calcutta of the Union—New Orleans.

And now, after a thousand and one persons have recorded their opinions of this city, what can I indite that will be new? Nothing—but I can give in addition to a few leading "fixed facts," my individual impressions, and here they are—First, as to its location. Had I not been told that it is one hundred miles from the Gulf of Mexico, and had I not seen that it occupies a bend in the Mississippi river, I should have imagined it located *nowhere*, since the surrounding country is flat, partly under water and desolate in the extreme. Its foundation stones are from two to five feet lower than the surface of the neighboring river at high water, and were it not for the extensive embankment which protects it, it could not exist in safety a single hour. As the market and exporting depot for the products of the finest valley in the world, and of three climates, its commercial position is all important, and each succeeding year, it seems to me, can only increase its business and its wealth.

In its general aspect, New Orleans reminds me of Quebec and Montreal, and this is not strange, since they were all founded by the French. The city is divided into three municipalities, the first of which is monopolized by the French and Creole population, and is ancient, gloomy and picturesque, with tile roofs, hanging street lamps, and cozy porticoes; the second municipality is chiefly in the hands of the Yankee race and abounds in handsome houses, substantial blocks of stores and warehouses, and portions of it are very much like the heart of Boston; and the third division of the town, which is sparsely settled, is the home of the Dutch and Irish. It is at all times a busy place, but during the winter it is pre-eminently so, and two single ideas seem to absorb the minds of the entire population—money and pleasure. The commission merchants drive their business with the utmost energy, cheered with the hope of leisurely spending the coming summer with their families at the north or on their plantations, far beyond the reach of yellow fever and cholera; and the petty tradesmen and mechanics, who are generally the permanent residents, do all they can during the day to earn their dollars, which they seldom fail to spend before the next morning, in having a good time at the theatre, the opera, the circus, the concert, the ten-pin alley, the ball room, the billiard saloon, the cafes, or the unnumbered gambling and drinking establishments. The leading hotels of the city (and the St. Charles and St. Louis are the two best) are on the grandest scale, richly furnished, so managed as to gratify every whim of appetite or taste, and like every thing else in this city, extravagant, to the ruination of all but the longest purses.

Here congregate, from all the southern and many of the northern States, beautiful women with small expectations, brought hither by hard-working fathers or brothers, and also another distinct class called "planters' daughters," who are chiefly distinguished for their white washed faces and immense fortunes consisting of negro property and plantations that have never been surveyed. They sip their coffee or smoke their cigars in bed, breakfast at twelve and dine at six, when parties or fancy balls occupy the night, and ancient gentlemen trot out their daughters on a venture, with pride and pleasure commendable. Everything is stylish, but all things human in fashionable hotel life stand upon a common level, even as does the city itself. The young men about town, the gamblers, the junior members and collecting clerks of New York, Boston, and Philadelphia houses and the adventurers, whom you may have seen dashing down the ball room in the waltz or polka, are the same who swarm in the mammoth drinking saloons, where appetite and alcohol reign supreme. To the eye, human life seems only one continued round of pleasure, but to the mind which looks below the surface, there are a thousand sources of anxiety and anguish, which are sure to have their hour of triumph in solitude and silence, or when death is on the breeze. But afer all, the Crescent City is not alone in its devotion to money and pleasure, and it is time that I should turn to its more peculiar characteristics.

By virtue of its well earned reputation as the "*Wet Grave*," it is of course well supplied with cemeteries. They may be found in all directions, and are among the lions of the town. Owing to the swampy nature of the earth however, such things as graves are nowhere seen, but in their stead we find brick, marble and granite tombs, or oven-like vaults, all constructed above ground. They are arranged by tiers in blocks or squares, with here and there isolated specimens, belonging to the rich and proud, and a walk among them in the narrow avenues, can never fail to make one appreciate the expression and idea suggested by "City of the Dead." Even when flooded with the blessed sunshine, these cemeteries are sad and desolate, and the feelings they inspire are only deepened by the common sight of weeping and praying mourners, and by the images and incense, the flowers and tapers and unmeaning inscriptions which meet the eye on every hand. By those who have deposited the remains of friends and relatives in these grave houses, they are of course held sacred and perhaps loved, but to those who have hoped, that when they came to die, they might have a clod of the valley for a pillow, and a covering of green turf, within sound of the country church-going bell, these southern cemeteries seem destitute of all comfort and cheerfulness. Upon some of them, money has been lavished with princely liberality, and yet the most touching tomb that I saw was built of brick, very old, all overgrown with moss, and was without an epitaph. To be remembered by the mosses of the earth alone, is indeed an unhappy fate.

Let us now return to the world-renowned Levee of New Orleans, which is the arena where the huge business of this city is transacted. It is at least three miles in length, and broad enough to marshal the armies of the world. Its northern boundary is a continuous line of stupendous warehouses, while it fronts upon the yellow and sullen Mississippi, where, clinging in constant fear, are the sail vessels, the steamboats and the flat-boats, which have come from any corner of the earth to pay their tribute to the chosen seat of commerce. To say nothing of the hourly arrivals of ships from the Gulf of Mexico and of steamboats from the interior, which congregate here by the hundred, only think of the departure in a single day, of twenty large ships and twenty-five steamboats. And then ascend to the upper-deck of one of these vessels and behold the landward scene! Sugar and cotton, cotton and sugar, flour from a hundred rivers, coal, pork and beef from the Ohio, lead and lumber from the upper Mississippi, furs from the Missouri, and cotton and sugar again from the Arkansas and Red rivers, teas from China, fruits from both the Indies, and the manufactures of every civilized nation, all mingled in one apparently boundless mass of conglomerate wealth. And then the negroes, hard working but jovial, in gangs of from five to a hundred, guided in their labors by little flags; the horses and mules and drays, clusters of trafficking planters and merchants, the hotel carriages and omnibusses, the fruit stands, organ grinders, peddlers of old clothes and shells, beggars and loafers—behold them numbering many thousands, all brought together as upon a single canvas, a *speaking* canvas too, for the ringing of bells, the shouting of sailors and boatmen, the songs of the slaves, (the only really happy people to be seen) with the accompanying hum of active life, conspire to create a *roar* which cannot be easily forgotten. Surely this Levee is one of the wonders of this wonderful age; but it must be seen, and that at high noon, to be fully appreciated.

The Public Squares of New Orleans are also peculiar to this city. They are not numerous nor large nor particularly elegant, but through every month in the year, they bloom with flowers, and on mid-winter afternoons present the gay and lively aspect of northern Parks on the first of June. The churches too, chiefly Roman Catholic, are interesting; the best of them, in style of architecture, and in their decorations, are antique, and remind the untraveled American of what he has read, respecting the Churches of the Old World; and here as well as in the shadow of St. Peter's in Rome, at the proper season, are enacted all the ceremonies of the Carnival. With the markets of the town I was disappointed. In regard to tropical fruits and wild game, they were most abundantly supplied, and aside from their *Frenchy* aspect and odor, they struck me as not unlike the leading markets of the Northern States, and by no means as entertaining to the stranger, as those of Montreal and Quebec. That places of amusement are abundant, has already been intimated, and that the theatres are open and extensively patronized even on Sunday night, proves the prevailing feelings, in regard to religion and morality, to be at the lowest ebb. But nowhere, in this country, can the opera be enjoyed to such perfection as in this city. As to the native population of the Crescent City, I must say that I have not fallen in love with them. Selfishness, vanity, and a limited knowledge of the world, seem to be the distinguishing features of the Creole race, and the Quadroons seem to occupy a debateable ground on the outskirts of the so-called good society. And finally, the great want of this city, is a better reputation; and since nature has done so much for it, it only requires to exchange what it has, for what it has not.

Intellectual culture should take the place of grossest sensualism, and a scientific system of drainage, the place of a most culpable spirit of neglect, in regard to clean streets.

As an American, it will not do for me to omit a passing allusion to the Battle of New Orleans. The famous field of action lies about four miles from the St. Charles Hotel; it is laved by the Mississippi river, flanked by a cypress swamp, and is at the present time occupied by a planter, who employs himself, all according to law, in "raising cane." The Eighth of January, 1815, was a sad day for Pakenham, and a proud one for Jackson, that most remarkable and fortunate man. The British force consisted of 12,000 regulars, while that of the Americans was composed chiefly of militia boys; but fortune favored the weak; more than two thousand of the enemy were killed or wounded, and less than a hundred of our men were compelled to lick the dust. During that battle it was, that the peculiar qualities of *gun cotton* were discovered and proven. And who can tell but what the Mississippi river obtained its first idea of *crevassing* New Orleans with its floods, from the military crevassa which nearly forty years ago poured the red-hot hail upon the invading army.

Had I the time I might enliven this letter by narrating a variety of local incidents that I have picked up in this city, but one, picturing human nature in bright colors, though with a *sable* pencil (pardon me sensible reader,) cannot be passed in silence. A negro man named Marshall, lately arrived here on his way from California to Claiborne parish in this State. He went to the far West, it appears, some two years ago with his master, who was taken sick last winter, near the Nevada mountains and died. Marshall took the utmost care of his master; was his faithful companion, nurse, and friend, and watched by him unceasingly until he breathed his last. There was nothing left to pay the funeral expenses and doctors' bills. Marshall set to work and labored hard until he managed to scrape together enough to settle these debts—amounting to eight hundred dollars. How few white men, near and dear relatives, would have done so much!

He gathered together his master's clothes and other personal effects, and, with about a thousand dollars that he had made, started home to his master's family, notwithstanding his knowledge that he was free in California, and the many inducements held out to him to remain there. He took the cheapest and most dangerous route back, going in a sailing vessel to Acapulco, and crossing Mexico, on horseback, from the former city to Vera Cruz—a very dangerous route. The American Consuls at both places took so much interest in him as to give him letters of recommendation, and to request of him to let them hear of him. He brought to this city several letters to persons living here or in the country, and which contained gold dust.

The faithful negro started home from this city on a Red River boat. He had letters from various persons in California to gentlemen of this city, recommending him, in the warmest terms, to their notice and protection, which were instantly accorded. An intimate friend of his master, wrote to his family stating that the unfortunate gentleman's last request was that his faithful servant should be emancipated and provided for by them as soon as he reached his home in Louisiana. From this incident, we may learn that the "tyranny of slavery" is not quite so demoralizing as some people imagine. There are *lights* as well as *shadows*, even under the system of slavery.

THE LOWER MISSISSIPPI.

SOME seven or eight years have elapsed since I last paid my respects, in person and with my pen, to the Lower Mississippi. I love it now, no better than I did then, for I am principled against loving any perpetually muddy and *remorseless* stream; but my *respect* for the Great River is very much enhanced, on account of its unbounded usefulness. With the Father of Waters I pretend to claim an intimate acquaintance, although I cannot, with one of the " oldest inhabitants" of this region assert, *that I have known it ever since it was a small creek.*

In coming from the Crescent City to Cairo, I drove dull care away, and took all things leisurely. I tested the quality of nearly every kind of steamboats, and went ashore for a day or two at every town that I thought worth visiting. And now for a description of the Eclipse and Illinois steamers, which are at the present time the best representatives of the two better classes of boats navigating the river. An English gentleman, Dr. Marshall Hall, whom I met on the first-named boat, remarked of it that, in his opinion, it was one of the three wonders of the United States—Niagara and the Levee of New Orleans being the other two. The Eclipse is a passenger craft, was built in Louisville, to which city she runs, and at a cost of $160,000. Her tonnage is 1200, her length 369 feet, and she draws, according to circumstances, from six to eleven feet. She makes two trips in a month, at an expense of $12,000 each—the wood alone costing $5000—has two hundred and fifty berths for first-class passengers, and the fare from city to city is thirty-six dollars, distance fourteen hundred miles.

She runs at the rate, up stream, of sixteen miles per hour, and the accommodations in every department vie with those of the very best hotels in the country, for all of which, including the choicest luxuries and light wines, there is no additional charge. The steamer Illinois belongs to another genus. She is a freight and passenger boat, and to the lover of quiet and plain comfort, and on account of her greater safety, is altogether preferable. She was built in Pittsburg, runs to St. Louis, and cost only $60,000. She performs one trip in a month, running about eight miles an hour, and the fare through is only twenty dollars. Her tonnage is rated at 800, while she carries 1500, and the character of her cargoes is diversified beyond conception. On her last trip down she carried of cattle alone nearly four hundred head, and when I was in her, she had, by way of variety, several foreign bulls and blood horses, any quantity of poultry for "home consumption," a pet deer or two which rambled where they listed; and directly under the boilers, which are near the bow of the boat, and all exposed to view, were a number of hogs, rooting quite happily in a bed of sand. She burns wood to the value of $3000 during each round trip, while her total expenses amount to $11,000,—the length of her heat being 1200 miles. Her own length is 303 feet, and she draws from three and a half to seven feet of water. Her table is plain but very neat, and the state-rooms spacious and comfortable; indeed so homelike is everything about her that the captain, a polite and substantial man, has the good sense to live with his family on board, as if in a dwelling on dry land.

That portion of the Mississippi valley lying between New Orleans and Baton Rouge is altogether the *sweetest* section of country in the United States, since it is here that the sugar-cane attains its greatest perfection and the largest quantity of sugar is made. Both sides of the Great river are lined with extensive plantations, and the same may be said of nearly all the bayous in western Louisiana, where are located the venerable, wealthy, and highly interesting French settlements of Attakapas and Opelousas, the last of which has been made classic by the genius of Longfellow in his "Evangeline." The surface of this whole sugar country is perfectly level, and the soil very rich and inexhaustible. The fields of sugar-cane which annually spring into rank luxuriance are very beautiful, while in all their borders are to be seen cypress swamps, lakes alive with the scarlet ibis and alligator, and live-oak forests that can be surpassed by no part of the world. Certain portions of this region are compared, by their sanguine and happy people, to the paradise of the antediluvian world, and truly with a shadow of propriety. All the residences that you see are pleasant and picturesque, and many of them have a stately bearing; the gardens which surround them, bloom almost perpetually with hedges of rose and hawthorn and with groves of the lemon and orange, and in their vicinity may always be seen the factory-looking sugar houses, with ther towering chimneys, and the neat white-washed cabins of the negroes,—all free from care and happy as they can wish to be. About all the sugar plantations there is a rural charm which never fails to interest the stranger; and though the levees which line the banks of the Mississippi for more than a hundred miles are indispensable as well as curious, the amount of ditching which has to be performed on some of the plantations is astonishing. Many of the estates are enormous, and I have heard of one which contained a thousand acres of land and had netted for its proprietor, in one year, the respectable sum of one hundred and fifty thousand dollars. But to dilate upon the many interesting particulars appertaining to the planting and the gathering of the sugar-cane and to the manifold mysteries of manufacturing and refining sugar, would occupy more time and space than I can now spare; and are not all these things recorded in the Encyclopedias? When performed by daylight and in a fine boat, the sail up this portion of the Mississippi is exceedingly interesting. All the men, women, and children whom you see at the various stopping-places appear happy, and about every spot there is an air of the picturesque. All through the winter the Cherokee rose sports itself luxuriantly on every plantation, and upon green lawns children play with their toys and throw the ball;—in continuous fields you see the cattle grazing, and droves of horses kicking up their heels; while the negroes, fat, hearty, and red-shirted, enliven every scene, as they drag down with their mules, to the shipping-places, the countless hogsheads of sugar and molasses. Of Baton Rouge it can be said, that it occupies the summit of the first bluff that you come to, in ascending the Mississippi; that it is a pretty town with bad hotels; that the State House is a handsome and imposing edifice commanding a very grand view of the Mississippi river and valley, and that it will be long remembered with veneration, for having been the home of Zachary Taylor.

From Baton Rouge I made an excursion of some fifty miles into the interior of the State, eastwardly, and so far as the mere journey was concerned, had a pleasant time. It was about the middle of March, and spring was bursting forth in all the gorgeousness peculiar to this southern clime. The accommodations, however, were most abominable, and though there were three hotels in the village where I spent one night, I was compelled, on taking my departure, to beg a little decent food from a private family. The few sugar plantations that I saw were well conducted, and the planters seemed to be thriving; but the cotton farms, which occurred chiefly in the pine woods, were small and in a neglected condition. The air was everywhere fragrant with flowers, but upon a large proportion of the scanty population was resting the blight of intemperance. At one place where I was forced to lodge, the landlord and his sons made the latter part of the night hideous, by a bacchanalian frolic, the earlier half having been devoted by them, with the family, to a ball which was given in the *Court-house* of the town.

Of the principal towns lying on the Mississippi, between Baton Rouge and this place, I have not much to say. Their names, as everybody knows, are Natchez, Vicksburg, and Memphis. They are all flourishing, supported by cotton, and located upon picturesque bluffs. Of the first, I remember to have heard it asserted that it was the county-seat of the wealthiest country in the Union, and that it numbers among its inhabitants one planter who is the owner of *four thousand* slaves. Of Vicksburg it may be said, that it is now a much more respectable place than formerly, and that a railroad leads therefrom to Jackson, the capitol of Mississippi, and the most inviting town therein. One incident worth mentioning, connected with it, is to this effect. A noted planter, who had more money than brains, took it into his head to give a grand *Sunday* dinner. He invited a hundred people, not one of whom thought proper to attend. He was disgusted, and by way of exhibiting his spleen, he summoned his slaves to the entertainment, and fed them right royally upon the luxuries which had been prepared. And his next step was, to command his overseers to give each one of his slaves a *strapping*, for fear that they might be spoiled by the indulgence he had shown them. Of Memphis it may be said, that it has recently been honored by the General Government with the donation of a Navy Yard, and is the only one in the country *into which* it would be impossible for a ship to sail, although they might be, and probably will be, *sent out* of it by the hundred. But my love for the olden times, carries me back to the city of Natchez. With "Natchez under the hill," ("now *as* then," a miserable spot,) or Natchez anywhere else, I have nothing to do; but I would recall and record what I remember of the Natchez tribe of Indians. They were worshippers of the Sun, and had a temple in which they kept a perpetual fire, and offered human sacrifices. They were friendly to the first French settlers of the country, but having been badly treated by them, they silently and secretly plotted and accomplished the destruction of great numbers of their enemies, the invaders of their country. The quaint and romantic Charlevoix was their chief historian, and from him we gather the following particulars: They lived, in 1720, in huts built of clay, mixed with straw, and covered with leaves and stalks of maize; their government was despotic, and their chiefs were proud but comparatively humane; their women were prëeminently profligate; they were fond of festivals, and offered in their temples the first fruits of every harvest; they also offered human sacrifices; and on the death of a chief, his warriors, to the number of one hundred, were put to death, that he might be followed to the "spirit land" with a retinue to do him honor. From other authors we learn, that in process of time they were subdued by the French, their women and children reduced to slavery, and the remnant of their warriors were sent to St. Domingo, or became amalgamated with the Creeks and Chickasaws.

There is one point on the Mississippi river which has been, and still is, subject to earthquakes, and those who have a fancy for such "institutions," would do well to spend a day in the village of New Madrid. Other points of interest that might be mentioned, are the mouths of the Red River and Washita, the Arkansas, the White and the Yazoo rivers. They are all very much alike in their alluvial character, sluggish, and generally muddy, running for the most part through uncultivated wildernesses, abounding in wild game and reptiles, with low and monotonous shores, fringed with the rankest vegetation, and teeming with the more common kinds of fish. Steamboats almost without number, small, savage and dirty affairs, navigate all their waters during the winter, and the amount of cotton which they annually float to market is very large. About each of these rivers an interesting book might be written, and to the lover of wild life and wild scenery, there are no rivers on the Continent that can excel the Red River and Arkansas. The Great Raft of the former, and the Hot Springs in the valley of the latter, will alone repay the traveller for the fatigue and dangers he must experience in visiting them.

To describe anew the scenery of the Lower Mississippi is not my intention. To all intelligent minds, its very name is identified with troubled and muddy waters, low and perpetually crumbling banks and continuous forests, where humanity is barely represented by the wood-chopper or the pioneer farmer; —with swift and flashy and dangerous steamboats, with sawyers and snags, with flat-boats and rafts, and with a restless and ever-moving population, whose traits and pursuits are almost infinite, and who (it needs no prophet's eye to see) are gradually transforming themselves into a body politic, which will eventually become the heart of the richest republican empire upon earth.

THE OHIO RIVER AND OVER THE MOUNTAINS.

Eight years ago, when I first sailed both up and down the Ohio, I attempted a description of its scenery and more poetical associations, but gave up the task in despair. I felt then, as I do now, that this river, like all the magnificent rivers of our land, can only be adequately portrayed in a series of chapters, and that in a single letter the tourist must confine himself to generalities, which are always unsatisfactory. But having, as opportunities occurred, heretofore touched upon nearly all the leading American rivers, I must at least devote a paragraph to the Ohio.

It is formed by the union of the Alleghany and Monongahela, which are deservedly the pride of Pennsylvania; while the Kanawha, with its pulpit cliffs, extensive salt works, and grand water-falls; the Cumberland, which flows through an agricultural region of surpassing richness; the Tennessee, with its gateway of mountains and rich country, and the lonely Wabash, all pour their waters into its uniform and placid current, which extends from Pittsburg to Cairo, one thousand miles. Its banks are generally precipitous, rising oftentimes into cliffs or bluffs three hundred feet in height, with bottom-lands of the greatest fertility. The forests, which everywhere cast their shadows upon it, consist of gigantic trees of almost every variety peculiar to the latitude; and the wooded islands which gem its bosom are numberless. The steamboats which ply upon it, vie, in every particular, with those of the Great Lakes and the Mississippi; and upon no river in the world can be found more extensive and beautiful farms, or a happier or more intelligent population. And what a brotherhood of cities and towns have sprung up all along its banks! They cannot, without a gazetteer, even be enumerated; but the honors of commerce are chiefly enjoyed by Pittsburg, the city of lumber, coal and iron; Cincinnati, the city of pork and wine; and Louisville, also a city of pork, as well as of chivalry and wit. In the second of these cities, it was once my fortune to spend the greater part of a year, and I always hear its name mentioned with pleasure. In my opinion, it is destined to be the largest and most wealthy place in the whole western country. Its founders and leading men came from New England, and in no other city can the indomitable will and elevated moral character of the Puritan blood, be more satisfactorily studied.

But alas! like too many of our superb rivers the more poetical and peculiar characteristics of the Ohio river are daily disappearing before the march of mammon. For this reason it is therefore, that when I would really enjoy the Ohio in its perfection, my mind reverts to those days, when it watered a comparative wilderness. And especially do I love to think of it, as it was seen and described by the great and good Audubon, who not only voyaged upon it at all seasons, but studied his delightful science upon its banks for many years. Then it was, that in the autumn, every tree was hung with long and flowing festoons of different species of vines, their richly colored fruit mingling with the yellow and deep green leaves, in such a manner as to surpass in brilliancy the gardens of the east. In floating down the stream in his skiff, the Naturalist met with no other ripple of the water, than that formed by the propulsion of his boat; and having his family with him, and an abundance of time at command, his enjoyment of the grand and beautiful scenery must have been truly exquisite. The fish that abounded in the stream, and the deer or turkeys that were killed along the shores, afforded him the best of food, and the nights that he spent by his camp fire, in the shadow of the huge buck-eye or sycamore were indeed "grand, gloomy and peculiar. No wonder then that he believed Nature had done more for this region than any other on the globe. Every day had its event, and though simple in their character, they made a deep impression upon his mind, and are more clearly descriptive of the virgin scenery of the Ohio, than all the set descriptions of all the writing travelers from Basil Hall and Harriet Martineau down to the last Guide Book and Fredericka Bremer. At one time the setting sun and the twilight hour, affected him with strong emotions; and the tinkling of bells told him the tired cattle were returning from their forest rambles to the settlements; and at another time the hooting of the great owl took his fancy captive and his dreams were of unvisited regions and of his future fame. Now the mellow-horn fell sweetly upon his ear heralding a keel boat laden with good things from New Orleans, on its slow passage up the stream, and then the fiddle, and sounds of laughter echoed over the waters from the rude deck of a flat boat, freighted with produce for emigrants, or a raft ornamented with rude flags and horns of the red deer and elk. At all times, the habits of many of the birds he has so charmingly described were studied and recorded. Here, the lonely cabin of the squatter met his eye, giving note of coming civilization; and there, the rude encampment of Indian hunters invited him to a "pow wow." Thanking his Maker for the blessing of existence, he pondered much and gratefully, upon the sufferings which had been previously endured by some of the best blood of good old Virginia in purchasing the safe navigation of the river; and with the toilsome lives of the earlier pioneers, and the daring deeds of the Regulators, who helped to free the country of its scoundrel population, he was quite familiar. When all these things are considered it is not to be wondered at, that, in the evening of his days, when the *golden bowl was breaking*, the noble Audubon, should have have said to others, as he said to me, when once I spent a most happy day under his roof on the Hudson,—"My recollections of the beautiful Ohio, are among the most cherished of my heart, and I would fain die upon its shore." But he died upon the margin of the Hudson. It was well that he should have won his brightest laurels on the banks of the fairest river of the west; and as he was a favorite of nature, and in her eye did live, it was more than well that the noblest river of the east should lave his burial place.

The journey from Pittsburg to Washington was performed by railroad, and the route lay up the Conemaugh, over the Alleghany mountains, down the Juniata and Susquehanna, and so across the country to the Potomac, having travelled, in a little less than four months, a distance of about eight thousand miles. I was accompanied during the entire tour by my wife, and though constantly exposed to the dangers of steamboat and rickety carriage travelling, it is indeed surprising, that not a single accident of moment has occurred to retard us on the way. The same remark is applicable to the long and frequent summer tours that I have performed in the Western, Northern and Eastern States, and through the neighboring British Provinces, and while few lovers of their country have had better opportunities than I, to view its magnificent scenery and study the character of its people, I cannot but hope my gratitude is equal to my rare good fortune.

But I would speak of our rushing journey through Pennsylvania. The Conemaugh is a picturesque stream, and though spring had just made her appearance in its lower valley, we found, as we proceeded that winter was still ruler among its tributaries on the mountains. Along its course we noticed a great number of coal mines, which seemed to be located at all sorts of elevations, and to see the coal trains coming out of the earth like living monsters, and wind downward as waywardly as the mountain streams, was a most curious and interesting spectacle. As the Pennsylvania canal followed our own course, it gave, with its boats and horses, its bridges and rude cabins, a pleasing variety to the panorama. Before reaching the summit of the mountain range, we ran through no less than four tunnels, the last one more than thirty-six hundred feet long, on emerging from which we were overtaken by a snow-storm. The tops of the hills were all covered with the pure element, the cedars and the pines were drooping under its weight, and from the surrounding cliffs hung, in a thousand fantastic forms, immense masses of solid ice. But the locomotive, and the men who managed it, and the conductors, paid no regard to the noble scenery and the storm; and onward and downward sped the train, its very movement reminding one of things unearthly,—

onward with the speed of the wind. And now we have reached the valley of the Juniata. A beautiful stream, and worthy of its fame! It springs from the earth where the red deer gives birth to its fawn; it passes by the hunter's cabin, springs over ledges of rock without number, sweeps through cultivated fields, tumbles over dams, and turns every mill-wheel it happens to meet, usurps the business of the canal, and floats its heavily laden boats, mirrors a great number of hills covered with pine, maple and oak, as well as many farms, all richly cultivated; rushes under picturesque bridges, races with the canal, enriches broad meadows, where cattle are grazing and horses are playing; laves the threshold of rural cabins, with children sporting beside them in wild glee; yields its treasures to the fishermen, wears upon its bosom the most charming of islands, perpetuates in its color, the emerald of summer, receives into its flood a hundred laughing brooks, teeming with trout, and finally waters a broad valley, where the yeoman tills his soil in peace, and looks with pride upon his lawn—like hills covered with sheep, while from many a grove is heard the pleasant singing of the birds. Onward, onward in our course. We cross, and at Harrisburg recross the superb Susquehanna, rush with increasing rapidity down the valley of the very beautiful Gunpowder river to Baltimore, and in two hours are at home. And thus endeth "a Winter in the South."

OCCASIONAL RECORDS.

THE SUGAR CAMP.

Among our more agreeable recollections of the wilderness are those associated with the making of *maple sugar*. Our first taste of this sweetest of woodland luxuries was received from the hands of an Indian, into whose wigwam we had wandered from our father's dwelling, on one of the Saturday afternoons of our boyhood. It was many years ago, and long before the frontier of Michigan was transformed into a flourishing member of the national confederacy. Since that time we have not only eaten our full proportion of the luxury in question, both in wigwam and cabin, but we have seen it extensively manufactured by the Indian, as well as the white man; and we now purpose to discourse upon the article itself, and upon a few incidents connected with its manufacture.

Maple sugar is made from the sap of a tree, known by the several names of rock maple, hard maple, and sugar maple, which is found in great abundance in various portions of the Union, but chiefly in the northern States. It is a lofty and elegantly proportioned tree, and its foliage is particularly luxuriant; and, when touched by the frosts of autumn, is pre-eminently brilliant. The wood is also highly esteemed for the beauty of its fibre, which consists of concentrical circles, resembling the eye of a bird; and hence the term *bird's*-eye maple.

Generally speaking, the sugar-making season commences early in April, is universally considered as one of festivity, and seldom continues more than four weeks. The sudden transition of the temperature from winter to spring is essential to its production, for at this season alone does the vital principal of the tree pass in large quantities from the roots into its branches. Hence it is that, while making this passage, the sap has to be withdrawn; and this is accomplished by making an incision in the tree some three feet from the ground, and receiving the liquid in a vessel prepared for the purpose. And it has been observed that, when a frosty night is followed by a dry and sunny day, the sap flows abundantly, at which times three or four gallons are obtained from a single tree in twenty-four hours. The process employed for converting the sap into sugar is perfectly simple, and consists in boiling it first into a syrup and then into a more tangible substance. Of this sugar there are two kinds, viz., the hard or cake sugar, and that of a friable character, which is produced by constantly stirring the thick syrup when it is becoming cool. The taste of the sap or juice, when taken from the tree, is just sweet enough to be noticed; and though we have never ascertained the quantity commonly obtained from a single tree, we have been told that a very fruitful tree, in a good season, may be made to yield five pounds of the best sugar. To the human palate this juice is not generally agreeable, but wild and domestic animals are said to be inordinately fond of it, and slake their thirst with it whenever they can. Although a sufficient quantity of maple sugar has never been manufactured in this country to rank it among our articles of exportation, it has, for many years past, been about the only sugar used by a large number of people—especially those who live in the more thickly-wooded districts of the States, and those inhabiting the northern and western frontiers of the United States and Canada. In the opinion of all who manufacture the article it is held in high estimation, both as a luxury and on account of its nutrition. In regard to this last quality, we believe it is superior to all other sugars; for we know, from personal observation, that when eaten by the Indian children, during the manufacturing season, they become particularly hearty, though exclusively confined to it as an article of food for weeks at a time.

From the very nature of the business, the making of maple sugar is commonly carried on in an encampment, and we now purpose to describe the various kinds with which we are acquainted, beginning, as a matter of course, with an Indian camp. We are speaking of the remote past, and of an encampment of Ottawa Indians, in one of the maple forests skirting the western shore of Green Bay. It is in the month of April, and the hunting season is at an end. Albeit, the ground is covered with snow, the noonday sun has become quite powerful, and the annual offering has been made to the Great Spirit, by the medicine men, of the first product of one of the earliest trees in the district. This being the preparatory signal for extensive business, the women of the encampment proceed to make a large number of wooden troughs to receive the liquid treasure, and, after these are finished, the various trees in the neighborhood are tapped, and the juice begins to run. In the mean time, the men of the party have built the necessary fires, and suspended over them their earthen, brass, or iron kettles. The sap is now flowing in copious streams, and from one end of the camp to the other is at once presented an animated and romantic scene, which continues, without interruption, day and night until the end of the sugar season. The principal employment to which the men devote themselves is that of lounging about the encampment, shooting at marks, and playing the moccasin game; while the main part of the labor is performed by the women, who not only attend to the kettles, but employ all their leisure time in making the beautiful birchen mocucks, for the preservation and transportation of the sugar when made; the sap being brought from the troughs to the kettles by the boys and girls. Less attention than usual is paid by the Indians at such times to their meals, and, unless game is very easily obtained, they are quite content to depend upon the sugar alone. If an Indian happens to return from the river with a fish, he throws it without any ceremony into the boiling sap, dipping it out, when cooked, with a ladle or stick; and therefore it is that we often find in the maple sugar of Indian manufacture the bones of a trout, or some more unworthy fish. That even a bird, a rabbit, or an opossum, is sometimes thrown into the kettle instead of a fish is beyond a doubt; and we are not positively certain that the civilized fashion of eating jelly with roast lamb, may not be traced to the barbarous custom of cooking animals in hot sap. That this sap itself, when known to be clear and reduced to the consistency of molasses, is a palatable article, we are ready to maintain against the world; and we confess that, when not quite so fastidious as now, we have often eaten it in truly dangerous quantities, even in the cabin of an Indian. As we have already intimated, the sugar season is dependent upon the weather; but, even when it is prolonged to four or five weeks, it continues from beginning to end to be one of hilarity and gladness. At such times, even the wolfish-looking dogs seem to consider themselves entitled to the privilege of sticking their noses into the vessels of sap not yet placed over the fire. And in this manner does the poor Indian welcome returning Spring.

It is now about the middle of June, and some fifty birchen canoes have just been launched upon the waters of Green Bay. They are occupied by our Ottawa sugar-makers, who have started upon a pilgrimage to Mackinaw. The distance is near two hundred miles, and as the canoes are heavily laden, not only with mocucks of sugar, but with furs collected by the hunters during the past winter, and the Indians are travelling at their leisure, the party will probably reach their desired haven in the course of ten days. Well content with their accumulated treasures, both the women and the men are in a particularly happy mood, and many a wild song is heard to echo over the placid lake. As the evening approaches, day after day they seek out some convenient landing-place, and, pitching their wigwams on the beach, spend a goodly portion of the night carousing and telling stories around their camp fires, resuming their voyage after a morning sleep, long after the sun has risen above the blue waters of the east. Another sunset hour, and the cavalcade of canoes is quiety gliding into the crescent bay of Mackinaw, and, reaching a beautiful beach at the foot of a lofty bluff, the Indians again draw up their canoes, again erect their wigwams. And, as the Indian traders have assembled on the spot, the more improvident of the party immediately proceed to exhibit their sugar and furs, which are usually disposed of for flour and pork, blankets and knives, guns, ammunition, and a great variety of trinkets, long before the hour of midnight. That the remainder of this night is devoted to feasting and dancing, and tumultuous recreation, is a matter of course. But the trader who would obtain from the Indians their more unique articles of merchandise, usually visits the encampment on the following morning, when he is always certain of obtaining from the young women, on the most reasonable terms, their fancy mocucks of sugar, all worked over with porcupine quills; and a great variety of beautifully worked moccasins, and fancy bags, made of the sweet-smelling deer skin. In about a week after their arrival at Mackinaw, the Ottawa Indians begin to sigh for the freedom of the wilderness; and, before the trader has left his bed some pleasant morning, there is nothing to be seen on the beach at Mackinaw but the smoking embers of a score or two of watch-fires.

We would now conduct our readers into the sugar camp of a Frenchman. It is situated in one of the maple forests of Michigan, on the banks of the River Raisin, and within half a mile of the rude, comfortable dwelling of the proprietor. Very much the same process is here pursued in making the sugar that we have already described, only that a large proportion of the labor is performed by the men and boys, the women participating in the employment more for the purpose of carefully packing away the sugar when made, and having a little romantic sport in the way of eating hot sugar in the aisles of the church-like forest. The season of winter with our Frenchman has been devoted almost exclusively to the pleasures of life, and the making of sugar is the first and probably the only really lucrative business which he ever transacts. By the term lucrative we mean a business which allows him to lay aside a little spare money; for, generally speaking (like the class to which he belongs in the north-west,) he is perfectly satisfied if the agricultural products of his small farm yield him a comfortable living. Maple sugar and maple molasses are considered by our friend and his family as among their greatest luxuries; and while he makes a point of taking a goodly quantity to market, he never fails to keep a plentiful supply of both under his own roof. In transporting his sugar (as well as all other marketable articles,) to the neighboring towns, he employs a rude two-wheeled vehicle, made exclusively of wood, and drawn by a Canadian pony. On his first visit to the town after the sugar season is ended, he will be accompanied by his entire family, decked in their more tidy garments; and, before his return home, you may be certain that the Catholic priest, whose church he regularly attends, will receive a handsome present of the newly-made sugar, with perhaps a small keg of the delicious maple syrup or molasses. And thus does the Frenchman of the frontier welcome the return of spring.

But we have spent some pleasant days in the sugar camps of the Dutch yeomanry on the eastern and southern side of the Catskill Mountains, and we must not omit to pay our respects to them. The very best sugar is made in this region, and much of it into solid cakes of various sizes, from one pound to twenty. It is manufactured here both for home consumption and the market, and the price which it has usually commanded during the last ten years has been about one "York shilling" per pound. The labor in this region is about equally divided between the women and the men, and considerable attention is devoted to the cultivation of the maple-tree. In cooling their sugar, or rather in performing the business called "sugaring off," the Dutch employ immense wrought-iron pans, which are undoubtedly a great improvement upon the Indian and French fashions, which are simply no fashions at all, since the kettles employed to boil the sugar are used to "cool it off."

But the Dutch of whom we are speaking, those especially who are more wealthy than their neighbors, have a very sensible mode of winding up their sugar-making labors by giving what they term a "*Sugar-bee,*" or party. The elements which go to make up one of these rustic entertainments it would be difficult to describe. We may mention, however, that every body is invited, old men and their wives, young men and maidens; that the principal recreation is that of dancing to the music of a fiddle; that a most sumptuous and excessively miscellaneous feast is spread before the multitude; that the people assemble in the afternoon, and generally succeed in getting home an hour or two *after* the break of day. That an abundance of maple sugar is met with on these occasions will be readily imagined, and we may add that, in those districts where temperance societies are unpopular, the sugar is taken considerably adulterated in whisky.

The last sugar-bee to which we had the pleasure of being invited, while once sojourning among the Catskills, was given by an old Dutchman who resided on the side of a mountain, some *ten* miles from our temporary abode. We started for his house about sundown, in a large lumber-wagon, which was packed by no less than eight buxom damsels and four young men besides ourself. Although a perfect stranger to nearly all the party, we were received as an old friend. The damsels were in high glee; we had a reckless driver and a span of capital horses, and of course the young men were not at all backward in their deportment. The first half of the road was very good, and, as we rattled along, the songs, uncouth and shrill, which were sung, awakened many a mountain echo. But while all this was going on, and other things which we have not time to mention, the sky became overcast, and in a short time it began to rain, and a most intense darkness settled upon the woods. Our driver became bewildered, and the first that *we* knew was that *he* had lost the road, and that our horses had halted directly in front of a huge stump. Having thus unexpectedly been brought to a stand, the male members of the party proceeded to reconnoitre, and one of them fortunately discovered a light at the distance of half a mile. Towards this light did the entire party direct their march, and about twelve o'clock succeeded in reaching a log-cabin, which was inhabited by an old hunter; and as the guests of this man the party, in a very disagreeable mood, spent the remainder of the night. Long before the mists had left the valleys on the following morning, the party had worked its way out of the woods, and for a week afterwards we were frequently complimented for the important part that we had taken in the last *sugar-bee*.

We cannot conclude this article without remarking that maple sugar of rare quality is manufactured in the States of Vermont, New Hampshire, and Maine; but as we have never visited that section of the Union in the spring we cannot, from personal observation, speak of the New England sugar camps. That the maple sugar usually offered for sale in the Boston and New York markets is chiefly brought from this section of country we know to be a fact, and it is one which forcibly illustrates the true idea of Yankee enterprise.

P. S.—Since writing the above, we have had the pleasure of reading an interesting description of a *maple sugar camp*, by the eminent ornithologist, Mr. Audubon, from which we gather the following particulars, viz., that the juice of the sugar maple was to him a most refreshing and delicious beverage; that it takes ten gallons of this juice to make one pound of grained sugar; that the best of the syrup is made at the close of the sugar season; and that the sugar maple is found in abundance from Maine to Louisiana, invariably growing on rich and elevated grounds.

ACCOMAC.

UPWARDS of two hundred years ago, the long peninsula, now divided into the counties of Accomac and Northampton, in Virginia, was known by the Indian name of *Acohawmack*. An extensive tribe of aborigines who occupied the country, bore the same title, and the meaning of the word is said to be, *People who live upon shell fish.* Next to a scanty record embodied in Captain John Smith's History of Virginia, the earliest printed account of this region may be found at the conclusion of a pamphlet written by one Colonel NORWOOD, of England, wherein he describes "*A Voyage to Virginia in* 1649." At the conclusion of his perilous voyage across the Atlantic, it was the author's misfortune to be wrecked upon one of the islands on the eastern shore of Accomac, and that, too, in the stormy month of January. To comment upon Norwood's well written and very interesting pamphlet, is not now our object; but we will remark, in passing, that this document, taken in connection with the county records of the peninsula, which extend as far back as the year 1632, and also with the ancient graveyards of the region, would furnish material for an exceedingly valuable and entertaining volume, and we are surprised that some enterprising antiquarian of Virginia has not, long before this, taken the matter in hand. It is our province to speak of *Accomac* (by which we mean the ancient dominion known by that name) as it appears to the traveller of the present day.

What the distance may be from Washington to the northern line of Accomac we cannot imagine, but we know that if the morning cars to Baltimore are punctual, and you are fortunate enough to meet the Whitehaven steamboat at Baltimore, at 8 o'clock, you may enjoy your next breakfast at Horntown, a few miles south of the Maryland line, and within the limits of Accomac. On board of the steamer which brought us down the bay, there was rather a scarcity of passengers, but among them were some intelligent gentlemen, from one of whom we gathered the following items of information. The entire length of the Chesapeake Bay, from Havre de Grace to Norfolk, is two hundred miles; in width it varies from five to twenty-six miles, and in depth from four to twenty-four fathoms. Its shores are low and level, with occasional bluffs, however, and its waters clear and of a greenish hue. It contains a great number of islands, some of which are exceedingly fertile, but destitute of all picturesque beauty. During the autumn and winter its shallower waters are filled with almost every variety of waterfowl; it is said to yield a larger quantity of oysters than any other section of the globe of the same size; and it is also famous for the abundance and quality of its shad, striped bass or rock-fish, its drum, sheeps-head, and a species of sea-trout. On approaching the Wicomoco river, an island of one thousand acres was pointed out to us, called Bloodsworth Island, which is the property of two men, who reside upon their domain, a pair of veritable hermits, who live upon fish and waterfowl, instead of cultivating their soil. Our attention was also directed to a neighboring island, which seemed to be in a state of high cultivation, and we were told that the owner thereof had refused the handsome price of one hundred dollars per acre for the entire island. With regard to Deal's Island and Dames Quarter, in this vicinity of the bay, we heard the following anecdote. The *original* name of the first was "Devil's Island," and that of the second, "Damned Quarter," as any one may see by referring to some of the older maps. Once upon a time, as the story goes, a Connecticut skipper, in his smack, chanced to make his course up the Chesapeake, and as he was a stranger in this region, he hailed nearly every vessel or boat he met, with a lot of questions. "What island is that?" inquired the Yankee, of a downward bound brig. "*Devil's Island*," was the brief reply; whereupon the stranger's conscience was a little disturbed. About an hour afterwards, "What island is that?" again vociferated the skipper; and a Chesapeake fisherman replied, "*Damned Quarter.*" At this intelligence, the Yankee was so much alarmed that he immediately made a sudden tack, and with his helm "hard up" started for the outlet of the bay, and was never heard of more in southern waters.

The peninsula of Accomac, as nearly as we can ascertain, varies in width from eight to twelve miles, and is not far from seventy miles long. Generally speaking, it is almost as level as the sea, the highest ground not attaining a greater elevation than some twenty feet. The soil is of a sandy character, and the forests, which are quite extensive, are composed chiefly of pine and oak. The country is almost entirely destitute of running streams, and nearly all the inlets, especially on the bay side, are lined with extensive marshes, where snakes, turtles, and lizards are particularly abundant. Along the sea side of Accomac lie a succession of sandy islands, which render the navigation dangerous, and between which and the main shore the water is shallow and far from clear. Two of the above islands, Assateague and Chingoteague, are inhabited by a peculiar people, of whom I shall have something to say in another place. The only villages in this district, properly so called, are Drummontown and Eastville; they are the county seats, and though bearing an ancient appearance, they contain some good houses, and are well worth visiting. You can hardly travel eight miles, in any direction, without coming to a post-office, which glories in a village name, and therefore appears on paper to much better advantage than in reality. In some parts of the country we frequently noticed houses which seemed to have been abandoned by their owners, as if the soil in the vicinity had been completely worn out, and could not be profitably cultivated. These household ruins, together with the apparent want of enterprise, which one notices everywhere, conspire to throw a gloom over the traveller's mind, thereby preventing him, perhaps, from fully appreciating the happiness which really prevails among the people. And these (as is the case, in fact, with every nook and corner of the world,) constitute the principal attraction of Accomac; for man by nature is a lover of his kind, and "we have all one human heart by which we live."

If we were called upon to classify the Accomacians, we would divide them into the gentry, the miscellaneous fraternity, and the slave population. The gentry are a comparatively small class, but the principal landholders of the district. They come of good old English families, and are highly intelligent and well educated. The houses they occupy are homely in appearance, but well supplied with all the substantials that can add to the pleasures of country life. They seem to think more of comfort than display, and are distinguished for their hospitality to strangers. The miscellaneous faternity, to which we have alluded, is more extensive. A very large proportion of them obtain their living from the sea, annually bringing up from its bed an immense quantity of oysters and clams, which they sell to the fishermen of Philadelphia and New York; but these fishermen not only send to market large quantities of fish, but during the autumn and winter months they make a good deal of money by killing waterfowl, which abound on all the shores of the peninsula. The more legitimate fishermen of Accomac, who number between thirty and forty voters, reside on the neighboring islands of Chingoteague and Assateague. They are an exceedingly hard, rude, and simple-hearted race, and a little more at home on the water than on the land. The dangers to which they wilfully expose themselves are truly astonishing, and almost lead one to suppose that they are web-footed. We have been told of one individual who, for want of a boat, once swam a distance of three miles in midwinter, merely for the purpose of examining the wreck of a brig which had been abandoned by its owners; and we have heard of others who had been upset at sea, a distance of ten miles from shore, but who have regained their mother earth with the ease and carelessness of wild geese. In the miscellaneous fraternity may also be included the mechanics of the country, and all such people as stage-drivers, dram-shop keepers, peddlers, and other kindred birds.

The slave population of this district is decidedly the most extensive, and, if we are to judge by their general deportment, and by what they say, they are undoubtedly by far the happiest class on the peninsula. We questioned them occasionally with regard to what we have been educated to look upon as a hard lot, but we never saw but one individual who succeeded in rousing our sympathies, and before he finished talking to us, we discovered that he was a scamp of the first water, and therefore not worthy of credit. Every negro in this section of country has the evening hours to himself, as well as the entire Sabbath, and, instead of being "lashed" into obedience, is constantly treated with the utmost kindness. Many of them, who choose to labor for themselves, have free permission to follow any employment they please; and we know of several individuals who earn thirty dollars per month by voluntary labor, and whose services are valued by their masters at only ten or fifteen dollars; so that the servant pockets fifty per cent. of his monthly earnings. But what proves more conclusively than anything else, that the black man's bondage is not unbearable, is the fact that they are the most moral and religious people of the country. They are, at the same time, the most polite and the most kindly spoken people that we have met with in our wanderings; and we verily believe that they would not break the imaginary chain which now binds them to their masters. We confess that we have a natural repugnance to the word *bondage*, but our dread of a mere idea cannot make us deaf to the eloquence of what we have *seen*. It is true, that our experience has not been extensive, but we cannot see that the slaves, so called, of this region, are any more to be pitied than the children of any careful and affectionate parent. A goodly number of the blacks in this region are free; and we know of one individual who is not only free, but the owner of no less than three farms.

And now, with regard to those traits which the Accomacians possess in common. In religion they are Methodists and Baptists, and in politics they belong to the rank and file of the unterrified Democracy. Those who are at all educated are highly educated; but of the twenty-five thousand souls who inhabit the peninsula, we suppose that not more than one thousand could distinguish the difference between the English and the Chippewa alphabet. In the two counties of Accomac and Northampton, the idea of even a weekly newspaper was never dreamed of. The people are fond of amusement, which consists principally of dancing and card-playing parties, and the Saturday of each week is usually appropriated as a holiday. Any event which can bring together a crowd is gladly welcomed, so that court days, training days, election days, the Fourth of July, Christmas day, New Year's day, and Thanksgiving day are among the white days of the unwritten calendar of the Accomacians. The roads of the country are all by nature very good, and the people exceedingly fond of going through the world as pleasantly as possible; so that each man who can own a horse is sure of owning a gig, and many of them are particularly unique and tottleish, something like a scow-boat in a gale of wind.

But the crowning peculiarity of this nook of the great world has reference to the custom of raising and taming wild horses. Like everything poetical connected with the habits of our people, this custom is rapidly becoming obsolete, and will soon be remembered merely as an idle and romantic tale. The very idea of having to do with wild horses excited our fancy the moment we heard the custom alluded to; and we made every effort to collect reliable information upon it, as it existed half a century ago. As good fortune would have it, we found out an intelligent and venerable gentleman, who supplied us with many interesting particulars. The "oldest inhabitant" to whom we allude, is the Rev. David Watts, of Horntown, who is now in the 82d year of his age, and the substance of his information is as follows:—

In the Atlantic Ocean, off the north-eastern shore of Accomac, lies a long and sandy island known by the name of Assateague. The distance from one extremity to the other is perhaps ten miles, and in reaching it you have to cross a bay that is perhaps eight miles wide. At the present time, there are only four families residing upon the island, one of them having charge of the lighthouse, the remaining three being devoted to the fishing business. From time immemorial it has been famous for its luxuriant grass, and from the period of the Revolution down to the year 1800, supplied an immense number of wild horses with food. When these animals were first introduced upon the island has not been ascertained, but it is said that they were the most abundant about half a century ago. At that period there was a kind of stock company in existence, composed principally of the wealthier planters residing on the main shore. The animals were of the pony breed, but generally beautifully formed and very fleet; of a deep black color, and with remarkably long tails and manes. They lived and multiplied upon the island without the least care from the hand of man, and, though feeding entirely on the grass of the salt meadows, they were in good condition throughout the year. They were employed by their owners, to a considerable extent, for purposes of agriculture, but the finer specimens were kept or disposed of as pets for the use of ladies and children. The prices which they commanded on the island varied from ten to twenty dollars, but by the time a handsome animal could reach New York or New Orleans, he was likely to command one hundred and fifty or two hundred dollars.

But by far the most interesting circumstance connected with the wild horses of Assateague had reference to the annual festival of penning the animals, for the purpose, not only of bringing them under subjection, but of selling them to any who might desire to purchase. The day in question was the 10th of June, on which occasion there was always an immense concourse of people assembled on the island from all parts of the surrounding country; not only men, but women and children; planters who came to make money, strangers who wished to purchase a beautiful animal for a present, together with the grooms or horse-tamers, who were noted at the time for their wonderful feats of horsemanship. But a large proportion of the multitude came together for the purpose of having a regular frolic; and feasting and dancing were carried on to a great extent, and that too upon the open sandy shore of the ocean, the people being exposed during the day to the scorching sunshine, and the scene being enlivened at night by immense bonfires, made of wrecked vessels or drift wood, and the light of the moon and stars. The staple business of these anniversaries, however, was to tame and brand the horses, which were usually cornered in a pen, perhaps a hundred at a time, when, in the presence of the immense concourse of people, the tamers would rush into the midst of the herd, and not only noose and halter the wild and untamed creatures, but, mounting them, at times, even without a bridle, would rush from the pen and perform a thousand fantastic and daring feats upon the sand. Few, if any, of these horsemen were ever killed or wounded while performing these exploits, though it is said that they frequently came in such close contact with the horses as to be compelled to wrestle with them, as man with man. But, what was still more remarkable, these men were never known to fail in completely subduing the horses they attempted to tame; and it was often the case that an animal which was as wild as a hawk in the morning could be safely ridden by a child at the sunset hour.

On his return from Accomac, which was visited at the special request of Joseph Gales, Esq., the writer went over to the good old-fashioned town of Norfolk and paid his respects to the famous Dismal Swamp in its vicinity. A most happy name is this, for a most unhappy looking place. It lies on the dividing line between Virginia and North Carolina, extending north and south a distance of thirty miles, and east and west about a dozen miles. It is an area of low submerged land, covered with a dense forest of pine, juniper and cypress, and all its more striking features, such as the green mosses which cover the fallen trees and cling around the roots of all, the grey mosses which hang from the branches of the cypress trees, the lonely lake and the water birds, reptiles and wild beasts which abound in every nook and corner, are in strictest keeping with the prevailing idea of gloom and desolation. And then, again, as is most natural, the stories and legends associated with the Dismal Swamp are anything but cheerful. The most authentic and pathetic one of all, and one which the poet Mcore has made the theme of a fine lyric, is to this effect:—a young man who lost his mind on the death of the girl whom he loved, disappeared from his friends and was never heard of afterwards. As he had frequently said, in his delirium, that the girl was not dead but gone in a canoe to the Dismal Swamp, it is supposed that he wandered into that dreary wilderness in search of the maid, and had died of hunger or from exposure in some of its dreadful morasses. But mammon has cut a canal through a portion of even the Dismal Swamp, and it cannot be long before every vestige of its primeval poetry will be forever gone.

THE FUR TRAPPERS.

THE unique brotherhood of men to whom we now direct the attention of our readers have always depended upon the fur trade alone for their support, and as the various fur companies of North America have flourished and declined, so have the trappers multiplied or decreased in numbers. The French, who were the founders of the fur trade on this continent, established themselves here in 1606, and the trapping fraternity may therefore claim the honor of having existed nearly two centuries and a half. To estimate the precise number of individuals composing this class at the present time would be an impossibility, occupying as they do a section of country extending from the Pacific Ocean to Hudson's Bay.

By the laws of our country they have ever been looked upon as aliens from the commonwealth of civilization, and by the Indian tribes as trespassers upon their natural and inherited privileges. The blood of the white man, though frequently considerably adulterated, invariably runs through their veins, and the great majority trace their origin to a French, Scottish, or Irish ancestry, it being an established and singular fact that trappers of pure American blood are exceedingly rare. Those of the far north commonly have the dark eyes and hair of the Canadian Frenchman, and those of the south-west the flaxen hair and broad brogue of the Scotchman or Irishman. The motives generally found to have influenced them in entering upon their peculiar life are exceedingly various, but among the more common may be mentioned a deeply-rooted love for the works of Nature in their primeval luxuriance, want of sufficient intelligence to prosecute a more respectable business, and a desire to keep out of the way of certain laws which they may have transgressed in their earlier days. They are usually men with families, their wives being pure Indian, and their children, of course, half breeds. They have what may be termed fixed habitations, but these are rude log cabins, located on the extreme frontiers of the civilized world. In religion, as a class, they are behind their red brethren of the wilderness, and their knowledge of books is quite as limited. Generally speaking, they spend about nine months roaming alone through the solitude of the forests and prairies, and the remaining three months of the year with their families or at the trading posts of the fur companies. As their harvest time is the winter, they are necessarily men of iron constitutions, and frequently endure the severest hardships and privations. Understanding as they do the science of trapping and the use of the gun more thoroughly than the Indian, they eclipse him in the business of acquiring furs, and from their superior knowledge of the civilized world, limited though it be, they realize much greater profits, and hence it is, that they are not only hated by the Indian but also by the traders. Their manner of dressing is ordinarily about half civilized, their buckskin hunting shirts and fur caps, of their own manufacture, appearing almost as picturesque as the blankets and plumes of the Indian himself. Like the Indians, too, they prefer richly-fringed leggins to pantaloons, and embroidered moccasins to shoes. To be perfectly free from every restraint both of body and mind, is their chief ambition, and to enjoy the freedom of the wilderness is their utmost happiness. Those who follow their trade among the mountains are commonly banded together in parties of half a dozen. They perform their long journey altogether upon horseback, and when among the mountains are as expert in scaling precipices, surmounting waterfalls, and buffeting snow-storms as the more hardy of the Indian tribes. They are expert horsemen, ride the best of animals, and take great pleasure, not only in decking themselves with ornaments, but also in caparisoning their horses in the most grotesque yet picturesque manner. The hardihood of these animals may be mentioned as something remarkable, for it is said that their only food during the winter months consists of what they can obtain from their own unaided exertions by burrowing in the snow, and stables are to them entirely unknown. As to the animals which all of them make it their business to capture, it may be mentioned that chiefest among them all is the beaver; but a goodly portion of their income is derived from the furs and peltries of the martin, otter, musk-rat, bear, fox, mink, lynx, wolverine, raccoon, wolf, elk, and deer, and the robes of the huge buffalo.

But let us describe the life of the trapping fraternity somewhat more minutely, in doing which we shall give an illustrative sketch of the career of a single individual, describing his departure from home, his sojourn in the wilderness, his return home, and his manner of spending his brief summer furlough.

It is a bright October morning, and about the threshold of the trapper's cabin there is an unusual stir. While the trapper himself is busily engaged in examining and putting in order his traps, packing away his powder and lead, with a number of good flints, giving the lock of his old rifle a thorough oiling, and sharpening his knives; his wife is stowing away in his knapsack a few simple cooking utensils, a small bag of tea and a little sugar, several pairs of moccasins and coarse woolen socks, and a goodly quantity of the sinewy material used in making snow-shoes. The fact that our friend is about to separate from his family for the most part of a year, makes him particularly kind to those about him; and, by way of manifesting his feelings, he gives into his wife's possession what little spare money he may have left in his pocket out of his earnings of the previous year, and allows his children to make as much noise as they please, even refraining from scolding them when they kick and abuse his favorite hunting dogs. All things being ready, night comes, and the trapper permits himself to enjoy another sleep in the midst of his household, but long before the break of day he has whistled to his dogs, and, with his knapsack on his back, has taken his departure for a stream that rises among the Rocky Mountains. If his course lies though a forest land he continues to travel on foot, taking his own leisure, killing a sufficient quantity of game to satisfy his wants, and sleeping at night upon his skins, under a canopy of leaves. If extensive water courses lie within his range, he purchases a canoe of some wandering Indians and plays the part of a navigator; and if he finds it necessary to cross extensive prairies, he obtains a pony, and, packing himself and plunder upon the animal, plays the part of an equestrian. When the first blast of December, accompanied by a shower of snow sweeps over the land, it finds our trapper friend snugly domiciled in a log shanty at the mouth of the river where he purposes to spend the winter, trapping for beaver.

And now all things are ready, and the trapper has actually entered upon his winter avocation. He has reconnoitered the valley in which he finds himself, and having ascertained the localities of the beaver, with their houses and dams, he forthwith manages to shoot a single male beaver, and having obtained from his glandulous pouch a substance called *castoreum*, he mixes it with a number of aromatics, and in three or four days he is supplied with a suitable bait and proceeds to set his traps. As the senses of the beaver are exceedingly keen, the business of the trapper requires experience and great caution, and he glides through the forests almost with the silence of a ghost; but, when a master of his calling, he seldom leaves a beaver village until, by his cunning arts, it has become depopulated. The war of extermination, as already intimated, begins at the mouth of the river, and with our friend, will only cease when he has reached the fountain-head, or the season for trapping comes to an end. The coldest winds may blow and the woods may be completely blocked with snow, but the trapper has mounted his snow-shoes, and day after day does he revisit and re-arrange his traps. If night overtake him when far removed from his shanty (which may be the case more than half the time,) he digs himself a hole in some sheltered snow bank, and, wrapped up in his blanket by the side of his solitary fire, spends a strangely comfortable night. When not engaged with his traps, he employs his time in drying and dressing his furs; or, as fancy may dictate, he shoulders his gun and starts out for the purpose of capturing a deer, a bear, or some of the beasts which are wont to howl him to sleep at the midnight hour. Venison and bear meat constitute his principal food, but he is particularly partial to the tail of his favorite beaver. The only human beings with whom he has any social intercourse during the long winter, are the poor wandering Indians who chance to visit him in his cabin; and at such times, many are the wild adventures and strange legends which they relate to each other around the huge fire of the trapper. And he now enjoys to perfection the companionship of his dogs. Companions, it is true, of another sort sometimes gather around his lonely habitation to relieve his solitude; for the snowy owl hoots and screams at night from the huge pine branch that reaches over his cabin, or perhaps an unmolested deer manifests its love of companionship by browsing the twigs in broad daylight almost at his very threshold. But now fair weather cometh out of the north, and the trapper begins to think that he has secured such a supply of furs as will guarranty him a comfortable support during the coming summer, and one by one he gathers in his traps. The crack of his rifle is now heard more frequently echoing through the woods, for he cares not to obtain more beaver skins even if he could, and he would obtain a sufficient number of miscellaneous furs to render his assortment complete. Heavy spring rains have set in, the water courses are nearly released from their icy fetters, and on issuing from his cabin, after a night of conflicting dreams, he finds that the neighboring stream has become unusually full. A single glance at its turbid waters is enough. He cuts down a suitable tree and builds him a canoe, and in this he stows away his furs and all his other plunder, and, seizing his paddle, he jumps into his seat, and with a light heart starts for his distant home.

The rains are over and gone, and although our voyager has already been ten days upon the waters, he has yet at least a thousand additional miles to travel. Rapids without number are to be passed, many a laborious portage must be made around huge waterfalls, and at least two months must elapse before he can moor his little barge in the haven where he would be. Day follows day, and his course is onward. All along his route the forest trees are bursting their buds and decking themselves with the livery of the vernal season, while the grasses and flowers of the prairies are striving to overreach each other as they loom into the pleasant sunshine. And then, too, the heart of our voyager is cheered by the singing of birds. When night comes, and he has lain himself down by his watch-fire on the shore, in some litle cove, he is lulled to sleep by the murmuring music of the stream. If, on a pleasant day when he is fatigued, he happen upon an Indian encampment and finds that an extensive ball-play or an Indian horse race, or any important medicine ceremony is about to occur, he tarries there for a few hours, and then, as his mind dwells upon the grotesque and laughable scenes he has witnessed, resumes his voyage in a more cheerful mood. Day follows day, and the stream upon which he is now floating is broad and deep, and sweeps onward as if rejoicing with pride for having triumphed over the obstacles of the wilderness, and is rapidly approaching the fields and the abodes of civilization. It is now the close of a day in the leafy month of June, and our voyager is gliding noiselessly into the quiet cove beside his cabin, and, uttering a loud whistle or whoop and firing his gun, his wife and children hasten to the shore, and—the trapper is at home!

The summer time, in the opinion of our trapper friend, is the season of unalloyed enjoyment, for it is then that he gives himself up to the gratification of all his desires. Having disposed of his furs and peltries at the nearest trading post for a few hundred dollars in cash, or its equivalent in merchandise, he deems himself independently rich, and conducts himself accordingly. In a fit of liberality, he orders his wife and children into his canoe and takes them upon a visit to the nearest frontier village or city, where he loads them with gewgaws, and the family spend a few days. The novelty of this visit soon passes away, and our trapper with his family are once more domiciled in their cabin. A week of inactivity then follows, and the trapper becomes as restless as a fish out of water. He is troubled with a kind of itching palm, and away he goes upon a vagabondizing tour among the hangers-on about the trading establishments, recounting to all who will listen to him his adventures in the wilderness, and spending the remainder of the summer after the manner of the idle and the dissipated. But the first frost brings him to his senses, and the trapper is himself again—for he is thinking of the wilderness.

ROCK CREEK.

It was a delightful autumnal morning in Washington City, and we had called upon a friend (who, like ourself, is a lover of nature,) and proposed that we should spend a day in the woods, whereupon he whistled for his handsome greyhound, and with our sketch-books in hand, we departed. We turned our faces towards *Rock Creek*, which rises in the central portion of Montgomery county, Maryland, and after running a distance of some fifteen miles, finally empties into the Potomac, between Washington and Georgetown. And now, before going one step further, we wish to inform the reader that it is not our intention to give a complete description of this charming stream: to accomplish that task faithfully it would be necessary for us to write a thousand poems and paint at least a thousand pictures, every one of which should be a gem. We purpose only to record the more prominent impressions which have been left upon our mind by the excursion to which we allude.

We struck the creek just without the limits of the city, and the first object that attracted our attention was "Decatur's tomb." This memorial of a departed naval hero occupies the summit of a picturesque hill, and is shaded from the sun by a brotherhood of handsome oak trees. It is built of bricks (which are painted white,) and resembles in shape a small Grecian temple without its columns, and is without any inscription. The remains of the commodore were originally deposited here, but his ashes have subsequently been removed to Philadelphia and deposited in his family vault. The land upon which this tomb is located is called Kalorama, and belongs to an estate originally owned by Joel Barlow, which fact is alone sufficient to give it a reputation; but it is somewhat more interesting to know that it was upon this spot of earth that Robert Fulton first tried his experiments while studying the science of steam navigation. This was at the time when Barlow and Fulton were on the most intimate terms of friendship, and Kalorama was Fulton's principal home. A gentleman residing in Georgetown informs us that he can well remember the time when an old wooden shed was standing in the vicinity of Rock Creek, where Fulton tried many of his experiments; and we are also informed that the parlour walls of Kalorama was once ornamented with fresco paintings executed by Fulton at the request of his friend Barlow. Subsequently to that period and while yet a member of Barlow's family, Fulton kept an account book, in which he recorded all his business transactions, and that curious and valuable relic of the departed engineer is now in the possession of a citizen of Washington, Joseph Gales, Esq., by whose politeness we are privileged to gratify our antiquarian readers with a brief description of the account book in question. It is of the size of an ordinary mercantile cash-book, and although only half filled with writing, it contains a record of business transactions occurring during the years 1809,–'10,–'11,–'12,--'13, and '14. It seems to have been kept with very little regard to method, but nevertheless contains a a great variety of items which are quite valuable in a historical point of view. On a fly-leaf for example, we have the following record :—

"1813. The dry-dock finished at the steamboat works in Jersey City on the 14th October. On that day, at 1 o'clock, the original North River steamboat entered for the first time, and I believe is the first vessel that has been in a dry-dock in the United States."

With regard to the name of the "original North River steamboat," we are not certain: but on the same leaf with the above, we find the following memorandum :—

"*Car of Neptune*—length of her bottom 157 feet; do. on deck 171 feet 6 inches; extreme width of the bottom 22 feet: do. on deck 26 feet."

And here, in passing, we will mention a few particulars respecting this *first* steamer and her *first* trip from New York to Albany, communicated to the public by one of her *first* passengers, John Q. Wilson, Esq., of the latter city. She had twelve births and they were all occupied, the fare being seven dollars, and the passage was performed in thirty-two hours. A quaker friend of Mr. Wilson hearing that he intended to venture upon the passage accosted him: "John, will thee risk thy life in such a concern? I tell thee, she is the most *fearful wild fowl living*, and thy father ought to restrain thee." Fulton himself was on board and his clear and sharp voice was heard above the strange noises of the machinery, and though he heard, on every hand, before starting, the jeers of the skeptical, he thought of the future and was not dismayed.

With a view of showing the profitableness of the steam-boating business in the olden times, we append the following:—

"Total number of passengers in the Raritan for 1809:

202 to Elizabethtown Point, at	4s.	each,	$101 00
1,480 to Amboy, at	8	do.	1,480 50
692 to Brunswick, at	12	do.	1,038 75
90 way			55 20
Total receipts			2,675 45

"Of this sum one-sixth, equal $445 90, to patentees."

Of the various persons with whom Fulton seems to have had extensive dealings, the principal one was Robert R. Livingston, from whom large sums of money were frequently received. The principal items under the head of 1813 (which seems to have been a very busy year), give one an idea of the extent of FULTON'S business, and is as follows:—

"Steamboats building and engaged:

2 from New Orleans to Louisville and St. Louis, Mississippi	$60,000
1 " Pittsburgh to Louisville, Ohio	25,000
1 " Richmond to Norfolk, James River	35,000
1 " Washington to Malbourg, Potomac	20,000
1 on Long Island Sound, from New York to Hartford	40,000
1 " East River ferry boat to Brooklyn	20,000
1, Petersburg	25,000
1, Elizabeth	30,000
1, Robert Fulton	26,000
1, Charleston	30,000
1, Cape Fear	22,000
Total	$332,000"

Another record which we find under the same head is this:

"Waters under the direction of B. H. Latrobe, or such of them as he shall have a steamboat on and in actual operation by January, 1815. Such as shall not have the funds raised for one boat within one year from May 1, 1813, shall be at the disposal of Livingston and Fulton.

"1st, Potomac, from Georgetown to Potomac Creek.

"2d, for the sounds from Charleston to Savannah.

"3d, from Pittsburg to Louisville.

"4th, the Cumberland from Nashville to Louisville.

"5th, the Tennessee to Louisville.

"For raising companies, funds, and establishing these, he has to have of each one-third of the patentee's rights."

Under the head of 1812, we find a statement giving the expenses of a North River steamboat (what one we know not,) which amounted to $610 per month, the boat making seventy-six trips. And as to wages, we gather that the captain received $50 per month; pilot, $35; engineer, $35; seamen and firemen, $20 each; cook, $16; servants, $14; and chambermaid, $8.

Another record readeth as follows:—

"*Gentlemen of influence in Cincinnati, Ohio.*—Jacob Burnet, Esq., Martin Baum, Esq., Jesse Hunt, General Findley, General Gano, Mr. Stanly."

The following we find under the head of "Notes on Steamboats:"—

"The Comet, constructed in Pittsburg in the spring of 1813, for Mr. Smith, is 52 feet long and 8 feet beam, cylinder 6¼ inches diameter, 18 inches stroke, vibrating motion, no condenser or air-pump. The water wheel in the stern, 6 feet diameter, 8 paddles, 2 feet 6 inches long and 11 inches wide. The boiler 14 feet long, 2 feet 6 inches wide, with a flue high, steam from 50 to 60 pounds to the inch square, 20 to 30 double stroke a minute. *This is Evans's idea of steam power by high steam. It was the Marquis of Worcester's* 120 *years ago; and Mr. Watts* 30 *years ago tried and abandoned it.*"

Another curious memorandum, which is without a caption, is as follows:—

"10,000 acres of pine land on Egg Harbor River, the property of Ebenezer Tucker, of Tuckerton, Burlington county, known by the name of Judge Tucker. Should this land produce only ten cords to an acre, it will be 1,000 to 100 acres, or 100,000 cords. The steamboats from New York will use 1,500 cords a year, or, for New York and Albany, 3,000 cords; thence 20 years would consume the wood of 6,000 acres, in which time, the first cut would grow up, and thus this 10,000 acres would perpetually supply the steamboats."

The longest record in this account book (like all the others,) is in Fulton's own handwriting, and entitled "*Livingston and Fulton* vs. *Lake Champlain boat.*" It occupies four closely written pages, is dated October 12, 1810, and signed by Robert

R. Livingston. It is an interesting document, but as the volume in question is about to be presented to the New York Historical Society, I will leave it with that honorable body to give it to the public in some of their publications.

But enough of this episode. Though Rock Creek may have been the birthplace of Fulton's steamboat idea, yet it is certain that, with all his fiery monsters at our command, we could never ascend this beautiful stream without the use of our legs, and we will therefore rejoin our companion and continue our pedestrian pilgrimage.

Our next halting-place, after we left Kalorama, was at an old mill, located in the centre of a secluded glen. With the humming music of its wheels, with the polite attentions of the *floury* miller, and the rustic beauty of his cottage and children, we were well pleased, but with the natural loveliness of the place we were delighted. A greater variety of luxuriant foliage we never before witnessed in so limited a nook of the country. From one point of view a scene presented itself which was indeed exquisite. We were completely hemmed in from the great world, and, in addition to the mill and the cottage, we had a full view of the stream, which was spanned by a rustic foot bridge, upon which a couple of children were standing and throwing pebbles in the water, while a few paces beyond a man was pulling to the shore a small boat laden with wood. On either hand, a number of proud-looking oaks towered against the sky, and by the water's edge in the distance stood a stupendous silver willow, literally white with age; and, to complete the picture, we had in one place a mysterious brick ruin, and in the foreground a variety of mossy rocks, upon which, in a superb attitude, stood our beautiful greyhound, watching a little army of minnows sporting in a neighboring pool. And with what great name does our reader imagine this beautiful place is associated? None other than that of the late John Quincy Adams, who became its purchaser many years ago, and to whose estate (as we believe,) it now belongs. And many a time, in other days, has that distinguished statesman spent the morning under the dome of the capitol in political debate, and the afternoon of the same day in this romantic glen, listening to the singing of the birds, which had built their nests in the branches of his own trees.

The roads which crossed the channel of Rock Creek, and frequently run for a long distance along its winding vale, are distinguished for their loneliness, and of course well adapted to please the poetic mind. Along many of them you might walk for miles without meeting a human being, but then you would be sure to frighten many a rabbit, and destroy the gossamer hammocks of unnumbered spiders. While passing along the road which took us from Adams' Mill further up the stream, we chanced to overtake a small negro boy (who was almost without any rags on his back, and whose straw hat looked as if the cows had feasted upon its brim,) with whom our companion held the following dialogue:—

"Boy, where are you going?"

"I'm gwine down to Mr. Pierce's."

And here—taking out his pencil, holding up his sketch-book, and looking very fiercely at the darkie—our friend exclaimed, "I'll sketch you, you rascal."

Whereupon the poor boy uttered a most frightful yell, and ran away in the greatest consternation, as if we had been a pair of murderers.

Our next stopping-place was at a cider mill, where an old negro, with the assistance of a mule, was grinding apples, and another man was pressing the sweet juice into a mammoth tub. A lot of boys, who were out on a chestnut gathering excursion, had discovered the mill, and having initiated themselves into the good graces of the darkies, were evidently enjoying a portion of Mr. Horace Greeley's celebrated "good time."

But it is now about noon, and we have reached that spot upon Rock Creek known as Pierce's Plantation. Here we found the ruins of an old saw-mill, and while transferring a portrait of it to our sketch-book, with its half decayed dam, and two or three hoary sycamores and elms, we discovered a boy in the act of fishing. We bowed to him as to a brother angler, and looking into his basket, we found snugly lying there no less than half a dozen handsome fall* fish, weighing from six ounces to a pound each. These we of course purchased, and then inquired of the boy if he knew of a house in that vicinity where we could likely have the fish cooked. He replied in the affirmative, whereupon we sent him to the dwelling he mentioned for the purpose of warning the inmates of our approach. On our arrival there we were warmly welcomed, and in due time we had the satisfaction of enjoying as finely cooked fish as ever tickled the palate of Izaak Walton or Sir Humphrey Davy. Not only were we waited upon with marked politeness, but were treated with an abundance of delicious currant wine and new cider, and for all this truly southern hospitality we could make no return, excepting in the way of gratitude.

But, pleasant as was our reception and repast at this Rock Creek cottage, our own mind was more deeply impressed with the exquisitely charming appearance of the cottage itself and surrounding buildings. It struck us as one of the most comfortable and poetical nooks that we ever beheld. It seemed to have everything about it calculated to win the heart of a lover of nature and rural life. Though situated on the side of a hill and embowered in trees, it commands a pleasing landscape; and as it was built upwards of one hundred years ago, it is interesting for its antiquity. Surmounted as it is with a pointed roof, green with the moss of years, and flanked by a vine-covered porch, the vegetation which clusters around it is so abundant that you can hardly discover its real proportions. And all the out-buildings are in strict keeping with the cottage itself. It is, upon the whole, one of the most interesting nooks to be found anywhere within an hour's ride of the capitol; and we can fully understand what a certain wealthy gentleman *felt* when he made the remark that this Rock Creek cottage was the only place he had ever seen which he would prefer to his

* The Fall Fish of Rock Creek is evidently identical with the Dace of Walton; it is really a beautiful and sweet fish, and well deserves its local reputation.

own, albeit his own residence is one of the most costly and beautiful in the District of Columbia.

The scenery of Rock Creek for several miles above the Pierce Plantation, is chiefly distinguished for its simple and quiet beauty. The whole vale in fact is remarkably luxuriant, and probably contains as great a variety of foliage as can be found in the same space in any section of the country. For miles and miles do the trees come together as if for the purpose of protecting the murmuring stream from the kisses of the sunlight, and even in September, birds and flowers are quite abundant; for here it is (it would seem) that summer lingers longest in the lap of autumn. And such vines, too, as cluster along the margin of this stream! The net-work which they have formed over the innumerable tiny waterfalls and the dark pools, is graceful beyond compare; and while happy children go there at times to gather the luscious grapes, we are certain that the little people of fairyland are well content with their allotted privilege of using the swing of the vine, while in the enjoyment of their midnight revels.

But we find that we are getting to be decidedly too poetical for our own safety and the comfort of our readers, and as the sun has long since passed the meridian, it is time that we should think of returning home. And, besides, as we shall return to the city by a different route from the one we came, we purpose to introduce to our readers one or two more "places of note" which are identified with Rock Creek.

And first as to the Rock Creek church, which lies somewhere between one and two miles eastward of the stream from which it derives its name. The original Rock Creek chapel was founded in the year 1719, and the bricks employed in its construction were brought from England. It became a parish church in 1726, at which time the glebe land (as at the present time, I believe) amounted to one hundred acres. It was rebuilt in the year 1768, the design having been made, it is said, by Washington, and many improvements added in the year 1808. The first rector of the church was the Rev. George Murdock, who officiated for thirty-four years; his successors were Rev. Alexander Williamson, Rev. Thomas Read, Rev. Alfred Henry Dashiels, Rev. Thomas G. Allen, Rev. Henry C. Knight, Rev. Levin I. Gills, Rev. Edward Waylen, and the present incumbent, Rev. William A. Harris. Of Mr. Read it is recorded that he presided over the church for forty years, during the whole of which time he was absent only *thirty* months; and with regard to Mr. Waylen, it may be stated that he compiled an interesting history of the Parish, which was published in 1845.

The appearance of Rock Creek church, as it now stands, is simply that of an old-fashioned but very comfortable brick church. It occupies the summit of a gentle hill, and is completely surrounded with a brotherhood of fine oak and chestnut trees. On every side of it tombs and grave-stones are quite abundant, and some of them are so very old as to be almost entirely hidden in the earth. Although we spent nearly an hour in this city of the dead, deciphering the various epitaphs, we only stumbled upon one which attracted our particular attention; it was a simple stone slab, covered with moss, upon which was this touching record:—

" *Grant, Lord, when I from death do wake,*
I may of endless life partake.
J. R.
1802."

And now, suppose our readers tarry with us for a few moments at the residence of a certain retired banker, which lies only a short distance from the Rock Creek church. With the elegant mansion and highly cultivated grounds, everybody must of necessity be pleased, for we believe that a more tasteful and superb place is not to be found in the country. It caps the summit of the loftiest hill in the vicinity of Washington, and while in one direction it commands a view of the Alleghany Mountains, in another lies spread out a complete panoramic view of the metropolis of the land, with a magnificent reach of the Potomac extending a distance of at least forty miles. To comment upon the spirits who preside over the mansion to which we have alluded is not our purpose, but we may mention in passing that among the numerous productions of art which adorn the interior, are two capital pictures by Morland, and a very fine landscape by Gainsborough. But enough. The sun is already near the horizon, and even now the latter half of our walk home must be by the light of the moon. And so much for a vagabondizing day on Rock Creek.

A VIRGINIA BARBECUE.

THE word *barbecue* is said to be derived from a combination of two French words, signifying *from the head to the tail*, or rather, "according to the modern," *the whole figure, or the whole hog*. By some, this species of entertainment is thought to have originated in the West India Islands. However this may be, it is quite certain that it was first introduced into this country by the early settlers of Virginia; and though well known throughout all the Southern States, it is commonly looked upon as a "pleasant invention" of the Old Dominion. The idea was evidently conceived by a rural population, and in a district where villages and the ordinary public buildings of the present time were few and far between. For purposes of business or pleasure, the people found it necessary, or advisable, to meet together in masses, at stated periods; and as these meetings were made a kind of rural festival, and as the animals served up on such occasions were commonly roasted entire, it was not unnatural that the feast should eventually have become known as a barbecue.

Of the genus barbecue, as it exists at the present time, we believe there are only two varieties known to the people of Virginia, and these may be denominated as social and political. The social barbecue is sometimes given at the expense of a single individual, but more commonly by a party of gentlemen, who desire to gratify their friends and neighbors by a social entertainment. At times, the ceremony of issuing written invitations is attended to; but, generally speaking, it is understood that all the yeomanry of the immediate neighborhood, with their wives and children, will be heartily welcomed, and a spirit of perfect equality invariably prevails. The spot ordinarily selected for the meeting is an oaken grove in some pleasant vale, and the first movement is to dispatch to the selected place a crowd of faithful negroes, for the purpose of making all the necessary arrangements. If the barbecue is given at the expense of half a dozen gentlemen, you may safely calculate that at least thirty servants will be employed in bringing together the good things. Those belonging to one of the entertainers will probably make their appearance on the ground with a wagon load of fine young pigs: others will bring two or three lambs, others some fine old whisky and a supply of wine, others the necessary table-cloths, plates, knives and forks, others an abundance of bread, and others will make their appearance in the capacity of musicians. When the necessaries are thus collected, the servants all join hands and proceed with their important duties. They first dig a pit, four feet wide, two or three deep, and as long as they require, into which they throw a quantity of wood, for the purpose of obtaining therefrom a bed of burning coals. This done, the more expert kitchen negroes proceed to roast (by laying them upon sticks across the fires) the various animals prepared for the occasion. In the meantime, all the other arrangements are progressing, such as spreading the white cloths upon the temporary board tables, and clearing a place for dancing. The guests begin to assemble about ten o'clock, and by noon there is hardly a tree within hailing distance of the centre of attraction, to which a horse is not fastened. The assembly is quite large; and white dresses and scarlet shawls are as numerous as the summer flowers upon the neighboring hills. Old men are here with their wives and daughters, in whose veins floweth the best of aristocratic blood; young husband with their wives; unmarried gentlemen with a bevy of laughing girls under their charge; and children of every age, from the wild and boisterous boy to little girls just old enough to totter after a butterfly. One, or perhaps two hours, are then spent by the multitude in playing rural games, in social converse, in telling stories, or in discussing the news of the day. Finally, the pigs and lambs have all been roasted, and the feast is ready; whereupon there followeth as busy and satisfactory a scene as can well be imagined. After it is ended, the negroes come into rightful possession of all the tables and the abundance of good things left over; and, having quietly invited a number of their friends, with their families, they proceed to enjoy their portion of the entertainment, which is generally concluded by a regular negro frolic, with banjo and fiddle, in a neighboring grove. In due time, after the more substantial feature of the barbecue has been enjoyed, the musicians are summoned to their allotted places, and the entire party of ladies and gentlemen proceed to trip the light fantastic toe. The exercise continues for hours, and white-haired men and little girls are seen wending their way through the intricate mazes of the country dance and the Virginia reel. As the sun nears the horizon, the more advanced members of the party quietly take their departure, leaving a cloud of dust behind them on the road. By the time the last day-flower has closed its petal, the young men and maidens have entire possession of the barbecue ground; and having wound up the last reel by the light of the newly-risen moon, they dismiss the musicians, gather together their hats and shawls, and with many a song and jest return to their several homes.

With regard to the political barbecue, we have to remark that it differs from the one already described only in the following particulars: It is generally gotten up by the leaders of one of the political parties, and speeches take the place of dancing, although ladies in considerable numbers are in attendance. Previous to the appointed day for the political barbecue, a placard is nailed to all the barn doors and blacksmith shops in the district or county where it occurs, to the effect that "several distinguished speakers will be present on the occasion," and that the people of all parties are invited to be present. If the entertainers on this occasion are of the Whig party, the first speech is delivered by a Whig orator, and it is no uncommon sight to see this gentleman standing literally *on the stump.* After he has taken his seat, he is usually followed by a brother orator of the Democratic party; and so, alternately, are the principles of the prevailing parties fully discussed. Generally, the greatest decorum exists, not only among the speakers but among the listeners; and if severe remarks are dropped in the heat of debate, they are not commonly considered of sufficient consequence to create a breach between personal friends. There are times, however, when even the political barbecue is concluded by a dance; but as the crowd is then particularly miscellaneous, the hilarity which usually prevails is apt to be a little too boisterous. When given in the autumn, new cider usually takes the place of more stimulating drinks (so far as the multitude are concerned, at any rate,) and when this is the case, it is very seldom that any improprieties occur. But a genuine Virginia barbecue, whether of a political or social character, is a rural entertainment which deserves far more praise than censure, and we know of none which affords the stranger a better opportunity of studying the character of the yeomanry of the Southern States.

RATTLESNAKES.

We believe that we have seen a greater number of these reptiles, in our various journeyings, and been more intensely frightened by them, than any other scenery-loving tourist or angler in the country, and hence the idea of our present essay. We shall record our information for the benefit of the general reader, rather than for the learned and scientific; beginning our remarks with what we know of the character of that really beautiful and magnanimous, but most deadly animal, which was adopted as the revolutionary emblem of our country, as the eagle is now the emblem of the Republic.

The rattlesnake derives its name from an instrument attached to its tail, consisting of a series of hollow scaly pieces which, when shaken, make a rattling or rustling noise. The number of these pieces or rattles are said to correspond with the number of years which the animal has attained, and some travellers assert that they have been discovered with thirty rattles, though thirteen is a much more common number. It is one of the most venomous serpents, and yet one that we cannot but respect, since it habitually makes honorable use of the singular appendage with which it is gitted. It never strikes a foe without first warning him of his danger. In form it is somewhat corpulent, has a flat heart-shaped head, and is supplied with fangs, varying from a half-inch to an inch in length, which lie hidden horizontally in the flesh of the upper jaw, and are capable of being thrown out like the blade of a knife. The venom emitted by it is so deadly that it has been known to cause the death of a human being in a very few hours, and to destroy a dog or cat in less than twenty minutes, and yet we have met with some half-dozen individuals in our travels who have been bitten by the rattlesnake without being seriously injured. Horses and cattle are known to become exceedingly terrified at its appearance, and generally speaking, when bitten, die in a short time, and yet we once saw a horse which was only troubled, in consequence of its bite, by a disease resembling the scurvy. The hair dropped off from the skin of the quadruped, and he looked horribly, if he did not feel so. As to the effect of this poison upon hogs, it has frequently been proven to be perfectly harmless, and we know it to be the custom in certain portions of the country, for farmers to employ their swine for the express purpose of destroying the rattlesnakes infesting their land. The effect of the rattlesnake's bite upon itself is said to be generally fatal. In regard to the antidote of this poison, we are acquainted with only one, besides that of stimulants used in some parts of the country, which is the plant commonly called the rattlesnake weed. Both the leaf and the root are employed, and applied internally as well as externally. This plant grows to the height of six or eight inches, has one stock and a leaf resembling in shape the head of the rattlesnake, and is almost invariably found in those sections of the country where the reptile abounds.

The courage of rattlesnakes is by no means remarkable, and it is but seldom that they will dispute the right of way with a man who is not afraid of them. They are sluggish in their movements, and accomplish the most of their travelling during the nocturnal hours. They feed upon almost every variety of living creatures which they can overpower. They are not partial to water, but when compelled to cross a river or lake, they perform the feat in a most beautiful manner, holding their heads about one foot from the surface, and gliding along at a rapid rate. They are affectionate creatures, and it is alleged that when their offspring are very young, and they are disturbed by the presence of man, the mothers swallow their little ones until the danger is past, and then disgorge them alive and writhing.

Another of their peculiarities consist in the fact, that they may be entirely disarmed by brandishing over their heads the leaves of the white ash, which are so obnoxious to their nervous system as to produce the most painful contortions of the body. When traveling at night in search of food, or for purposes of recreation, as it may be, they have a fashion of visiting the encampments of hunters, and it has been ascertained that the only way of keeping them at a respectable distance is to encircle the camp with a rope, over which they are afraid to crawl;—and it has frequently happened to hunters, in a snake country, that on awaking after a night of repose, they have discovered on the outside of their magic circle as many as a dozen of the charming creatures, carefully coiled up and sound asleep. It is also related of this snake, that it has the power of throwing off or suppressing a disagreeable effluvium, which is quite sickening to those who come within its range. If this be true it occurs chiefly in the month of August, when the weather is sultry and the snake is particularly fat. That this snake has the power of *charming*, as some writers maintain, may be true, but we know not of an authenticated instance. That it may have a very quiet way of stealing upon its prey seems to us much more plausible—but upon this fact we are non-committal. As to their power of *hissing*—that also is an undecided question. In regard to their manner of biting we can speak with more confidence. They never attack a man without first coiling themselves in a graceful manner, and instead of jumping they merely extend their bodies, with the quickness of thought, towards their mark, and if they do not reach it, they have to coil themselves again for a second effort, and when they hit a man at all, it is generally on his heel, for the bruising of which they have the authority of the Scriptures. Although they possess the power of inflicting almost instantaneous death, they seldom attack man excepting in self-defence. When about to bite, their eyes sparkle like fire, their bodies become bloated with rage, their heads and necks alternately flatten and distend, and their lips contract and expand, so that their appearance is then most horrible.

But while the rattlesnake is a formidable enemy to man, the

deer and the blacksnake seem to be at enmity with him. Whenever a buck discovers a rattlesnake in a situation which invites an attack, he loses no time in preparing for battle. He approaches to within ten or twelve feet of the snake, then leaps forward and aims to sever the body with his sharp hoofs. The first onset is commonly successful; if otherwise, the buck repeats the trial till he cuts the snake in twain. The rapidity and fatality of his skilful manœuvre leave but a slight chance for his victim either to escape or inject poison into his more alert antagonist.

The rattlesnake also finds a dreaded opponent in the blacksnake. Such is its celerity of motion, not only in cunning, but entwining itself around its victim, that the rattlesnake has no way of escaping from his fatal embrace. When the black and rattlesnakes are about to meet for battle, the former darts forward at the height of his speed, and strikes at the head of the latter with unerring certainty, leaving a foot or two of the upper part of the body at liberty. In an instant he encircles him in five or six folds; he then stops and looks the strangled and gasping foe in the face, to ascertain the effect produced upon his corseted body. If he shows signs of life, the coils are multiplied, the operator all the while narrowly watching the countenance of the helpless victim. Thus the two remain some thirty minutes, when the executioner slackens one coil, noticing at the same time whether any signs of life appear; if so, the coil is resumed and retained, until the incarcerated snake is entirely lifeless.

The rattlesnake is peculiar to the American continent. Four varieties alone are known to naturalists, three of which are found in the United States, and one in South America. In the States bordering on the Gulf of Mexico, they attain the length of seven and eight feet, and a diameter of three or four inches; the males having four fangs, and the females only two. These are characterized by a kind of diamond figure on the skin, and are partial to the low or bottom lands of the country. Those found in the Middle and Northern States are called the common or banded rattlesnakes, and are altogether the most abundant in the Union. They vary in length from two and a half to four feet, and are partial to mountainous and rocky districts. There is also a very small, but most dangerous variety, called the ground rattlesnakes, which are found on the sterile and sandy prairies of the West, and to a limited extent in the barren districts of the South. In Canada they are almost unknown, and even in the more thickly settled States of the Union, they are rapidly becoming extinct. As to their value, it may be stated, that their oil and gall are highly prized in all sections of the Union, for medicinal purposes, and by the Indians and slave population of the South, their flesh is frequently employed as an article of food, and really considered sweet and nourishing.

The attachment of the Aborigines to this famous reptile is proverbial: among nearly all the tribes, even at the present day, it is seldom disturbed, but is designated by the endearing epithet of *grandfather.* It is recorded, however, by the early historians, that when one tribe desired to challenge another to combat, they were in the habit of sending into the midst of their enemy the skin of a rattlesnake, whereby it would appear to have been employed as an emblem of revenge. And as to the origin of the rattlesnake, the old men among the Cherokees relate a legend to the following effect, which, the reader will notice, bears a striking analogy to the history of our Saviour. A very beautiful young man, with a white face, and wrapped in a white robe, once made his appearance in their nation, and commanded them to abandon all their old customs and festivals, and to adopt a new religion. He made use of the softest language, and everything that he did proved him to be a good man. It so happened, however, that he could make no friends among them, and the medicine men of the nation conspired to take away his life. In many ways did they try to do this—by lashing him with serpents and giving him poison, but were always unsuccessful. But in process of time the deed was accomplished, and in the following manner. It was known that the good stranger was in the habit of daily visiting a certain spring, for the purpose of quenching his thirst and bathing his body. In view of this fact, the magicians made a very beautiful war-club, inlaid with bone and shells, and decorated with rattles, and this club they offered to the Great Spirit, with the prayer that he would teach them how to destroy the stranger. In answer to the prayer, a venomous snake was created and carefully hidden under a leaf by the side of the spring. The stranger, as usual, came there to drink, was bitten by the snake, and perished. The Cherokee nation then fell in love with the snake, and having asked the Great Spirit to distinguish it, by some peculiar mark, from all the other snakes in the world, he complied, by transferring to its body the rattles which had made the club of sacrifice so musical to the ear, and so beautiful to the eye. And from that rattlesnake are descended all the poisonous snakes now scattered through the world.

We commenced this article with the determination of not writing a single paragraph (for the above legend, after a fashion, is historical,) which could be classed with the unbelieving things called "Snake Stories," but the following matter-of-fact, though disconnected anecdotes, may not be unacceptable to our readers.

We were once upon a fishing expedition among the mountains of North Carolina, with two other gentlemen, when it so happened that we concluded to spend the night in a deserted log cabin, belonging to one of the party. By the light of a large fire, we partook of a cold but comfortable supper, and after talking ourselves into a drowsy mood, we huddled together on the floor, directly in front of the fire-place, and were soon in a sound sleep. About midnight, when the fire was out, one of the party was awakened by a singular rattling noise, and having roused his companions, it was ascertained beyond a doubt, that there were two rattlesnakes within the room where we were lying. We arose, of course, horrified at the idea, and as we were in total darkness, we were afraid even to move, for fear of being bitten. We soon managed, however, to strike a light, and when we did so, we found one of our visitors on the hearth, and the other in the remotest corner of the room. We killed them, of course, with a most hearty relish, and in the morning another of the same race, just without the threshold of the cabin. The reptiles had probably left the cabin just before our arrival, and on returning at midnight, had expressed their displeasure at our intrusion upon their abode, by sounding their rattles.

On another occasion we were of a party of anglers who killed a rattlesnake on one of the mountains overlooking Lake George, (where this reptile is very abundant,) and after its head had been cut off and buried, one of the party affirmed that there was not a person present who could take the dead snake in his hand, hold it out at arm's length, and give it a sudden squeeze, without dropping it to the ground. A wager was offered, and by the most curious and courageous of the party was accepted. He took the snake in his hand and obeyed the instructions, when the serpentine body suddenly sprang, as if endowed with life, and the headless trunk struck the person holding it, with considerable force upon the arm. To add that the snake fell to the ground most suddenly, is hardly necessary. We enjoyed a laugh at the expense of our ambitious friend, but the phenomenon which he made known, remains to this day unexplained. Since that time we have been led to believe that there is not one man in a thousand who would have the fortitude to succeed in the experiment above mentioned.

A paper recently read before the Boston Society of Natural History, by Dr. W. J. Burnett, on the character and habits of the rattlesnake, contains among others, the following interesting particulars. The Doctor had been experimenting on two or three specimens of this animal, and announces the discovery of numerous embryo poisonous fangs in the jaws of the snake, immediately behind the outward fangs. The use of these hidden weapons of destruction appears to be, to supply the place of the biting fangs of the serpent, when they get broken off or worn out in service. It also appears that the long fangs, (two in number,) which are used in inflicting the deadly bite of the rattlesnake, are naturally shed every few years, when they are not injured by accident or wear, and the reserve fangs are sufficiently numerous to meet the worst emergencies. From minute microscopical examination of the structure of these teeth, Dr. B. concludes that there are two canals in each fang, only one of which conveys the poison to the wound. Respecting the character of the poison itself, the Doctor remarks as follows:

There is good reason to believe that its action is the same upon all living things, vegetables as well as animals. It is even just as fatal to the snake itself as to other animals, for one specimen that we have heard of, after being irritated and annoyed in its cage, in moving suddenly, accidentally struck one of its fangs into its own body, when it soon rolled over and died, as any other animal would have done. Here, then, we have the remarkable, and perhaps unique physiological fact, of a liquid secreted directly from the blood, which proves deadly when introduced into the very source (the blood) from which it was derived.

In order to scrutinize, by the aid of a microscope, the operation of this deadly agent on the blood, Dr. Burnett stupified one of the fiercest of his snakes, by dropping chloroform upon his head.

Twenty-five or thirty drops being allowed to fall on his head, one slowly after the other, the sound of his rattle gradually died away, and in a few minutes he was wholly under the agent. He was then adroitly seized behind the jaws, with the thumb and finger, and dragged from the cage, and allowed to partially resuscitate; in this state a second person held his tail, to prevent his coiling around the arm of the first, while a third opened his mouth, and with a pair of forceps pressed the fang upwards, causing a flow of poison, which was received on the end of the scalpel. The snake was then returned into the cage.

Blood was next extracted from the finger, for close microscopical examination. The smallest quantity of the poison being presented to the blood between the glasses, a change was immediately perceived; the corpuscles ceased to run together, and remained stagnant, without any special alteration of structure. The whole appearance was as though the vitality of the blood had been suddenly destroyed, exactly as in death from lightning. This agrees also with another experiment performed on a fowl, where the whole mass of the blood appeared quite liquid, and having little coagulable power.

Dr. Burnett is of opinion, that the physiological action of the poison of a rattlesnake in animals is that of a most powerful sedative, acting through the blood on the nervous centres. He supports this position by the remarkable fact, that its full and complete antidotes are the most active stimulants, and alcohol, in the form of rum or whiskey, is the first. This remedy is well known at the South, and there are some twenty-five authentic cases on record, proving that a person suffering from the bite of a rattlesnake, may drink from one to two quarts of clear brandy, and eventually recover.

A WESTERN PIONEER.

It was about twenty years ago, on a bright November morning, that a large covered wagon, drawn by four horses, came to a halt in front of the office of the Receiver of Money for the Public Lands in the village of Monroe, territory of Michigan. The wagon in question contained implements of husbandry, a plentiful stock of provisions, and all the household furniture of a family consisting of an old man and his wife, three sons, and two daughters; and their outside possessions were comprised in a small but miscellaneous herd of cows, oxen, sheep, and hogs. The head of this family was a New York farmer in indigent circumstances, who had conceived the idea of making himself a home in what was then the wilderness of Michigan. All the money he had in the world was one hundred dollars, and with this he purchased at the land-office a tract of eighty acres of uncultivated land, which he had never seen, but upon which he was about to locate with his family. The honest and independent deportment of this emigrant enlisted the feelings of the Receiver, and he accordingly extended an invitation to him and his party to spend the night under his roof. The invitation was accepted, and after a "lucid interval" of comfortable repose, and cheered by a warm breakfast, the emigrating party respectfully took leave of their entertainer, and started upon their dreary pilgrimage.

The distance they had to travel was one hundred and eighty miles. As the roads were new and rough, they plodded along, day after day, at a slow rate, and with much difficulty; took their meals in the open air, and spent their nights under a tent, with only a few heavy quilts to protect them from the dampness of the ground. While upon this journey they were overtaken by cold weather, and, in fording one of the many streams which crossed their route, the venerable emigrant had one of his legs frost-bitten, which resulted, after much delay and trouble in sending for a physician, in its amputation. His life was spared, however, and in due time, in spite of the calamity which had befallen them, the emigrants were encamped upon their "land of promise."

Having thus reached the end of their journey, the first thing to be done was to erect a suitable dwelling wherein to spend the winter; and, the father of the family having been rendered almost helplesss by his misfortune, the labor of building it devolved exclusively upon his sons, the youngest of whom was a mere boy. Animated by a most noble spirit, they fell to work without any delay, and in the course of ten days had accomplished their first task, and were the masters of a comfortable log-cabin. It stood on the sandy knoll of an "oak opening," and in the immediate vicinity of a sparkling rivulet. The only evidences of civilization which surrounded them were the stumps, and chips, and decaying branches which covered the site of their labors; but the emigrants had a home, and though a rude and apparently comfortless one, they were satisfied, if not happy.

The winter days passed rapidly away; and, while the disabled emigrant did little more than keep himself warm by his huge wood-fire, his sons were felling the trees on every side, and doing their utmost to enclose their domain. And at night, when gathered at the evening meal, or in a circle around their hearth, and the newly-cut wood was hissing under the influence of the bright flame, they would talk over the pleasures of other days, experienced in a distant portion of the land, and cherish the hope that the future had even more happiness in store. Within their cabin was to be found the spirit of genuine religion, and as the hopeful music of woman's voice was there, and their hearts were bound together by the cords of a holy family love, they were indeed happy.

It was now the spring-time of the year, a warmer tint was in the sky, and the wilderness was beginning to blossom like the rose. The birds were building their nests, and their sweet minstrelsy was heard throughout the air; and there, too, was the tinkling of bells, for the cattle sought their food in the remote dells, and returned at the sunset hour, with their udders teeming full. The brush and waste wood of the "girdled clearings" were gathered into heaps and burnt—in the daytime forming fantastic columns of smoke, and at night making the midnight darkness, save where the flame was particularly brilliant, more profound. And then the plough was brought forth, and made to try its strength in turning up the virgin soil. Our emigrant friend has now entirely recovered from his late disaster, and, having manufactured for himself an artificial leg, he begins to think it time for him to lend a helping hand towards accelerating the improvements of his "farm." The smell of the ploughed field has given him a thrill of pleasure, and he determines to try what he can accomplish in the way of planting corn. This effort proves successful, and, as he becomes accustomed to the use of his new member, he takes the lead in most of the farming operations, and thinks no more of his past sufferings than of the fact that he is what many people are pleased to term a poor man.

As industry and virtue are almost invariably followed by prosperity, we must not wonder at the future career of our Western pioneer. Five years have passed away, and, as his crops have been abundant, we find him the possessor of half a thousand acres of valuable land instead of one hundred. He has also gathered the means to build himself a new frame house; and, as the "harvest is past and the summer ended," his barns are filled to overflowing. On every side are spread out extensive fields, and his hired men may be counted by the dozen. They have gathered in the crops, and, after a brief furlough, a portion of them will take possession of the barns, and devote themselves to the flail, while the remainder will enter some neighboring woodland with their axes, and proceed in their laborious work of destruction. Winter comes, and still the sounds of the flail and the axe are heard in the barn and in the forest. The coldest of winds may blow, and the snow may fall so as to bury the fences, but what matter? The genius of health reigns supreme. All the day long, and at night, huge fires are blazing in the dwelling of the pioneer; his larder is filled with an abundance of the good things of life, and his numerous cattle are more comfortably housed than himself when he first came into the wilderness. Spring has returned once more, and a new life has not only been instilled into the earth, but also into the blood of man.

It is now the delightful season of midsummer, and we see before us, basking in the sunshine, a domain of two thousand acres of land, in the highest state of cultivation. Capping the summit of a hill stands a spacious and elegant mansion, surrounded with outhouses, and bespeaking the possessor to be a man of opulence and taste. In one direction, fading away to a great distance, lie a succession of fields waving with golden grain; in another, hill beyond hill of the deep green and graceful corn; in another we see a magnificent meadow, with hundreds of cattle and horses and sheep quietly grazing or sporting in their glee; and in another direction an almost impenetrable forest, where the black-walnut, the white-wood, the oak, and the hickory strive to excel each other in the respective attributes of beauty and might. And this is the home and the domain of the Western pioneer. Less than a mile distant from his mansion stands a charming village, from which arises a single spire, pointing to the Christian's home. The pastor of that church is the youngest son of our friend the pioneer. Within said village, too, may be seen an "Eagle Hotel," and a "New York Store," which are both the property of his two elder sons. At their expense, a public school has also been established within the village. The country around is intersected with good roads, along which the heavily-laden wain pursues its snail-like course, and the mail coach rattles along with its panting horses, nine passengers on the inside, and a deep coating of dust on the boot and everything outside. Plenty and peace have taken possession of the land, and the pioneer of other days has become the nabob of the present time.

PLANTATION CUSTOMS.

We profess to be neither a defender nor an advocate of slavery, but circumstances having brought us into frequent communication with the colored population of the Southern States, we have the satisfaction of knowing that our opinions, concerning their condition, whether correct or not, are the result of personal observation. We do indeed consider the institution an evil, but we consider the fanaticism of the North a much greater evil. By birth and education a Northern man, we willingly acknowledge that we started upon our first journey through the Southern States, harboring in our breast an unreasonable number of prejudices against the institution already mentioned. The tables, however, are now completely turned. Aside from the abstract idea which has ever and will ever trouble us, we have seen but little to mourn over and regret, but rather observed much, touching the happiness of the negro and especially his customs, which we cannot but commend and admire. Instead of commenting upon these customs in a general manner, we propose to give an idea of them by describing two specimens—the negro manner of spending the Christmas Holidays, and the prominent features of one of their Corn Huskings.

The scene of our first description is a plantation in the interior of South Carolina. Within hailing distance of the planter's mansion is a collection of picturesque cabins, where are domiciled his negroes, numbering in all about one hundred souls. It is early morning and the day before Christmas. The slaves have obtained their accustomed holiday, which is to last until the close of the year, and they are now on the point of carrying to the market of some neighboring town the products they may have obtained from their allotted plots of ground during the bygone season. All the means of conveyance belonging to the plantation have been placed at their disposal, and the day has arrived when they are to receive in hard money, or merchandise, the fruit of their own industry, irrespective of their obligations to their masters. The excitement among them is unusual, and is participated in by all—men, women, and children. All things being ready, the sable fraternity are upon the move, and as they enter upon a road winding through a succession of picturesque woods, we will glance at some of the characters belonging to the cavalcade. The leader thereof is probably the most industrious and frugal of the whole brotherhood, and he is taking to market, in a double wagon drawn by two horses, some two or three bales of cotton, which he will dispose of for one hundred and fifty dollars. The next vehicle is also a wagon, and in it are two or three old women, who have under their especial protection an assortment of poultry which it is their intention to exchange with the village merchant for any little conveniences that they may need, or any fancy articles that they may desire. Directly behind these we have a noisy party of girls and boys, who are footing their way to market more for the frolic or freedom of the thing than any desire to obtain money, albeit we doubt not that some of the boys may have stowed away in one of the wagons an occasional fox or coon skin which have accidentally come into their possession by means of their cunningly-devised traps. In another wagon, drawn by a pair of mules, we notice a load of articles, including a supply of rudely-wrought agricultural implements, a few bags of corn and other grain, and a neatly-dressed hog, with his hoofs pointing to the sky. We now have a venerable negro, mounted upon an equally venerable horse, his only saddle consisting of a large bag of choice seeds, which he has been permitted to glean from his master's fields at the end of the harvest. And coming in the rear, is the miscellaneous portion of the procession, who ramble along, so far as their appearance is concerned, somewhat after the manner of a party of bedlamites, but as joyous and light-hearted as if they were the lords instead of the serfs of creation. And so much for the appearance of our friends on their way to market.

The thousand and one incidents which occur at the town, interesting and unique as they are, we will leave to the imagination of our readers. Towards the close of the day the party return to their cabins upon the plantation, and although some of the more indiscreet may have imbibed an undue quantity of the intoxicating beverage, the majority of them are as circumspect in their deportment as could be expected. And then, on their arrival home, commences the long-anticipated frolic of Christmas Eve. The banjoes and fiddles are brought forth, and devoting themselves most heartily to the pleasures of dancing, singing, and discussing the acquisitions made during the day, the hours of night are soon numbered, and the revelry is only concluded by the approach of day.

Two hours after sunrise on Christmas morning they are all out of their beds and moving about with considerable activity, considering their loss of sleep, and a new order of things is about to occur. The house servants, and such of the field hands as think their services may be needed, place themselves in the way of the master and mistress of the plantation, and cheerfully perform any necessary work which may be allotted to them. This done, they return to their cabins, and plan the various means of enjoying themselves. Those old women, and others who are religiously disposed, jump into a wagon and drive to some neighboring church to hear the story of the Saviour. Others, who have relatives belonging to another plantation, start off upon a friendly visitation. Some, who have a passion for shooting, and have either borrowed or purchased the necessary fusees, depart upon an excursion into the woods; while others, who are particularly covetous, and have already experienced the satisfaction of owning a little property, remain about the premises for the purpose of accomplishing some newly-conceived scheme, which will most likely result at no distant day in their purchasing their freedom. As Christmas is passed, so are the remaining days of the week, an arrangement having been made among the negroes, that a portion of them should take turns with another portion, so that the necessary labor of the plantation might not be neglected. At the commencement of the year, the regular order of business is resumed upon the plantation, and so continues with occasional interruption until another Christmas arrives, to the entire satisfaction, both of master and slave.

The rural custom denominated *corn husking* or *corn shucking*, is peculiar to the Southern States. It occurs at night, in the autumn of the year, is participated in by negroes alone, and has for its main object the husking and the gathering into barns of the yellow maize or corn. And the locality of our present description is a plantation in the State of Georgia.

Intelligence having previously been circulated throughout the district, that a husking is to occur on a certain night, at a certain plantation, the first step is to prepare for the contemplated meeting. The corn yielded by the present harvest is hauled in from the surrounding fields, and deposited in huge heaps, immediately around the crib or barn into which it is eventually to be deposited. The roof of the crib having been built so as to be easily removed, and for the purpose of allowing the corn to be thrown into the building from a considerable distance, it is accordingly transferred to some out-of-the-way place, there to remain until re-appropriated to its legitimate use after the husking is ended. The next step is to bring together at convenient points around the barn and the stacks of corn, huge quantities of light wood, which is to be employed for the several purposes of tempering the night air, affording necessary light, and rendering the approaching scene as cheerful as possible. And while all these preparations are being made by the men, others of quite as much importance are occupying the attention of all the women belonging to the plantation, whose business it is to prepare the feast which necessarily follows the husking; while the children are probably spending their time in clearing away the rubbish from a level spot of ground in the vicinity of the bonfires, where it is more than probable we may yet have the pleasure of witnessing a negro dance.

Night has settled upon the world, and the whole space enclosed by the planter's mansion and his almost innumerable outhouses, is filled with a hum of talking and laughing voices—the loud talking and the hoarse laughing of perhaps two hundred negroes, exclusive of women and children. The torch is now applied to the piles of dry wood, and by the brilliant light of the several fires the *huskers* move to their allotted places around the corn house and seat themselves upon the ground. They are divided into what might be termed four divisions (occupying or flanking the several sides of the house,) each one of which is "*headed*" by one of the smartest men in the company, whose province it is not only to superintend his division, and with the assistance of several boys to throw the corn, as it is husked, into the crib, but to take the lead in the singing which, among the blacks, always accompanies the business of husking corn. A signal is given, and the whole party fall to work as if their very lives depended upon their handling a specified quantity of the white and yellow grain. At the same instant commences a mingled sound of shouting and singing voices, which presently swell into a loud and truly harmonious chorus, and the husking scene is in its prime. The very fires seem elated with the singular but interesting prospect which they illumine, and shoot their broad sheets of flame high into the air. Song follows song, in quick succession, and in every direction piles of beautiful corn seem to spring out of the earth as if by magic, and with the quickness of magic are transferred into the great receptacle, which is itself rapidly becoming filled. Rude indeed are the songs they sing, the words are improvised and the ideas are simple, but there is a pathos and harmony in the chorus which fails not to delight the ear. Amusing stories are occasionally told, and then resoundeth far over the quiet fields sleeping in moonlight, boisterous peals of laughter. One, two, three, and perhaps four hours have elapsed, and it is now midnight, when the announcement is made by some patriarch of the company that the corn is all husked, and the crib is nearly full. One more song is called for, during the singing of which the roof is replaced upon the corn house, and after congregating around the fires, partly with a view of comparing notes as to the amount of labor performed, but more especially for the purpose of drying the sweat from their sable faces, the entire party of huskers move to the spacious kitchen attached to the planter's mansion.

And here an entirely new scene presents itself to our view. Board tables have been spread in every available corner, and even in the more sheltered portions of the adjoining yard, and everywhere is displayed a most sumptuous entertainment, consisting not only of the substantials of life, strangely served up in the form of a thick soup, but abounding even in luxuries. Good whisky and perhaps peach brandy is supplied in reasonable quantities, and the women, having finished their allotted duties, now mingle with the men, and the feasting company presents as merry and happy a picture of rural life as can well be imagined. Each negro devotes himself to his particular mess, and somewhat after the manner of the aborigines. Jokes of questionable elegance and delicacy are uttered to a considerable extent, and many compliments paid to the "*lib'ral and magnan'mous massa ob dis plantation.*" On such occasions, as might not be supposed, acts of decided impropriety seldom occur, and it is not often that a sufficient quantity of spirit is imbibed, either materially to injure the health or produce intoxication. In this particular, even the "*down-trodden*" slaves, as they are called, may often set a worthy example for the imitation of those who occupy a more elevated rank in society.

We now come to describe the concluding scene of the corn-husking entertainment, which consists of a dance upon the spot cleared away by the boys in the vicinity of the late fires, which are replenished for further use. The scraping of fiddles and the thumping of banjos having been heard above the clatter of *spoons, soup-plates*, and *gourds*, at the various supper tables, a new *stampede* takes place, and the musicians are hurried off to the dancing ground, as if this were deemed the climax of earthly happiness. "On with the dance, let joy be unconfined." But there seemeth no need of the poet's advice on the present occasion, for the sable congregation now assembled, seem animated with an almost frantic excitement. The dance is the famous "*Virginia Reel*," and at least a hundred individuals have formed themselves in their proper places. No sooner do the instruments attain the necessary pitch, than the head couples dash into the arena, now slowly and disdainfully, now swiftly and ferociously, and now performing the *double shuffle* or the *pigeon-wing*. Anon they come to a stand, while others follow, and go through the same fantastic performances, with the addition perhaps of an occasional leap or whirl. The excitement is becoming more intense than ever, and it is evident that those whose business it is to stand still, are actually dancing in their shoes. Louder than ever wails the music—order is followed by confusion—and in the madness of the dance there is no method. The brilliant watch-fires cast a ruddy glow upon the faces of the dancers, and when, as it sometimes happens, an individual chances to wander without the circle, his leaping and uncouth figure pictured against the sky, resembles more the form of a lost spirit than a human being. Music, dancing, shouting, leaping, and laughing, with other indescribable antics, are mingled together in a most unique manner, constituting a spectacle only equalled by the midnight dances of painted savages. For hours does this frolic continue, and perhaps is only brought to an end by the crowing of a cock, or the first glimpse over the eastern hills, of coming day. And then comes the breaking up of the assembly, so that by the usual breakfast hour, the negroes have reached the several plantations to which they belong, and after spending rather an idle day, are ready for any other *husking* to which they may be invited, and which their masters will permit them to attend.

DEATH IN THE WILDERNESS.

MIDWAY between the St. Louis River and Sandy Lake, in the territory of Minnesota, is to be found one of the largest and most forbidding of tamarack swamps. It has always been a thing of dread, not only to the Indians, but also to the traders and voyageurs, for directly across its centre runs the portage trail leading from the waters of Lake Superior to those of the Upper Mississippi. For a goodly portion of the year it is blocked up with snow, and during the summer is usually so far covered with water as only occasionally to afford a little island of coarse vegetation. It is so desolate a place as to be uninhabited even by wild animals, and hence the pleasures of travelling over it are far from being manifold. In fact, the only way in which it can be overcome during the vernal months is by employing a rude causeway of logs for the more dangerous places; and as it happens to be directly on the route of a portage over which canoes and packs of furs are annually transported to a considerable extent, we cannot wonder that it should frequently be the scene of mishaps and accidents. We distinctly remember to have seen evidences to prove this, when once crossing the swamp, for all along the trail were the skeletons of canoes, which had been abandoned by their owners, together with broken paddles and remnants of camp furniture. But the most interesting object that we witnessed in this remote corner of the wilderness was a rude wooden cross, surmounting a solitary grave. And connected with this grave is the following story, obtained from one who assisted at the burial.

It was a summer day, and many years ago, when a stranger made his appearance at the Sault St. Marie. He reported himself as coming from Montreal, and anxious to obtain a canoe passage to the head waters of the Mississippi. He was a Frenchman, of elegant address, and in easy circumstances, so far as one could judge from his stock of travelling comforts. His name and business, however, were alike unknown, and hence a mystery attended him. Having purchased a new canoe and a comfortable tent, he secured the services of four stalwart Chippeways, and started upon his western pilgrimage. He sailed along the southern shore of Lake Superior, and as its unique features developed themselves to his view one after another, he frequently manifested the gratification he experienced in the most enthusiastic manner, thereby increasing the mystery which surrounded him. Wholly unacquainted with the language spoken by his companions, he could only converse with them by signs; and though they could not relate to him the traditions associated with the sandstone cliffs, mountains, and beautiful islands which they witnessed, they did everything in their power to make him comfortable. They entered his tent and built his watch-fire at night, supplied him with game and fish, and, during the long pleasant days, when skimming over the blue waters, entertained him with their romantic but uncouth songs. In due time, they reached the superb and most picturesque St. Louis River, surmounted its waterfalls by means of many portages, entered and ascended one of its tributaries, and finally drew up their canoe at the eastern extremity of the portage leading over the tamarack swamp.

The spot where the voyageurs landed was distinguished for its beauty, and as they arrived there in the afternoon, they concluded that a better place could not be found to spend the night. The tent of the stranger was therefore erected, and while the Indians busied themselves in preparing the evening meal, the former amused himself by exploring the immediate vicinity of the encampment. He wandered into a neighboring swamp, for the purpose of obtaining a few roots of the *sweet flag*, of which he was particularly fond, and on his return to the tent, ate an unreasonable quantity of what he had collected. On that night he was taken sick, and while endeavoring to account for heart-burning and severe pains that he experienced, he pulled out of his pocket a specimen of the root he had eaten, and handed it to the Indians. They were surprised at this movement, but on examining the root they found it to be a deadly poison, whereupon they managed to inform the stranger that he had made a great mistake, and would probably loose his life. This intelligence was of course received with amazement and horror, and the unhappy man spent a most agonizing night. At daybreak he was a little better, and insisted upon immediately continuing his journey. The voyageurs obeyed, and packing up their plunder, started across the portage in single file. The excitement which filled the mind of the stranger seemed to give new energy to his sinews, and he travelled for about an hour with great rapidity; but by the time he reached the centre of the tamarack swamp his strength failed him, and he was compelled to call a halt. Upon one of the green islands, already mentioned, the Indians erected his tent, and, with all the blankets and robes belonging to the company, made him as comfortable as possible. The hours of the day were nearly numbered; the stranger had endured the severest agony, and he knew that he was about to die! He divested himself of his clothes, and, with all his papers and other personal property, motioned that they should be placed in a heap a few paces from the door of his tent. His request was obeyed. He then handed them all the money he had, and despatched all his attendants upon imaginary errands into the neighboring woods, and when they returned they found the heap of clothes and other property changed into heaps of ashes. They supposed the sick man had lost his reason, and therefore did not deem his conduct inexplicable. They only increased their kind attentions, for they felt that the stream of life was almost dry. Again did the stranger summon the Indians to his side, and pulling from his breast a small silver crucifix, motioned to them that they should plant upon his grave a similar memento; and hiding it again in the folds of his shirt, cast a lingering and agonizing look upon the setting sun, and in this manner breathed his last.

By the light of the moon the Indians dug a grave on the spot where the stranger died, into which they deposited his remains, with the crucifix upon his breast. At the head of the grave, they planted a rude cross made of the knotty tamarack wood, and after a night of troubled repose, started upon their return to the Sault St. Marie, where they finally recounted the catastrophe of their pilgrimage. And such is the story that we heard of the lonely cross in the northern wilderness surmounting the remains of the nameless exile.

THE CANADIAN RECLUSE.

Of the many singular characters which we have met with in our various travels, we remember none with more pleasure, and even wonder, than the hero of this chapter. In company with three friends, we were upon a fishing cruise along the northern shore of the river St. Lawrence, above the Saguenay, and having on a certain afternoon steered our little craft into a cove at the mouth of a brook, for the purpose of obtaining fresh water, we were surprised to find ourselves in the immediate neighborhood of a rude but comfortable log cabin. Curiosity led us to visit the cabin, and introduce ourselves to the proprietor. We did so, and were not only warmly welcomed, but were invited to tarry with our new acquaintance until the next day, and, had we not accepted the invitation, the following particulars would not now be made public.

The individual under consideration was a Frenchman, and a native of Quebec. He was above the medium height, about forty years of age, graceful in his manners, active in mind and body, and altogether just the character to rivet the attention of the most casual observer. He was wholly ignorant of the world, having never been out of his native city, excepting when he took up his abode in this out-of-the-way corner of the country, where, at the time we met with him, he had been secluded for nearly twenty years. He had a wife (but no children,) who was as much like himself in appearance and character as nature could well allow her to be. He was illiterate, but possessed an attachment to botany which was truly remarkable. His cabin had only two lower rooms and one garret, and yet the best of the three was exclusively appropriated to a collection of plants, gathered from the neighboring hills and mountains, and numbering several hundred varieties, together with large moose horns, furs, and other forest curiosities. He knew not the generic name of a single specimen, and yet he could expatiate upon their beauty in the most interesting manner, showing that he loved them with intense affection. To the discovery and cultivation of plants he told us he was in the habit of devoting more than half of his time, whereupon we asked him from what source he obtained his living. He informed us that, having inherited the large tract of land upon which he resided, he had come here for the purpose of getting a living out of *that*. On casting our eyes about, and finding nothing for them to rest upon but mountains of solid rock, where even pine trees hardly had the courage to grow, we thought his reply somewhat mysterious. He smiled at our perplexity, and then told us that he had two or three profitable salmon fishing-grounds within a mile of his house, which were rented to Quebec fishermen, and yielded him all the necessaries of life, and that he obtained his fresh meats with his own hands from the forest.

Had we been inclined to doubt any of the assertions of our friend in regard to his good living, all such doubts would have been most assuredly dispelled by what we witnessed and enjoyed before closing our eyes on the night in question. Having taken us to the fishing-ground lying nearest to his cabin, for the purpose of letting us see how the salmon were taken in the circular set nets (into which they swam on their way up stream when the tide was high, and from which they were taken by hundreds when the tide was low,) he picked out a splendid twenty pound fish, and piloted us back again to his dwelling. He then excused himself from further waiting upon us, and begging us to amuse ourselves by *examining his plants*, or doing anything else we pleased, he informed us that he must assist his wife in preparing our supper. We bowed our most willing assent, and as the sun was near setting, we ascended a neighboring knoll for the purpose of enjoying the extensive prospect which presented itself to view.

We were looking towards the south, and across that portion of the noble St. Lawrence where it is without an island, and its shores are twenty-five miles apart. The retinue of clouds around the setting sun were remarkably brilliant, and were distinctly mirrored on the tranquil bosom of the river. In the distance we could barely discover the southern shore, forming a long narrow line of purple; about a dozen miles to the eastward one solitary ship lay floating, at the mercy of the tide, and in the foreground was the cabin of our entertainer, partly hidden from our view by a few stunted trees, and apparently hemmed in by inaccessible mountains, while before the cabin lay extended some half-dozen immense mongrel dogs, which were the only living creatures, besides ourselves, tending to animate the lonely scene. Silently communing with our own hearts, we watched with peculiar interest the coming forth, one after another, of the beautiful stars, and we could not but think of our distant homes, and of the ties which bound us to the absent and loved. One moment more, and we heard a loud halloo, which came from the lungs of our Canadian friend, who informed us that supper was ready, whereupon we descended to the cabin at a pace bordering upon a run.

And such a supper! Our host presided; and while two of his guests were seated on either side, the hostess occupied the opposite end of the table from her husband. She could not speak a word of English, and of course uttered all her apologies in French; and though the husband pretended to talk English, we begged him to remember that his guests all understood French, and that he had better converse as nature dictated. No objections were made, and we proceeded to business. The table was literally loaded; and, whilst the matron poured out a capital cup of coffee, the host overwhelmed the plates of his guests with various kinds of meat, most of which were fried or broiled almost to a crisp. We gave vent to our curiosity by inquiring the names of the dishes we were eating. From this moment, until the truly delicious feast was ended, the talking was all performed by the Canadian botanist, and the substance of his remarks may be stated as follows:—

"That meat, in the blue platter, gentlemen, was cut from the hind-quarters of the biggest *black bear* ever seen among the mountains. He weighed over four hundred pounds, and was as savage as he was fat and big. I was climbing along the edge of a hill, about a week ago, for the purpose of securing a small yellow flower that I had discovered hanging from a rock, when the bear in question came running out of the mouth of his den, and saluting me with a long scratch on the back, I gave him a stab in the belly, and tumbled myself down the offset in the most hasty manner imaginable. I always take my gun with me when I go into the woods, and when I reached the bottom of the hill I looked out for the bear, and, discovering him on a stump some twenty yards off, I gave him a shot, and he made at me with the fires of revenge and rage in his eye. I climbed up a small tree, and while the rascal made an unsuccessful attempt to follow me, I reloaded my gun, and sent another charge directly into his mouth, which gave him a bad cough, and in a short time he staggered a few paces from the tree, and fell to the ground quite dead. *I then went back to the cliff to secure my yellow flower*, and during that afternoon, by the aid of my pony, dragged the bear to my cabin.

"In that dish, with a piece broken from the edge, gentlemen, you have a mixture of *moose tongue*, *moose lip*, and *moose brains*. I spent nearly a month moose-hunting last winter, in company with a couple of Indians, and though the snow was deep, the crust hard, our snow-shoes in good order, our dogs brave and strong, and moose were numerous, we only killed about sixteen. I only brought home the heads (while the Indians were satisfied with the skins and haunches;) but I was more than paid for all my trouble, in the way of hard travelling and cold sleeping, for, in one of the moose-yards that we visited, *I found a specimen of pine which I had never seen before.* It was very soft and beautiful, and I think the book men of England would give a good deal of money if they could have it in their great gardens.

"As to that meat in the white dish, which you all seem to eat with such a relish, I think you will be surprised to learn that it is nothing but *beaver's tail.* To my taste it is the sweetest meat in the world, and I am only sorry that this valuable animal is becoming so very scarce in this section of country. My present stock of beaver's tail came from the shore of Hudson's Bay, and, though I bought it of an Indian, I had to pay him as much for the tails as the fur company paid him for the skins of his animals. I never trapped for beaver myself, but I have for otter, and often have great sport in killing seals, which are very abundant in the St. Lawrence, and afford to the Indians pretty good food during the hard winters. The only thing that I have against the beaver is, that he has a fashion, I am told, *of cutting down for his house such beautiful trees as the birch, mulberry, willow, and poplar, before they are half grown.*

"As to the salmon upon which you have been feasting, gentlemen, you know as much about that particular individual as I do, since you saw him while in his native element. The men who hire my fishing grounds pay me so much for every fish they take, and sell them at a great profit in Quebec, and even in Montreal. From the fisheries on this shore the people of Canada are exclusively supplied with salmon, and when we have had a good season our merchants manage to send over to the United States, in a smoked condition, a good many thousand. As to taking them with those pretty little flies, which you gentlemen always carry in your pocket-books, I never could understand how you manage to deceive so sensible a fish as the salmon. Of one thing I am certain; if you expect to take any of the salmon in this region with those little lines and hooks, you will be much mistaken. You will have to go down to the Saguenay, where I am told the fish do not know any better than to be deceived by your cunning arts. But if I were ever to follow fishing as you do, it seems to me that instead of red, yellow, and blue feathers, I should cover my hooks *with the bright berries and buds which you may find upon some trees even during the fishing season.*"

This last remark of our host convinced us that he was indeed possessed with a ruling passion, and we of course gratified ourselves by humoring him to the length of our patience. He not only monopolized the conversation during supper, but he did most of the talking until bed-time. We spent the night under his roof, sleeping upon bear-skins, spread on the floor; and after an early breakfast, we bade him adieu, and pursued our course down the St. Lawrence.

TRIP TO WATCH HILL.

Once on a time just as the sun had risen above the eastern hills, which look down upon the Thames, at Norwich, Connecticut, the prettiest sail-boat of the place left her moorings, and with a pleasant northerly breeze started for the Sound. Her passengers consisted of six gentlemen, all equipped in their sporting jackets, and furnished with fishing tackle, and their place of destination was Watch Hill, which is a point of land in Rhode Island, extending into the Atlantic, a few miles from Stonington. We were on a fishing frolic, as a matter of course; and a happier company, I ween, were never yet afloat, for the sport of a morning breeze. What with the story, the jest, the iced lemonade and exquisite cigar, the minutes glided by as swiftly and unobserved as the tiny waves around us. Now we met a solitary fisherman, towing for bass, and as we hailed him with a friendly shout, and passed by, he began to talk in an under tone, and his voice did not die away until we had turned a point. What would I not give for an accurate record of that old man's life! Anon, we witnessed the soothing picture of a well-conducted farm, with its green-girt cottage, spacious barns, neat and flowing fields, and its horses and oxen, cows, sheep, hogs, and poultry. Now we saw some noble men, such as Vernet delighted to paint, hauling the seine, and, as the "fruit of all their toil" were thrown upon the sand, their flipping forms reflected back the sunlight, reminding us of—anything the reader may be pleased to imagine. Now, we were overtaken and tossed about by a steamer bound to New Haven; and then we sailed in company with a boat, a sloop, and schooner; meeting others beating up, from Boston, New York, and Philadelphia. And the termination of this pleasing panorama was composed of Gale's Ferry, the commanding town, fort, and momument of Groton, together with the city of New London, among whose anchored shipping floated the saucy Revenue Cutter, and at whose docks were chained a goodly number of storm beaten whalers.

Having taken in "our stores," and obtained from the fish-market a basket of bait, we again hoisted sail, "bound first to Commit Rock," and "binding" ourselves to capture all of the watery enemy which might tempt the power or dexterity of our arms.

When about three miles from New London, all eyes were attracted by a beautiful craft on our lee, laden with a party of ladies and gentlemen. "They're going towards a reef!" exclaimed our captain; and no sooner had the words escaped his lips, than the stranger struck, and stove a hole through her bottom. We were just in time to save the party from a watery grave; and when we had landed them in safety on the beach, we were well repaid for our trouble by the consciousness of having done a good act, and by the thankful words and benignant smiles of the ladies fair. A dozen minutes more and we were within oar's length of the fishing rock. "All ashore, that's coming!" shouted our mate as he stood on the rock, when we all leaped out, and plenty of line being given her, the boat swung to, and "like a cradled thing at rest," floated upon the waves. Then commenced the sport. The breeze was refreshing, and the breath of the salt sea-foam buoyed up our spirits to a higher pitch, and gave new vigor to our sinews. The youngest of the party was the first who threw his hook, which was snapped in the twinkling of an eye. Another trial, and a four-pound blackfish lay extended upon the rock. Another and another, until four-score, even-numbered, came following after. Tired of the sport, two of the party entered the boat, and hoisted sail for a little cruize. Half an hour had elapsed, when the steady breeze changed into a gale, capsizing within hailing distance a fishing boat with two old men in it. Hanging on, as they were, to the keel of the boat, (which having no ballast, could not sink,) their situation was extremely dangerous, as there was not a vessel within two miles. The poor men beckoned to us to help them; but as our boat was gone, we could not do so. For one long hour did they thus hang "midway betwixt life and death," exposed to the danger of being washed away by the remorseless surge, or swallowed up, as we were afterwards told, by a couple of sharks, which were kept away only by the hand of Providence. This incident tended to cool our ardor for fishing, and as we were satisfied with that day's luck, we put up our gear, during which time the boat arrived, and we embarked for the Hill. We made one short turn however, towards the boat which had picked up the fishermen, as we were anxious to tell them why we did not come to their relief. We then tacked about, and the last words we heard from our companions were: "Thank you—thank you—God bless you all," and until we had passed a league beyond Fisher's Island, our little vessel "carried a most beautiful bone between her teeth."

At sunset we moored our little boat on the eastern shore of Paucatuck Bay. On ascending to the Watch Hill hotel, we found it to be a large, well-furnished house, and our host to be a fat and jolly Falstaff-ish sort of man, just suited to his station. At seven o'clock we sat down to a first rate blackfish supper, then smoked a cigar, and while my companions resorted to the bowling alley, I buttoned up my pea-jacket, and sallied forth on an "exploring expedition." As I stood on the highest point of the peninsula, facing the south, I found that the light-house stood directly before me, on the extreme point, that a smooth beach faded away on either side, the left hand one being washed by the Atlantic, and that on the right by the waters of Fisher Island Bay, and that the dreary hills in my rear were dotted by an occasional dwelling. The breeze had died away, and the bright, full moon was in the cloudless sky. Many sails were in the offing, and also the Providence and Stonington steamboats bound to New York. The scenery around me, and the loveliness of the sky, with its galaxy of stars, caused me to forget myself, and I wandered far away upon the shore now gazing with wonder and admiration into the cerulean vault of Heaven, or into the still deeper blue of the mighty sea, and now repeating one of the sacred songs of the sweet singer of Israel. Now, a thousand images of surpassing loveliness darted across my vision, as I thought of God—of an eternal life in heaven—of love, divine and human; and then there came a weight upon my spirit, as I remembered the powers of darkness, and the miseries engendered by our evil passions. In that communion with the mysteries of the universe, strongly blended as they were, I felt that I could wander on without fatigue, until the whole earth should be trodden by my pilgrim feet. But the chilly air and the fading night warned me to retrace my steps, and in an hour I had reached my home.

When the sun arose from his ocean-bed on the following morning, surrounded by a magnificent array of clouds, I was up, and busily engaged preparing for a day's fishing,—first, and before breakfast, for bluefish, then for blackfish, and lastly for bass. While my companions were asleep, I went out with an old fisherman, and by breakfast time had captured thirty bluefish, weighing about two pounds a piece. The manner of catching these is to tow for them with a long line, the bait being a piece of ivory attached to a strong hook. They are a very active and powerful fish, and when hooked, make a great fuss, skipping and leaping out of the water.

At nine o'clock our party were at anchor on a reef about one mile off, and for the space of about two hours we hauled in the blackfish as fast as possible, many of them weighing eight to ten pounds a piece. For them you must have a small straight hook, and for bait, lobsters or crabs. A broiled blackfish, when rightly cooked, is considered one of the best of salt water delicacies.

But the rarest of all fishing is that of catching bass, and a first-rate specimen I was permitted to enjoy. About eleven o'clock, I jumped into the surf-boat of an old fisherman, requesting him to pull for the best bass ground with which he was acquainted. In the mean time my friends had obtained a large boat, and were going to follow us. The spot having been reached, we let our boat float, wherever the tide and wind impelled it, and began to throw over our lines, using for bait the skin of an eel six inches long. Those in the neighboring boat had fine luck, as they thought, having caught some dozen five-pounders, and they seemed to be perfectly transported because nearly an hour had passed and I had caught nothing. In their glee they raised a tremendous shout, but before it had fairly died away, my line was suddenly straightened, and I knew that I had a prize. Now it cut the water like a streak of lightning, although there were two hundred feet out, and as the fish returned I still kept it taut; and after playing with him for about forty minutes, I succeeded in drowning him, then hauled up gradually, and with my boat hook landed him in the boat safe and sound. The length of that striped bass was four feet two inches, and his weight, before cleaned, fifty-eight pounds. You can easily imagine the chop-fallen appearance of my brother fishermen, when they found out that "the race is not always to the swift, nor the battle to the strong." At three o'clock in the afternoon, a piece of that fish tended to gratify the appetite which had been excited by his capture.

Satisfied with our piscatorial sports, we concluded to spend the rest of the day quietly gathering shells upon the beach; but causes of excitement was still around us. No sooner had we reached the water's edge, than we discovered a group of hardy men standing on a little knoll, in earnest conversation, while some of them were pointing towards the sea. "To the boat! to the boat!" suddenly shouted their leader, when they all descended with the speed of Swiss mountaineers, and on reaching a boat which had been made ready, they pushed her into the surf, and three of them jumped in, and thus commenced the interesting scene of hauling the seine. There was something new and romantic to us in the thought, that the keen and intelligent eye of man could even penetrate into the deep, so far as to designate the course of travel of the tribes of the sea. And when the seine was drawn, it was a glorious and thrilling sight to see those fishermen tugging at the lines, or leap into the surf, which sometimes completely covered them, to secure the tens of thousands of fish which they had caught. There was a grace and beauty about the whole scene, which made me long for the genius of a Mount or Edmonds.

A little before sunset, I was again strolling along the shore, when the following incident occurred. You will please return with me to the spot. Yonder, on that fisherman's stake, a little sparrow has just alighted, facing the main. It has been lured away from the green bowers of home by the music of the sea, and is now gazing, perhaps with feelings kindred to my own, upon this most magnificent structure of the Almighty hand. See! it spreads its wing, and is now darting towards the water —fearless and free. Ah! it has gone too near! for the spray moistens its plumes! There—there it goes, frightened back to its native woodland. That little bird, so far as its power and importance are concerned, seems to me a fit emblem of the mind of man, and this great ocean an appropriate symbol of the mind of God.

The achievements of the human mind "have their passing paragraphs of praise, and are forgotten." Man may point to the Pyramids of Egypt, which are the admiration of the world, and exclaim, "Behold the symbol of my power and importance!" But most impotent is the boast. Those mighty mysteries stand in the solitude of the desert, and the glory of their destiny is fulfilled in casting a temporary shadow over the tent of the wandering Arab.

The achievements of the Almighty mind are beyond the comprehensions of man, and lasting as his own eternity. The spacious firmament, with its suns, and moons, and stars; our globe, with its oceans, and mountains, and rivers; the regularly revolving seasons; and the still, small voice continually ascending from universal nature, all proclaim the power and goodness of their great original. And everything which God has created, from the nameless insect to the world of waters,—the highway of nations,—was created for good,—to accomplish some omnipotent end. As this ocean is measureless and fathomless, so is it an emblem, beautiful but faint, of that wonderful Being, whose throne is above the milky-way, and who is himself from everlasting to everlasting. But see, there is a heavy cloud rising in the west, the breeze is freshening, flocks of wild ducks are flying inland, and the upper air is ringing with the shrill whistle of the bold and wild sea-gull, whose home is the boundless sea; therefore, as my friend Noble has somewhere written, "the shortest homeward track's the best."

Still in the present tense would I continue. The witching hour of midnight has again returned. A cold rain-storm has just passed over, the moon is again the mistress of a cloudless sky, but the wind is still raging in all its fury.

"I view the ships that come and go,
Looking so like to living things.
O! 'tis a proud and gallant show
Of bright and broad-spread wings,
Making it light around them, as they keep
Their course right onward through the unsounded deep."
Dana.

God be with them and their brave and gallant crews. But, again:

"Where the far-off sand-bars lift
Their backs in long and narrow line,
The breakers shout, and leap, and shift,
And send the sparkling brine
Into the air; then rush to mimic strife;
Glad creatures of the sea, and full of life."—*Ibid.*

But I must stop quoting poetry, for as "a thing of beauty is a joy forever," I should be forever writing about the sea. Heavens! what a terrible song is the ocean singing, with his long white hair streaming in the wind! The waving, splashing, wailing, dashing, howling, rushing, and moaning of the waves is a glorious lullaby, and a fit prelude to dream of the sea.

At an early hour on the following day, we embarked for home, but a sorry time we did have of it, for the winds were very lazy. We were ten hours going the distance of twenty-two miles. It was now sunset, and we were becalmed off Gale's

Ferry. Ashore we went, resolved to await the coming of the Sag Harbor steamboat, which usually arrived about nine o'clock, and by which we were, finally, taken in tow. Snugly seated in our boat, and going at the rate of eighteen miles an hour, we were congratulating ourselves upon an early arrival home, and had already begun to divide our fish. But, alas! at this moment the painter broke; the steamer, unconscious of our fate, still sped onward, while we sheered off towards the shore, *almost disgusted* with human life in general—for our boat was large, and we had but one oar. But what matter? We were a jolly set, and the way we gave three cheers, as a prelude to the song of "Begone Dull Care," must have been startling to the thousand sleeping echoes of hill, forest, river, and glen.

Having crept along at snails' pace about one mile, we concluded to land, and, if possible, obtain a place to sleep, and something to eat; for not having had a regular dinner, and not a mouthful of supper, we were half starved. With clubs in our hands, to keep off hobgoblins and bull-dogs, we wended our way towards a neighboring farm-house, where we knocked for admittance. Pretty soon, a great gawky-looking head stuck itself out of an upper window, to which we made known our heartfelt desires, receiving, in return, the following answer:—"My wife is sick—hain't got any bread—you can go in the barn to sleep if you want to;" and we turned reluctantly away, troubled with a feeling very nearly allied to anger. "Come, let's off in this direction," exclaimed one of the party, "and I'll introduce you to my old friend, Captain Somebody;"—and away we posted, two by two, across a new-mown field. Presently, our two leaders were awe-stricken by the sudden appearance of something white, which seemed to be rising out of the earth, beside a cluster of bushes, and the way they wheeled about, and ran for the river, (accompanied by their fellows, whose fright was merely sympathetic,) was "a caution" to all unbelievers in ghosts and other midnight spectres.

At last we halted to gain a little breath; an explanation was made; and our captain forthwith resolved to *investigate* the matter. He now took the lead, and on coming to the mysterious spot, discovered *an old blind white horse*, who had been awakened by the noise, and, following the instinct of his nature, had risen from his lair, to be better prepared for danger. I doubt whether the echoes are yet silent, which were caused by the loud and long peals of laughter which resounded to the sky. Being in a strange land, without chart or compass, we could not find the mortal dwelling-place of Captain Somebody, and so we changed our course of travel.

We stopped at another house, farther on, but to save our lives we could not obtain an interview, although we entered the hen-coop, and set the hens and roosters a cackling and crowing—the pig-pen, and set the hogs a squealing—while a large dog and two puppies did their best to increase and prolong the mighty chorus. If our farmer friend did not deem himself transported to Bedlam, about that time, we imagine that nothing on earth would have the power to give him such a dream. Our ill-luck made us almost desperate, and so we returned to the boat, resolved to row the whole distance home, could we but find an extra oar.

It was now eleven o'clock, and the only things that seemed to smile upon us were the ten thousand stars, studding the clear, blue firmament. Anon, a twinkling light beamed upon our vision; and, as we approached, we found it to proceed from a little hut on an island, where the Thames lamp-lighter and his boy were accustomed to pass the night, after their work was done. Having again concluded to land, we received a hearty welcome, as the host proved to be an old acquaintance of our captain and mate. "Have you anything to eat?" was almost the first question of every tongue. "No, nothing but this barrel of crackers, and some cheese," exclaimed the man of light. "And we," shouted one of our crew, "have plenty of fish,—can't we have a chowder?" "Ay, ay; a chowder, a chowder it shall be!" were the words which rang aloud to the very heavens. A wherry was dispatched to the main-land, to the well-known habitation of the old fisherman, for the necessary iron pot and bowls, and for the potatoes and onions, which were dug for the occasion; also for the pork, the pepper, and salt; all which, added to our biscuit and black-fish, nicely cleaned and prepared, constituted a chowder of the very first water. There was one addition to our company, in the person of the old fisherman; and our appearance, as we were seated in a circle on the floor, each with a bowl of thick hot soup in his hands, constituted a picture rich and rare. After we were done, it was acknowledged by all, that a better meal had never been enjoyed by mortal man. In about thirty minutes from this time, the odd one of the company bade us "good night," and the midnight brotherhood resigned themselves to sleep. The last sounds I heard, before closing my eyes, were caused by the regular opposition steamboats from New York, as they shot ahead almost as "swift as an arrow from a quivering bow."

The first faint streak of daylight found us on board our boat, homeward bound, wafted on by a pleasant southerly breeze. At the usual hour, we were all seated at our respective breakfast tables, relating our adventures of the excursion just ended.

A WEEK IN A FISHING SMACK.

ON a pleasant Monday morning, in other days, I started from Norwich, Connecticut, bound to New London, and from thence to any other portion of the world where I might have some sport in the way of salt-water fishing. In less than an hour after landing from the steamboat, I had boarded the handsome smack Orleans, Captain Keeney, and by dint of much persuasion, secured a berth on board to accompany him on a fishing voyage. In addition to my previous preparation, I had only to purchase a Guernsey shirt and tarpaulin; and by the time I was regularly equipped, the sails were hoisted, and we were on our course for Nantucket. An intimate acquaintance was soon formed between myself and crew, which consisted of the master, two sailors, and the cook. The whole time that I spent in their company was six days, as I reached home on the following Saturday evening. The incidents that I met with were somewhat new, as a matter of course, and I employed a few moments of every evening, during my absence, in briefly recording the events of the past day; and that medley I now put together as a literary chowder.

Monday Evening. My observations to-day have been limited to our little vessel, in consequence of a dense fog, which drenched us to the skin, and seems likely to continue us in this state of preservation. I have obtained some information, however, concerning the character of an interesting class of men, which may be new to you. Smack-fishermen are a brave, hardy, honest, and simple-hearted race, and, as my captain tells me, spend nine-tenths of their time "rocked in the cradle of the deep." Their vessels, or smacks, are generally of about forty tons burden; the number of those which supply New York and Boston with fish is said to be near a thousand, and they are all at home anywhere on the coast between the Kennebeck and the Delaware. Of the perils which these fishermen endure, and the privations they suffer, how little is known or thought by the great world at large! Yet I believe there is as much genuine happiness in their lives, as in those of any other class. Their fathers were fishermen before them, and as they themselves have mostly been born within hearing of the surf, they look upon the unsounded deep as their fitting home, their only home, and would not part with it for a palace or a crown. Four is the usual number of a smack's crew, and the master is invariably called a skipper. Most of them are worthy husbands and fathers, whose families are snugly harbored in some convenient seaport, with enough and to spare of the good things of life. They are a jovial set of men, hailing each other upon the ocean as friends, and meeting upon land as brothers. Each skipper thinks his craft the handsomest and swiftest that floats, and very exciting are the races they sometimes run. Their affection for their own vessel is like that of the Arab for his steed, and like the Arab, too, they have been known even to weep over the grave of a favorite craft.

The kinds of fish which they mostly bring to market are shad, salmon, lobsters, mackerel, cod, bluefish, haddock, blackfish, porgees, bass, and halibut. The first three are generally purchased of local fishermen, but all the rest are caught by themselves. The haunts of the blackfish are rocky reefs, those of the bass and bluefish in the vicinity of sandy shoals or tide rips, and those of the remainder in about fifteen fathom water. These are the varieties they capture by way of business, but when in a frolicksome mood, they frequently attack a swordfish, a shark, or black whale; and thrilling, indeed, and laughable withal, are the yarns they spin concerning these exploits.

As to their mode of living, while at sea, it is just what it should be, and what they would have it, although it would be "positively shocking" to a Bond Street gentleman of leisure.

But they always possess a good appetite, which is what money cannot purchase, and without which the greatest delicacy in the world would be insipid or loathsome. Fish, sea-biscuit, corned beef and pork, potatoes, onions, and pancakes, constitute their provisions, and what besides these would a reasonable man desire ? It is with a mixture of some of these, that a *chowder* is concocted, and where can anything more delicious be found, even at the tables of the Astor and Tremont ? And with these ingredients, moreover, they manage very well to keep body and soul together, unless a storm on a rock-bound coast happens to make a sudden separation.

I have just been on deck, and must say that I resume my pen with a heavier heart. The fog has not dispersed in the least, a regular gale of wind is blowing from the north, and the waves, seemingly in a revengeful mood, are tossing our bark about, as if the skipper, like the Ancient Mariner, had shot another albatros. But like a fearless man, as he is, he stands at the helm, watching the sails with a steady eye, and the men with their storm-jackets on are standing by, muttering something about the coming darkness, and a reef somewhere on our lee. Never before have I so distinctly understood the force of the Psalmist's simile, when he compares a wave to a drunken man reeling to and fro. Both have it in their power to cause a mighty mischief, and both become exhausted and perish,—one upon a sandy beach, and the other, sweeping over the peninsula of time, finds a grave on the shore of eternity. Heavens! how the wind whistles, and the waters roar! Ay, but a still small voice do I hear, and I lay me down to sleep, with a prayer upon my lips, and a feeling of security at my heart, as I place implicit confidence in Him who holdeth the ocean in the hollow of his hand.

Tuesday Evening. I was awakened out of a deep sleep this morning by the following salutation from the skipper, as he patted me on the shoulder. "It's a beautiful morning, and you ought to be up;—the fog is gone, and the wind is down; won't you come up and take the helm awhile, so that the boys and I may obtain a little sleep before reaching the fishing-ground, which will be about ten o'clock?" I was delighted to accept the invitation, and in a very short time the sailors were asleep, and I in my new station, proud as a king, and happy as a boy. Would that I could describe the scene that fascinated my eyes as I lay there upon the deck, with one hand resting on the rudder, and my other hand grasping a Claude glass! I felt as I once felt before, when standing on the famous precipice of Niagara, that then, more than ever, I desired God to be my friend. I also felt, that I could remain upon the ocean forever. More earnestly than ever did I long for a complete mastery of the pictorial art. The fact of being out sight of land, where the blue element announced that the ocean was soundless, filled my soul with that "lone, lost feeling," which is supposed to be the eagle's, when journeying to the zenith of the sky. The sun had just risen above the waves, and the whole eastern portion of the heavens was flooded with exquisite coloring from the deepest crimson to the faintest and most delicate purple, from the darkest yellow to an almost invisible green; and all blended in forms of marvellous loveliness. A reflection of this scene was also visible in the remaining quarters of the horizon, and it is before me now. Around me the illimitable deep, whose bosom is studded with many a gallant and glittering ship,

——— that have the plain
Of ocean for their own domain.

The waves are lulling themselves to rest, and a balmy breeze is wandering by, as if seeking its old grandfather, who kicked up the grand rumpus last night; whereby I learn, that the offspring of a "rough and stormy sire," are sometimes very beautiful and affectionate to the children of men. But look! even the dwellers in the sea and of the sea are participating in the hilarity of this bright summer morning! Here, a school of herring are skipping along like a frolicsome party of vagabonds as they are,—and yonder a shark has leaped out of the water, to display the symmetry of his form and the largeness of his jaw, and looking as if he thought, "that land-lubber would make me a first rate breakfast;" there, a lot of porpoises are playing "leap-frog," or some other *outlandish* game; and, a little beyond them, a gentleman sword-fish is swaggering along to parts unknown, to fight a duel in cold blood with some equally cold-blooded native of the Atlantic; and now, a flock of gulls are cleaving their course high overhead, bound to the floating body perhaps of a drowned mariner, which their sagacity has discovered a league or two away:—and now, again, I notice a flock of petrels, hastening onward to where the winds blow and the waves are white. Such are the pictures I beheld in my brief period of command. It may have been but fancy, but I thought my little vessel was trying to eclipse her former beauty and her former speed. One thing I know, that she "walked the water like a thing of life." I fancied, too, that I was the identical last man whom Campbell saw in his vision, and that I was then bound to the haven of eternal rest. But my shipmates returning from the land of Nod, and a certain clamor within my own body having caught my ear, I became convinced that to break my fast would make me happier than anything else just at that time, and I was soon as contented as an alderman at five P. M. About two hours after this, we reached our fishing-place, which was twenty miles east of Nantucket. We then lowered the jib and topsail, and having luffed and fastened the mainsheet, so that the smack could easily float, we hauled out our lines and commenced fishing, baiting our hooks with clams, of which we had some ten bushels on board. Cod fishing (for we were on a codding cruize,) is rather dull sport; it is, in fact, what I would call hard labor. In six hours we had caught all the skipper wanted, or that the well would hold, so we made sail again, bound to New York; and at supper-time the deck of our smack was as clean and dry as if it had never been pressed save by the feet of ladies. At sunset, however, a fierce southerly wind sprang up, so that we were compelled to make a harbor; and just as I am closing this record, we are anchoring off Nantucket, with a score of storm-beaten whalers on our starboard bow.

Wednesday Evening. The weather to-day has been quite threatening, and the skipper thought it best to remain at our moorings; but with me the day has not been devoid of interest; for, in my sailor garb, I have been strolling about the town, studying the great and solemn drama of life, while playfully acting a subordinate part myself. This morning, as it happened, I went into the public graveyard, and spent an hour conning over the rude inscriptions to the memory of the departed. In that city of the dead I saw a number of the living walking to and fro, but there was one who attracted my particular attention. He was a sailor, and was seated upon an unmarked mound, with his feet resting upon a smaller one beside it, his head reclined upon one hand, while the other was occasionally passed across his face, as if wiping away a tear. I hailed him with a few kind questions, and my answer was the following brief tale:—

"Four years ago I shipped aboard that whaler, yonder, leaving behind me, in a little cottage of my own, a mother, a wife, and an only boy. They were all in good health, and happy; and, when we were under sail, and I saw from the mast-head how kindly they waved their handkerchiefs beside my door, I, too, was happy, even in my grief. Since that time I have circumnavigated the globe, and every rare curiosity I could obtain, was intended for my dear ones at home. Last Saturday our ship returned, when I landed, hastened to my dwelling, and found it locked. The flagging in my yard attracted my notice, and I thought it strange that the rank grass had been suffered to grow over it so thickly. The old minister passed by my gate, and running to him, I inquired for my family. 'Oh, Mr. B.,' said he, 'you must bless the Lord;—he gave them to you, and he hath taken them away.' And as the thought struck me, my suffering, sir, was intense. And there they are, my wife and child, and, a step or two beyond, my poor old mother. Peace to their memories!"

Such is the substance of the simple story I heard in the Nantucket graveyard, and I have pondered much upon the world of woe which must have been hidden in the breast of that old mariner.

This island of Nantucket is in many particulars, an interesting place. It is said to derive its name from the *Nauticon* Indians, its original proprietors. It was discovered by Bartholomew Gosnold, in 1602, but not settled until fifty years after. It is fourteen miles long, and contains about thirty thousand acres of level and poor land, which every year is washing away. Like its sister island, Martha's Vineyard, it produces grapes in abundance; but as everybody knows, it is supported by the whale fishery. The first whale ever killed by its inhabitants, was killed in 1672, within the limits of the present harbor, but the regular business which has made the island wealthy and celebrated, did not commence until 1690.

After dinner to-day, I strolled into the company of some fishermen who were going after bass and bluefish, and in a short time I had captured, with my own hands, two big bass and some dozen bluefish—which I packed in ice as a present for New York friends.

At my present time of writing, which is near ten o'clock at night, we are weighing anchor, and the skipper tells me we shall be in New York by to-morrow's sunset. An hour before coming on board this evening, I lounged into a sailor boarding-house, and mingled as freely with a company of whalemen there, as if I had ever been a member of the craft. I heard a great deal that interested me, and was sorry that I could not remain longer. There were some in that company lately arrived from every portion of the world, and yet they were engaged in the same business, and had journeyed on the same mighty highway of nations. One was descanting upon the coral islands of the torrid zone; another upon the ice-mountains of the Arctic Sea; a third was describing the coast of California; and another the waters that lave the eastern shore of Asia. The more I listened to these men, the more did the immensity of ocean expand before my mind, and in the same proportion was I led to wonder at the wisdom of the Almighty.

I have just been on deck, and find that we are on the way to our desired haven, wafted by a steady and pleasant breeze. Our course is between Martha's Vineyard and Rhode Island, which is a route studded with islands and seaports, that now appear in the cool starlight like enchantment.

Thursday Evening. Instead of coming through the Sound last night, we headed our vessel outside of Long Island, and after a delightful sail, have realized our skipper's promise, for we are now floating beside the market in New York. The reason assigned for taking the outside course was, that the fish would keep better, on account of the greater coldness of the water. Nothing of peculiar interest has happened to us to-day, except the meeting with a wreck off Sandy Hook. It was the hull of a large ship, whose name we could not discern. It had a very old appearance, and from the moss and sea-weed that covered it, we supposed it must have been afloat for many months, the plaything of the waves. "Man marks the earth with ruin," but who is it that scatters such splendid ruins upon the ocean? And a thousand remorseless surges echo back the answer: "To us belong the glory of those deeds." If that wreck had language, what a strange, eventful history would it reveal! Its themes would be,—home and all its treasures lost; the sea, and all its dangers; the soul, and all its agonies; the heart, and all its sufferings. But when we multiply all this as fast as time is multiplying it, we cannot but realize the idea, that human life is but a probationary state, and that sorrow and sighing are our earthly inheritance.

Friday Evening. After portioning out my fish this morning, and sending them to my friends, I put on my usual dress, and having obtained a six hours' furlough, set off towards Broadway, where, between the reading rooms and the studios of a few artists, I managed to spend my time quite pleasantly. At noon, we embarked for home, and had a delightful time, passing through the East River, and that pleasing panorama from the city to the Sound never appeared more beautiful.

It is now quite late, and I have been on deck all the evening alone. In a thoughtful mood I fixed my eyes upon the stars, and my spirits were saddened by the continual murmur of the sea. Of what avail, thought I, is all this excitement? Is it to be my destiny to sail for a few brief years longer upon the ocean of life, and, when the death-tempest overtakes me, to pass away unloved and unremembered? If not an honored name, can I not leave behind me one—that will be cherished by a few, to whom I have laid bare my heart, when I was younger and happier than I am now?

Saturday Evening. We anchored off New London to-day, in time for me to take the evening steamer for Norwich. When I parted with my "shipmates," I shook each one affectionately by the hand, and thought that I might travel many years without finding a brotherhood of nobler men. I reached home as the eight o'clock bells were ringing, and was reminded that another week of precious time was forever gone. That it must be remembered as an unprofitable one, I cannot believe, for I feel that my soul has been enlarged and my heart humbled, by listening to the teachings of the mighty deep.

A CHIP FROM BLOCK ISLAND.

Of all the islands that lie off the coast of the United States, the most interesting, to my mind, is Block Island. Nantucket, in a commercial point of view, is of more importance, and Martha's Vineyard, I remember perhaps with more pleasure, because I first visited it by the advice of Daniel Webster; Long Island may well be proud of Montauk Point, but its proportions are too vast; the sandy islands off the Southern States abound in a greater variety of game, but in many particulars none of them can compare with Block Island. It lies at the junction of Long Island Sound and Narragansett Bay, and is washed by those waters of the Atlantic which are perpetually blue. It is twenty-one miles from Montauk Point, twenty-five from Watch Hill, thirty from Newport, and about fifty from Martha's Vineyard. Its dimensions are eight miles by three, and every year is diminishing its size. At its northern extremity, where stands a double light-house, a sandy bar shoots out for a mile and a half, under water, upon the end of which, the oldest inhabitants of the island allege that they have gathered berries. Clay bluffs, rising to the height of one and two hundred feet, alternate with broad stretches of white beach in forming its shores; its surface is undulating to an uncommon degree, and almost entirely destitute of trees, the highest hill lying south of the centre, rising more than four hundred feet; and by way of atoning for its want of running streams, it has two handsome lakes, one of which is of fresh water and the other of salt water; the former shallow and abounding in yellow perch, and the latter, which covers some two thousand acres, being sixty-five feet deep and well supplied at all times with white perch and good oysters.

The original name of Block Island was *Monasses*, a word of the Narragansetts—to which tribe of Indians it once belonged. The white man who discovered and first landed upon it was a Dutch navigator, named Adrian Block, whose name it now bears. This event occurred upward of two hundred years ago, and soon thereafter the Puritans took a fancy to it, and having sent over from Plymouth a delegation of leading men, negotiated a purchase from the Narragansetts chiefs. From this good stock do the present inhabitants of Block Island claim to have descended. In 1658, the General Court of Massachusetts granted all their right and title to the island to John Endicott and three others. In 1672, it was made a township by the name of New Shoreham; and in 1690, the French made a descent upon it and carried off some of its people. The present inhabitants purport to number in all about fifteen hundred souls, and with very few exceptions are a race of hardy fishermen and sea-faring men. In what is called worldly wisdom they are perhaps fifty years behind the present progressive age. From their isolated position they are peculiar in their habits, and, caring nothing for the world at large, and possessing an abundance of the necessaries of life, they are clannish and independent to a degree quite remarkable. Among their eccentricities may be mentioned that of dining at *eleven* o'clock. Their whole domain is cut up into small farms, upon all which are planted comfortable dwellings, and hardly any of the able-bodied men are without a small landed estate. The houses are usually surrounded with stone walls, and instead of gates or bars, the stile is in common use; and in the vicinity of nearly every dwelling is a slight frame-work upon which their fish are dried in the sun. In religion they are Baptists, associated and free-will, having a unique old church; and if the majority are not devout men, they respect all sacred things. They are temperate in their habits, and not addicted to the vanity of dancing and other nightly fandango doings which are so common among the poorer classes of all countries.

In their intercourse with each other, they are particularly amiable and obliging, never spending money for labor, but helping each other on all occasions for naught; but they are apt to deport themselves among strangers as if jealous of their time and property. The richest among them are perhaps worth ten thousand dollars, while few are worth less than one thousand dollars; and when their funds are not packed away in old bags, they are found deposited in the banks at Newport. All their provisions, excepting flour, tea, coffee, and sugar, they produce on their own lands, and their own private looms furnish them with clothing. Nearly all the inhabitants are natives of the island,—some of them indeed who are more than fifty years old, boast that they never spent a night upon any other spot of earth,—and the some half dozen individuals who have become naturalized are called "emigrants." The rudiments of a common school education they all possess, and though, like sensible men, they seem to care little for politics and despise politicians; yet they are prompt in performing their election duties, and on more than one occasion have they decided the elections of their State. The present Lieutenant Governor of Rhode Island, was once a fisherman, and is a native and resident of Block Island. The people have no newspaper and are content with a weekly mail.

Though the chief business of this island is fishing, and all the inhabitants are fishermen, yet its agricultural resources are not to be despised. The soil is naturally good, though there is not an acre of *level* land on the whole island,—but by a free use of sea-weed it is made extremely rich and productive. Better potatoes and corn I have never seen in the United States, —the latter article they grind in windmills,—and all garden vegetables are abundant and of superior quality. Various kinds of grass grow luxuriantly. The horses are small but tough, the oxen large and used for every variety of draughting, and the cows and hogs and sheep of good common stocks. The bogs which are scattered over the island, supply the inhabitants with fuel, and the smoke of a peat fire, in spite of its poetical associations, is by no means aromatic. Poultry of all kinds is exceedingly plentiful, and the geese, turkeys, and chickens, which are so highly praised on the tables at Newport, are taken to that place from Block Island by the ton.

With regard to the treasures of the sea, I am informed that they are taken throughout the year. Codfish, both in winter and summer, large bluefish during the summer and autumn, bass in the autumn, tautog in summer, and lobsters in the spring and autumn. When the fishing-smacks are on hand from New York and other cities, the fish are transferred in a fresh state from the Block Island boats to the smacks, which often pay their way with merchandise instead of cash; and when this is not the case, the cod and bluefish are dried and pickled for exportation.

The only sporting fish to be found here, is the bluefish; and when snugly seated in a Block Island boat, with two intelligent Islanders to talk with, and a stiff breeze blowing, the man who cannot be happy, for an afternoon, must be hard to please. During the two last hours that I had the pleasure of spending in this manner, I caught with an ivory squid twenty-five bluefish, the largest weighing fourteen pounds, and the smallest five. I have been surprised to learn, when trolling for these fish, that the fishermen could tell when a school was coming by the sense of *smell* alone. It would appear that when these fish have been feeding, they sink to the bottom and remain quiet; but just before starting after a new supply of food, they disgorge what may be left in their stomachs, and it is this oily substance which forms what is called a *slick*, and emits the smell alluded to. The bluefish is a very voracious creature, feeding upon everything it can master; but then it finds a master in the porpoise, and when these make their appearance, the bluefish vanish to the depths profound. At ordinary times, however, they are to be seen skipping along the surface by millions, and it is a common sight to see a fleet of fifty of the Island boats trolling at one time. On such occasions, they frequently sail five or six miles from shore; and if a returning whale ship happens to come in sight, (and this is a frequent occurrence,) and has a pilot-flag at her mast, the races to board the ship are sometimes exciting. The victorious man—for all Block Islanders are pilots—after boarding his ship, sends his boat home by his partner, and after taking the ship to her desired haven or the main coast, receives a fee of thirty or forty dollars, and trusts to chance for a passage home.

The only craft which the people of Block Island recognize as worth possessing is a smallish affair, deep, sharp at both ends, with two masts and two small sails. Nothing could be more simple, nothing ride the waves more gracefully, and nothing more safe; they are all built on the island, after a model one hundred and fifty years old, and out of lumber imported from the main shore. They sometimes venture one or two hundred miles out to sea, and experience very rough weather, and yet it is stated that not a single one has ever been lost when managed by an experienced man. But while the *shipping* of Block Island is first-rate of its kind, I am compelled to speak of its harbor as most indifferent. It lies on the eastern side of the island, and "faces the *loudest* music" of the Atlantic, and all that Nature has done for it is to pile up a few boulders at the end of a small point of sand. In calm weather a few piles, kept down by stones, answer the partial purpose of a wharf, but when a storm approaches, every boat afloat is hauled up high and dry, and all sea business is suspended. At such times, to arrive or depart from Block Island is equally impossible; and then it is that the stranger there, by lounging around the fish-houses with the fisherman, has a capital chance to hear them spin their uncouth but pleasant yarns.

The majority of people who have hitherto visited Block Island for pleasure have made it a stopping-place when out upon a yachting-cruise; but matters are now so arranged that you may go from Newport in the mail-boat (a Block Islander) during the summer, on every Thursday, wind and weather permitting, and from Stonington on Tuesday and Friday of every week, in a comfortable sloop commanded by Captain Fitch, an experienced and obliging sailor. On arriving at the island, your luggage, if in as many pieces, will be taken up to the hotel by half a dozen fishermen, who, in their kindness, make no demand for their services. When in the mood, and you understand it is not for pay, they will treat you with great respect; but the moment you begin to attempt the patron, they begin to be suspicious and treat you with coldness. The one hotel which receives all strangers, is a much more comfortable affair than you would expect in such a place. The position is commanding, and though the rooms are small, the beds are clean, and the table bountiful, neat, and tasteful. The landlord's name is Card, and all who have ever paid him a visit agree in calling him a *trump*. The view of the ocean from his house is truly magnificent; and while you have on the one hand a superb beach for surf-bathing, and where more than one old whale has been stranded, you have on the other a rocky shore where many hours may be pleasantly spent gathering the delicate plants that are nourished by the sea, or in sending the fancy to revel among the mountains and valleys of the wonderful world of waters. But for the scenes that can only be described by such words as day-break, sunrise, twilight, and moonlight, I know of no place that can surpass the Block Island Hotel.

The climate of Block Island is severe but healthful. Fogs are at times heavy and continuous, and the winter storms have been described to me as terrific. On questioning one of the ancient mariners about the health of the island, he replied as follows:—"We never die, sir; we dry up and are blown away."

And now for a legend appertaining to this curious and interesting island. With all their intelligence the inhabitants are somewhat superstitious, and I can safely assert that I have never conversed with a single native who did not, in some degree at least, believe in the *Fire Ship*, about which there are a thousand and one stories in circulation. The story, in its most common form, seems to be a blending of authentic facts, with atmospheric appearances and a belief in the supernatural. I tell the tale as it was told to me, and I may add, in passing, that I have in my possession some articles of old china-ware, which many people on Block Island believe, without a doubt, to have been brought from the ship in question. But to the legend.

Many, many years ago a ship called the *Palantine* sailed from Holland, with a large number of Dutch passengers, bound to a new home in North America. Soon after leaving port, it became generally known that many of the passengers were wealthy, and had a large amount of gold and silver in their possession. Three weeks elapsed, when the captain and his crew conceived the idea of enriching themselves by plundering and murdering the inoffensive and unsuspicious persons in their power. They first reported their provisions spoilt, but managed to sell hard biscuits for a guinea each. This process was at length suspended, and then disease and famine had full sway. The winds were favorable, all were not yet dead, and lo! the ship was floating off Block Island.

The few passengers who still survived might still live to tell their tale of woe, and so the ship must be destroyed, with all her living freight. The captain and his crew piled their ill-gotten wealth in their two yawls, and having scuttled and set fire to the ship, they embarked for the neighboring island, where they landed, just as the great mass of flame sank hissing into the deep. The pirates told the islanders a plausible story, and for many months they lived in a house which is still pointed out to the curious stranger—but is a mere ruin. The pirates quarreled, separated, and left for parts unknown. For many years thereafter, the house was deserted by all persons of flesh and blood, but thickly peopled with ghosts,—with pale women in white, old men reduced to skeletons, and children with bloody faces, and whenever they made their appearance at the witching time of night, there were heard the most frightful cries of anguish. In process of time, however, the spectres all disappeared; but of late years, whenever a great storm is about to lash the ocean into fury, the *Fire Ship* is distinctly seen in the offing; her hull a mass of cinders, and her sails, sheets of pure flame. Many old men have looked upon this phantom many times, and some of them allege that they have seen the sufferers imploring Heaven for succor, and heard their shrieks of despair.

SALMON FISHING.

I like the society of fish, and as they cannot with any convenience to themselves visit me on dry land, it becomes me in point of courtesy to pay my respects to them in their own element.—William Scrope.

Of the genuine salmon, we believe there is but one distinct species in the world; we are sure there is but one in the United States. From its lithe beauty, its wonderful activity, and its value as an article of food, it unquestionably takes precedence of all the fish which swim in our waters.

The variety of which we speak is a slender fish, particularly solid in texture, and has a small head and delicate fins. The upper jaw is the larger, while the tip of the under jaw in the female has an upward turn. The back is usually of a bluish color, the sides of a silvery hue, and the belly pure white, while along the centre of its body runs a narrow black stripe. The scales are small, and the mouth is covered with small, but stout and pointed teeth. A few dark spots are dispersed over that part of the body above the lateral line, and the females usually exhibit a larger number of these spots than the males. The tail of the young salmon is commonly forked, while in the adult fish it is quite square. To speak of the salmon as a bold biter, and a handsome fish, or of his wonderful leaping powers, would be but to repeat a thrice-told tale.

And now for a few words on some of the habits of the salmon. He is, unquestionably, the most active of all the finny tribes, but the wonderful leaps which he is reported to have made are all moonshine. We have seen them perform some

GROUP OF CAME FISH.

superb somersets, but we never yet saw one which could scale a perpendicular waterfall of ten feet. That they have been taken above waterfalls three or four times as high we do not deny; but the wonder may be dispensed with, when we remember that a waterfall seldom occurs, which does not contain a number of resting-places for the salmon to take advantage of while on his upward journey.

Contrary to the prevailing opinion, we contend that the salmon is possessed of a short memory. While fishing in a small river on a certain occasion, owing to the bad position in which we were placed, we lost a favorite fly, and it so happened that in about one hour afterwards a fish was taken by a brother angler, in whose mouth was found the identical fly that we had lost.*

This fish is a voracious feeder, and an epicure in his tastes, for his food is composed principally of small and delicate fish, and the sea-sand eel; but it is a fact that the *surest* bait to capture him with is the common red worm.

The salmon is a shy fish, and as he invariably inhabits the clearest of water, it is always important that the angler's movements should be particularly cautious; and in throwing the fly, he should throw it clear across the stream, if possible; and after letting it float down for a few yards he should gradually draw it back again, with an upward tendency.

Like all other fish that swim near the surface of the water, the salmon cannot be eaten in too fresh a condition; and, judging from our own experience, they may be eaten three times a-day, for a whole season, and at the end of their running time they will gratify the palate more effectually than when first brought upon the table.

The process of spawning has been described by various writers, and the general conclusion is as follows. On reaching a suitable spot for that purpose, the loving pair manage to dig a furrow some six feet long, in the sand or gravel, into which the male ejects his milt, and the female her spawn; this they cover

* This is by no means an uncommon circumstance.—*Ed.*

with their tails, and leaving this deposit to the tender mercies of the liquid elements, betake themselves to the sea whence they came. This spawning operation usually occupies about ten days, and takes place in the autumn; and when the spring-time comes the salmon are born, and, under "their Creator's protection," are swept into the sea, where they come to their natural estate by the following spring, and ascend their native rivers to revisit the haunts of their minnowhood. And it is a singular fact, that the salmon leaves the sea in an emaciated condition, acquires his fatness while going up a river, and subsequently return to the sea for the purpose of recruiting his wonted health and beauty.*

The salmon is a restless fish, and seldom found a second time in exactly the same spot; but his principal travelling time is in the night, when the stars are shining brightly and all the world is wrapt in silence.

The salmon come up from the sea during a flood or a freshet, and in ascending a river, they invariably tarry for a short time in all the pools of the same. Their object in doing this has not been clearly defined; but is it unreasonable to suppose that they are influenced by the same motives which induce a human traveller to tarry in a pleasant valley? The only difference is, that when the man would resume his journey he waits for a sunny day, while the salmon prefers a rainy day to start upon his pilgrimage. The best places to fish for salmon are the shallows above the deep pools; and it is a settled fact, that after you have killed a fish, you are always sure to find in the course of a few hours another individual in the same place. It would thus seem that they are partial to certain localities. Another thing that should be remembered is, that salmon never take the natural fly while it is in a stationary position, or when floating down stream; hence the great importance of carrying the artificial fly directly across the stream, or in an upward oblique

* The propagation of salmon at Galway and elsewhere by artificial means, which is now carried on most successfully, will throw much light on the habits of this fish.

direction. When you have hooked a salmon, it is a bad plan to strain upon him in any degree, unless he is swimming towards a dangerous ground, and even then this is an unsafe experiment. The better plan is to throw a pebble in front of him, for the purpose of frightening him back, and you should manage to keep as near his royal person as practicable. Another peculiarity of the salmon is the fact that (excepting the shad,) it is the only fish which seems to be perfectly at home in the salt sea, as well as in the fresh springs among the mountains. It is also singular in the color of its flesh, which is a deep pink, and the texture of its flesh is remarkably solid: the latter circumstance is proved by the fact that you cannot carry a salmon by the gills, as you can other fish, without tearing and mutilating him to an uncommon degree.

In olden times there was hardly a river on the eastern coast of the United States, north of Virginia, which was not annually visited by the salmon; but those days are for ever departed, and it is but seldom that we now hear of their being taken in any river south of Boston. They frequented, in considerable numbers, the Susquehanna, the Delaware, and North rivers, but were eminently abundant in the Connecticut and the Thames. On the former stream it used to be stipulated by the day-laborer, that he should have salmon placed upon his table only four times in the week; and we have been told by an old man residing on the latter stream, that the value of three salmon, forty years ago, was equal to one shad—the former were so much more abundant than the latter. But steamboats and the din of cities, have long since frightened the salmon from their ancient haunts, and the beautiful aborigines of our rivers now seek for undisturbed homes in more northern waters. Occasionally even at the present time, the shad fishermen of the Merrimac and Saco succeed in netting a small salmon; but in the Androscoggin, Kennebec, and Penobscot, they are yet somewhat abundant, and these are the rivers which chiefly supply our city markets with the fresh article.

As the ice melts away in the spring, says Dr. J. V. C. Smith, in his interesting little book on the Fishes of Massachusetts, they rush to the rivers from the ocean; and it is an undeniable fact, confirmed by successful experiments, that they visit, as far as possible, the very streams in which they were born. When undisturbed, they swim slowly in large schools near the surface; yet they are so timid, that if suddenly frightened, the whole column will turn directly back towards the sea. It has also been proven that a salmon can scud at the surprising velocity of thirty miles an hour. The young are about a foot long when they visit the rivers for the first time; and at the end of two years, according to Mr. Smith, they weigh five or six pounds, and attain their full growth in about six years. When running up the rivers they are in a fat condition; after that period, having deposited their spawn, they return to the sea, lean and emaciated. In extremely warm weather, and while yet in the salt water, they are often greatly annoyed by a black and flat-looking insect, which is apt to endanger their lives. As soon, however, as they reach the fresh water, this insect drops off, and they rapidly improve.

The streams which these fish ascend are invariably distinguished for their rocky and gravelly bottoms, for the coldness and purity of their water, and for their rapid currents. Those which afford the angler the most sport are rather small and shallow, and empty into tide-water rivers; while in these they are chiefly taken with the net. The tributaries of the Androscoggin, Kennebec, and Penobscot, having all been blocked up with mill-dams, the salmon is only found in the principal estuaries; and as these are large and deep, they are of no value to the angler, and will not be many years longer even to the fishermen who capture them for the purpose of making money. So far as our own experience goes, we only know of one river, within the limits of the Union, which affords the angler good salmon fishing, and that is the Aroostook, in Maine. We have been informed, however, that the regular salmon is taken in many of those rivers, in the northern part of New York, which empty into Lake Ontario, and the upper St. Lawrence, but we are compelled to doubt the truth of the statement. Such may have been the case in former times, but we think it is not so now. Salmon are not taken at Montreal, and it is therefore unreasonable to suppose that they ever reach the fountain-head of the St. Lawrence; this portion of the great river is too far from the ocean, and too extensively navigated, and the water is not sufficiently clear. That they once ascended to the Ottawa river and Lake Ontario we have not a doubt, but those were in the times of the days of old. Another prevailing opinion with regard to salmon we have it in our power decidedly to contradict. Mr. John J. Brown, in his useful little book entitled the "American Angler's Guide," makes the remark, that salmon are found in great abundance in the Mississippi and its magnificent tributaries. Such is not the fact, and we are sure that if "our brother" had ever caught a glimpse of the muddy Mississippi, he would have known by intuition that such *could* not be the case. Nor is the salmon partial to any of the rivers of the far South, as many people suppose, not being known in any river emptying into the Gulf of Mexico; so that the conclusion of the whole matter is just this, that the salmon fisheries of the United States proper are of but little consequence when compared with many other countries on the globe, which fact will be an everlasting disgrace to the generation which has sanctioned the unwise and unchristian doings of the millers and factors of the country. When we come to speak of our territories, however, we have a very different story to relate, for a finer river for salmon does not water any country than the mighty Columbia—that same Columbia where a certain navigator once purchased a ton of salmon for a jack-knife. But that river is somewhat too far off to expect an introduction in our present essay, and we will therefore take our reader, by his permission, into the neighboring provinces of Canada, New Brunswick, and Nova Scotia.

Before proceeding another step, however, we must insert a paragraph about the various methods employed to capture the salmon. The Indians, and many white barbarians, spear them by torchlight; and the thousands sent to market in a smoked condition are taken in nets and seines of various kinds. But the only instruments used by the scientific angler are a rod and reel, three hundred feet of hair or silk line, and an assortment of artificial flies. Our books tell us that a gaudy fly is commonly the best killer, but our own experience inclines us to the belief that a large brown or black hackle, or any neatly made grey fly, is much preferable to the finest fancy specimens. As to bait-fishing for salmon we have never tried it—we care less about it than we know, and we know but very little. Next to a delicately made fly, the most important thing to consider is the leader of the line, which should be made of the best material (a twisted gut,) and at least five feet in length. But if the angler is afraid of wading in a cold or even a deep stream, the very best of tackle will avail him nothing. It is but seldom that a large salmon can be taken, without costing the captor a good deal of hard labor, and a number of duckings. And when the character of the fish is remembered, this assertion will not appear strange. Not only is the salmon a large fish, but he is remarkable for his strength and lightning quickness. Owing to his extreme carefulness in meddling with matters that may injure him, it is necessary to use the most delicate tackle, in the most cautious and expert manner. To pull a salmon in shore, immediately after he has been hooked, will never do; the expert way is to give him all the line he wants, never forgetting in the meantime that it must be kept perfectly taut. And this must be done continually, in spite of every obstacle, not only when the fish performs his splendid leaps out of the water, but also when he is stemming the current of the stream, trying to break the hook against a rock, or when he has made a sudden wheel, and is gliding down the stream with the swiftness of a falling star. The last effort to get away which I have mentioned, is usually the last that the salmon makes, and it is therefore of the highest importance that the angler should manage him correctly when going down. Narrow rifts, and even waterfalls, do not stop the salmon; and bushes, deep holes, slippery bottoms, and rocky shores, must not impede the course of the angler who would secure a prize. And though the salmon is a powerful fish, he is not long-winded, and by his great impatience is apt to drown himself much sooner than one would suppose. The times most favorable for taking this fish are early in the morning and late in the afternoon; and when the angler reaches his fishing ground and discovers the salmon leaping out of the water, as if too happy to remain quiet, he may then calculate upon rare sport. As to the pleasure of capturing a fine salmon, we conceive it to be more exquisite than any other sport in the world. We have killed a buffalo on the head waters of the St. Peter's river, but we had every advantage over the pursued, for we rode a well-trained horse and carried a double-barreled gun. We have seen John Cheney bring to the earth a mighty bull moose, among the Adirondac mountains, but he was assisted by a pair of terrible dogs, and carried a heavy rifle. But neither of these exploits is to be compared with that of capturing a twenty pound salmon, with a line almost as fine as the flowing hair of a beautiful woman. When we offer a fly to a salmon, we take no undue advantage of him, but allow him to follow his own free will; and when he has hooked himself, we give him permission to match his strength against our skill. We have sat in a cariole and driven a Canadian pacer at the rate of a mile in two minutes and a half, on the icy plains of Lake Erie, and, as we held the reins, have thought we could not enjoy a more exquisite pleasure. That experience, however, was ours long before we had ever seen a genuine salmon; we are somewhat wiser now, for we have acquired the art of driving through the pure white foam even a superb salmon, and that, too, with only a silken line some hundred yards in length.

One of the most fruitful salmon regions for the angler to visit, lies on the north shore of the Gulf of St. Lawrence, between the Saguenay and the Godbout river, in Labrador. A few years ago, however, there was good fishing to be had in Mal Bay river, above the Saguenay, and also in the Jacques Cartier, above Quebec, but good sport is seldom found in either of those streams at the present time. But the principal tributaries of the Saguenay itself (particularly the river St. Margaret) afford the rarest of sport, even now. The streams of this coast are rather small, but very numerous, and without a single exception, we believe, are rapid, cold, and clear. They abound in waterfalls, and though exceedingly wild, are usually quite convenient to angle in, for the reason that the spring freshets are apt to leave a gravelly margin on either side. The conveniences for getting to this out-of-the-way region are somewhat rude, but quite comfortable and very romantic. The angler has to go in a Quebec fishing-smack, or if he is in the habit of trusting to fortune when he gets into a scrape, he can always obtain a passage down the St. Lawrence in a brig or ship, which will land him at any stated point. If he goes in a smack, he can always make use of her tiny cabin for his temporary home; but if he takes a ship, after she has spread her sails for Europe, he will have to depend upon the hospitality of the Esquimaux Indians. At the mouths of a few of the streams alluded to, he may chance to find the newly-built cabin of a lumberman, who will treat him with marked politeness; but he must not lay the "flattering unction" to his soul that he will receive any civilities from the agents of the Hudson's Bay Company whom he may happen to meet in that northern wilderness.

A large proportion of these streams runs through an unknown mountain land, and are yet nameless; so that we cannot designate the precise localities where we have been particularly successful; and we might add that the few which have been named by the Jesuit missionaries can never be remembered without a feeling of disgust. Not to attempt a pun, it can safely be remarked that those names are decidedly *beastly;* for they celebrate such creatures as the hog, the sheep, and the cow. The salmon taken on this coast vary from ten to forty pounds, though the average weight is perhaps fifteen pounds. They constitute an important article of commerce, and it is sometimes the case that a single fisherman will secure at least four hundred at one tide, in a single net. The cities of Montreal and Quebec are supplied with fresh salmon from this portion of the St. Lawrence, and the entire valley of that river, as well as portions of the Union, are supplied with smoked salmon from the same region. The rivers on the southern coast of the Gulf of St. Lawrence are generally well supplied with salmon, but those streams are few and far between, and difficult of access. But a visit to any portion of this great northern valley, during the pleasant summer time, is attended with many interesting circumstances. Generally speaking, the scenery is mountainous, and though the people are not very numerous, they are somewhat unique in their manners and customs, and always take pleasure in lavishing their attentions upon the stranger. The weeks that we spent voyaging upon the St. Lawrence we always remember with unalloyed pleasure; and if we thought that fortune would never again permit us to revisit those delightful scenes, we should indeed be quite unhappy.

The most agreeable of our pilgrimages were performed in a small sail-boat, commanded by an experienced and very intelligent pilot of Tadousac, named Oavington, and our companions were Charles Pentland, Esq., of L'anse a-l'eau, on the Saguenay, and David Price, Esq., of Quebec. We had everything we wanted in the way of "creature comfort;" and we went everywhere, saw everybody, caught lots of salmon, killed an occasional seal, and tried to harpoon an occasional white porpoise; now enjoying a glorious sunset, and then watching the stars and the strange auroras, as we lay becalmed at midnight far out upon the deep; at one time gazing with wonder upon a terrible storm, and then again, happy, fearless, and free, dashing over the billows before a stiff gale.

Some of the peculiar charms of fly-fishing in this region are owing to the fact, that you are not always sure of the genus of your fish even after you have hooked him, for it may be a forty or twenty pound salmon, and then again it may be a salmon-trout or a four pound specimen of the common trout. The consequence is, that the expectations of the angler are always particularly excited. Another pleasure which might be mentioned is derived from the queer antics and laughable yells of the Indians, who are always hanging about your skirts for the express purpose of making themselves merry over any mishap which may befall you. The only drawback which we have found in fishing in these waters is caused by the immense number of musquitos and sand-flies. Every new guest is received by them with particular and constant attention: their only desire, by night or day, seems to be to gorge themselves to death with the life-blood of those who "happen among them." It actually makes our blood run cold to think of the misery we have endured from these winged tormentors.

Even with the Gulf of St. Lawrence before our mind, we are disposed to consider the Bay of Chaleur the most interesting salmon region in the British possessions. This estuary divides Lower Canada from New Brunswick, and as the streams emptying into it are numerous and always clear, they are resorted to by the salmon in great numbers. The scenery of the bay is remarkably beautiful, the northern shore being rugged and mountainous, presents an agreeable contrast to the southern shore, which is an extensive lowland, fertile, and somewhat cultivated. The principal inhabitants of this region are Scotch farmers, and the simplicity of their lives is only equalled by their hospitality; and upon this bay, also, reside the few survivors of a once powerful aboriginal nation, the Micmac Indians. But of all the rivers which empty into the Bay of Chaleur, there is not one that can be compared to the Restigouche, which is its principal tributary. It is a winding stream, unequal in width, and after running through a hilly country, it forces its way through a superb mountain gorge, and then begins to expand in width until it falls into its parent bay. The scenery is most beautiful, the eye being occasionally refreshed by the appearance of a neat farm, or a little Indian hamlet. The river is particularly famous for its salmon, which are very abundant and of a good size. But this is a region which the anglers of our country or the Provinces, with few exceptions, have not yet taken the trouble to visit, and many of the resident inhabitants are not even aware of the fact that the salmon may be taken with the fly. The regular fishermen catch them altogether with the net, and the Indians with the spear; and it is a singular fact that the Indians are already complaining of the whites for destroying their fisheries, when it is known that a single individual will frequently capture in a single day a hundred splendid fellows, and that, too, with a spear of only one tine. It is reported of a Scotch clergyman who once angled in "these parts," that he killed three hundred salmon in one season, and with a single rod and reel. A pilgrimage to the Restigouche would afford the salmon fisher sufficient material to keep his memory busy for at least one year. The angler and lover of scenery who could spare a couple of months, would find it a glorious trip to go to the Bay of Chaleur in a vessel around Nova Scotia, returning in a canoe by the Restigouche and the Salmon river, which empties into the St. John. His most tedious portage would be only about three miles long, (a mere nothing to the genuine angler,) and soon after touching the latter river he could ship himself on board of a steamboat, and come home in less than a week, even if that home happened to be west of the Allegheny mountains. The Nipisiguit and the Miramichi, are also glorious streams for the salmon fisher; but like the Restigouche, they have been elsewhere described in these pages more particularly than would be proper in this essay.

Of all the large rivers, indeed, of New Brunswick, we know not any which will not afford the fly fisherman an abundance of sport. Foremost among them, we would mention the St. John, with the numerous beautiful tributaries which come into it below the Great Falls, not forgetting the magnificent pool below those falls, nor Salmon river, the Tobique and the Aroostook. The scenery of this valley is truly charming, but the man who would spend a summer therein must have a remarkably long purse, for the half-civilized white people of the region have, or had a few years ago, a particular passion for imposing upon travellers, and charging them the most exorbitant prices for the simple necessaries they might need. The salmon of the St. John are numerous, but rather small, seldom weighing more than fifteen pounds. The fisheries of the Bay of Fundy, near the mouth of the St. John, constitute an important interest, in a commercial point of view. The fishermen here take the salmon with drag-nets, just before high water:

the nets are about sixty fathoms long, and require three or four boats to manage them. The fish, at one time, were all purchased at this particular point, by one man, at the rate of eighty cents a-piece, large and small, during the entire season.

We now come to say a few words of Nova Scotia, which is not only famous for its salmon, but also for its scientific anglers. In this province the old English feeling for the "gentle art" is kept up, and we know of fly fishermen there, a record of whose piscatorial exploits would have overwhelmed even the renowned Walton and Davy with astonishment. The rivers of Nova Scotia are very numerous, and usually well supplied with salmon. The great favorite among the Halifax anglers is Gold river, a cold and beautiful stream, which is about sixty miles distant from that city, in a westerly direction. The valley of the stream is somewhat settled, and by a frugal and hard-working Swiss and German population, who pitched their tents there in 1760. It is fifteen years since it was discovered by a strolling angler, and at the present time there is hardly a man residing on its banks who does not consider himself a faithful disciple of Walton. Even among the Micmac Indians, who pay the river an annual visit, may be occasionally found an expert fly fisher. But, after all, Nova Scotia is not exactly the province to which a Yankee angler would enjoy a visit, for cockney fishermen are a little too abundant, and the ways of the people, in some particulars, are not over agreeable. The fishing season commences in this province at least a month earlier than in New Brunswick.

Having finished our geographical history of the salmon and his American haunts, we will take our leave of him, by simply remarking (for the benefit of those who like to preserve what they capture) that there are three modes for preserving salmon:—first, by putting them in salt for three days, and then smoking, which takes about twelve days; secondly, by regularly salting them down, as you would mackerel; and, thirdly, by boiling and then pickling them in vinegar. The latter method is unquestionably the most troublesome, but at the same time the most expeditious; and what can tickle the palate more exquisitely than a choice bit of pickled salmon, with a bottle of Burgundy to float it to its legitimate home?

P. S. In the foregoing chapter I have alluded to the Godbout, and Nepisiguit rivers as among the very best known to American anglers for salmon fishing; and though I have elsewhere fully described the latter streams, the following particulars respecting them both, extracted from private letters are worth recording.

In April, 1853, H. Stephens, Esq., wrote to me from Montreal respecting the *Godbout* in Labrador, as follows:—

"My trip last year was one of complete success. I killed, with my own rod, seventy-two salmon, the largest of which weighed twenty-two and a half pounds, with five others over sixteen pounds. I have secured from Sir George Simpson, the Governor of the Hudson's Bay Co., the exclusive right to the best river in the Gulf of St. Lawrence, (the Godbout) and you must be a dull sportsman, if you do not have the satisfaction of killing, at least, fifty salmon, and I have no doubt you have done enough in this way to know the full pleasure of this sport.

"I can take up the same schooner I had last year for four or five dollars per day, including our men, and I think the whole expense will not exceed one hundred and fifty dollars each, and if we take another companion, it will, of course, reduce it to one hundred dollars. You will require to be here on the 4th of June to sail from Quebec on the 5th, and if we avail ourselves of the whole fishing season, should stay until the 20th of July, it can be arranged, however, so that you can leave at an earlier date on your return.

"I have full appointments, such as tents, kettles, &c., in fact, no general officer was ever better provided in this respect, and all you will require to provide will be your bedding and musquito nets for sleeping. I have a complete specific that will keep off all flies during the day.

"At this point last year in one of the best pools, I killed, assisted by a friend, ten salmon in two hours and a half, all upon single gut, of an average weight of at least twelve pounds.

At this point of the game we were 'used up,' and suspended our sport for rest and refreshments, killing in the afternoon five more, making up a glorious day's sport, and I can almost fancy myself now standing upon that beautiful pool, rod in hand, the click of the reel vibrating in my ear as the noble salmon makes his first rocket-like plunge."

In another letter describing his luck during the season of 1853, Mr. Stephens writes as follows:—

"My last trip proved the most successful sporting expedition in salmon fishing that I have made, I went, as usual, the three preceding years to the Godbout River, was absent from home only thirty-one days, fished the river eighteen days, and killed fifty-three salmon, the largest weighing nineteen and a half pounds. This, taking into account the time employed, I think you will acknowledge, to be very fine sport, particularly when I tell you, that thirty of those salmon were killed with a fourteen foot trout-rod and single gut casting line, and, hereafter, I am prepared to recommend to all true sportsmen the propriety of adopting a light elastic rod, certainly not over fifteen feet in length, and the use of the single gut only, and you will find, that this mode of fly-fishing for salmon, brings into play such a complete and delicate exercise of art, that your sport becomes doubly interesting. The Godbout River, I think, is one of the best rivers for salmon fishing with fly, in the Gulf of St. Lawrence, nevertheless it is attended with some little inconvenience and trouble to reach it, when once accomplished, you meet with ample return in the fine sport it affords. Your outfit must be complete in leaving Quebec, with a good safe schooner of some fifty or one hundred tons, on board of which you must be supplied with two skiffs, tents, with full camp equipage, in short, everything that your own convenience may seem to require for a life in the woods, totally excluded, for the time being, from the rest of the world; thus appointed with acceptable companions, and a voyage of three or four days from Quebec, you will be safely landed at the Godbout, when your sport will only be limited by the proper exercise of the art of fly-fishing. My experience of past years would fix the 10th of June as the most desirable period for sailing from Quebec."

In February, 1853, Moses H. Perley, Esq., of St. John, New Brunswick, gave me the following particulars respecting the *Nipisiguit.*

"This is the best river we have. The salmon can only go twenty-five miles up the river from the sea, being there stopped by very high falls. There is good fishing at several points on the river, but the best place, to my fancy, is at the Papineau Falls, seven miles from Bathurst, with a fair road for a wagon. The fishing begins in June. At that time the white sea trout of the Gulf are found abundantly in the river, of large size. But the best salmon fishing is in July, the height of the season is understood to be from the 20th of July to the 10th of August, after which the grilse, (small salmon under 5 lbs.) come in plentifully, until the close of the season. Among the exploits that have been performed by personal friends I may mention fifty-eight salmon by one in ten days; by another, in six weeks, one hundred and seventy, and by another in the whole season, three hundred and twenty. There are seldom more than ten or a dozen fishers on the Nipisiguit each season, and there is fishing enough for all. To be sure of sport, you should give yourself ample time, as the river may not be in condition when you arrive. The best fishing is of course immediately after a rain-storm, as each freshet in the river brings up a large run of fish *clean* from the sea.

"There is no end to the trout fishing on the river, and they are of large size. But two days would give you enough of that, if you followed it up. I tried it two mornings for a few hours, caught one hundred each day and then cried enough. It very soon ceases to be sport, especially when you know there are salmon and grilse in the immediate vicinity."

I do not agree with Mr. Perley in pronouncing the Papineau Falls the best spot on the river, but A. P. Bradbury, Esq., of Bangor, thinks with him, and thus mentions his sport there in 1853. "My friend Mr. Carr and myself remained upon the ground nineteen days, and in that time killed forty-three fish, the largest weighing only seventeen pounds. The longest time occupied in landing a fish was two hours, he having sulked one hour of that time. The shortest time was about twenty minutes.

Besides these, we caught a large number of trout weighing from one to four pounds, which gave us fine sport. Altogether, we enjoyed our trip exceedingly. Many times, during our sojourn on the banks of the Nipisiguit, did we make '*Lanman's Camp*,' a shelter from sun and rain, nor did we omit his health in our *schnapps*."

But I cannot take leave of my friend Mr. Perley, without quoting in full another of his private piscatorial letters, which runneth as follows:—

WIGWAM, BURNT CHURCH POINT,
MIRAMACHA BAY, *Aug.* 5, 1853.

"I have been here three days, and three happier days I scarce ever spent.

"In the first place, my wigwam is a superb one—twenty feet by sixteen, and a perfect picture, inside and out. It stands on a grass plat, in a clump of young firs, fifty yards from the sea-shore. I have four Indians—young men and first rate attendants. Two of them cook admirably. As to the materials for cooking, we (Coley and self,) have now in camp the following stock:

Salmon—fresh, salted, smoked and preserved.
Trout—bass—lobsters, and "a pile" of oysters.
Ham, pork, bread, biscuit, &c., &c.
Blueberries and raspberries, by the pailful.
Fresh mackerel, (this moment arrived.)
A brace of plover.
Cod, haddock, and halibut.

"Two days ago, Coley made his debut as a fly-fisher, and caught forty-eight trout; a pretty good beginning. I caught a hundred and thirteen—the largest weighed just two pounds, when cleaned. Yesterday, Coley caught sixty-two trout, and I caught a hundred and five—the young scamp caught fish for fish with me the first half hour. As yet he has not broken a line or lost a fly.

"You know, Coley is grave and quiet—he had not been here twelve hours, until the Indians dubbed him, "Sagamon chiche," *the little chief;* and by that name he is now called altogether. To-day he has been out shooting with a long legged Indian, and fired away any amount of powder and shot—result—the two plover aforesaid.

"My happiness would be complete if you were here for a day or two. What a change from New York or Washington! Such a delicious air, pure sea-water, atmosphere warm but bracing. At this moment I am stronger and more vigorous than at any time during the last three years.

"It is now an hour to sunset, and the cook wants to know what I will have for supper. Last night I had boiled mackerel, not half an hour caught. I caught six sea trout about an hour ago, so here they go, with new potatoes and an egg.

"At this moment I think Coley the happiest fellow in this world. He has on a *red* shirt—is stretched out on a *blue* blanket—a white blanket about his feet, and my gray shawl under his head. He holds Harper for July in one hand, and is dipping the other into a pail of blueberries standing beside him. One of my flags, St. George's Cross, hangs above him; while guns, fishing-rods, nets, spears, shot-belts, landing-nets, game-bags, fishing baskets, &c., are placed about the camp in most picturesque fashion, but most perfect order.

"To-day, I went over to the fishing station at Portage Island. A small fleet of green bottomed schooners were cruising off and on—they showed no colors, it is therefore impossible to say with certainty to what nation they belonged; but "I guess" they were Yankees and no mistake. It is a little over six miles from the station to my camp; the canoe, with a fine breeze, came over in exactly thirty-seven minutes. They sail beautifully. The quantity of salmon put up this year at Portage Island, is something almost fabulous. Just now they are putting up lobsters in thousands. The salmon are nearly done; that fishery closes by law on the 15th instant.

"The Micmacs hold a grand Festival at this place every year on St. Anne's day, (26th July)—this festival lasted a week this year and is just over. There were five hundred Indians here; among them visitors from Cape Breton and Bay Chaleur. Most of these have departed; but some thirty or forty revellers remain, who still keep it up among the residents here. Daily pic nics to gather berries, with dancing and gambling nearly all night, make out the twenty-four hours, quite as well as among those who move in higher circles, yet follow the same amusements.

"*Saturday morning, August* 6. This morning at day light, an Indian arrived from New Castle with my letters and papers —a goodly pile. This morning is very hot, and but for the delicious sea breeze would be unbearable. The little waves are "lapping" on the smooth sand-beach, and all nature seems pleased and happy. I have just bought a splendid salmon for half a dollar, which is two pence more than the established price, the market rate being two and four pence. The English shilling passes at one and three pence, so I just paid forty-seven cents for the salmon.

"*Sunday, August* 7. In the cool of the evening, Coley and I caught thirty-seven trout, and at sunset I received a party of visitors from Miramachi. Such a night as we put in! Such songs, speeches, toasts and uproar, I never heard. They all slept in camp on the fir boughs, and a more comfortable set of gentlemen you never saw anywhere. We have had an excellent breakfast, and now they are out fishing in a boat belonging to the Indians. Whilst I stay in camp and look after dinner.

Bill of Fare settled thus:

Boiled salmon—oyster sauce.
Fried bass.
Lobster, cold.
Fried trout.
Pork chips.
Cold ham.
Boiled shoulder of pork.
New potatoes, string beans, Windsor beans, carrots, beets.
Snipe and plover.
Blueberries and raspberries.

"Neither the Astor nor the National ever turned out a better breakfast thon we had this morning, and I have no fears for the dinner. The wigwam is a perfect picture to-day, the most stylish and sporting thing I ever saw."

TROUT FISHING.

It carries us into the most wild and beautiful scenery of nature; amongst the mountain lakes and the clear and lovely streams that gush from the higher ranges of elevated hills, or make their way through the cavities of calcareous rocks.

SIR HUMPHREY DAVY.

WERE it not for the salmon we should pronounce the trout the most superb game-fish in the world. As the case now stands, however, we are inclined to believe that he has delighted a greater number of anglers than any other inhabitant of the "liquid plain." The characteristics of this charming fish are so well know that we shall not, on this occasion, enter upon a scientific description either of his person or habits. In all the particulars of beauty, of color and form, of grace, of activity, of intelligence and flavor, as before intimated, he has but one rival. He always glories in the coldest and purest of water, and the regions of country to which he is partial are commonly distinguished for the wildness of their scenery; and therefore it is that to the lover of nature this imperial fish has ever been exceedingly dear. Their period of spawning is in the autumn, and they recover as early as February, thereby remaining in season a part of the winter, as well as the entire spring and summer—though the trouting months, *par excellence*, are May and June.

In weight, even when fully grown, the different varieties of trout run from four ounces to sixty pounds, and of the different distinct species found in the United States and Canada, we are acquainted only with the following!—

The Common, or Brook and River Trout.—There is hardly a cold and rocky stream in any part of the New England or Northern States, or among the mountains of the Middle and Southern States, where this species is not found in abundance. In regard to weight, they ordinarily vary from three or four ounces to two pounds; and in color, according to the character of the brook or river which they inhabit. So apparent is the difference of color in this family, that, in the several sections of the country where they are found, they are designated by the names of silver or fall trout, as in Lake George; and the black trout, as in many of the smaller lakes or Ponds of New England. The only *civilized* mode employed by our people for taking them is with the hook; but, while the scientific angler prefers the artificial fly (with an appropriate reel,) large numbers are annually destroyed by the farmer's boys with the common hook and red worm. As to the heathenish mode of netting this beautiful fish, we can only say that it merits the most earnest condemnation of every gentleman. The common trout is proverbially one of the most skittish of all the finny tribes; but when he happens to be a little hungry, he is fearless as the hawk, and at such times often leaps into the air as if for the purpose of defying the cunning of his human enemies. According to our experience, the best bait for early spring fishing is the common worm; but for June, July, and August, we prefer the fly. Sometimes, however, a minnow is preferable to either. The great charm of fly fishing for trout is derived from the fact that you then see the movement of your fish, and if you are not an expert hand, the chances are that you will capture but one out of the hundred that may rise to your hook. You can seldom save a trout unless you strike the very instant that he leaps. But, even after this, a deal of care is required to land him in safety. If he is a half-pounder, you may pull him out directly; but if larger than that, after fairly hooking him, you should play him with your whole line, which, when well done, is a feat full of poetry. The swiftness with which a trout can dart from his hiding-place after a fly is truly astonishing; and we never see one perform this operation without feeling an indescribable thrill quivering through our frame. The fact that this is the only fish in the world which nature has designated by a row of scarlet spots along the sides, would seem to imply that she deemed it the perfection of her finny creations, and had, therefore, fixed upon it this distinguishing mark of her skill.

The Salmon Trout.—Under this head we include all those fish of the trout genus which are found only in those lakes of our country having no connection whatever with the sea. The fish now under consideration resembles, in its general appearance, the legitimate salmon, but is totally unlike it in several particulars. The salmon trout, for example, varies in weight from three to sixty pounds; and if everybody is to be believed, they have been taken in some of our waters weighing upwards of one hundred pounds. They are of much less value than the real salmon as an article of food, there being nothing at all delicate in the texture or flavor of a mammoth fish. As sporting fish, too, they are of little value, for they love the gloom of deep water, and are not distinguished for their activity. The names, besides its own, by which this fish is recognised, are the lake trout and the Mackinaw trout; and, by many people who ought to know better, they are often confounded with the genuine salmon. As is the case with the salmon, they are seldom or never found in any of our rivers, but chiefly in the lakes of the northern and northwestern States of the Union, being found in the greatest numbers at the Straits of Mackinaw, in Lake Superior, Lake George, and the other lakes of the Empire State, and in Moosehead Lake.

The Sea Trout.—Our idea of this fish is that it is quite at home in the "deep, deep sea," but rather partial to the brackish waters of large rivers and the inland bays of the American coast. And also that they vary in weight from three to fifteen pounds, and ought to be highly prized as a game fish, their flesh being of a rosy hue, and excellent, and their courage and strength allied to those of their more aristocratic cousin—the salmon. Like the salmon and common trout, too, they scorn the more common baits of fishermen, and possess a decided taste for the fly, albeit thousands of them are taken with the shrimp and minnow. The waters where they mostly abound are those of the lower St. Lawrence and its tributaries, the bay of Cape Cod, all along the southern shore of Barnstable, the entire shore of Martha's Vineyard, and the bays Delaware and Chesapeake. So much for the varieties of trout with which we are personally acquainted.

It now behooves us to record some of our experience in trout fishing, but we have already published in our books of travel, and elsewhere, quite as many *fish stories* as will be readily believed. We shall, therefore, content ourselves, on this occasion, with a brief description of our favorite localities.

As a matter of course, the first place that we mention in this connection is Sault St. Marie, which, for many reasons, is an exceedingly attractive place. In the first place, it is the outlet to Lake Superior, the largest body of fresh water on the globe. It is also the western terminating point of the lake navigation of the north. From the earliest periods of our history to the present time, it has been, as it were, the starting-place for all the fur expeditions by land which have ever penetrated the immense wilderness bordering on Hudson's Bay and the Arctic Ocean. The fall of the river St. Marie at the spot called the Sault, is nearly twenty-five feet within the space of half a mile, so that from a canoe at the foot of the rapid it presents the appearance of a wall of foam. The width of it is reputed to be one mile, and on the British side are several beautiful islands, covered with hemlock, spruce, and pine, pleasingly intermingled with birch. The bed of the river at this point consists chiefly of colored sand-stones, the depth varies from ten to perhaps one hundred feet, and the water is perpetually cold, and as clear as it is possible for any element to be. But what makes the Sault particularly attractive to the angler, is the fact that the common trout is found here in good condition throughout the year. They are taken with the fly, and from boats anchored in the more shallow places of the river, as well as from the shore. We have known two fishermen to spend an entire day in a single reef, or at one anchorage, and in spite of sunlight and east winds, have known them to capture more than a cart-load of the spotted beauties, varying in weight from half a pound to three and four. How it is that the fish of this region always appear to be in season has never been explained, but we should imagine that, either they have no particular time for spawning, or that each season brings with it a variety peculiar to itself. Those of the present day who visit Sault St. Marie for the purpose of throwing the fly, ought to be fully prepared with tackle and that of the best quality. With regard to the *creature comforts* obtainable in the village of Sault St. Marie, they will be as well supplied as in any other place of the same size equally remote from the civilized centre of the world. And when the pleasures of trout fishing begin to subside they can relieve the monotony of a sojourn here by visiting the Indians in their wigwams, and seeing them capture (with nets, in the pure white foam) the beautiful white fish; they may also with little difficulty visit the copper mines of Lake Superior, or if they would do their country service (provided they are Americans,) they may indite long letters to members of Congress on the great necessity of a ship canal around the falls or rapids of St. Mary.

And now for the island of Mackinaw. For an elaborate description of this spot we refer our readers to any of the numerous travellers who have published its praises, not forgetting by way of being *impartial* an account from our own pen already before the public. The time is rapidly approaching, we believe, when this island will be universally considered one of the most healthful, interesting, convenient, and fashionable watering-places in the whole country. And the naturalists, not to say the angler, will find here the celebrated Mackinaw trout in its greatest perfection. And when the Detroit and Chicago steamer runs into the little crescent harbor of the island for the purpose of landing the traveller, and he discovers among the people on the dock some half-dozen wheelbarrows laden with fish four feet long and weighing fifty or sixty pounds, he must not be alarmed at finding those fish to be Mackinaw trout, and not sturgeon, as he might at first have imagined. The truth is, the very size of these fish is an objection to them, for, as they have to be taken in deep water, and with a large cord, there is far more of manual labor than sport in taking them. But when one of these monsters happens to stray towards the shore where the water is not over fifty feet, it is then, through the marvellously clear water, exceedingly pleasant to watch their movements as they swim about over the beds of pure white sand. As before intimated, the Mackinaw trout is far inferior to the common trout as an article of food, and to the white fish almost infinitely so.

The Mackinaw trout (as is the case with all salmon trout) is in fine condition throughout the winter months; and the Indians are very fond of taking them through the ice. Their manner of proceeding is to make a large hole in the ice, over which they erect a kind of wigwam, so as to keep out the light; and, stationing themselves above the hole, they lure the trout from the bottom by an artificial bait, and when he comes sufficiently near pick him out with a spear; and they are also taken with a hook. The voraciousness of the Mackinaw trout at this season is said to be astonishing; and it is recorded of a Canadian fisherman, that, having lost all his artificial bait by being bitten to pieces, he finally resorted to a large jack-knife attached to a hook which he had in his pocket, and which was swallowed by a thirty pound fish. Another anecdote that we have heard touching this mode of winter fishing, is as follows, and shows the danger with which it is sometimes attended. An Indian fisherman, of renown among the tribes of Lake Superior, while fishing on this lake in the manner above mentioned, at a considerable distance from the shore, was once detached with a cake of ice from the shore and carried into the lake by the wind, and was never heard of more. Such a death as he must have met with it would be difficult to describe.

But we cannot leave Mackinaw without making a passing allusion to the fish whose Indian name is *ciscovet*. It is a handsome fish, unquestionably of the trout family, a bold biter, richly flavored, and very beautiful both in symmetry and color. They are not very abundant, and are altogether the greatest fishy delicacy of this region, excepting the white fish.

They weigh from five to ten pounds, and are remarkable for their fatness. At the Island of Mackinaw the common trout is not found at all, but in all the streams upon the main shore of Lake Michigan, which is only a short distance off, they are very abundant and very large.

Another trouting region whose praises we are disposed to sing, is that of northern New York, lying between Lake George and Long Lake. All the running waters of this section of country are abundantly supplied with common trout, and all the lakes (which are numerous) with salmon trout. The scenery everywhere is of the wildest and most imposing character. The two branches of the noble Hudson here take their rise, and almost every rood of their serpentine courses abounds in rapid and deep pools, yielding common trout of the largest size. But the angler who visits this region must not expect to be feasted with the fashionable delicacies of the land, or spend his nights in luxuriantly furnished rooms; he must be a lover of salt pork, and well acquainted with the yielding qualities of a pine floor. To those of our readers who would become better acquainted with the region alluded to, we would recommend the interesting description of Charles F. Hoffman, Esq., and the spirited, though somewhat fantastic ones of J. T. Headley, Esq.

In the "times of old" we have enjoyed ourselves exceedingly in making piscatorial pilgrimages among the Catskill and Shandaken Mountains, but their wilderness glory is rapidly departing. We can now only recommend this region as abounding in beautiful as well as magnificent scenery. Now, while we think of it, however, we have one little incident to record connected with Shew's Lake, which beautifies the summit of one of the Catskills. Having once caught a large number of small common trout in a stream that ran out of this lake, we conceived the idea that the lake itself must of necessity contain a large number of full-grown fish of the same species. With this idea in view, we obtained the services of a mountaineer, named Hummel, and tried our luck at the lake, by the light of the moon, with set-lines and live minnows. During the night we caught no less than forty-two trout, averaging in weight over a pound a-piece. We were of course greatly elated at this success; and, having enjoyed quite a romantic expedition, we subsequently published an account of the particulars. A few days after this, a party of anglers residing in the town of Catskill saw what we had written, and immediately posted off to Shew's Lake, for the purpose of spending a night there. They did so, and also fished after the same manner that we did, and yet did not capture a single trout. They of course returned home considerably disgusted, and reported that the lake in question was covered with dead eels, that the water was alive with lizards, that they saw the glaring eyes of a panther near their watch-fire, and that *we* had been guilty of publishing a falsehood. It now becomes us to deny, and in the most expressive tone, this rough impeachment, although we fully confess that there still hangs a mystery over our piscatorial good fortune.

If the anglers of New York city are to be believed, there is no region in the world like Long Island for common trout. We are informed, however, that the fish are here penned up in ponds, and that a stipulated sum per head has to be paid for all the fish captured. With this kind of business we have never had any patience, and we shall therefore refrain from commenting upon the exploits or trespassing upon the exclusive privileges of the cockney anglers of the empire city.

But another trouting region, of which we can safely speak in the most flattering terms, is that watered by the two principal tributaries of the river Thames, in Connecticut, viz., the Yantic and the Quinnebaug. It is, in our opinion, more nearly allied to that portion of England made famous by Walton in his *Complete Angler*, than any other in the United States. The country is generally highly cultivated, but along nearly all its very beautiful streams Nature has been permitted to have her own way, and the dark pools are everywhere overshadowed by the foliage of overhanging trees. Excepting in the immediate vicinity of the factories, trout are quite abundant, and the anglers are generally worthy members of the gentle brotherhood. When the angler is overtaken by night, he never finds himself at a loss for a place to sleep; and it has always seemed to us that the beds of this region have a "smell of lavender." The husbandmen whom you meet here are intelligent, and their wives neat, affable, and polite, understanding the art of preparing a frugal meal to perfection. Our trouting recollections of this section of New England are manifold, and we would part with them most unwillingly. Dearly do we cherish, not only recollections of scenery and fishing, but of wild legends and strange characters, bright skies, poetic conceptions, and soul-instructing lessons from Nature. Yes, and the secret of our attachment to the above-mentioned streams may be found in the character of these very associations. What intense enjoyment would not Father Walton have derived from their wild and superb scenery! The streams of England are mostly famous for the bloody battles and sieges which they witnessed for many centuries, and the turreted castles which they lave tell us eventful stories of a race of earth-born kings. But many of the streams of our country, even in these days, water a virgin wilderness, whose only human denizens are the poor but noble Indian tribes, who live, and love, and die in their peaceful valleys; and the unshorn forests, with the luxuriantly magnificent mountains, sing a perpetual hymn of praise to One who is above the sky, and the King of kings.

Of all the New England States, however, (albeit much might be written in praise of Vermont and New Hampshire, with their glorious Green and White Mountains,) we believe that Maine is altogether the best supplied. In the head-waters of the Penobscot and Kennebec, the common trout may be found by the thousand; and in Moosehead Lake, as before stated, salmon trout of the largest size and in great numbers. This is even a more perfect wilderness than that in the northern part of New York, and it is distinguished not only for its superb scenery, but its fine forests afford an abundance of large game, such as moose, deer, bears, and wolves, which constitute a most decided attraction to those disciples of the gentle art who have a little of the fire of Nimrod in their natures.

The Middle States of the Union are also not without their

attractions to the angler. In the Juniata, the most picturesque stream in Pennsylvania, and in the tributaries of the Youghagany and Cheat rivers in Virginia, I have caught trout by the hundred,—beautiful trout and large. Like those in nearly all our mountain districts, the accommodations for shelter and food are poor among the Alleghanies; but the log-cabins are picturesque, the sable pilots whom you have to employ interesting to study, and purer air or mellower sunshine are nowhere to be enjoyed.

Another region towards which we would direct the attention of our readers, is that portion of Canada lying on the north shore of the St. Lawrence. At the mouth of all the streams here emptying into the great river, and especially at the mouth of the Saguenay, the sea trout is found in its greatest perfection. They vary from five to fifteen pounds, and are taken with the fly. But what makes the fishing for them particularly interesting is the fact, that when the angler strikes a fish it is impossible for him to tell, before he has seen his prize, whether he has captured a salmon trout, a mammoth trout, common trout, (which are here found in brackish or salt water,) or a magnificent salmon, glistening in his silver mail.

BASS FISHING.

We delight, as all the world has long well known, in every kind of fishing, from the whale to the minnow.—CHRISTOPHER NORTH.

THE beautiful fish now chosen for our "subject theme" is a genuine *native American*, and ranks high among the game fish of the country. When fully grown, he is commonly about fifteen inches long, two inches in thickness, and some five inches broad, weighing perhaps five or six pounds. He belongs to the perch family, has a thick oval head, a swallow tail, sharp teeth, and small scales. In color, he is deep black along the back and sides, growing lighter and somewhat yellowish towards the belly. He has a large mouth, and is a bold biter, feeds upon minnows and insects, is strong and active, and, when in season, possesses a fine flavor. He spawns in the spring, recovers in July, and is in his prime in September.

The black bass is peculiarly a Western and Southern fish, and is not known in any of the rivers which connect immediately with the Atlantic Ocean. They are found in great abundance in the upper Mississippi and its tributaries, in all the great lakes excepting Superior, in the upper St. Lawrence, especially at the Thousand Islands, the tributaries of the Ohio, in Lake Champlain and Lake George, and nearly all the smaller lakes of New York. In portions of the last-named State they are called the Oswego bass, in the southwest the black perch, and in the northwest, where they are most abundant, the black bass. In nearly all the waters where they abound has it been our good fortune to angle for this fish, and his very name is associated with much of the most beautiful scenery in the land. Our own experience, however, in bass fishing, is chiefly identified with Lake George, Lake Erie, Lake Michigan, and the upper Mississippi, and to these waters alone it is our purpose to devote a few paragraphs.

And first, as to the beautiful "Horicon" of the North. Embosomed as it is among the wildest of mountains, and rivaling, as do its waters, the blue of heaven, it is indeed all that could be desired, and in every particular worthy of its fame. Although this lake is distinguished for the number and variety of its trout, I am inclined to believe that the black bass found here afford the angler the greatest amount of sport. They are taken during the entire summer, and by almost as great a variety of methods as there are anglers; trolling with a minnow, however, and fishing with a gaudy fly from the numerous islands in the lake, are unquestionably the two most successful methods. As before intimated, the bass is a very active fish, and, excepting the salmon, we know of none that perform, when hooked, such desperate leaps out of the water. They commonly frequent the immediate vicinity of the shores, especially those that are rocky, and are seldom taken where the water is more than twenty feet deep. They commonly lie close to the bottom, rise to the minnow or fly quite as quickly as the trout, and are not as easily frightened by the human form.

The late William Caldwell, who owned an extensive estate at the southern extremity of Lake George, was the gentleman who first introduced us to the bass of the said lake, and we shall ever remember him as one of the most accomplished and gentlemanly anglers we have ever known. He was partial to the trolling method of fishing, however, and the manner in which he performed a piscatorial expedition was somewhat unique and romantic. His right hand man on all occasions was a worthy mountaineer, who lived in the vicinity of his mansion, and whose principal business was to take care of the angler's boat, and row him over the lake. For many years did this agreeable connection exist between Mr. Caldwell and his boatman, and, when their fishing days were over, was happily terminated by the deeding of a handsome farm to the latter by his munificent employer. But we intended to describe one of Mr. Caldwell's excursions.

It is a July morning, and our venerable angler, with his boatman, has embarked in his feathery skiff. The lake is thirty-three miles long, and it is his intention to perform its entire circuit, thereby voyaging at least seventy miles. He purposes to be absent about a week, and having no less than half a dozen places on the lake shore where he can find a night's lodging, he is in no danger of being compelled to camp out. His little vessel is abundantly supplied with fishing tackle, as well as the substantials of life, and some of its liquid luxuries. He and *Care* have parted company, and his heart is now wholly open to the influences of nature, and therefore buoyant as the boat which bears him over the translucent waters. The first day his luck is bad, and he tarries at a certain point for the purpose of witnessing the concluding scene of a deer hunt, and hearing the successful hunter expatiate upon his exploits and the quality of his hounds. On the second day the wind is from the south, and he secures no less than twenty of the finest bass on the lake. On the third day he also has good luck, but is greatly annoyed by thunder showers, and must content himself with one of the late magazines which he has brought along for such emergencies. The fifth and sixth days he has some good fishing, and spends them at Garfield's landing (for the reader must know that there is a tiny steamboat on Lake George,) where he has an opportunity of meeting a brotherhood of anglers, who are baiting for the salmon trout; and the seventh day he probably spends quietly at Lyman's Tavern, in the companionship of an intelligent landscape painter (spending the summer there,) arriving at home on the following morning.

As to our own experience in regard to bass fishing in Lake George, we remember one incident in particular which illustrates an interesting truth in natural history. We were on a trouting expedition, and happened to reach the lake early in June, before the bass were in season, and we were stopping with our friend Mr. Lyman, of Lyman's Point. The idea having occurred to us of spearing a few fish by torchlight, we secured the services of an experienced fisherman, and, with a boat well supplied with *fat pine*, we launched ourselves on the quiet waters of the lake about an hour after sundown. Bass were very abundant, and we succeeded in killing some half dozen of a large size. We found them exceedingly tame, and noticed, when we approached, that they were invariably alone, occupying the centre of a circular and sandy place among the rocks and stones. We inquired the cause of this, and were told that the bass were casting their spawn, and that the circular places were the beds where, the young were protected. On hearing this, our conscience was somewhat troubled by what we had been doing, but we resolved to take one more fish and then go home. We now came to a large bed, around the edge of which we discovered a number of very small fish, and over the centre of the bed a very large and handsome bass was hovering. We darted our spear, and only wounded the poor fish. Our companion then told us, that if we would go away for fifteen minutes, and then return to the same spot, we should have another chance at the same fish. We did so, and the prediction was realized. We threw the spear again, and again failed in killing our game, though we succeeded in nearly cutting the fish in two pieces. "You will have the creature yet; let us go away again," said my companion. We did so, and lo! to our utter astonishment, we again saw the fish, all mutilated and torn, still hovering over its tender offspring! To relieve it of its pain, we darted the spear once more, and the bass lay in our boat quite dead; and we returned to our lodgings on that night a decidedly unhappy man. We felt, with the *ancient mariner*, that we "*had done a hellish deed*," and most bitterly did we repent our folly. Ever since that time have we felt a desire to atone for our wickedness, and we trust that the shade of Izaak Walton will receive our humble confession as an atonement. The bass that we took on the night in question, owing to their being out of season, were not fit to eat, and we had not even the plea of palatable food to offer. The maternal affection of that black bass for its helpless offspring, which it protected even unto death, has ever seemed to us in strict keeping with the loveliness and holiness of universal nature.

And now with regard to Lake Erie. We know not of a single prominent river emptying into this lake in which the black bass is not found in considerable numbers. The sport which they yield to the disciples of Walton at the eastern extremity of the lake, has been described by George W. Clinton, Esq., of Buffalo, in a series of piscatorial letters, published in the journals of that city; and, as we would not interfere with him while throwing the fly in his company on the same stream, neither will we trespass upon that literary ground which he has so handsomely made his own. When, however, we hear the green waves of Lake Erie washing its western shores, we feel that we have a right to be heard, for in that region, when it was for the most part a lonely wilderness, did we first behold the light of this beautiful world. With the windings of the Sandusky, the Maumee, the Huron, and the Detroit rivers, we are quite familiar, and we know that they all yield an abundance of black bass; but with the river Raisin, we are as well acquainted as a child could be with its mother's bosom. Upon this stream was the home of our boyhood, and at the bare mention of its name, unnumbered recollections flit across the mind, which to our hearts are inexpressibly dear.

Even when a mere boy we esteemed the black bass as a peer among his fellows, and never can we forget our first prize. We had seated ourself at the foot of an old sycamore, directly on the margin of the River Raisin, and among its serpent-like roots we were fishing for a number of tiny rock bass that we had chanced to discover there. We baited with a worm, and while doing our utmost to capture a two-ounce fish, we were suddenly frightened by the appearance of a black bass, which took our hook, and was soon dangling in the top of a neighboring bush. Our delight at this unexpected exploit was unbounded, and, after bothering our friends with an account of it until the night was far spent, we retired to bed, and in our dreams caught the same poor fish over and over again until morning. From that day to this, rivers and fish have haunted us like a passion.

Like the trout, the black bass seems to be partial to the more romantic and poetical places in the rivers which they frequent. On the River Raisin, for example, we used to enjoy the rarest of sport at an old and partly dilapidated mill-dam, which was covered with moss, and at the foot of which were some of the nicest "deep holes" imaginable. Wherever the timbers of the dam formed a "loop-hole of retreat," there we were always sure of finding a bass. And we also remember an old mill, in whose shadowy recesses, far down among the foundation timbers, the bass delighted to congregate, and where we were wont to spend many of our Saturday afternoons; but our favorite expeditions were those which occupied entire days, and led us along the banks of the Raisin, in the vicinity of its mouth, and far beyond the hearing of the mill-wheel or the clink of the blacksmith's anvil. At such times, the discovery of old sunken logs was all that we cared for, for we knew that the bass delighted to spend the noontide hours in their shadow. And when we could borrow a canoe, and obtain a foothold on the extreme point of a wooded island, so as to angle in the deep dark holes, we seldom failed in realizing all the enjoyment that we anticipated. And, if we chanced to come across a party of fishermen drawing the seine, we were sure to forget our promise to our parents to return home before sundown, and, far too often for a good boy, did we remain with them even until the moon had taken her station in the sky. To count the fish thus captured, and to hear the strange adventures and exploits talked over by these fishermen, was indeed a delightful species of vagabondizing; and we usually avoided a very severe scolding by returning home "with one of the largest bass ever caught in the river," which we may have taken with the hook or purchased of the fishermen. But we are talking of the "times of the days of old," and as we remember that the glories of the River Raisin, in regard to its scenery and its fish, are forever departed, we hasten to other waters.

In fancy we have now crossed the peninsula of Michigan, or

rather compassed it by means of the splendid steamers which navigate the waters of Huron and Michigan, and we are now on the banks of the river St. Joseph. This is a small river, and unquestionably one of the most beautiful in the western world. It runs through an exceedingly fertile country, abounds in luxuriant islands, is invariably as clear as crystal, and in its course winding to an uncommon degree. It is navigable for small steamboats to the village of Niles, fifty miles from its mouth, and for batteaux somewhere about fifty miles further towards its source. Early in the spring it abounds in the more common varieties of fresh-water fish, but throughout the summer and autumn it yields the black bass in the greatest abundance.

Our piscatorial experience upon the St. Joseph has not been very extensive, but we deem it worthy of a passing notice. We were on our way to the "Far West," and had been waylaid in the beautiful village of Niles by one of the fevers of the country. The physician who attended us was a genuine angler, and we believe that our speedy recovery was owing almost entirely to the capital fish stories with which he regaled us during that uncomfortable period. Be that as it may, one thing we very clearly remember, which is this: that we enjoyed for one afternoon, some of the most remarkable bass fishing in his company that we have ever experienced. It was in September, and we commenced fishing at three o'clock. We baited with live minnows, fished with hand lines, and from a boat which was firmly anchored at a bend of the river, and just above a long and very deep hole, two miles above the village of Niles. Our lines were upwards of a hundred feet long, and as the current was very rapid, the pulling in of our minnows was performed with little trouble. The sun was shining brightly, and the only sounds which floated in the air were the singing of birds, the rustling of the forest leaves, and the gentle murmuring of the waters as they glided along the luxuriant banks of the stream. We fished a little more than two hours, but in that time we caught no less than ninety-two bass, a dozen of which weighed over five pounds, and the great majority not less than two pounds.

Such remarkable luck had never been heard of before in that vicinity, and of course, for several days thereafter the river was covered with boats; but, strange to say, nearly all the anglers returned home disappointed. On a subsequent occasion, the doctor and his patient made another trial at their favorite spot, but succeeded in taking only a single fish, from which circumstance we came to the conclusion that we had actually cleared that portion of the river of its fishy inhabitants.

Before quitting the St. Joseph, we ought to state that its beautiful tributaries, the Pipe Stone and the Paw-Paw, afford a superior quality of bass, and that no pleasanter fishing-ground can anywhere be found than at the mouth of the parent river itself. With regard to the other principal rivers of Western Michigan, we can only say that the Kalamazoo and the Grand river are not one whit behind the St. Joseph in any of those charms which win the affections of the angler and the lover of nature.

We come now to speak of the Upper Mississippi, in whose translucent water, as before stated, the black bass is found in "numbers numberless." Not only do they abound in the river itself and its noble tributaries, but also in the lakes of the entire region. The only people who angle for them, however, are the travellers who occasionally penetrate into this beautiful wilderness of the Northwest. Generally speaking, the bass, as well as all other kinds of fish, are taken by the Indians with a wooden spear, and more to satisfy hunger than to enjoy the sport. The angler who would cast a fly above Fort Snelling must expect to spend his nights in an Indian lodge instead of a white-washed cottage, to repose upon a bearskin instead of a bed (such as Walton loved) which "smells of lavender," and to hear the howl of the wolf instead of a "milk-maid's song."

In all the lakes and streams of Florida, Alabama, and Mississippi, the black bass are abundant, constituting, indeed, the only genuine game of the region; but they are there erroneously called trout. They attain in Florida the weight of fifteen pounds and are good eating.

As our piscatorial recollections of the Upper Mississippi are not particularly interesting, and as it is attracting much attention at the present time, (1849) under the new name of *Minnesota*, or *Turbid Water*, we shall conclude our essay with the following general description.

According to the final provisions of the Act of Congress which has lately transferred this extensive wilderness into a Territory of the United States, it is bounded on the north by the British possessions, on the east by Lake Superior and the State of Wisconsin, on the south by the State of Iowa, and on the west by the Missouri river and the extensive possessions of the Indians. The surface of the country is generally level, and it has been estimated that at least two-thirds of its area consists of prairie land, the remainder being forest. Much of the soil is fertile, and easy of cultivation. It is watered by no less than six of the most superb rivers on the face of the earth—the Mississippi and Missouri, River Au Jacques, the St. Peter's, or Minnesota River, the Red River, emptying into Hudson's Bay, and the St. Louis, emptying into Lake Superior. Were it not for the Falls of St. Mary (a canal having been built around those of Niagara,) a vessel sailing from the city of New York, by the St. Lawrence and the great lakes, might deposit her merchandise almost within its very heart; while it is a well-known fact that a New Orleans steamer may, by the Mississippi and Missouri rivers, transport the products of the South to its more remote extremities. The two facts, that Minnesota is laved by the waters of the largest lake in the world, and that in its very centre are located at least a thousand lesser lakes, which constitute the fountain-head of the Father of Waters, are in themselves sufficient to give it a world-wide reputation. In addition to all this, the climate of this territory is all that could be desired. The winters are, indeed, somewhat long and cold, but they are regular; and, as to the summers, we have never witnessed any that were to us so bracing and delightful. The dreaded ague is a stranger in this region, and the very night airs seem to increase the strength of the voyageurs and Indian traders, who, for ths most part, are the only civilized inhabitants of the domain. Game is found in the greatest abundance, from the buffalo to the deer and the grouse, and there is no region in the world where can be found a greater variety of fresh-water fish.

The Indian population is by far the most extensive now existing within its limits, but the nations are only two in number, the Chippewas and the Sioux. The wrongs which these unfortunate children of the wilderness have for many years past endured from the more unprincipled traders are among the blackest crimes of the white man, and it is to be most sincerely hoped that a new order of things will now be brought about which may in some slight degree atone for those wrongs. To us, who have been a devoted lover of the red man, even from childhood, the fact that the race is literally withering from the land of their fathers is indeed depressing and sickening. With all his faults, we dearly love the poor neglected and deeply-wronged Indian, and we verily believe that our beloved country can never prosper, as it might, until we have done something to atone for the unnumbered outrages committed against the race by our more unworthy citizens. But we are wandering.

With regard to the towns or villages existing at the present time in Minnesota, we can offer but little. So far as we now remember, they consist of only three: Fond du Lac, on the St. Louis, a mere trading post; St. Peter's, at the mouth of the river of that name, distinguished as the site of Fort Snelling, as being within five or six miles of the Falls of St. Anthony, and at the head of steamboat navigation; and the hamlet of St. Paul, which is on the west side of the Mississippi, only about six miles below the mouth of the St. Peter's. The fact that the last-named place has been selected as the seat of government of the new Territory renders it of some interest. It is situated on a bluff which rises some fifty feet above the Mississippi, and, though flanked by a thinly-wooded, or rather prairie country, the soil is fertile, and the scenery both up and down the Mississippi is exceedingly beautiful. Unlike that running south of the Missouri, this portion of the great river is invariably translucent, and for many reasons is interesting to an uncommon degree. Steamboats drawing only a few inches of water navigate this portion of the river during the whole summer. When we visited St. Paul (1846) the majority of its dwellings, if not all, (numbering not more than half a dozen,) were built of logs, and, though very comfortable, were not particularly showy. At that time, too, the only business carried on there was that of trading with the Indians. Our most vivid recollections of the place are associated with a supper that we enjoyed in the cabin of the principal trader. We had lost ourself in travelling by land from Lake St. Croix to the village, and for many hours before our arrival we had been in a particularly hungry mood. We entered St. Paul just as the sun was setting; and it so happened that, on the very outskirts of the place, we chanced to kill a couple of young coons. A portion of one of these animals, fried in its own fat, with a dish of tea, constituted our supper, and a more truly satisfactory supper we have hardly ever enjoyed, albeit we have been quite an extensive traveller in the wilderness. If the citizens of St. Paul only welcomed their newly-appointed Governor by giving him a coon supper, we feel confident that he was well pleased with the reception.

As to the agricultural products, we cannot speak with much confidence. Wild rice, we know, grows in great abundance, and is the staple article of food with the Indians. For corn, the climate is considered rather cold; but potatoes and the more common vegetables grow to perfection. In many parts the maple-tree predominates, and a fine sugar is produced in considerable quantities. The principal timbers are pine and a dwarfish oak. The only Alpine region of Minnesota is that which lies upon Lake Superior, and the beautiful mountains which here kiss the blue of heaven are invariably covered with a miscellaneous forest; and, if half the stories we have heard are true, they must abound in the valuable minerals of copper and silver.

Those of our readers who may desire further information in regard to the Territory of Minnesota would do well to consult the following authorities, viz., General Pike, who travelled through the region in 1806; Henry R. Schoolcraft's Travels, both in 1820 and 1832; Major Long, who visited Leech Lake in 1823; and M. Nicolet, whose map of the region is exceedingly valuable.

ROCK FISHING.

Of recreations, there is none
So free as fishing is alone;
All other pastimes do no less
Than mind and body both possess:
My hands alone my work can do,
So I can fish and study too.
ISAAK WALTON.

WE consider the rock-fish, or striped bass, one of the finest game fish to be found in American waters. From all that we can learn, it is peculiar to this country, and to particular sections, not being found farther north than Maine, nor farther south than the Carolinas or Georgia, where it is known as the rock-fish. It varies in weight from six ounces to one hundred pounds; and though a native of the ocean, it spends a portion of every year in the fresh water rivers—yet it seems to be partial to the mouths of our larger estuaries. Our naturalists have pronounced it a member of the perch family, and doubtless with scientific propriety; but we have seen a bass that would outweigh at least four score of the largest perch found in the country. The rock is a thick-set and solid fish, having a strong bony mouth, and sharp teeth. In color, it varies from a deep green on the back to a rich silvery hue on the belly, and its scales are large and of a metallic lustre. But the distinguishing feature of this fish consists in the striped appearance of its body. Running from the head nearly to the tail, there are no less than eight regularly marked lines, which in the healthy fish are of a deep black. Its eyes are white, head rather long, and the under jaw protrudes beyond the upper one, somewhat after the manner of the pike. The strength of the bass is equal to that of the salmon, but in activity it is undoubtedly inferior. As an article of food, it is highly valued, and in all the Atlantic cities invariably commands a good price.

The spawning time of this fish we have not positively ascertained, though we believe it to be in the spring or early summer. The New York markets are supplied with them throughout the year, but it is unquestionably true that they are in their prime in the autumn. The smaller individuals frequent the eddies of our rivers, while those of a larger growth seem to have a fancy for the reefs along the coast. On the approach of winter, they do not strike for the deep water, but find a residence in the bays and still arms of the sea, where they remain until the following spring. They begin to take the hook in April, and, generally speaking, afford the angler any quantity of sport until the middle of November. For the smaller fish at the North, the shrimp and minnow are the most successful baits; and for the larger individuals nothing can be better than the skin of an eel, neatly fastened upon a squid. The river fisherman requires a regular equipment of salmon tackle, while he who would capture the monsters of the ocean, only needs a couple of stout Kirby hooks, a small sinker, a very long and heavy line, a gaff hook, and a surf boat. But those who capture the bass for lucrative purposes, resort to the following more effectual methods: first by using set-lines, and secondly, by the employment of gill-nets and the seine. The sport of taking a twenty-pound bass in a convenient river is allied to that of capturing a salmon, but as the former is not a very skittish fish, the difficulties are not so great. As before intimated, all our Atlantic rivers, from the Penobscot to the Savannah, are regularly visited by the bass; but we are inclined to believe that they are found in the greatest abundance and perfection along the shores of Connecticut, Rhode Island, Massachusetts, and Maine. At any rate, our own experience has been confined to this region; and though we remember with unfeigned pleasure our success in taking the larger varieties along the shores of Martha's Vineyard, at Montauk Point, and in the vicinity of Watch Hill, yet we are disposed to yield the palm to Block Island. This out-of-the-way spot of the green earth belongs to Rhode Island, comprises a whole county of that State, and lies about forty miles from the main shore. It is nine miles in length, and varies in width from three to four miles. It is quite hilly, with an occasional rocky shore, contains a number of salt-water ponds, and is covered with a scanty growth of trees and other vegetation. The male inhabitants, numbering only a few hundred souls, are devoted exclusively to the fishing business, and they are as amiable and honest at heart, as they are rude and isolated in their manner of life. Block Island sailors frequently find their way to the remotest quarters of the globe, though few who were born upon the island ever become entirely weaned from its ocean-girt shores. The Block Island fishermen build their own smacks, and as these are about the only things they do manufacture, they have acquired remarkable skill in building swift vessels, which are also distinguished for their strength and safety.

The pleasantest time to kill bass at Block Island is in the month of October, and immediately after a severe gale, for then it is that the larger fish seek a sheltering place between the reefs and the shore. And if the angler would be certain of success, he ought to be upon the water before sunrise, or at the break of day. He must have only one companion, a stalwart Block Islander, whose duty it shall be to steady the boat, as she dashes along upon the restless bosom of the ground-swell, so that, with his legs carefully braced, he can throw his squid to a great distance, instead of being thrown himself into the sea. And if an occasional shark should stray into the vicinity of his boat, he must not suffer himself to be alarmed, for a single discharge from the fisherman's pistol (which he usually carries for that purpose) will be sure to frighten the monster out of his way. Gulls without number, large and small, of a dark-gray and a pure white, will be sure to fly screaming above his head, and their wild chorus will mingle well with the monotonous war of the waves as they sweep upon the shore. The fatigue attendant upon this mode of fishing is uncommonly great; and if the angler should happen to strike a forty-pounder, he will be perfectly satisfied with that single prize; but if his luck should lie among the smaller variety he ought to be content with about half a dozen specimens, weighing from ten to fifteen pounds, which would probably be the result of the morning's expedition. On returning to the shore, the angler will find himself in a most impatient mood for breakfast; but with a view of enhancing the anticipated enjoyment, he should first throw aside his clothes and make a number of plunges in the pure white surf, which will cause him to feel as strong and supple as a leopard.

We did think of commenting upon Block Island as a most fitting place to study the mighty ocean, for the waves which wash its shores come from the four quarters of the globe. It so happens, however, that we have just been reading a passage in an admirable little volume entitled "*The Owl Creek Letters*," (the author is a man after our own heart,) which was written at Block Island, and we are sure the passage in question would "take the wind out of any sail" that our pen might produce. The passage alluded to is as follows:—

"Men speak of our 'mother the earth.' But I never could appreciate the metaphor. A hard mother is old Terra. She refuses us food, save when compelled by hard struggling with her, and then yields it reluctantly. She deceives us too often, and finally takes us, when worn and weary, only by the difficult digging of a grave.

"But the ocean is mother-like, singing songs to us continually, and telling a thousand legends to our baby ears. She casts up toys to us on every shore, bright shells and pebbles. (What else do we live for?) True, maniac as she is, she sometimes raves madly and hurls her children from her arms, but see how instantly she clasps them again close, close to her heaving bosom, and how calmly and quietly they sleep there—as she sings to them—nor wake again to sorrow."

As to bass fishing in the vicinity of New York, where scientific anglers are abundant, it affords us pleasure to give our readers the following account, written at our request by G. C. Scott, Esq., who is distinguished for his love and practical knowledge of the gentle art.

"The weather and the tide are in our favor, and the moon all right—for this planet, you must know, always gives the bass an excellent appetite and great activity. Speaking of its influence upon the appetite of fish, reminds me that those in the waters near the ocean bite best when the moon is new; whilst salt water fish which are up the creeks and near to fresh water, are killed in the greatest number during high tides, and immediately after a hard 'nor'-easter,' when the wind has shifted to the north-west. You may prove these facts without going half a dozen miles from old Gotham, and I have always noticed that it is better fishing in the 'Kills' and at the hedges of Newark Bay, as well as at those in the lower part of the Bay of New York, when the tide is high; while the fishing at King's Bridge and the mouth of Spiting Devil is always best at extreme low tides.

"As we are out after bass, suppose we 'make a day of it,' and first try the bridge at Haerlam Dam. Being an angler yourself, you know of course that much depends upon bait, and we will want to use the best. As it is the month of August, we will purchase a few shedder crabs in the market; and if we find shrimp necessary, we can procure enough of them at either of the fishing-grounds. During the spring, I use shad roes for bass bait; but in summer, and until the first of October, I prefer shedder crab; after that, I use shrimp and soft-shell clams. Some anglers prefer shrimp at all seasons, as it is well known that small bass are more generally taken with them; but for my part, give me shedder crabs enough, and I will agree to forego the use of all other kinds of bait for bass. Next, you may want to know how to rig your tackle. Where we are going to-day, you want nothing but a good bass rod, reel, and float, with a single gut leader, to which you fasten a hook and attach it to the line one-third of its length from the hook. Use your float only when the tide runs slowly, for bottom-fishing is the best for large fish, unless you troll for them when you use a squid and fish in the Bronx with regular trolling tackle, of sufficient strength to land a fish weighing one hundred and fifty pounds, for they are sometimes caught there of that weight, but generally from thirty to eighty pounds.

"Well, having arrived at King's Bridge, and as it is about ebb tide, we will first see what we can kill from the east bridge. I like bridge fishing, for it is so fine to pay out line from; and then in striking a fish thirty yards off, there is so much sport in playing him, and your being such a distance above the water, you generally fasten him at the first bite. Reel off! reel off! you have struck him! There! give him play, but feel his weight and let him contend for every inch of line that you give him, or he will take the whole of it without exhausting himself, and you will lose him. Keep him in slack water, and after playing him until you kill him, land him on the shore, for he is too heavy to risk your tackle in raising him to the bridge. And now, having fished out the last of the ebb and the turn, until the tide runs too fast to use a float, just step into this punt and we will anchor out near to the edge of the current, by the first island below the mill, and fish in the current without the float, until the tide turns, when we will make for the mouth of the Spiting Devil, and fish fifty rods below it in the Hudson.

"Now, my friend, this day's sport may be considered a fair criterion for these grounds. We have taken between twenty and thirty bass, but there is only one that weighs over five pounds, and their average weight will not vary much from half that. To-night we will troll in the Bronx, for if the sky be clear, the bass will bite sooner at a squid 'by the light of the moon' than in the day-time; and there is very little use in stopping to try M'Comb's Dam, as the sport will not be first-rate there until the Croton aqueduct is finished and the coffer dam is torn away, so that the fish may have a clear run and unobstructed passage between the East and Hudson rivers. It is supposed that this will be effected next year, when M'Comb's Dam will retrieve its lost honors, and furnish one of the best places for sport in this vicinity to those who prefer bridge fishing.

"Having given you a taste of the sport on the waters bounding this island on the north and east, let us to-day fasten our punt to the lower hedges of New York Bay, and try the difference between 'bottom fishing,' and that 'with the float.' I will remark, in passing, that it is better to anchor your punt about a rod above the hedge and fish towards the hedge without a float, than to fasten your boat to the hedge, as commonly practised, and fish with a float; for you will notice that while you, in the old way, are continually reeling up and making casts, I am feeling for them with a moving bait towards the bottom, and as near the hedges as I can venture without getting fast. And then when I strike, I am sure to fasten them as they turn from me for the shelter of the hedge. I can also better play my bait without the danger of too much slack. You will see also that I kill the largest fish.

"Let us now up anchor and way for the Kills and to the reef opposite Port Richmond. Here the fish are about as large as those at the hedges we just left. The tide is nearly full, and we will fish without the float until it is about to turn, when we will move over to the Jersey shore, about fifty rods below the mouth of Newark Bay. Here, as the tide is just in the turn, we can fish an hour of the ebb with floats, when it will be best to try bottom-fishing again. Well, if you are tired of killing younglings, varying from one to three pounds, let us put the punt about and prepare for a beautiful row up to the third, ourth, and fifth hedges in Newark Bay—trying each one—and we may strike some fish that will try our tackle. Change your leader for a heavier one, and let go the anchor, for we are three rods above the hedge. The water is quite slack, and we will try the float until the tide ebbs a little more and the current becomes more rapid. There, sir, what think you of that? He feels heavy—see him spin! take care of your line or he'll get foul, as I cannot govern him, and it will be with great difficulty that I keep him out of the hedge. What a splendid leap! I'll see if I can turn him—here he comes—take the landing net—there! there, we have him, and I will bet the champagne that he weighs nearer twenty pounds than ten!

"Thus, my friend, having shown you the principal grounds, and informed you of the bait and tackle to be used in killing bass in this vicinity, I hope that you will not be at loss for piscatorial sport when trying your skill in the waters of old Gotham."

It is now time that we should say something about bass or rock fishing in the South. The only streams frequented by this fish, of which we have any personal knowledge, are the Potomac and Roanoke, though we have heard many wonderful stories related of the James River and the Great Pedee. In speaking of the Potomac we are sorely tempted to indite an episode upon the beautiful and magnificent sweeps which this river makes after it leaves the gorge of Harper's Ferry until it loses itself in Chesapeake Bay, and also upon its historical associations, among which the genius of Washington reigns supreme—but it is our duty to forbear, for we should occupy too much time.

Unquestionably, the finest rock-ground on the Potomac is the place known as the Little Falls, about four miles above Georgetown. At this point the river is only fifty yards wide, and as the water descends not more than about ten feet in running three hundred yards, the place might be more appropriately termed a schute than a fall. The banks on either side are abrupt and picturesque; the bed of the stream is of solid rock, and below the rapids are a number of inviting pools, where the water varies from forty to sixty feet in depth. The tides of the ocean reach no further up the Potomac than this spot, and though the rockfish are caught in considerable numbers at the Great Falls, (which are ten miles farther up the river, and exceedingly romantic,) yet they seem to be partial to the Little Falls, where they are frequently found in very great numbers. They follow the shad and the herring in the spring, but afford an abundance of sport from the 1st of May until the 4th of July, though they are caught in certain portions of the Potomac through the year, but never above the Great Falls. The rock of this portion of the Potomac vary in weight from two to eighteen or twenty pounds, and it is recorded of the anglers and business fishermen, that they frequently kill no less than five hundred fish in a single day. The favorite bait in this region is the belly part of the common herring, as well as the shiner and minnow; but it is frequently the case that a common yellow-flannel fly will commit sad havoc among the striped beauties. A stout rod, a large reel and a long line, are important requisites to the better enjoyment of rock-fishing at this point; but as the good standing-places are few in number, many anglers resort to boat-fishing, which is here practised with pleasure and profit. Of the many scientific anglers who visit the Little Falls during the spring and summer, the more expert ones come from Washington; and of one of these a story is related that he once killed no less than eighty handsome rockfish in a single afternoon. He occupied a dangerous position upon two pointed rocks in the river, (one foot upon each rock and elevated some five feet above the water,) and fished in a pool that was some seventy feet down the stream, while the fish were landed by an expert servant stationed on the shore about thirty feet below the spot occupied by the angler. The gentleman alluded to is acknowledged to be the most successful angler in this region, and in an occasional conversation with him, we have obtained a goodly number of piscatorial anecdotes. One or two of them are as follows:—

On one occasion, while playing a good-sized rockfish, it unfortunately ran around a sharp rock, and by cutting the line made its escape, carrying off the angler's float, and a favorite fly. On the third day after this event a boy who was playing on the river about half a mile below the falls, happened to see a cork darting hither and thither across the surface of the water, and immediately went in pursuit of the life-like piece of wood. After many twistings and turnings and a long row, he finally overtook it, and to his utter astonishment he landed in his boat a very handsome five pound bass. He recognized the fly as the one commonly employed by our angler, to whom the fly, the float, and the fish, were promptly delivered by the honest boy.

Another and a similar incident was as follows:—

Our angling friend had lost another float, by the obstinacy of a fish. About a week after this mishap a fisherman who had a "trot line" set across the river at Georgetown, for the purpose of taking catfish, saw a great splashing in the water near the middle of his line, and on hastening to the spot he had the pleasure of pulling up a very handsome twelve pound bass. After faring sumptuously upon the fish, the fortunate individual took it into his head that the tackle belonged to *the* angler of the falls, whereupon he delivered it to our friend, accompanied with a statement of the manner in which he made the discovery. The distance travelled by that fish, with a hook in his mouth, was four miles, and it was by the merest accident that his leading-string had become entangled with the "trot line."

The angling-ground at the Little Falls is annually rented by the proprietors to a couple of men named Joe Paine and Jim Collins, who are the presiding geniuses of the place, and have been such for upwards of twenty years. They pay a rent of seventy dollars per annum, and as they receive from fifty cents to five dollars from every angler who visits them, and as they are occasionally troubled with as many as thirty individuals per day, it may readily be imagined that their income is respectable. Some of Collins' friends allege that he has several thousand dollars stowed away in an old pocket-book, which it is his intention to bequeath to a favorite nephew, he himself being a bachelor. The reputation of Jim Collins in this section of country is very extensive, and that this should be the case is not at all strange, for he is a decided original. He is about fifty years of age, measures six feet five inches in height, and the offshoots from the four prongs of his body number *twenty-four* instead of twenty, as in ordinary mortals; I mean by this, that his fingers and toes number no less than twenty-four. Notwithstanding this bountiful supply of appendages, Jim Collins has a great antipathy to useful labor, and is as averse to walking as any web-footed animal. Fishing and sleeping are his two principal employments; and that he is a judge of good whisky, none of his acquaintance would have the hardihood to doubt. The taking of small fish he considers a business beneath his dignity, and the consequence is that his tackle consists of a miniature bed-cord, with a hook and cedar pole to match, and his bait a whole herring. He commonly fishes in a boat, and the dexterity with which he "*Kawallups*" the fish upon his lap is truly astonishing. But if you would see Jim Collins in his glory, wait until about the middle of a June afternoon, after he has pocketed some fifteen dollars, and he is sunning himself, with pipe in mouth, upon the rocks, absorbed in *fishy contemplations*. His appearance at such times is allied to that of a mammoth crane, watching (as he does his cockney brethren of the craft) the movements of a lot of half-fledged water birds.

During the fishing season he is generally actively employed, but the remainder of his time he spends about the Little Falls, as if his presence were indispensable to the safe passage of the waters of the Potomac through this narrow gorge. That Jim Collins should have met with many queer mishaps, during a residence of twenty years on the Potomac, may be readily imagined; but we believe the most unique adventure of which he has ever been the victim, happened on this wise. The substance of the story is as follows:—

Our hero is a great lover of "sturgeon meat," and for many years past it has been a habit with him to fish for that huge leather-mouthed monster, with a large cord and sharp grappling hooks, sinking them to the bottom with a heavy weight, and then dragging them across the bed of the stream; his sense of touch being so exquisite, that he can always tell the instant that his hooks have struck the body of a sturgeon, and when this occurs, it is almost certain that the fish becomes a victim to the cruel art. In practising this mode of fishing, Jim Collins invariably occupies a boat alone, which he first anchors in the stream. On one occasion he had been fishing in this manner for a long time without success, and for the want of something more exciting, he had resorted more frequently than usual to his junk bottle. In process of time, however, he found the exercise of fishing decidedly a bore, but as he was determined not to give up the sport, and at the same time was determined to enjoy a quiet nap, he tied the cord to his right arm, and lounged over on his back for the purpose of taking a snooze. There was an unusual calmness in the air and upon the neighboring hills, and even the few anglers who were throwing the fly at the Falls, did so in the laziest manner imaginable. While matters were in this condition, a sudden splash broke the surrounding stillness, which was immediately followed by a deafening shout, for it was discovered that a sturgeon had pulled poor Collins out of his boat into the swift stream, and he was in great danger of leading him off to the residence of *David Jones*. At one moment the fisherman seemed to have the upper hand, for he pulled upon his rope, and swore loudly, sprawling about the water like a huge devil fish; but in another instant the fellow would suddenly disappear, and an occasional bubble rising to the surface of the stream was all the evidence that he was not quite drowned. This contest lasted for some fifteen minutes, and had not the sturgeon finally made his escape, Jim Collins would have been no more. As it happened, however, he finally reached the shore, about two hundred yards below the Falls, and as he sat upon a rock, quite as near the river Styx as he was to the Potomac, he lavished some heavy curses upon the escaped sturgeon, and insisted upon it, that the best hooks that man ever made were now for ever lost. Years have elapsed since this occurrence took place, and when the ancient fisherman "hath his will," he recounts the story of this catastrophe with as brilliant a fire in his eye as that which distinguished the countenance of Coleridge's particular friend, the "Ancient Mariner."

Before closing this essay, it is proper that we should allude to the beautiful scenery that the angler will enjoy in going to and returning from the Little Falls. The entire region, in fact, known by the name of Cooney, and comprehending some fifteen miles of the Potomac, is particularly picturesque, but is at the same time said to be the most barren and useless portion of Virginia. In visiting the falls you have to pass over a kind of wooded and rocky interval, and by an exceedingly rough road, which is annually submerged by the spring freshets. The water here sometimes rises to the height of fifty feet, and often makes a terrible display of its power; on one occasion the water came down the valley with such impetuosity that a certain wall, composed of rocks six or eight feet square, and united together with iron, was removed to a distance of many rods from its original position. To the stranger who may visit the Little Falls, we would say, forget not on your return to Washington, the superb prospect which may be seen from the signal tree on the heights of Georgetown. From that point the eye comprehends at one glance, the church spires and elegant residences of Georgetown, the Metropolis of the land, with its capitol and numerous public buildings, and the more remote city of Alexandria, with a reach of the magnificent Potomac, extending a distance of at least thirty miles. The best time to look upon this prospect, is at the sunset hour, when the only sounds that fill the air are the shrieking of swallows, and the faintly heard song of a lazy sailor far away upon the river, where perhaps a score of vessels are lying becalmed, while on the placid stream a retinue of crimson clouds are clearly and beautifully reflected. Scenes of more perfect loveliness are seldom found in any land; and these we never witness without being reminded of the great and good Daniel Webster, with whom we have spent many summer mornings at the Little Falls, and also of his distinguished and intimate friend, the Hon. John F. Crampton, in whose society it is our good fortune frequently to throw the fly or spin the bait in these latter days.

PIKE FISHING.

If so be the angler catch no fish, yet hath he a wholesome walk to the brookside, and pleasant shade by the sweet silver streams.—ROBERT BURTON.

THE Pike is a common fish in all the temperate, and some of the northern regions of the world; but in no country does he arrive at greater perfection than in the United States. For some unaccountable reason he is generally known in this country as the pickerel; and we would therefore intimate to our readers that our present discourse is to be of the legitimate pike. In England, he is known under the several names of pike, jack, pickerel, and luce. His body is elongated, and nearly of a uniform depth from the head to the tail; the head is also elongated and resembles that of the duck; his mouth is very large and abundantly supplied with sharp teeth, and his scales are small and particularly adhesive; the color of his back is a dark brown, sides a mottled green or yellow, and belly a silvery white. The reputation of this fish for amiability is far from being enviable, for he is called not only the shark of the fresh waters, but also the tyrant of the liquid plain. He is a cunning and savage creature, and for these reasons even the most humane of fishermen are seldom troubled with conscientious scruples when they succeed in making him a captive. Pliny and Sir Francis Bacon both considered the pike to be the longest lived of any fresh water fish, and Gesner mentions a pike which he thought to be two hundred years old. Of these ancient fellows, Walton remarks, that they have more in them of state than goodness, the middle-sized individuals being considered the best eating. The prominent peculiarity of this fish is his voraciousness. Edward Jesse relates that five large pike once devoured about eight hundred gudgeons in the course of three weeks. He swallows every animal he can subdue, and is so much of a cannibal that he will devour his own kind full as soon as a common minnow. Young ducks and even kittens have been found in his stomach, and it is said that he often contends with the otter for his prey. Gessner relates that a pike once attacked a mule while it was drinking on the margin of a pond, and his teeth having become fastened in the snout of the astonished beast, he was safely landed on the shore. James Wilson once killed a pike weighing seven pounds, in whose stomach was found another pike weighing over a pound, and in the mouth of the youthful fish was yet discovered a respectable perch. Even men, while wading in a pond, have been attacked by this fresh-water wolf. He is so much of an exterminator, that when placed in a small lake with other fish, it is not long before he becomes "master of all he surveys," having depopulated his watery world of every species but his own. The following story, illustrating the savage propensity of this fish, is related by J. V. C. Smith. A gentleman was angling for pike, and having captured one, subsequently met a shepherd and his dog, and presented the former with his prize. While engaged in clearing his tackle, the dog seated himself unsuspectingly in the immediate vicinity of the pike, and as fate would have it, his tail was ferociously snapped at by the gasping fish. The dog was of course much terrified, ran in every direction to free himself, and at last plunged into the stream. The hair had become so entangled in the fish's teeth, however, that it could not release its hold. The dog again sought the land, and made for his master's cottage, where he was finally freed from his unwilling persecutor; but notwithstanding the unnatural adventure of the fish, he actually sunk his teeth into the stick which was used to force open his jaws.

The pike of this country does not differ essentially from the pike of Europe. His food usually consists of fish and frogs, though he is far from being particular in this matter. He loves a still, shady water, in river or pond, and usually lies in the vicinity of flags, bulrushes, and water-lilies, though he often shoots out into the clear stream, and on such occasions frequently affords the riflemen good sport. In summer he is taken at the top and the middle, but in winter at the bottom. His time for spawning is March, and he is in season about eight months in the year. In speaking of the size of this fish, the anglers of Europe have recorded some marvellous stories, of which we know nothing, and care less. In this country they vary from two to four feet in length, and in weight from two to forty pounds; when weighing less than two pounds, he is called a jack. As an article of food he seems to be in good repute; but since we once found a large water-snake in the stomach of a monster fish, we have never touched him when upon the table. He suits not our palate, but as an object of sport we esteem him highly, and can never mention his name without a thrill of pleasure.

In this place we desire to record our opinion against the idea that the pike and muskalounge are one and the same fish. For many years we entertained the opinion that there was no difference between them, only that the latter was merely an overgrown pike. We have more recently had many opportunities of comparing the two species together, and we know that to the careful and scientific observer, there is a marked difference. The head of a muskalounge is the smallest; he is the stoutest fish, is more silvery in color, grows to a much larger size, and is with difficulty tempted to heed the lures of the angler. They are so precisely similar in their general habits, however, that they must be considered as belonging to the pike family. They are possibly the independent, eccentric, and self-satisfied nabobs of the race to which they belong; always managing to keep the world ignorant of their true character, until after their days are numbered.

We will now mention one or two additional traits, which we had nearly forgotten. The first is, that the pike is as distinguished for his abstinence as for his voracity. During the summer months, his digestive organs seem to be somewhat torpid, and this is the time he is out of season. During this period he is particularly listless in his movements, spending nearly all the sunny hours basking near the surface of the water; and as this is the period when the smaller fry are usually commencing their active existence, we cannot but distinguish in this arrangement of nature the wisdom of Providence. Another habit peculiar to this fish is as follows:—During the autumn, he spends the day-time in deep water, and the night in the shallowest water he can find along the shores of river or lake. We have frequently seen them so very near the dry land as to display their fins. What their object can be in thus spending the dark hours, it is hard to determine: is it to enjoy the warmer temperature of the shallow water, or for the purpose of watching and capturing any small land animals that may come to the water to satisfy their thirst? We have heard it alleged that they seek the shore for the purpose of spawning, but it is an established fact that they cast their spawn in the spring; and, besides, the months during which they seek the shore as above stated, are the very ones in which they are in the best condition, and afford the angler the finest sport. Autumn is the time, too, when they are more frequently and more easily taken with the spear, than during any other season. And as to this spearing business, generally speaking, we consider it an abominable practice; but in the case of the savage and obstinate pike, it ought to be countenanced even by the legitimate angler.

We have angled for pike in nearly all the waters of this country where they abound. The immense quantity of book lore that we have read respecting the character of pike tackle, has always seemed to us an intelligent species of nonsense—a kind of literature originally invented by tackle manufacturers, or up-start cockney foreigners, who follow book-making as a trade. Our own equipment for pike fishing we consider first-rate, and yet it consists only of a heavy rod and reel, a stout linen line, a brass leader, a sharp Kirby hook, and a landing-net. For bait we prefer a live minnow, though a small shiner, or the belly of a yellow perch, is nearly as sure to attract notice. We have taken a pike with a gaudy fly, and also with an artificial minnow, but you cannot depend upon these allurements. Sinkers we seldom use, and the fashionable thing called a float we utterly abominate. We have fished for pike in almost every manner, but our favorite method has ever been from an anchored boat, when our only companion was a personal friend, and a lover of the written and unwritten poetry of nature. This is the most quiet and contemplative method, and unquestionably one of the most successful ones; for though the pike is not easily frightened, it takes but a single splash of an oar when trolling, to set him a-thinking, which is quite as unfortunate for the angler's success as if he were actually alarmed. Another advantage is, that while swinging to an anchor you may fish at the bottom, if you please, or try the stationary trolling fashion. To make our meaning understood, we would add, that an expert angler can throw his hook in any direction from his boat, to the distance of at least a hundred feet, and in pulling it in, he secures all the advantages that result from the common mode of trolling. The pike is a fish which calls forth a deal of patience, and must be humored; for he will sometimes scorn the handsomest bait, apparently out of mere spite; but the surest time to take him is when there is a cloudy sky and a southerly breeze. Live fish are the best bait, as we have before remarked, though the leg of a frog is good, and in winter a piece of pork, but nothing can be better than a shiner or a little perch; and it might here be remarked, that as the pike is an epicure in the manner of his eating, it is invariably a good plan to let him have his own time, after he has seized the bait. As to torchlight fishing for pike, though unquestionably out of the pale of the regular angler's sporting, it is attended with much that we must deem poetical and interesting. Who can doubt this proposition when we consider the picturesque effect of a boat and lighted torch, gliding along the wild shores of a lake, on a still, dark night, with one figure noiselessly plying an oar, and the animated attitude of another relieved against the fire-light, and looking into the water like Orpheus into hell? And remember, too, the thousand inhabitants of the liquid element that we see, and almost fancy to be endowed with human sympathies. What a pleasure to behold the various finny tribes amid their own chosen haunts, leading, as Leigh Hunt has exquisitely written,

> "A cold, sweet, silver life, wrapped in round waves,
> Quickened with touches of transporting fear!"

In some of the Northern States, fishing for pike with set lines through the ice, is practised to a great extent. The lines are commonly attached to a figure four, by which the fisherman is informed that he has a bite, and if he has many lines out, and the fish are in a humor to be captured, this mode of fishing is really very exciting. Especially so, if the ice is smooth, and the fisherman can attend to his hooks, with a pair of sharp skates attached to his feet.

Another mode for catching pike in the winter, and which we have seen practised in the lakes and rivers of Michigan, is as follows. You cut a large hole in the ice, over which you erect a tent or small portable house; and after taking a seat therein, you let down a bait for the purpose of alluring the fish, and as they follow the hook, even to your feet, you pick them out with a sharp spear. In the St. Lawrence they are also taken through the ice, but there the bait and hook are only employed, the spear being exclusively used for torch-light fishing.

But it is time that we should change the tone of our discourse, and mention the favorite waters of the American pike. The largest we have ever seen were taken in the upper Mississippi, and on the St. Joseph and Raisin rivers of Michigan, where they are very abundant. They are also found in nearly all the streams emptying into Lakes Michigan, Erie, and Ontario;—also, in the Ohio and its tributaries. We have heard of them in the upper St. Lawrence, and know them to abound in Lake Champlain, and in a large proportion of the lakes and rivers of New England. A very pretty lady once told us that she had seen a pike taken from Lake Champlain, which was as long as the sofa upon which we were seated together, conversing upon the gentle art of fishing, and the tender one of love. Pike

WINTER FISHING ON THE ST. LAWRENCE.

fishing with the hook we have not practised to a very great extent. Our angling experience has been chiefly confined to the smaller lakes of Connecticut, particularly those in the vicinity of Norwich. Our favorite resort has been Gardner's Lake, whose shores are surrounded with pleasant wood-crowned hills, teeming with partridge and woodcock, and the Sabbath stillness which usually reigns about it is seldom broken, save by the dipping oar, or the laugh of the light-hearted fisherman. Dearly indeed do we cherish the memory of the pleasant days spent upon this picturesque lake; and we hope it may never be used for any other purpose than to mirror the glories of heaven, and never be visited by any but genuine sportsmen and true-hearted lovers of Nature. Preston Lake is another beautiful sheet of water near Norwich, which reminds us of a night adventure. A couple of us had visited it for the purpose of taking pike by torch-light, having brought our spears and dry-pine all the way from Norwich in a one-horse wagon. It was a cold but still autumnal night, and as we tied our horse to a tree in an open field, we had every reason to anticipate a "glorious time." So far as the fish were concerned, we enjoyed fine sport, for we caught about a dozen pike, varying from one to four pounds in weight; but the miseries we subsequently endured were positively intolerable. We had much difficulty in making our boat seaworthy, and, in our impatience to reach the fishing-grounds, we misplaced our brandy bottle in the tall grass, and were therefore deprived of its warming companionship. About midnight, a heavy fog began to rise, which not only prevented us from distinguishing a pike from a log of wood, but caused us to become frequently entangled in the top of a dry tree, lying on the water. Our next step, therefore, was to go home, but then came the trouble of finding our "desired haven." This we did happen to find, for a wonder, and having gathered up our plunder, started on our course over the frosty grass after our vehicle and horse. We found them, but it was in a most melancholy plight indeed. Like a couple of large fools, we had omitted to release the horse from the wagon, as we should have done, and the consequence was that he had released himself, by breaking the fills and tearing off the harness, and we discovered him quietly feeding a few paces from the tree to which we had fastened him. What next to do we could not in our utter despair possibly determine; but after a long consultation, we both concluded to mount the miserable horse, and with our fish in hand actually started upon our miserable journey home. Our fish were so heavy, that we were compelled at the end of the first mile to throw them away, and as the day was breaking, we entered the silent streets of Norwich, pondering upon the pleasures of pike fishing by torch-light, and solemnly counting the cost of our nocturnal expedition.

But the most successful pike fishing we ever enjoyed was at Crow Wing, on the upper Mississippi. We were spending a few days with an isolated Indian trader of the wilderness, round whose cabin were encamped about three hundred Chippewa Indians. Seldom was it that we allowed a night to pass away without trying our luck with the spear, and as a dozen canoes were often engaged in the same sport, the bosom of the river presented a most romantic and beautiful appearance. Each canoe usually contained two or three individuals, and our torches, which were made of dried birch bark, threw such a flood of light upon the translucent water, that we could see every object in the bed of the river with the utmost distinctness. Beautiful indeed were those fishing scenes, and when the canoes had floated down the river for a mile or two, the homeward-bound races that followed between the shouting Indians, were exciting in the extreme. And what added to *our* enjoyment of this sporting, was the idea that to grasp the hand of a white man, (besides that of our host,) we should have to travel one hundred miles through a pathless wilderness. We seldom took any note of time, and sometimes were throwing the spear even when the day was breaking. The largest fish that we saw taken at Crow Wing weighed upwards of forty pounds, and we have known five spearmen to take seventy pike and muskalounge in a single night.

But we must curtail our pike stories, for we purpose to append to our remarks a few interesting observations upon that and a kindred fish, which have been kindly furnished to us by a genuine angler, and valued friend, John R. Bartlett, Esq.

The pike bears the same relation to the finny tribes that the hyena and jackal do to animals, the vulture to birds, or the spider to insects—one of the most voracious of fishes. He feeds alike on the living or dead; and even those of his own brethren which are protected by nature against the attacks of other fish, find no protection against him. It is remarkable in the economy of animals, that while nature provides her weaker and smaller creatures with the means of defence against the stronger ones, she has, at the same time, furnished some of the latter with weapons, apparently for the very purpose of overcoming the feeble, however well they may be guarded. Thus, the pike, with its immense jaws, armed with innumerable teeth, is able to seize and crush every kind of fish. Its own kind do not escape, for instances are frequent when a pike of three or four pounds is found in the stomach of one of twelve or fifteen pounds weight.

It is interesting to notice the habits of the pike, which an angler may easily do in still, clear water. They have been characterized as a solitary, melancholy, and bold fish. Never are they found in schools, or even in pairs, as most other fish are, nor are they often seen in open water, where other fish would discover them, and avoid their grasp. When in open water, they lie very near the bottom, quite motionless, appearing like a sunken stick. Their usual and favorite place of resort is among the tall weeds, where they cannot be seen. Here they lie, as it were, in ambush, waiting the approach of some innocent, unsuspecting fish, when they dart forth with a swiftness which none of the finny tribe can attain, seize their harmless victim, and slowly bear it away to some secluded spot. Here they crush their prey with their immense jaws, and leisurely force it into their capacious stomachs. Often, when angling for the pike with a live perch, from a wharf so far raised above the water that we could see every object for twenty feet on either side, a pike has so suddenly darted from a cluster of weeds, beyond the range of our vision, that the first intimation we had of his presence was, that he had seized our bait.

On one occasion, when angling in the St. Lawrence, where pike are very abundant, we put a minnow on our hook, and threw our line towards a mass of weeds, in the hope of tempting a perch to take it. Not many minutes had elapsed before our silvery minnow had tempted the appetite of one, which soon conveyed him to his maw. Knowing that our game was sure, we let him play about, first allowing him to run to the extent of our line, and then drawing him towards us, when, on a sudden, a pike shot from his hiding-place and seized the perch. We were obliged to let the fellow have his own way, and give him all the time he wanted to swallow the perch, when, with a good deal of difficulty, we succeeded in disabling him, and to tow him in triumph to the shore. The perch weighed a pound and a half; the pike ten pounds.

The long and slender form of the pike, tapering towards the head and tail, enables him to move with great rapidity through the water, while his smooth and finless back facilitates his movements through the weeds or marine plants. Thus has nature provided this fish with a form adapted to its habits, and with large and well-armed jaws, to give it a pre-eminence among the finny tribes which inhabit the same waters. We have often thought why so great an enemy, so great a devourer of his race, should be placed among them, favored by so many advantages. May it not, nay, must it not be for some wise purpose? It is known how very prolific fishes are, and unless some way was provided to lessen the number, our inland waters could not contain the vast numbers which a few years would produce. Most fish live on each other, others on decomposing substances floating about. It is not always the largest that prey on each other, for the sturgeon is one of the largest fresh-water fish, and he subsists on decomposing matter or minute fish. A few pike placed in a lake, would very effectually prevent an over-population. May it not, then, be so ordered, that the inhabitants of the seas, which are not so favored as those who dwell on the earth's surface, and who have a great variety of food to supply their wants, may have the means of providing their own sustenance by an immense increase of their own species?

Blaine observes that "the abstinence of the pike and jack is no less singular than their voracity; during the summer months their digestive faculties are somewhat torpid, which appears a remarkable peculiarity in pike economy, seeing it must be in inverse ratio to the wants of the fish, for they must be at this time in a state of emaciation from the effects of spawning. During the summer they are listless, and affect the surface of the water, where in warm sunny weather they seem to bask in a sleepy state for hours together. It is not a little remarkable, that smaller fish appear to be aware when this abstinent state of their foe is upon him; for they who at other times are evidently impressed with an instinctive dread of his presence, are now swimming around him with total unconcern. At these periods, no baits, however tempting, can allure him; but on the contrary, he retreats from everything of the kind. Windy weather is alone capable of exciting his dormant powers. This inaptitude to receive food with the usual keenness, continues from the time they spawn, until the time of their recovery from the effects of it."

The peculiarity above noticed does not entirely apply to the pike of the Northern States, and particularly of the great lakes and rivers whose waters are not so sensibly affected by the heat of summer as shallow water is. In the smaller streams he lies in the listless state described by Mr. Blaine, but when he can reach the deep water he always does so.

Pike are found in all the lakes and inland waters of the Northern and Middle States of the Union. In the great lakes they grow to an enormous size. No fish is better known throughout Europe and the northern parts of Asia. In colder climes he attains the largest size, and is said by Walkenburg to disappear in geographical distribution with the fir. In our waters they are taken of all sizes, from four or five pounds to fifty or sixty. Their haunts are generally among the weeds or marine plants near the shore, or in deep bays where the water is not made rough by winds, and in all parts of rivers. They are rarely found on rocky bottoms or bars. A high wind and rough sea often drives them from their weedy haunts into deeper water. From wharves where bass are only taken on ordinary occasions, pike will bite with avidity when a severe gale is blowing, and the water is in a disturbed state.

This fish, according to Donovan, attains a larger size in a shorter time, in proportion to most others. In the course of the first year it grows eight or ten inches; the second, twelve or fourteen; the third, eighteen or twenty inches. Some pike were turned into a pond in England, the largest of which weighed two and a half pounds. Four years after, the water was let off, when one pike of nineteen pounds, and others of from eleven to fifteen, were found. Mr. Jesse, in his Gleanings of Natural History, relates certain experiments by which he shows that the growth of pike is about four pounds a year, which corresponds with the growth of those before stated.

The various books on sporting give numerous instances of pike weighing from thirty to forty pounds, taken in England, though an instance is mentioned in Dodsley's Register for 1765, of an enormous pike weighing one hundred and seventy pounds, which was taken from a pool near Newport, England, which had not been fished in for ages. In Ireland and Scotland, they are found larger than in England. In the Shannon and Lough Corrib, they have been found from seventy to ninety-two pounds weight. At Broadford, near Limerick, one was taken weighing ninety-six pounds. Another was caught by trolling in Loch Pentluliche, of fifty pounds; and another in Loch Spey, that weighed one hundred and forty-six pounds. But these are small in comparison with a pike, which is stated by Gesner (and from him quoted by most writers on fish) to have been taken in a pool near the capital of Sweden, in the year 1497, which was fifteen feet in length, and weighed three hundred and fifty pounds. Under the skin of this enormous fish was discovered a ring of Cyprus brass, having a Greek inscription round the rim, which was interpreted by Dalburgus, Bishop of Worms, to signify: "I am the fish first of all placed in this pond, by the hands of Frederic the Second, on the 5th of October, in the year of grace 1230;" which would make its age two hundred and sixty-seven years. The ring about his neck was made with springs, so as to enlarge as the fish grew. His skeleton was for a long time preserved at Manheim.

During the past summer which we spent on the banks of the St. Lawrence, we had frequently tried the spool-trolling, and always with success. Sometimes we would use two lines, one seventy the other one hundred and twenty feet in length. On the longer one we had the best success, and our bait would be seized three times, when on the shorter one it would be but once; it being farther from the boat, the movements of which through the water, and the noise of the oars, drove the fish off. From experience we are satisfied that long trolling-lines are the best. Bass will seize a fly or spoon at a few feet distance, but a pike will not. We have tried the experiment, when trolling for pike, to attach to one hook a bait of pork and red flannel, a very common bait, and to the other a brass spoon. The latter was invariably seized first, for the reason, that it made more show in the water. Neither resembled a fish, fly, or any living creature, but curiosity or hunger attracted the fish to the strange bait gliding through the water, which they seized, paying with their lives the penalty for so doing.

There is a large fish of the pike species commonly called the muskalounge or maskalunge before spoken of, of what specific character is not well understood by naturalists. Their habits and their haunts are the same as those of the pike, and they attain a larger size than any fish of our inland waters. We have seen them carried by two men of ordinary height, with a pole running through the gills and supported on the shoulders of the men. In this position the tail of the fish dragged on the ground. Forty or fifty pounds is not an unusual weight for them, and instances are known when much larger ones have been caught. Muskalounge are generally taken in seines, seldom with the hook. Their size is so large that the ordinary baits of anglers would be no temptation to them. In the several opportunities which we have had to examine the stomachs of the fish, we have invariably found within them fish of very large size, such as no angler would ever think of putting on his line. The largest perch we ever saw, about fifteen inches in length, was taken from the paunch of a muskalounge, and we have often seen catfish, perch, and other fish weighing from one to two pounds, taken from them; but in no instance small fish; and hence anglers have not taken them, as few would angle with live bait of that size, where there are no fish but these which would take it.

The most exciting sport we ever had on the St. Lawrence, was capturing a muskalounge. It was a regular battle, such only as salmon anglers enjoy when they hook a twenty-pounder. As the method was very different, we will state the particulars.

A friend and ourself took a small skiff, with one trolling line, intending to take turns at the oars, and proceeded at once to a favorite spot among the "Thousand Islands."

We held the trolling line with a spoon hook attached, while our companions pulled the oars. We sailed among the secluded places, wherever weeds were seen below the surface of the water, and were rewarded with good sport by taking several fine pike, weighing from six to fifteen pounds, which we managed to secure with ease, save the largest, which gave us some trouble. We then thought we would try deeper water, in the hope of tempting larger fish. A few windings among the clusters of small islands brought us to the channel of the river, when we directed our companion to increase the speed of the skiff, determined that the curiosity of no fish should be satisfied, without first tasting our gilded spoon. We pulled for half a mile, when the river wound suddenly round an island, which presented a bold shore, from the rushing of the river's current. The tall forest-trees extended to the very brink of the river, over which they hung, throwing a deep shadow on the water. This quiet spot looked as though it might be an attractive one for some solitary fish, and we accordingly took a sweep around the foot of the island. Scarcely had we entered the deep shade spoken of, when we felt a tug at our line, which was so strong that we supposed our hook had come in contact with a floating log or fallen tree. Our companion backed water with his oars to relieve our hook, when another violent pull at our line convinced us that it was no log, but some living creature of great weight. Our line was already out its full length of one hundred and fifty feet; no alternative was therefore left but to give my fish more line by rowing after him.

This we did for a few minutes, when we began to pull in the slack of our line, some fifty feet or more, when we felt the fish. The check was no sooner felt by him than he started forward with a velocity scarcely conceivable in the water, bringing the line taut, and the next moment our skiff was moving off stern foremost towards the river's channel. We soon perceived that our fish had turned his head up stream, and as the water was deep, there was no danger of his coming in contact with weeds or protruding rocks. We therefore allowed him to tow us for about five minutes, when he stopped. Then quickly backing water with our oars, and taking in our line, we carefully laid it over the skiff's side, until we had approached within twenty feet of our fish. We then gave him another check, which probably turned his head, for he again darted off in a contrary direction down stream. We pulled our skiff in the same direction as fast as possible to give the fish a good run before checking him again, but he soon had the line out its full length, and was again towing our skiff after him with more rapidity than before. This did not last long, however, for we then took the line and hauled towards him to lessen our distance. He made another slap, when we managed to keep the line taut, and with our oars moved towards him. Our victim now lay on the surface of the water with his belly upward, apparently exhausted, when we found him to be a muskalounge, between five and eight feet in length. We had no sooner got him alongside than he gave a slap with his tail and again darted off the whole length of the line, taking us once more in tow. His run was now short, and it was evident he was getting tired of the business. Again the line slacked, and we drew the skiff up to the spot where he lay turned upon his back.

He now seemed so far gone that we thought we might draw

him into our skiff, so we reached out our gaff and hooked him under the jaw, while my companion passed his oar under him. In this way we contrived to raise him over the gunwale of the skiff, when he slid to its bottom. We then placed our foot at the back of his head to hold him down, in order to disengage our hook, which passed through his upper jaw. No sooner had we attempted this than he began to flap about, compelling us to give him room to avoid his immense jaws. Every moment seemed to increase his strength, when our companion seized an oar in order to dispatch him, while we took out our knife for the same purpose. The first blow with the oar had only the effect to awaken our fish, which, taking another and more powerful somerset, threw himself over the gunwale of our skiff, which was but a few inches above the water, and with a plunge disappeared in the deep water at our side. We had scarcely recovered from our surprise, when we found the line drawn out again to its full length, save a few tangles and twists, which had got into it in the struggle between us and our fish. We determined to trifle no longer with the fellow, with our small skiff, but to make for the shore and there land him. A small island a short distance from us, seemed to present a convenient place, and here, without further ceremony, we pulled, towing our fish after us. We leaped into the water about ten feet from the shore, and tugged away at my victim, who floated like a log upon the water, while my companion stood by with an oar to make the capture more sure this time. In this way we landed him in safety just one hour and a quarter after he was first hooked. This muskalounge weighed forty-nine pounds, and had within him a pike of three pounds weight, a chub, partially decomposed, of four pounds, and a perch of one and a half pounds, which appeared to have been but recently swallowed; yet this fish's appetite was not satisfied, and he lost his life in grasping at a glittering bauble. Any person who has ever killed a pike of ten pounds or upwards, can readily imagine the strength of one five times that weight.

The great strength of these fish was shown in a sporting adventure which happened to a friend of mine when out a few evenings since, spearing by torchlight. The person alluded to had never before tried his hand with the spear, although he was a skillful angler. On this occasion he had killed several fish, which he secured without trouble. He was then in about six or eight feet of water, when he discovered a large fish, either a very large pike or muskalounge. He planted himself with one foot below the flaming torch, the other a little behind, when he plunged his spear into the huge fish that lay so quietly before him; but whether he was so deceived in the depth of the water, or whether he had not braced himself properly in the boat, is not known, at any rate he struck the fish, which darted off like lightning, taking the spear with him, as well as him who threw it. For the gentleman, probably deceived by the depth of the water, had reached forward too far and thereby lost his balance. So over he went head foremost, holding on to the spear. But he was satisfied without following the fish further, which escaped with the long spear, neither of which could be again seen. The gentleman made the best of his way into the skiff. Two days after a large muskalounge floated ashore several miles below the spot where the event took place, with the spear still clinging to him, just before the dorsal fin.

But the scenic attractions of the Thousand Islands, are quite equal to its attractions piscatorial. That portion of the St. Lawrence so named, extends from Lake Ontario about forty miles down the river; and while the upper part is eleven miles wide, it gradually narrows as you descend, and is said to contain sixteen hundred islands. They are of every form and size, and while the larger ones are covered with well tilled farms, the great majority are composed of a few rocks, a little earth, and a pleasing variety of northern trees. On one of them are the picturesque ruins of an old fort, by the side of another are a couple of sunken men-of-war hulls, while upon others may occasionally be seen, mournful Indian graves. Muskalounge, pike, and black bass, are the principal game fish taken here, and to angle among these islands, when autumn is in its prime, seems more like enchantment than reality. The waters vary in depth from five to eighty feet, flow at the rate of three miles an hour, and though generally ice-bound during the long winters of this latitude, there is one spot, between two islands near the north shore, which is never frozen on account of a warm spring which bubbles from the bottom of the stream; and what is more, local Indian legends may be picked up among these charming islands, and rare characters, in the way of habitan fishermen and hunters, be stumbled upon, which will make the remembrance of the place perennial.

FISHING IN GENERAL.

We have, indeed, often thought that angling alone offers to man the degree of half-business, half-idleness which the fair sex find in their needle-work or knitting, which employing the hands, leaves the mind at liberty, and occupying the attention, so far as is necessary to remove the painful sense of a vacuity, yet yields room for contemplation, whether upon things heavenly or earthly, cheerful or melancholy.—SIR WALTER SCOTT.

IN the preceding articles we have given the public the substance of our experience in regard to our five favorite fish, the salmon, trout, pike, rock, and black bass. On the present occasion we purpose to embody within the limits of a single article, our stock of information upon the remaining fish of the United States, which properly come under the jurisdiction of the angler. We shall proceed in our remarks after the manner of the dictionary-makers, and shall take up each variety without any regard to their order, but as they may happen to come into our mind.

The Perch.—With two members of this family alone are we personally acquainted, viz. the yellow perch and the white perch. The first is a beautiful fish, and found in nearly all the waters of the Northern and Middle States, and probably as well known throughout the world as any of the finny tribes. Its predominating color is yellow; it has an elegant form, is a bold biter, varies in weight from four ounces to a pound, (although occasionally found in New England weighing two pounds;) has a dry and sweet flesh, but ill adapted to satisfy the cravings of a hungry man on account of its bones, which are particularly numerous, hard and pointed. They generally swim about in *schools*, and yet at the same time are not at all distinguished for their intelligence, being invariably allured to destruction by the most bungling anglers, and the more common kinds of bait. They spawn in the spring, and recover, so as to be in fine condition, early in the autumn. They delight in clear rivers or lakes, with pebbly bottoms, though sometimes found on sandy or clayey soils. They love a moderately deep water, and frequent holes at the mouths of small streams, or the hollows under the banks. With regard to the white perch we have only to say that it is well described by its name, is a migratory fish, found in nearly all the rivers of the Atlantic coast, from Boston to Norfolk; but particularly abundant in the Delaware, Susquehanna and Potomac; and they weigh from six ounces to one pound, are in season during the spring and summer, are capital as an article of food, and afford the entire brotherhood of anglers an abundance of sport. As touching the name of the fish now before us, we desire to chronicle our opinion respecting an important instance in which it has been misapplied. Many years ago, while reading the remarkable and intensely interesting work of Audubon on the birds of America, we chanced upon the description of a fish, found in the Ohio, to which he gave the name of white perch. Subsequently to that period, while sojourning in the city of Cincinnati, we happened to remember Mr. Audubon's description, and one morning visited the market for the purpose of examining the fish. We found them very abundant, and were informed that they commanded a high price. On examining the fish, however, in view of certain doubts that we had previously entertained (for we knew that the white perch of the books was a native of salt water,) we found it to be not a legitimate white perch, but simply the fish known in Lake Erie as the fresh water sheepshead, and in New York as the growler. But this misapplication of the term perch is not peculiar to the residents on the Ohio, for we know that, throughout the Southern States where the black bass is found, it is universally called the black perch or trout; and that in the vicinity of Boston and Nahant the miserable little fish called the conner is there designated as a black perch.

That there are several varieties of the real perch besides those mentioned, we do not deny, but we feel confident that the above correction cannot be refuted.

The Muskalounge and Pickerel.—Both of these fish are peculiar to the United States, and especially to the Great Lakes, and the waters of the St. Lawrence and Mississippi. The former belongs unquestionably to the pike family, although commonly weighing from twenty to forty pounds, while many people affirm that it is only an overgrown pike. They are valued as an article of food, and, by those who are fond of killing the most savage of game at the expense of much labor, they are highly appreciated. The best and about the only valuable account of this fish that we have ever seen, was written by George W. Clinton, Esq., and published in the Buffalo Commercial Advertiser. As to the fish which we call the pickerel, we have to say that it occupies a position somewhere between the trout and perch; that it is a favorite with the anglers of Lake Champlain, Lake Erie, and Lake Michigan, and with those also who practise the gentle art along the borders of the Ohio and the Tennessee. It is an active fish, of a roundish form, with large mouth and sharp teeth, and covered with small scales, the predominating colors being a dark green and yellowish white. The name which it bears is the one so generally applied, but erroneously, to the legitimate pike. It is also the same fish known in the South-west as the salmon, but as unlike the peerless creature of the far North as a grey wolf is unlike a deer. As is the case with the muskalounge, the pickerel is among the first of the finny tribes that run up our Western rivers early in the spring; and in the waters of Lake Champlain and the St. Lawrence they are found herding with the yellow perch, and we believe that in some districts they are considered as belonging to the perch family.

The Catfish.—This fish is distinguished for its many deformities, and is a great favorite with all persons who have a fancy for muddy waters. In the Mississippi they are frequently taken weighing upwards of one hundred pounds; and while they are taken in all the tributaries of that river, it has been ascertained that they decrease in size as you ascend towards the north. They are also found in the tributaries of Lake Erie. They are taken with any kind of bait; and as they are very strong, the best of tackle is invariably necessary. This fish is also found in many of the lakes of New England, where they seldom weigh more than two pounds, being there known as the horn or bull pout, owing to a peculiar pectoral thorn with which they are adorned. Their flesh, though not particularly sweet, is said to be easily digested, and they are often sought for by people with weak stomachs. But it has always seemed to us that it required a very *powerful* stomach to eat a piece from one of the mammoths of the Western waters.

As to the remaining fresh-water fish of the country, we will content ourself by merely mentioning the names of those which are known to our anglers, to wit: the chub, dace, white bass, sunfish, roach, bream, and rock bass. The fish called in Virginia and Maryland the fall fish, is identical with the dace. In the waters of the West the mullet, fresh water sheepshead, and sucker, are found in immense numbers, but they are all exceedingly poor eating, and as sporting fish are of no account. The sturgeon, we believe, is found almost everywhere, and known to almost everybody.

There is a fish found in Florida which belongs to the bass family, abounds in all the rivers, lakes, and springs of this State, is a bold biter, reaches the weight of fifteen pounds, has a white and sweet flesh, and is taken in very much the manner employed by northern anglers in capturing the pike, and with similar artificial baits. This fish is called a trout, but is in reality a variety of the black bass. The fish known as the *gar-pike* is universal in this country and though not eaten, is frequently captured for the mere sport. Its natural history is peculiar and of great interest to naturalists. At the present time it is found exclusively in North America, and yet the fossils of the old world prove that it was once cosmopolite in its geographical distribution. It is supposed to be a link connecting the fish with the reptile, since it is the only fish known which has the power of moving its head on the neck freely, in all directions.

We now come to our favorites of the ocean and tide-water rivers; and the first fish that we mention is the *black fish*, or *tautog*, as it was called by the Mohegan Indians. It is a stationary inhabitant of the salt water, and usually found upon reefs and along rocky shores. It is taken all along the Atlantic coast between New York and Boston, but it has been known north of Cape Cod only within a few years; its legitimate home is Long Island Sound. It is an active, bold, strong, and tough fish, highly esteemed as an article of food, and, like the cod, is brought to the principal markets in floating cars, in which confinement they are said to fatten. They are by no means a handsome fish, and their scales are so adhesive as to be taken off only with the skin. They are a summer fish, being taken as early as April, and no later than October. A three-pounder is considered a good fish, but we have often taken them weighing ten pounds, and have seen them weighing fifteen pounds. They are generally taken with the hand line, and no better bait can be employed than the lobster or soft crab.

The Sheepshead.—This is a thickset but rather handsome fish, and, for the sweetness of its flesh, highly esteemed. They are seldom seen in the New York market, but very common in the Charleston and Mobile markets, from which we infer that they are partial to southern waters. They vary in weight from three pounds to fourteen; live exclusively upon shellfish, and invariably command a high price. They are popular with the anglers, for they swim in shoals, and are captured with but little trouble. They are most abundant in the Gulf of Mexico. Another popular fish, peculiar to southern States, is the *Blue Bream*, which takes the fly, and attains the weight of one pound, but is only found in fresh water streams or lakes. The *Drum* is also a noted southern fish. It is the largest *scale* fish that we have, and derives its name from a noise it is in the habit of making during the spawning season. It is the most abundant on the coasts of the Carolinas and Georgia, is taken ten months in the year, but only takes the hook during the *love* season.

The Blue Fish.—The name of this glorious fish reminds us

of the ground swell, and sends through our whole frame a thrill of pleasure. They are a species of mackerel, attaining in certain places the weight of a dozen pounds. They swim in shoals, and are taken with a trolling line and an ivory squid. Our favorite mode for taking them has ever been from a small boat with a hand line, though many people prefer taking them from a sail-boat when running before a breeze. They are quite as active a fish as we have ever seen, and the strength of their jaws is so great that we have known them to bite off a man's finger. When fresh and fat we consider them quite as delicate as the real mackerel, and much better than the black fish. They are found on the sea-coast as far south as Norfolk (where they are called tailors,) but they are particularly abundant along the shores of Connecticut and Rhode Island. In some places we have often found them so numerous, that we have seen a dozen of them darting after our squid at the same instant. They are in season during the whole of summer and autumn.

Another capital fish that we have caught "all along shore," between New York and Cape Cod, is the *weak fish*, or *squeteague*. It never comes into the fresh water rivers, and usually makes its appearance about harvest time. Its habits are similar to those of the striped bass, and in appearance it closely resembles the *ciscovet* of Lake Superior. They commonly weigh from three to five pounds, though they have been taken weighing nearly ten. They are bold biters, and highly esteemed for their sweetness.

With regard to the remaining fish found on our seabord we are disposed to be brief. The *mackerel* we esteem, and have had rare sport in taking them, but we look upon them as the exclusive property of our merchants. The *halibut* we admire, but fear, for he reminds us of one of the most fatiguing piscatorial adventures we ever experienced, when we hooked a thirty-pounder in the Atlantic, one hundred miles off Nantucket. As to the *cod*, we have only to say that we have caught them off Nahant by the hundred, and never wish to catch any more; like the *mackerel*, we consider them the exclusive property of the mercantile fraternity. With the *king fish* and *drum* we are wholly unacquainted. The *tom cod* and *conner* or *blue perch* we despise, and our antipathy to snakes has always caused us to avoid the *eel*. Of the *sea bass* and *paugee*, if we knew what to say, we would indite a long paragraph, for we esteem them both. As to the *shad* and *sea sturgeon*, we shall dismiss them with an angler's scorn, for they know not what it is to take the hook. The *pollock*, by the way, is another pleasant fish to capture, and is associated, in our minds, with many most happy days spent with Daniel Webster, in his own yacht, off Marshfield. And now that we have reached the bottom of our last page (devoted to the finny tribes,) we are reminded of the very peculiar but sweet and valuable fish, which are ever found only at the bottom of the sea—the *flounder* and *flat-fish*. Many a time and oft have we taken them both with the hook and spear, and we can pay them no higher compliment than by mentioning the fact that they are particular favorites with the distinguished painter, *William S. Mount, Esq.*, of Long Island.

Indian Legends.

THE SHOOTING METEORS.

Among the Indians who live upon the north-eastern shore of Lake Huron, a remnant of the Iroquois, it is believed that the heavens contain only four meteors which have the power of shooting through the sky. It is thought they severally occupy the four quarters of the compass, and that they never perform their arrowy journey excepting for the purpose of warning the Huron Indians of approaching war. The meteors in question, or Pun gung-nung, are recognized by their peculiar brilliancy, and universally considered the Manitoes or guardian spirits of the entire Indian race. They came into existence at the same period of time which witnessed the creation of Lake Huron itself, and the legend which accounts for their origin is distinguished for the wild and romantic fancies of the aborigines. I obtained it from a chief named *On qwa-sug*, or Floating Wood.

It was the winter time, and an Indian with his wife and two children, a daughter and a son, were living in a wigwam on a bleak peninsula of the Great Lake. The game of that section of country had nearly all disappeared, and the fish were spending the season in such deep water, that it was quite impossible to secure any of them for food. Everything seemed to go wrong with the poverty-stricken Indian, and he was constantly troubled with the fear that the Master of Life intended to annihilate his family and himself by starvation. He expressed his anxiety to his wife, and was surprised to hear her answer with a song.

Nearly half a moon had passed away, and the sufferings of this unfortunate family were melancholy in the extreme. Whole days did the father spend roaming through the forests, with his bows and arrows, and on four several evenings had he returned without even a pair of tiny snow-birds for a supper. The ill-luck which attended him in his expeditions made him very miserable, but he was frequently astonished and alarmed, on such occasions, by the conduct of his wife and children. When he gave them an account of his ill luck in obtaining game, instead of manifesting any anxiety, they usually ran about the wigwam with their fingers on their mouths, and uttering a singular moan. He noticed with fear that they were becoming greatly emaciated for the want of food. So deeply grieved was the poor man, that he almost resolved to bury himself in the snow and die. He made a better resolution and again went out to hunt.

On one occasion he had wandered into the woods to an unusual distance, and, as fortune would have it, was successful in finding and shooting a single rabbit. With the speed of a deer did he return to his cabin (with his braided shoes over the crusted snow,) but he now met with a new disappointment. On entering his lodge he found the fire entirely out, and the simple utensils for cooking all scattered about in great confusion; but what was far more melancholy, his wife and children were gone, and he knew not where to find them. The more he thought upon what had happened for many days past, the more bewildered did he become. He threw down his game almost in despair, and hurried out of his cabin in search of his missing family. He looked in every direction, but could see no signs of their appearing, and the only noise that he could possibly hear was a singular and most doleful moan, resembling the wail of a loon, which seemed to come from the upper air. By a natural instinct he raised his eyes towards the heavens, and beheld perched upon the dry limb of a tall tree, which stood a short distance off, all the members of his family. He shouted with delight at the unexpected spectacle, and, rushing towards the tree, told his wife and children that they must come down, for he had killed a rabbit, and they would now have a good feast. But again was he astonished to find his words unheeded. Again did he beseech them to come down, but they replied not a single word, and looked upon him with eyes that seemed made of fire. And what was still more wonderful, it was evident that they had thrown aside their beaver and deer-skin dresses, and were now decked out in newly fashioned robes, made of the fur of the white fisher and the white fox. All this was utterly inexplicable, and the poor husband re-entered his lodge, bewildered and perplexed to a marvelous degree.

Then it was that the idea entered his head that he would try an experiment, by appealing to the hunger of his obstinate wife and children. He therefore cleaned the rabbit and boiled a sweet soup which he carried out, and with which he endeavored to allure his friends to the earth. But this attempt was all in vain. The mother and her children expressed no desire for the food, and still remained upon the tree, swaying to and fro like a flock of large birds. Again in his wretchedness was he about to destroy himself, but he took the precaution to appropriate the soup to its legitimate purpose. Soon as this business was accomplished, he relapsed into his former state of melancholy, from which he was suddenly aroused by the moans of his wife, which he was sure had an articulate tone. Again was he riveted to his standing place under the magic tree, and from the moaning of his wife he gathered the following intelligence. She told him that the Master of Life had fallen in love with her and her two children, and had therefore transformed them all into spirits, with a view of preparing them for a home in the sky. She also told him that they would not depart for their future home until the coming spring, but would, in the meantime, roam in distant countries till the time of his own transportation should arrive. Having finished her communication, she and her children immediately commenced a song, which resembled the distant winds, when they all rose gracefully from the tree, and leaning forward upon the air, darted away across the lake toward the remote South.

A cheerless and forlorn moon did the poor Indian spend in his lonely lodge on the margin of the Great Lake. Spring came, and just as the last vestige of snow had melted from the woods, and at the quiet evening hour, his spirit-wife again made her appearance, accompanied by her two children. She told her husband that he might become a spirit by eating a certain berry. He was delighted with the idea, and, complying with her advice, he suddenly became transformed into a spirit, and having flown to the side of his wife and children, the party gradually began to ascend into the air, when the Master of Life thought proper to change them into á family of Shooting Stars. He allotted to each a particular division of the heavens, and commanded them to remain there forever, as the guardians of the great nation of Lake Huron.

THE MAIDEN OF THE MOON.

The following legend was obtained from the lips of a Chippewa woman named Penaqua, or the Female Pheasant, and I hardly know which to admire most, the simple beauty of the plot, or the graphic and unique manner of the narrative, of which, I regret to say, I can hardly give a faithful translation.

Among the rivers of the North, none can boast of more numerous charms than the St. Louis, and the fairest spot of the earth which it waters is that where now stands the trading post of Fond du lac. Upon this spot, many summers ago, there lived a Chippewa chief and his wife, who were the parents of an only daughter. Her name was Weesh—Ko-da-e-mire, or the Sweet Strawberry, and she was acknowledged to be the most beautiful maiden of her nation. Her voice was like that of the turtle-dove, and the red deer was not more graceful and sprightly in its form. Her eyes were brilliant as the star of the northern sky, which guides the hunter through the wilderness, and her dark hair clustered around her neck like grape vines around the trunk of the tree they loved. The young men of every nation had striven to win her heart, but she smiled upon none. Curious presents were sent to her from the four quarters of the world, but she received them not. Seldom did she deign to reply to the many warriors who entered her father's lodge, and when she did, it was only to assure them that while upon earth she would never change her condition. Her strange conduct astonished them, but did not subdue their affection. Many and noble were the deeds they performed, not only in winning the white plumes of the eagle, but in hunting the elk and the black bear. But all their exploits availed them nothing, for the heart of the beautiful girl was still untouched.

The snows of winter were all gone, and the pleasant winds of spring were blowing over the land. The time for making sugar had arrived, though the men had not yet returned from the remote hunting grounds, and in the maple forests bright fires were burning, and the fragrance of the sweet sap filled all the air. The ringing laugh of childhood and the mature song of women, were heard in the valley, but in no part of the wilderness could be found more happiness than on the banks of the St. Louis. But the Sweet Strawberry mingled with the young men and maidens of her tribe, in a thoughtful mood and with downcast eyes. She was evidently bowed down by some mysterious grief, but she neglected not her duties; and though she spent much of her time alone, her buchère-bucket was as frequently filled with the sugar juice as any of her companions.

Such was the condition of affairs, when a party of young warriors from the far North came upon a frolic to the St. Louis River. Having seen the many handsome maidens of this region, the strangers became enamored of their charms, and each one succeeded in obtaining the love of a maiden, who was to become his bride during the marrying season of summer.

The warriors had heard of the Sweet Strawberry, but, neglected by all of them, she was still doomed to remain alone. She witnessed the happiness of her old playmates, and, wondering at her own strange fate, spent much of her time in solitude. She even became so unhappy and bewildered that she heeded not the tender words of her mother, and from that time the music of her voice was never heard.

The sugar making season was now rapidly passing away, but the brow of the Sweet Strawberry was still overshadowed with grief. Everything was done to restore her to her wonted cheerfulness, but she remained unchanged. Wild ducks in innumerable numbers arrived with every southern wind, and settled upon the surrounding waters, and proceeded to build their nests in pairs, and the Indian maiden sighed over her mysterious doom. On one occasion she espied a cluster of early spring flowers peering above the dry leaves of the forest, and, strange to say, even these were separated into pairs, and seemed to be wooing each other in love. All things whispered to her of love, the happiness of her companions, the birds of the air, and the flowers. She looked into her heart, and inwardly praying for a companion whom she might love, the Master of Life took pity upon her lot and answered her prayer.

It was now the twilight hour, and in the maple woods the Indian boys were watching their fires and the women were bringing in the sap from the surrounding trees. The time for making sugar was almost gone, and the well-filled mocucks, which might be seen in all the wigwams, testified that the yield had been abundant. The hearts of the old women beat in thankfulness, and the young men and maidens were already beginning to anticipate the pleasures of wedded life and those associated with the sweet summer time. But the brow of the Sweet Strawberry continued to droop, and her friends looked upon her as the victim of a settled melancholy. Her duties, however, were performed without a murmur, and so continued to be performed until the trees refused to fill her buchère-bucket with sap, when she stole away from the sugar camp and wandered to a retired place to muse upon her sorrows. Her unaccountable grief was very bitter, but did not long endure; for, as she stood gazing upon the sky, the moon ascended above the hills and filled her soul with a joy she had never felt before. The longer she looked upon the brilliant object, the more deeply in love did she become with its celestial charms, and she burst forth into a song—a loud, wild, and joyous song. Her musical voice echoed through the woods, and her friends hastened to ascertain the cause. They gathered around her in crowds, but she heeded them not. They wondered at the wildness of her words, and the airy-like appearance of her form. They were spell-bound by the scene before them, but their astonishment knew no limits when they saw her gradually ascend from the earth into the air, where she disappeared, as if borne upward by the evening wind. And then it was that they discovered her clasped in the embraces of the moon, for they knew that the spots which they saw within the circle of that planet were those of her robe, which she had made from the skins of the spotted fawn.

Many summers have passed away since the Sweet Strawberry became the Maiden of the Moon, yet among all the people of her nation is she ever remembered for her beauty and the mystery of her being.

THE GHOSTLY MAN-EATER.

There is an idea existing among the Chippewa Indians, which corroborates a statement made by the early travellers on this continent relative to the belief that there once existed among the aboriginal tribes, a species of vampire, or ghostly man-eater. The Chippewas do not assert that there ever lived more than one of these unearthly beings; but they pretend that such an one did, and does exist, and that he has his residence upon an island in the centre of Lake Superior—which island can never be seen by mortal man, excepting when darkness has settled upon the world. The stories they relate of his appearance and deeds, are horrible in the extreme, and resemble much the creations of a mind suffering under the influence of the nightmare. For example, they describe this monster as possessing the material appearance of the human form—but of such a nature as not to be susceptible to the touch. He is said to have the body of a serpent, with human legs and arms—all supplied with immense nails, which he employs for the double purpose of digging up the earth, and dissecting the bodies upon which he feeds; his head is like that of a wolf, and his teeth of a peculiar sharpness.

The deeds which he performs are worthy of his personal appearance—and some of them are as follows: When the Indian mother, during a long journey, has lost her infant child, and placed it on the rude scaffold, that she may return to it at some future day, the Ghostly Man-Eater only waits until she is fairly out of his sight, and then proceeds to the sacred place, and feasts himself upon the tender flesh and blood of his victim.

And therefore it is, that the traveler sometimes sees, in the remote wilderness, fragments of human bones scattered on the ground, as if a wolf had been suddenly interrupted, while devouring his prey. But the Man-Eater sometimes enters the house, or half-buried receptacle of the dead; and, after digging his way to the decaying body, coils himself up, as if in delight, and gluts his appetite with the unholy food. How it is that he travels, with lightning speed, from one distant place to another, has never been ascertained; but the strange sounds which the Indian occasionally hears, high in the air above his wigwam, is thought to be the song of the Man-Eater, as he hurries upon the wings of the wind, from a recent banquet, to his mysterious island on the lake.

But I once heard a legend in the Chippewa country, which accounted for the origin of the man-eating monster—and I now record it in the English tongue, for the benefit of those who feel an interest in the mythology of the Indian, and the peculiarities of his mind. The individual from whom I obtained this story was named Ka-yon-kee-me, or the Swift Arrow; and his words, as near as we can remember them, were as follows:—

I ask the white man to listen. At an early period in the history of the world, an old Indian hunter and a little boy who was his grandson, lived in an isolated cabin on the north shore of Lake Superior. They were the only remnants of a once powerful tribe of Indians, whose name is not now remembered. It was the middle of a long and dreary winter, and the entire country was covered with snow, to the height of the tallest wigwam. The section of country where resided the hunter and child was particularly desolate, and destitute of almost every species of game; and whilst the former was too feeble to wander far, after the necessary food, the latter was too young and inexperienced. The very wood which the unequal pair collected to keep them warm, was brought to their cabin with the greatest difficulty; and the thought occasionally entered the old man's mind, that the Great Spirit was about to give him up to the pains of starvation. He uttered not a murmur, however; but, as he reflected upon his impending fate, he bit his lips with a scornful smile.

One, two, and three days had passed away and the old man, as well as the child, had not tasted a particle of food. But, on the evening of the fourth day, the boy came tottering into the comfortless lodge and threw at the feet of his grandfather the lifeless body of a white partridge, which he had fortunately killed with his own arrow. Immediately was the bird divested of its feathers —and, while yet its very blood was warm, it was devoured by the starving man and child. Sweet was the slumber of the noble boy on that night—but, as the story goes, that aged man was visited by a dreadful dream at the same time, which made him a maniac.

Another day was nearly gone, and the unhappy pair were standing in front of their wigwam watching the western sky, as the sun enlivened it with his parting beams. The old man pointed to the bright picture, and told the boy that there was the gateway to the Spirit Land, where perpetual summer reigned, and game was found in great abundance. He spoke too of the child's father and mother, and of his little brother, whom he described as decked out in the most beautiful of robes, as they wandered through the forests of that distant, shadowy land. The boy, though suffering with the pangs of hunger, clapped his little hands in glee, and told his grandfather that it would make him very happy if he could go to the land of perpetual summer. And then it was that the old man patted the boy upon his head, and told him that his desires should be realized before the sun again made its appearance above the snow-covered mountains and plains of the east.

It was now the hour of midnight. Intensely cold was the wind which swept over the wilderness, but the sky was very blue, and studded with many stars. No sound broke upon the air, save the occasional groan of the ice along the lake shore, and the hissing whisper of the frost. Within the Indian lodge, which was the very home of desolation, the child was sweetly sleeping, enveloped in his robes, while the old man bent over the burning embers as if in despair. Some inhuman thought had crazed his brain, and he was nerving himself for an unheard of crime. One moment more, and in the dim light of that lonely lodge, gleamed the polished blade of a flinty weapon—a sudden groan was heard—and the Indian maniac was feeding upon the body of his child.

I have given the white man a sorrowful history, but it is one which the Chippewa nation believe. On the morning which followed the event I have now narrated, a party of Indian hunters came to the cabin of the unknown man, and they found him lying dead upon the ground, with the mangled remains of the boy at his side. This was the most terrible deed which ever happened in the Chippewa country—and the one which so greatly offended the Great Spirit, that he pronounced a curse upon the man who had destroyed his child for food—and he, therefore, doomed him to live upon the earth forever, tormented with an appetite which nothing can ever appease, but the decaying flesh of the human race.

THE FIRE-WATER SACRIFICE.

The historical tradition which I am now to narrate, is said to have occurred at an early day on the extreme western point of what is now called Drummond's Island, in the northern waters of Lake Huron. I obtained it from the lips of Kah-ge-ga-gah-bowh, or *Upright Standing*, a young chief of the Chippeway nation, who assured me that it commemorated the first introduction of the baneful Fire-water into the Indian country.

It was the afternoon of a pleasant day in the autumn-time, when a trading canoe landed on Drummond's Island, in the immediate vicinity of a Chippewa village. It belonged to a French trader, and was laden with a barrel of whisky, which he had brought from the lower country. Soon as he had deposited his barrel upon the beach, he called together the men of the village, and told them that he had it in his power to supply them with a beverage which would make them exceedingly happy, and that he was willing to supply them with what they wanted, provided they would give into his hands all the furs they had in their possession. A bargain was consequently made, and while the entire population of the village were quaffing the baneful fire-water, the trader packed away his treasures in the canoe, and under cover of the night, started upon his return to Detroit.

The moon and stars came forth in the northern sky, and the only sound which broke the solitude of the wilderness, issued from the Indian village, where the medicine man and the chief, the Indian mother and her infant, were shouting and dancing and fighting in a delirium of madness. The carousal did not end until the break of day, and soon as the sun was fairly risen above the horizon, it was rumored in every wigwam that a young hunter, named Ne-mo-a-Kim, or *Purple Shell*, had taken the life of a brother hunter, who happened to be his dearest friend. An apparent gloom rested upon every countenance, and as the more aged Indians reflected upon the sudden disappearance of the trader, and upon the headache which many of them endured, they became greatly enraged, and attributed the calamity which had befallen them to the burning water. But the trader who had brought it to them was beyond their reach; so they buried the murdered man with appropriate honors, and then announced that a council should be immediately held to decide upon the fate of the murderer. Blood for blood was demanded by the relatives of the deceased; the time-honored law of the Chippewas could not be evaded, and a delegation was appointed to prepare Ne-mo-a-Kim for the sacrifice. His lodge was entered by the ministers of death, but Ne-mo-a-Kim was not there. They hunted for him in all the wigwams of the village, but nowhere could he be found. The old men who had suffered with him in the remote wilderness, and had never known him to be guilty of a cowardly deed, now shook their heads in sorrow and disappointment. Another council was held, another ancient law remembered, and it was again decided that the only relative and brother of Ne-mo-a-Kim should suffer in his stead. The name of that brother was Ma-Ko-nah, or *The Unbending Pine*, and when they informed him of his fate, he uttered not a murmur, but demanded that his execution should take place on the following night at the rising of the moon.

And now for another scene in our strange story. The sun has long been absent from the western sky, and once more has the solemn midnight settled upon the world. The inhabitants of the Indian village have assembled upon a level green. Firmly in the earth have they planted a stake, on either side of which are burning a couple of huge fires, while at the distance of about one hundred feet may be discerned a crowd of eight or ten young men, who are bending their bows and straightening their arrows for the cruel deed. A small white cloud makes its appearance above the horizon, and a murmur of excitement issues from the crowd of human beings. The proud form of an Indian is now seen marching across the green, when the name of Ma-Ko-nah is whispered from ear to ear, and an unearthly shout ascends into the upper air. The heroic man stands before the stake, and looks with scorn upon the withes lying at his feet. The people have confided in his bravery, and they will not humble his proud spirit by resorting to the disgraceful implements of security. Upon his naked breast has the Indian hero painted the uncouth figure of a swan, as a certain mark for the arrows which are to deprive him of life. Around his waist has he carefully adjusted his richest robe, and by a motion of his hand, has signified his intention of delivering a speech; an intense silence reigns throughout the surrounding multitude, and Ma-Ko-nah thus addresses his cowardly brother, whose spirit he imagines to be hovering near.

"Willingly do I die for you, my brother, but you have disgraced your nation. Your name will hereafter be hissed at by the little boys, when they pick up the purple shells on the lake shore. I am going to the Spirit Land, and while I shall be happy in the possession of every good, you will be despised by all who learn your history. Your food will be bitter, and the ground upon which you will have to sleep will always be uneven, and covered with thorns and stones. You are a coward, my brother; but Ma-Ko-nah is a brave man, and not afraid to die."

Loud and long was the shout which replied to this proud speech. All things were now ready, and the fatal moment, when the rim of the moon should appear above the distant waters, was nigh at hand. Another snowy cloud floated into view, and just as the signal to fire was about to be given by the great medicine man, Ne-mo-a-Kim suddenly burst through the crowd, and threw himself upon the ground before his brother Ma-Ko-nah. To describe the confusion which followed were quite impossible. It were sufficient to know that Ma-Ko-nah was released from his obligation, and while he was to continue in the land of the living, his repentant brother was to perish. But though he now yielded himself as a willing sacrifice, his integrity had been doubted, and the lately untouched thongs were used to bind him to the stake. All things were again ready, the signal was given, the loud twang of the bow-strings pulled at the same instant was heard, and the Chippewa murderer was weltering in his own blood.

The night was far spent, the silence of the grave rested upon the wilderness village, and all the Indians, save one, were asleep in their wigwams. But Ma-Ko-nah was filled with grief, and the remaining hours of that night did he spend in his lodge, mourning over the body of his unfortunate and only brother. His father and mother were both dead, and so also was his wife, and the heart of Ma-Ko-nah was very desolate. So endeth the story of The Fire-Water Sacrifice.

ORIGIN OF THE CATAWBA INDIANS.

THERE was a time when the world was an unbroken waste of rocks, hills, and mountains, save only one small valley, which was distinguished for its luxuriance, and where reigned a perpetual summer. At that time, too, the only human being who inhabited the earth was a woman, whose knowledge was confined to this valley, and who is remembered among the Catawbas as the mother of mankind. She lived in a cavern, and her food consisted of the honey of flowers, and the sweet berries and other fruits of the wilderness. Birds without number, and the wild streams which found a resting-place in the valley, made the only music which she ever heard. Among the wild animals, which were very numerous about her home, she wandered without any danger; but the beaver and the doe were her favorite companions. In personal appearance she was eminently beautiful, and the lapse of years only had a tendency to increase the brightness of her eyes and the grace of her movements. The dress she wore was made of those bright green leaves which enfold the water lilies, and her hair was as long as the grass which fringed the waters of her native vale. She was the ruling spirit of a perennial world, for even the very flowers which bloomed about her sylvan home were never known to wither or die. In spite of her lonely condition, she knew not what it was to be lonely; but ever and anon a strange desire found its way to her heart, which impelled her to explore the wild country which surrounded her home. For many days had she resisted the temptation to become a wanderer from her charming valley, until it so happened, on a certain morning, that a scarlet butterfly made its appearance before the door of her cave, and by the hum of its wings invited her away. She obeyed the summons, and followed the butterfly far up a rocky ravine, until she came to the foot of a huge waterfall, when she was deserted by her mysterious pilot, and first became acquainted with the emotion of fear. Her passage of the ravine had been comparatively smooth; but when she endeavored, in her consternation, to retrace her steps, she found her efforts unavailing, and fell to the ground in despair. A deep sleep then overcame her senses, from which she was not awakened until the night was far spent; and then the dampness of the dew had fallen upon her soft limbs, and for the first time in her life did she feel the pang of a bodily pain. Forlorn and desolate indeed was her condition, and she felt that some great event was about to happen, when, as she uncovered her face and turned it to the sky, she beheld, bending over her prostrate form, and clothed in a cloud-like robe, the image of a being somewhat resembling herself, only that he was more stoutly made, and of a much fiercer aspect. Her first emotion at this strange discovery was that of terror; but as the mysterious being looked upon her in kindness, and raised her lovingly from the ground, she confided in his protection, and listened to his words until the break of day.

He told her that he was a native of the far off sky, and that he had discovered her in her forlorn condition while travelling from the evening to the morning star. He told her also that he had never before seen a being so soft and beautifully formed as she. In coming to her rescue he had broken a command of the Great Spirit, or the Master of Life, and, as he was afraid to return to the sky, he desired to spend his days in her society upon earth. With joy did she accept this proposal; and, as the sun rose above the distant mountains, the twain returned in safety to the luxuriant vale, where, as man and woman, for many moons, they lived and loved in perfect tranquillity and joy.

In process of time the woman became a mother; from which time the happiness of the twain became more intense, but they at the same time endured more troubles than they had ever known before. The man was unhappy because he had offended the Master of Life, and the mother was anxious about the comfort and happiness of her newly-born child. Many and devout were the prayers they offered the Great Spirit for his guidance and protection, for they felt that from them were to be descended a race of beings more numerous than the stars of heaven. The Great Spirit had compassion on these lone inhabitants of the earth; and, in answer to their prayers, he caused a mighty wind to pass over the world, making the mountains crowd closely together, and rendering the world more useful and beautiful by the prairies and valleys and rivers which now cover it, from the rising to the setting sun. The Master of Life also told his children that he would give them the earth and all that it contained as their inheritance; but that they should never enjoy their food without labor, should be annually exposed to a season of bitter cold, and that their existence should be limited by that period of time when their heads should become as white as the plumage of the swan. And so endeth the words of the Catawba.

THE LONG CHASE.

It was a summer day, and my birchen canoe, paddled by a party of Chippewa Indians, was gliding along the southern shore of Lake Superior. We had left the Apostle Islands, and were wending our way towards the mouth of the Ontonagon, where we intended to spend the night. Behind us reposed in beauty the Emerald Islands, in our front appeared the Porcupine Mountains, the sky above was without a cloud, and the waste of sleeping waters was only broken by the presence of a lonely swan, which seemed to be following in our wake, apparently for the sake of our companionship. I was delighted with the scene which surrounded me, and having requested my comrades to refill their pipes from my tobacco-pouch, I inquired for an adventure or a story connected with this portion of the lake. I waited but for a moment, when the chief of the party, *O-gee-maw-ge-zhick*, or Chief of the Sky, signified his intention by a sudden exclamation, and proceeded with the following historical tradition:

The Indian warrior of other days seldom thought that distance ought to be considered when he went forth to battle against his enemies, provided he was certain of winning the applause of his fellow men. Fatigue and hunger were alike looked upon as unimportant considerations, and both endured without a murmur.

The white man had not yet become the owner of this wilderness, and our nation was at war with the Ircquois, who had invaded our territory. At this time it was that a party of six Iroquois runners had been sent by their leading chiefs from Ke-wa-we-non, on the southern shore of Lake Superior, to examine the position of the Chippewas, who were supposed to be on an island called Moo-ne-quah-na-kon-ing. The spies having arrived opposite the island where their enemies were encamped (which island was about three miles from the main shore,) they built a war-canoe out of the bark of an elm tree, launched it at the hour of midnight, and, having implored the god of war to smile upon them and keep the lake in peace, they landed on the island, and were soon prowling through the village of the unconscious Chippewas.

They were so cautious in all their movements, that their footsteps did not even awaken the sleeping dogs. It so happened, however, that they were discovered, and that, too, by a young woman, who, according to ancient custom, was leading a solitary life previous to becoming a mother. In her wakefulness she saw them pass near her lodge and heard them speak, but could not understand their words, though she thought them to be of the Na-do-was tribe. When they had passed, she stole out of her own wigwam to that of her aged grandmother, whom she informed of what she had seen and heard. The aged woman only reprimanded her daughter for her imprudence, and did not heed her words. "But, mother," replied the girl, "I speak the truth; the dreaded Na-do-was are in our village; and if the warriors of the Buffalo Race do not heed the story of a foolish girl, their women and their children must perish." The words of the girl were finally believed, and the warriors of the Crane and Buffalo tribes prepared themselves for the capture. The war-whoop echoed to the sky; and the rattling of bows and arrows was heard in every part of the island. In about an hour, the main shore was lined with about eight hundred canoes, whose occupants were anxiously waiting for the appearance of the spies. These desperate men, however, had made up their minds to try the mettle of their oars to the utmost, and, as the day was breaking, they launched their canoe from a woody cove, shot round the island, and started in the direction of the Porcupine Mountains, which were about sixty miles distant. Soon as they came in sight of the Chippewas, the latter became quite frantic, and, giving their accustomed yell, the whole multitude started after them swift as the flight of gulls. The mighty lake was without a ripple; and the beautiful fish in its bosom wandered about their rocky haunts in perfect peace, unconscious of the dreadful strife which was going on above. The canoes of the pursued and the pursuers moved with magic speed. The Iroquois were some two miles ahead, and while they strained every nerve for life, one voice rose high into the air, with a song of invocation to the spirits of their race for protection; and, in answer to their petition, a thick fog fell upon the water, and caused great confusion. One of the Chippewa warriors laid down his paddle, seized his mysterious rattle (made of deer's hoof,) and, in a strange, wild song, implored the spirits of his race to clear away the fog, that they might only see their enemies. The burthen of the song was:—

"Mon e-tou ne bah bah me tah wah
Ke shig ne bah bah me tah goon
Ah bee ne nah wah goom me goon
Men ke che dah awas—awas."

Which may be translated as follows:—

"Spirit! whom I have always obeyed,
Here cause the skies now to obey,
And place the waters in our power.
We are warriors—away, away."

Just as the last strain died upon the air, the fog quickly rolled away, and the Iroquois spies were discovered hastening towards the shore, near Montreal river. Then came the fog again, and then departed, in answer to the conflicting prayers of the nations. Long and awfully exciting was the race. But the Great Spirit was the friend of the Chippewa, and just as the Iroquois were landing on the beach, four of them were pierced with arrows, and the remaining two taken prisoners. A council was then called, for the purpose of deciding what should be done with them; and it was determined that they should be tortured at the stake. They were fastened to a tree, and surrounded with wood, when, just as the torch was to be applied, an aged warrior stepped forth from the crowd of spectators, and thus addressed the assembly:—

"Why are you to destroy these men? They are brave warriors, but not more distinguished than we are. We can gain no benefit from their death. Why will you not let them live, that they may go and tell their people of our power, and that our warriors are numerous as the stars of the northern sky." The council pondered upon the old man's advice, and there was a struggle between their love of revenge and love of glory; but both became victorious. One of the spies was released, and, as he ascended a narrow valley, leading to the Porcupine Mountains, the fire was applied to the dry wood piled round the form of the other; and in the darkness of midnight, and amid the shouting of his cruel enemies, the body of the Iroquois prisoner was consumed to ashes. The spot where the sacrifice took place has been riven by many a thunderbolt since then, for the god of war was displeased with the faint-heartedness of the Chippewa, in valuing a name more highly than the *privilege* of revenge; and the same summer, of the following year, which saw the humane Chippewa buried on the shore of Superior, also saw the remains of the pardoned spy consigned to the earth on the shore of Michigan.

Thus ended the legend of Shah-gah-wah-mik, one of the Apostle Islands, which the French named La Pointe, and which was originally known as Moo-ne-quah-na-kon-ing. The village stood where the old trading establishment is now located; and among the greenest of the graves in the hamlet of La Pointe is that where lie the remains of the Indian girl who exposed herself to reproach for the purpose of saving her people.

THE LONE BUFFALO.

AMONG the legends which the traveler frequently hears, while crossing the prairies of the Far West, I remember one which accounts in a most romantic manner for the origin of thunder. A summer-storm was sweeping over the land, and I had sought a temporary shelter in the lodge of a Sioux, or Dacotah Indian on the banks of the St. Peter's. Vividly flashed the lightning, and an occasional peal of thunder echoed through the firmament. While the storm continued my host and his family paid but little attention to my comfort, for they were all evidently stricken with terror. I endeavored to quell their fears, and for that purpose asked them a variety of questions respecting their people, but they only replied by repeating, in a dismal tone, the name of the Lone Buffalo. My curiosity was of course excited, and it may readily be imagined that I did not resume my journey without obtaining an explanation of the mystic words; and from him who first uttered them in the Sioux lodge I subsequently obtained the following legend:—

There was a chief of the Sioux nation whose name was the Master Bear. He was famous as a prophet and hunter, and was a particular favorite with the Master of Life. In an evil hour he partook of the white man's fire-water, and in a fighting broil unfortunately took the life of a brother chief. According to ancient custom blood was demanded for blood, and when next the Master Bear went forth to hunt, he was waylaid, shot through the heart with an arrow, and his body deposited in front of his widow's lodge. Bitterly did the woman bewail her misfortune, now mutilating her body in the most heroic manner, and anon narrating to her only son, a mere infant, the prominent events of her husband's life. Night came, and with her child lashed upon her back, the woman erected a scaffold on the margin of a neighboring stream, and with none to lend her a helping hand, enveloped the corpse in her more valuable robès, and fastened it upon the scaffold. She completed her task just as the day was breaking, when she returned to the lodge, and shutting herself therein, spent the three following days without tasting food.

During her retirement the widow had a dream, in which she was visited by the Master of Life. He endeavored to console her in her sorrow, and for the reason that he had loved her husband, promised to make her son a more famous warrior and medicine man than his father had been. And what was more remarkable, this prophecy was to be realized within the period of a few weeks. She told her story in the village, and was laughed at for her credulity.

On the following day, when the village boys were throwing the ball upon the plain, a noble youth suddenly made his appearance among the players, and eclipsed them all in the bounds he made, and the wildness of his shouts. He was a stranger to all, but when the widow's dream was remembered, he was recognized as her son, and treated with respect. But the youth was yet without a name, for his mother had told him that he should win one for himself by his individual prowess.

Only a few days had elapsed, when it was rumored that a party of Pawnees had overtaken and destroyed a Sioux hunter, when it was immediately determined in council that a party of one hundred warriors should start upon the war-path and revenge the injury. Another council was held for the purpose of appointing a leader, when a young man suddenly entered the ring and claimed the privilege of leading the way. His authority was angrily questioned, but the stranger only replied by pointing to the brilliant eagle's feathers on his head, and by shaking from his belt a large number of fresh Pawnee scalps. They remembered the stranger boy, and acknowledged the supremacy of the stranger man.

Night settled upon the prairie world, and the Sioux warriors started upon the war-path. Morning dawned, and a Pawnee village was in ashes, and the bodies of many hundred men, women, and children were left upon the ground as food for the wolf and vulture. The Sioux warriors returned to their own encampment, when it was ascertained that the nameless leader had taken more than twice as many scalps as his brother warriors. Then it was that a feeling of jealousy arose, which was soon quieted, however, by the news that the Crow Indians had stolen a number of horses and many valuable furs from a Sioux hunter as he was returning from the mountains. Another warlike expedition was planned, and as before, the nameless warrior took the lead.

The sun was near his setting, and as the Sioux party looked down upon a Crow village, which occupiod the centre of a charming valley, the Sioux chief commanded the attention of his braves and addressed them in the following language:

"I am about to die, my brothers, and must speak my mind. To be fortunate in war is your chief ambition, and because I have been successful you are unhappy. Is this right? Have you acted like men? I despise you for your meanness, and I intend to prove to you this night that I am the bravest man in the nation. The task will cost me my life, but I am anxious that my nature should be changed and I shall be satisfied. I intend to enter the Crow village alone, but before departing, I have one favor to command. If I succeed in destroying that village, and lose my life, I want you, when I am dead, to cut off my head and protect it with care. You must then kill one of the largest buffaloes in the country and cut off his head. You must then bring his body and my head together, and breathe upon them, when I shall be free to roam in the Spirit-land at all times, and over our great prairie-land wherever I please. And when your hearts are troubled with wickedness remember the Lone Buffalo."

The attack upon the Crow village was successful, but according to his prophecy the Lone Buffalo received his death wound, and his brother warriors remembered his parting request. The fate of the hero's mother is unknown, but the Indians believe that it is she who annually sends from the Spirit-land the warm winds of spring, which cover the prairies with grass for the sustenance of the Buffalo race. As to the Lone Buffalo, he is never seen even by the most cunning hunter, excepting when the moon is at its full. At such times he is invariably alone, cropping his food in some remote part of the prairies; and whenever the heavens resound with the moanings of the thunder, the red man banishes from his breast every feeling of jealousy, for he believes it to be the warning voice of the Lone Buffalo.

LEGENDS OF MACKINAW.

The original Indian name of this island was Mich-il-i-mack-i-nack, signifying the mammoth turtle. It is a beautiful spot of earth, and its origin is accounted for by the following Ottawa legend:

When the world was in its infancy, and all the living creatures were wandering over its surface from their several birth places, for a permanent home, it so happened that a multitude of turtles came to the southern shore of Lake Erie. They found the country generally level, and were delighted with the muddy waters of the lake, and also with the many stagnant rivers and ponds which they discovered in its vicinity. But while the race were generally satisfied with their discoveries, and willing to remain where they were, the mammoth leader of the multitude resolved upon extending his journey to the north. He was allured to this undertaking by a strange light of exceeding loveliness (supposed to be the Aurora Borealis,) which he had frequently observed covering the horizon. He endeavored to obtain a few companions for his intended pilgrimage but without success. This disappointment did not dishearten him, however, and as he remembered that the summer was only half gone, he determined to depart alone. Long and very circuitous was his journey, and many, beautiful and lonely, the bayous and swamps where he frequently tarried to rest himself and obtain refreshment. Summer, and nearly the whole of autumn were now passed, and the travelling turtle found himself on a point of land which partially divided the two lakes of Huron and Michigan. Already he had been numbed by chilly winds, but his ambition was so great that he still persisted in his foolish pilgrimage. The day on which he made his final launch upon the waters, was particularly cold and desolate, and it so happened that in the course of a few days his career was stopped by the formation of an icy barrier, which deprived him of life and left him, a little black spot, on the waste of frozen waters.

Spring returned once more, but while the ice gradually dissolved itself into beautiful blue waves, the shell of the turtle was fastened to a marine plant or tall reed, and in process of time became an island, which the Indians appropriately named Mich-il-i-mack-i-nack, or the Mammoth Turtle.

The individual from whom I obtained the above story was an Ottawa Indian; and he told it to me as we sat together on the brow of the arched rock which has, from time immemorial, been considered the principal natural curiosity of Mackinaw.

The following legend I obtained from the same source, and, like the majority of Indian stories, it is uncouth and unnatural; but interesting for the reason that it bears a curious analogy to a certain passage in the Old Testament. But this remark is applicable, I believe, to the early traditions of nearly all the aboriginal nations of North America. But to the tradition:

Very many winters ago, the sun was regularly in the habit of performing his daily circuit across the heavens, and when the stars made their appearance in the sky, he invariably descended into an immense hole supposed to be located in the remote west. But in process of time it so happened that a chief of the Ottawas committed an unheard of crime against the person of his only daughter, and the Master of Life became so offended, that he caused a mighty wind to come upon the earth, whereby the rocky hills were made to tremble, and the waters which surround them to roar with a dreadful noise. During this state of things, which lasted for one whole day, the sun shot through the heavens with an unsteady motion, and when it had reached the zenith suddenly became fixed, as if astonished at the red man's wickedness. All the people of the Ottawa nation were greatly alarmed at this phenomenon, and while they were gazing upon the luminary, it gradually changed into the color of blood, and with a dreadful noise, as if in a passion, it fell upon the earth. It struck the northern shore of Mackinaw, formed the cavity of the Arched Rock, and so entered the earth, from which it issued in the far east, at an early hour on the following morning, and then resumed its usual journey across the heavens.

Many, very many winters have passed away since the last-mentioned incident occurred, and it is true that even the present race of Indians can seldom be persuaded to approach the brow of the Arched Rock. Never have I heard of one who was sufficiently bold to walk over the arch, though the feat might be easily accomplished by any man with a steady nerve. The shores of the island of Mackinaw are almost entirely abrupt —and their general altitude is about one hundred and fifty feet; but the summit of the Arched Rock has been estimated to be at least two hundred feet above the water. In connection with the above stories, I might introduce a description of the island they commemorate, but such a description has already been published in my "Summer in the Wilderness."

GREEN-CORN CEREMONIES OF THE CHEROKEES.

My main object in the present paper is to record a complete account of the ceremonies which were once practised by the Cherokee Indians, in connection with their principal agricultural pursuit of raising maize or Indian corn. For the great majority of my facts I am indebted to Mr. Preston Starritt, of Tennessee. While this is the case, however, I beg my readers to understand that I shall speak of the tribe in question as it existed in the times of old, when its members were the sole proprietors of the southern Alleghanies. Let us, then, banish from our minds the unhappy relations which brood over the Cherokees at the present time, and, by the aid of our fancy, mingle with the nation as it existed in its pristine glory.

The snows of winter have melted from the mountain peaks, the rains are over and gone, the frosts are out of the ground, and the voice of the turtle is heard in the land. The beautiful valley to which we have journeyed is entirely surrounded with mountains, about five miles square, watered by a charming stream, and inhabited by two thousand aborigines, who are divided into seven clans, and located in seven villages. The ruling men of the tribe have signified to their people that the period for planting corn has arrived, and that they must gather themselves together for the purpose of submitting to the annual ceremonies of purification. For doing this they have a double object: they would, in the first place, expunge from their bodies every vestige of all the colds and diseases with which they may have been afflicted during the past winter; and, in the second place, they would propitiate the Great Spirit, so as to secure his blessing upon the crops which they are about to deposit in the ground. The moon being now at its full, and a fitting location having been selected, the chiefs and magicians congregate together, and the preliminary measures are thus managed. A magic circle is made to keep out all evil spirits and enemies, and the medicine men then proceed to walk in single file, and with measured steps, completely around the spot which they would render sacred, and which is generally half a mile in diameter, marking their route by plucking a single leaf from every tree or bush which they may happen to pass, all these leaves being carefully deposited in a pouch carried for the purpose. In the mean time, the brotherhood of chiefs have not been unemployed, for while the most aged individual of all has been making a collection of roots, the remainder have built a rude dam, and thereby formed a pond or pool of water on the creek which invariably waters the sacred enclosure. The entire population of the valley are now summoned to the outskirts of the sacred enclosure, and a general invitation extended to all to approach and join the chiefs and magicians in the rite they are about to perform; it being understood, however, that no man, under penalty of death, shall venture to participate, or who has left a single wrong unrevenged, or committed any unmanly deed, and no woman who has given birth to a child since the preceding full moon. In the centre of the sacred ground, and in the vicinity of the pool, a large fire is now made, around which the multitude are congregated. The night is clear, and the moon and stars are flooding the earth with light. An earthen pot is now placed upon the fire, the roots gathered by the old chief, numbering seven varieties, are placed therein, also the leaves plucked by the magicians, when the pot is filled with water by seven virgins, who are promoted to this honor by the appointment of the senior chief. After the contents of the pot have been thoroughly boiled, and a most bitter but medicinal beverage been made, all the persons present are called upon to take seven sips of the bitter liquid, and then directed to bathe no less than seven times in the neighboring pool, the waters of which have been rendered sacred by the incantations of the priests. All these things being done, the multitude assemble around the fire once more, and, to the music of a strange wild singing, they dance until the break of day, and then disperse to their several homes. The friendship of the Great Spirit has now been secured, and therefore, as opportunity offers, the Indians proceed to loosen their ground, as best they may, and then plant their corn. This labor is performed chiefly by the women, and the planted fields are considered as under their especial charge. Though planted in the greatest disorder, they keep their cornfields entirely free of weeds, and the soil immediately around the corn in a loose condition. At every full moon they are commonly apprehensive that some calamity may befall their crop, and, by way of keeping the Great Spirit on their side, the women have a custom of disrobing themselves, at the dead hour of night, and of walking entirely around the field of corn.

And now that the sunshine and showers of summer are performing their ministry of good in bringing the corn to its wonted perfection, it may be well to make the reader acquainted with the following facts: As the Indians purify themselves and perform all their religious rites only when the moon is at its full, so do they refrain from plucking a single ear of corn until they have partaken of their annual harvest or green-corn feast. This feast occurs on that night of the full moon nearest to the period when the corn becomes ripe; and, by a time-honored law of the nation, no man, woman, or child is ever permitted, under penalty of death, to pluck a single roasting-ear. So rigidly enforced is this law that many Cherokees are known to have lost their lives for disobeying it, while many families have suffered the pangs of hunger for many days, even while their fields were filled with corn, merely because the harvest moon had not yet arrived, and they had not partaken of their annual feast. If a full moon should occur only one week after the corn has become suitable to pluck, the Indians will not touch a single ear until the next moon, even if it should then be so hard as to require pounding before becoming suitable for food. During the ripening period the cornfields are watched with jealous care, and the first stalk that throws out its silken plume is designated by a distinguishing mark. In assigning reasons for this peculiar care, the Indians allege that until the harvest feast has taken place the corn is exclusively the property of the Great Spirit, and that they are only its appointed guardians; and they also maintain that, when the corn is plucked before the appointed moon has arrived, the field which has thus been trespassed upon is sure to be prostrated by a storm or be afflicted with the rot; and therefore it is that they are always greatly alarmed when they discover that a cornfield has been touched, as they say, by the Evil One.

But the harvest moon is now near at hand, and the chiefs and medicine men have summoned the people of the several villages to prepare themselves for the autumnal festival. Another spot of ground is selected, and the same sanctifying ceremony is performed that was performed in the previous spring. The most expert hunter in each village has been commissioned to obtain game, and while he is engaged in the hunt the people of his village are securing the blessing of the Great Spirit by drinking, with many mystic ceremonies, the liquid made from seven of the most bitter roots to be found among the mountains. Of all the game which may be obtained by the hunters, not a single animal is to be served up at the feast whose bones have been broken or mutilated; nor shall a rejected animal be brought within the magic circle, but shall be given to those of the tribe who, by some misdeed, have rendered themselves unworthy to partake of the feast. The hunters are always compelled to return from the chase at the sunset hour, and long before they come in sight of their villages they invariably give a shrill whistle, as a signal of good luck, whereupon the villagers make ready to receive them with a wild song of welcome and rejoicing.

The pall of night has once more settled upon the earth, the moon is in its glory, the watch-fire has been lighted within the magic circle, and the inhabitants of the valley are again assembled together in one great multitude. From all the cornfields in the valley the magicians have collected the marked ears of corn, and deposited them in the kettles with the various kinds of game which may have been slaughtered, from the bear, the deer, and the turkey, to the opossum, the squirrel, and the quail. The entire night is devoted to eating, and the feast comes not to an end until all the food has been dispatched, when, in answer to an appropriate signal from the medicine men, the bones which have been stripped of their flesh are collected together and pounded to a kind of powder, and scattered through the air. The seven days following this feast are devoted to dancing and carousing, and at the termination of this period the inhabitants of the valley retire to their various villages, and proceed to gather in their crops of the sweet maize or Indian corn.

THE OVERFLOWING WATERS.

A TRADITION OF THE CHOCTAWS.

THE world was in its prime, and time rolled on with its accustomed regularity. The tiny streams among the hills and mountains shouted with joy, and the broad rivers wound their wonted course along the peaceful valleys. Many a tall oak had grown from the acorn, spread its rich foliage to the summer winds, decayed with age, and mingled with its mother earth. The moon and stars had long made the night-skies beautiful, and guided the Indian hunter through the wilderness. The sun which the red man calls the glory of the summer time, had never failed to appear at his appointed periods. Many generations of men had lived and passed away.

In process of time the aspect of the world became changed. Brother quarreled with brother, and cruel wars frequently covered the earth with blood. The Great Spirit saw all these things and was displeased. A terrible wind swept over the wilderness, and the red men knew that they had done wrong, but they lived as if they did not care. Finally a stranger prophet made his appearance among them, and proclaimed in every village the news that the human race was to be destroyed. None believed his words, and the moons of summer again came and disappeared. It was now the autumn of the year. Many cloudy days had occurred, and then a total darkness came upon the earth, and the sun seemed to have departed forever. It was very dark and very cold. Men laid themselves down to sleep, but they were troubled with unhappy dreams. They arose when they thought it was time for the day to dawn, but only to see the sky covered with a darkness deeper than the heaviest cloud. The moon and stars had all disappeared, and there was constantly a dismal bellowing of thunder in the upper air. Men now believed that the sun would never return, and there was great consternation throughout the land. The great men of the Choctaw nation spoke despondingly to their fellows, and sung their death songs, but those songs were faintly heard in the gloom of the great night. It was a most unhappy time indeed, and darkness reigned for a great while. Men visited each other by torch-light. The grains and fruits of the land became mouldy, and the wild animals of the forest became tame and gathered around the watchfires of the Indians, entering even the villages.

A louder peal of thunder than was ever before heard now echoed through the firmament, and a light was seen in the North. It was not the light of the sun, but the gleam of distant waters. They made a mighty roar, and, in billows like the mountains, they rolled over the earth. They swallowed up the entire human race in their career, and destroyed everything which had made the earth beautiful. Only one human being was saved, and that was the mysterious prophet who had foretold the wonderful calamity. He had built him a raft of sassafras logs, and upon this did he float safely above the deep waters. A large black bird came and flew in circles above his head. He called upon it for aid, but it shrieked aloud, and flew away and returned to him no more. A smaller bird, of a bluish color, with scarlet eyes and beak, now came hovering over the prophet's head. He spoke to it, and asked if there was a spot of dry land in any part of the waste of waters. It fluttered its wings, uttered a sweet moan, and flew directly towards that part of the sky where the newly-born sun was just sinking in the waves. A strong wind now arose, and the raft of the prophet was rapidly borne in the same direction which the bird had pursued. The moon and stars again made their appearance, and the prophet landed upon a green island, where he encamped. Here he enjoyed a long and refreshing sleep, and when morning dawned he found that the island was covered with every variety of animals, excepting the great *Shakanli*, or mammoth, which had been destroyed. Birds, too, he also found here in great abundance. He recognized the identical black one which had abandoned him to his fate upon the waters, and, as it was a wicked bird and had sharp claws, he called it *Ful luh-chitto*, or bird of the Evil One. He also discovered, and with great joy, the bluish bird which had caused the wind to blow him upon the island, and because of its kindness to him and its beauty, he called it *Puch che-yon-sho-ba*, or the soft-voiced pigeon. The waters finally passed away, and in process of time that bird became a woman and the wife of the prophet, from whom the people now living upon the earth are all descended. And so endeth the story of The Overflowing Waters.

THE NAMELESS CHOCTAW.

There once lived in the royal Indian town of *E-ya-sho* (Ya-zoo) the only son of a war chief, who was eminently distinguished above all his fellows for his elegant form and noble bearing. The old men of the nation looked upon him with pride, and said that he was certainly born to occupy a high position as a warrior. He was also an eloquent orator, and none ever thought of doubting his courage. But, with all these qualities, he was not allowed a seat in the councils of his nation, because he had not distinguished himself in war. The renown of having slain an enemy he could not claim, nor had he ever been fortunate enough to take a single prisoner. He was universally beloved, and, as the name of his childhood had been abandoned according to an ancient custom, and he had not yet succeeded in winning a name worthy of his ability, he was known among his kindred as the Nameless Choctaw.

In the town of E-ya-sho there also once lived the most beautiful maiden of her tribe. She was the daughter of a hunter, and the betrothed of the Nameless Choctaw. They met often at the great dances, but, because she hoped to become his bride, she treated him as a stranger. Often, too, did they meet at the setting of the sun, but then they listened to the song of the whippoorwill or watched the rising of the evening star, when each could hear the throbbing of the other's heart. They loved with a wild passion and were very happy. At such times one thought alone entered their minds to cast a shadow. It was this: They knew that the laws of their nation were unalterable, and that she could not become his bride until he had won a name. She knew that he could always place at the door of her lodge an abundance of game, and would deck her with the most beautiful of shells and wampum; but all this availed them nothing; that he must go upon the war-path was inevitable. She belonged to a proud family, and she never would consent to marry a man who had not a loud sounding name, and who could not sit in the councils of her people. She was willing to become his bride at any time, and therefore left him, by his prowess, to decide upon that time.

It was now midsummer and the evening hour. The Nameless Lover had met his promised bride upon the summit of a small hill, covered with pines. From the centre of a neighboring plain arose the smoke of a large watch-fire, around which were dancing a party of four hundred warriors. They had planned an expedition against the Osages, and the present was the fourth and last night of the preparation ceremonies. Up to that evening the Nameless Choctaw had been the leader in the dances, and even now his absence was only temporary, for he had stolen away to express his parting vows to his beloved. The last embrace was given, and then the maiden was alone upon the hill-top, looking down in sadness upon the dancing warriors, among whom she beheld none who commanded more attention than the being whom she loved.

Morning dawned, and the Choctaw warriors were upon the war-path leading to the country of their enemies, far up on the headwaters of the Arkansas. Upon that stream they found a cave, and in that cave, because they were on a praire land, they secreted themselves. Two men were then selected to act as spies, one of whom (the Nameless Choctaw,) was to reconnoitre in the west and the other in the east. Night came, and the party in the cave were discovered by an Osage hunter, who had traveled thither for the purpose of sheltering himself until morning from the heavy dews. By the light of the stars did he then travel to the nearest village, and having warned his people of the proximity of their enemies, they hurried in a large body to the cave. At its mouth they built a fire, and when the sun rose in the horizon the entire party of

Choctaws had been smothered to death by the cunning of their enemies.

The Choctaw spy who had journeyed towards the east, had witnessed the surprise and unhappy fate of his brother warriors, and, returning to his own country, he called a council and revealed the sad intelligence. As to the fate of the Nameless Choctaw, who had journeyed to the westward, he knew that he too must have been overtaken and slain. Upon the heart of one being this last intelligence fell with a most heavy weight, and the promised bride of the Nameless Lover pined in melancholy grief. From the night on which she was made wretched, she began to droop, and before the reigning moon had passed away she died, and was buried on the identical spot where she had parted with her lover.

But what became of the nameless Choctaw? It was not true that he had been overtaken and slain. He was indeed discovered by the Osages, and far over the prairies and across the streams was he closely pursued. For many days and through the watches of many nights did the race continue, but the Choctaw warrior finally made his escape. His course had been exceedingly winding, and when he came to a pause he was astonished to find that the sun rose in the wrong quarter of the heavens. Everything appeared to him wrong and out of order, and the truth was he became a bewildered and forlorn man, and everywhere did he wander. He found himself at the foot of a mighty range of mountains, which were covered with grass and unlike any that he had ever before seen.

It so happened, however, at the close of a certain day, that he sauntered into a wooded valley, and having built him a rude bower and killed a rabbit, he lighted a fire and prepared himself for one quiet meal and a night of repose. Morning dawned, and he was still in trouble. Many moons passed away and the Choctaw was still desolate and forlorn. It was now summer, and he called upon the Great Spirit to make his pathway plain; and having hunted the forests for a spotted deer, and slain her, on a day when there was no wind he offered a sacrifice, and that night supped upon a portion of the animal's sweet flesh. His fire burnt brightly, and though somewhat forlorn, he found that his heart was at peace. But now he hears a footstep! A moment more, and a snow-white wolf of immense size is crouching at his feet, and licking his torn moccasins. "How came you in this strange country?" inquired the wolf; and the poor Indian related the story of his unsuccessful exploit and subsequent escape. The wolf took pity upon the Choctaw and told him that he would conduct him in safety to the country of his kindred; and on the following morning did they take their departure. Long, very long was the journey, and many and very wild and turbulent the streams which they had to cross. The wolf helped the Choctaw to kill game for their mutual sustenance, and by the time that the moon for weeding the corn had arrived, the nameless Choctaw had entered his native village again. This was on the anniversary of the day he had parted with his betrothed, and he was sorely grieved to find his people mourning her untimely death. Time and fatigue had so changed the returned Choctaw that his relatives and friends did not recognize him, and he chose not to reveal himself. From many a mouth, however, did he learn the story of her death, and many a wild song, to the astonishment of all his friends, did he sing to the memory of the departed, whom he called by the beautiful name of IMMA, or the idol of warriors. And on a cloudless night did he wander to the grave of his beloved, and at a moment when the Great Spirit cast his shadow upon the moon (alluding to an eclipse) did he throw himself thereon and die. For three nights thereafter were the inhabitants of the Choctaw village alarmed by the continual howling of a wolf, and when it ceased, the pine forest, upon the hill where the lovers were resting in peace, took up the dismal howl or moan, and has continued it to the present time.

THE SPIRIT SACRIFICE.

It was midsummer, and there was a terrible plague in the wilderness. Many a Chippewa village on the borders of Lake Superior had been depopulated. The only band of the great northern nation which had thus far escaped, was the one whose hunting grounds lay on the northern shore of the St. Mary's River. Their principal village stood upon a gentle promontory overlooking the Great Lake, immediately at the head of the *Sault* or Falls, and at this village the chiefs and warriors of the tribe were assembled in council. Incantations of every possible description had for many days been performed, and yet nightly tidings were received, showing that the fatal disease was sweeping over the land, like the fires of autumn over the prairies. The signs in the sky, as well as these tidings, convinced the poor Indians that their days were numbered. It was now the last night of their council, and they were in despair. They knew that the plague had been sent upon the earth by the Great Spirit, as a punishment for some crime, and they also knew that there was but one thing that could possibly appease his anger. And what was this? The sacrifice of the most beautiful girl of her tribe. And such was the decree, that she should enter her canoe, and throwing away her paddle, cast herself upon the waters just above the *Sault.*

Morning dawned, and loud and dismal beyond compare, was the wail of sorrow which broke upon the silent air. Another council was held, and the victim for the sacrifice was selected. She was an only child, and her mother was a widow, feeble and infirm. They told the maiden of her fate, and she uttered not a repining word. The girls and women of the village flocked around their long-loved companion, and decked her hair and her neck with all the brightest wampum, and the most beautiful feathers and shells that could be found in all the tribe. The time appointed for the sacrifice was the sunset hour; and as the day was rapidly waning, the gloom which pervaded the entire village gradually increased, and it even seemed as if a murmuring tone mingled with the roar of the mighty waterfall. The day had been one of uncommon splendor, and as the sun descended to the horizon, a retinue of gorgeous clouds gathered around him, and the great lake, whose waters receded to the sky, was covered with a deeper blue than had ever before been seen.

All things were now ready, and the Indian maiden was ready for the sacrifice. In silence was she conducted to her canoe, and loud was the wail of lamentation. It died away; and now, to the astonishment of all the peeple, a strange echo came from over the waters. What could it mean? A breathless silence ensued, and even the old men listened with fear. And now a louder and clearer continuation of the same echo breaks upon the air. A speck is seen upon the waters. The sun has disappeared, and a small canoe is seen rapidly approaching, as if from the very spot where the orb touched the waters. The song increases; and as the fairy-like canoe sweeps mysteriously over the watery waste, it is now seen to contain a beautiful being, resembling a girl, clothed in a snow-white robe. She is in a standing attitude, her arms are folded and her eyes are fixed upon the heavens. Her soul is absorbed in a song, of which this is the burden:

> "I come from the Spirit land,
> To appease the Great Spirit,
> To stay the plague,
> And to save the life of the beautiful Chippewa."

Onward she came, and her pathway lay directly towards the mighty rapids. With utter astonishment did the Indians look upon this unheard of spectacle, and while they looked they saw the canoe and its spirit voyager pass directly into the foam, where it was lost to them for ever. And so did the poor Indians escape the plague.

The St. Mary is a beautiful river; and during the summer time its shores are always lined with lilies, large, and of a marvelous whiteness; and it is a common belief among the Chippewas, that they owe their origin to the mysterious spirit, from whose mutilated body they sprang. And so endeth the Legend of the Spirit Sacrifice.

THE PEACE-MAKER.

The following story was obtained by the writer, directly from the lips of a Seneca Indian, and the hero is said to have been the grandfather of the celebrated orator Red Jacket.

THERE was a time when all the Indian tribes in the world were at war with the great Seneca nation, whose hunting-grounds were on the borders of Lake Ontario. So fearful had they become of their enemies, that the bravest hunters and warriors never left their wigwams without bending their bows, and little children were not permitted by their mothers to gather berries or hickory nuts in the neighboring woods. The head chief of the nation at that time, was *Sa-go-you-wat-ha*, or *Always Awake*. He was a good man, and being sorely grieved at the unhappiness of his people, he conceived the idea of securing a permanent peace. It was true, he said, that his father had been a cruel and unpopular chief, but he did not think it right that the generation which followed his father should be made miserable for crimes never committed by them. And therefore it was that he prayed to the *Great Ha-nee* to tell him, in a dream, what he must do to accomplish his end. Night came, and in spite of his name, *Always Awake* fell into a deep sleep and had a dream.

He was told that in the direction whence came the warm winds of summer, and distant from his village a journey of one moon, there was a very large mountain. On the summit of that mountain, as he was told, were living a few people from all the nations of the earth, excepting the Senecas. The place alluded to was called the *Mountain of Refuge*, and it was so sacred a place, that its soil had never been wet with human blood, and the people who lived there, were the peculiar favorites of the Great Ha-nee, and were the law-makers of the world.

The dream also told the Seneca chief, that he could secure a permanent peace only by visiting the sacred mountain; but as the intervening distance was so great, and his trail would be only among enemies, the dangers of the expedition would be very numerous. By travelling at night, however, and sleeping in the day time, the task might be accomplished, and he was at liberty to try *his* fortune.

Always Awake pondered a long time upon this strange vision, but finally determined to start upon the appointed expedition. Great was the fatigue that he endured, and oftentimes he was compelled to satisfy his hunger with the roots and berries of the forest. Many a narrow escape did he make from his enemies; but in due time he reached the Mountain of Refuge. He was warmly welcomed among the Indians of the mountain, and when he told his story and talked of peace, they honored him with many a loud shout of applause. A council was held, and a decree passed, to the effect that the important question at stake should be settled by another council composed of the head chiefs of all the Indian nations in the land. The fleetest runners were employed to disseminate the news, and at the appointed time the council of chiefs was held. They formed themselves into a confederacy, and with one exception, the nations of the wilderness became as one people, and so continued until the white man crossed the great waters and taught them the vices which have almost consumed them from the face of the earth. The only nation that would not join the confederation was the Osage nation, and because of their wickedness in so doing, they were cursed by the Great Ha-nee, and have ever since been a by-word and a reproach among their fellows.

And when the Seneca chief returned to his own country, he was very happy. His trail through the forests and over mountains was lined with bonfires, and in every village that he tarried, he was feasted with the best of game. One moon after he returned to his people he died, and was buried on the banks of the beautiful lake where he lived; and ever since that time the Great Ha-nee has permitted his people to live upon the land inherited from their fathers.

ORIGIN OF THE DEER.

A SHAWNEE LEGEND.

WA-PIT-PA-TASKA, or the Yellow Sky, was the daughter of a Shawnee or Snake hunter. His lodge was not one of the handsomest in the village where it stood, but the paths leading to it were more beaten than those leading to any other, for the daughter of the hunter was a great favorite among the young men of her tribe. The exploits of those who sought her hand had no charms for her ear, and her tastes were strangely different from those common among women. She knew that she had not many years to live upon the earth, and her dreams had told her she was created for an unheard-of mission. There was a mystery about her being, and none could comprehend the meaning of her evening songs. On one condition alone did she avow her willingness to become a wife, and this was, that he who became her husband should never, under any circumstances, mention her name. If he did so, a sad calamity would befall him, and he would forever thereafter regret his thoughtlessness. By this decree was the love of one of her admirers greatly enhanced, and before the summer was gone the twain were married and dwelt in the same lodge.

Time flew on and the Yellow Sky sickened and died, and her last words were that her husband should never forget her admonition about breathing her name. The widower was very unhappy, and for five summers did he avoid his fellow-men, living in solitude, and wandering through the forests alone. The voices of autumn were now heard in the land, and the bereaved husband had, after his many journeyings, returned to the grave of his wife, which he found overgrown with briers and coarse weeds. For many moons had he neglected to protect the remains of his wife, and he now tried to atone for his wickedness by plucking up the briers and covering the grave with a soft sod. In doing this he was discovered by a stranger Indian, who asked him whose grave it was of which he was taking so much care? "It is the grave," said he, "of *Wa-pit-pa-taska;*" and hardly had the forbidden name (which he thoughtlessly uttered,) passed from his lips, before he fell to the earth in a spasm of great pain. The sun was setting, and his bitter moans echoed far through the gloomy woods, even until the darkness settled upon the world.

Morning came, and near the grave of the Yellow Sky a large buck was quietly feeding. It was the unhappy husband, whom the Great Spirit had thus changed. The trotting of a wolf was heard in the brake, and the deer pricked up his ears. One moment more, and the wolf started after the deer. The race was very long and painful, but the deer finally escaped. And thus from a man came into existence the beautiful deer, or *mu-rat-si;* and because of the foolishness of this man, in not remembering his wife's words, the favorite animal of the Shawnee has ever been at the mercy of the wolf.

LEGEND OF THE WHITE OWL.

It was in the country of the Winnebagoes, or people of the turbid water, and there was a great scarcity of game. An Indian hunter, while returning from an unsuccessful expedition, at the sunset hour, chanced to discover in the top of a tree a large white owl. He knew that the flesh of this bird was not palatable to the taste, but as he thought of his wife and children, who had been without food for several days, he concluded to bend his bow and kill the bird. Hardly had he come to this determination, before he was astonished to hear the owl speaking to him in the following strain: "You are a very foolish hunter. You know it is against the laws of your nation to kill any of my tribe, and why should you do wrong because you happen to be a little hungry? I know that your wife and children are also hungry, but that is not a good reason for depriving me of life. I too have a wife and several children, and their home is in the hollow of an old tree. When I left them a little while ago, they were quite as hungry as you are, and I am now trying to obtain for their enjoyment a red squirrel or a young opossum. Unlike you, I have to hunt for my game only at night, and if you will go away and not injure me, I may have it in my power to do you a kindness at some future time."

The Indian hunter was convinced and he unbent his bow. He returned to his wigwam, and after he had told his wife what had happened to him, she told him she was not sorry, for she had been particularly fortunate in gathering berries. And then the Indian and his family were contented, and game soon afterwards became abundant in the land.

Many seasons had passed away, and the powerful nation of the Iroquois were making war upon the Winnebagoes. The hunter already mentioned had become a successful warrior and a chief. He was a mark for his enemies, and the bravest among them started upon the war-path for the express purpose of effecting his destruction. They hunted him as they would the panther, but he always avoided their arrows. Many days of fatigue had he now endured, and, believing that his enemies had given up the chase, he stopped, on a certain evening, to rest himself and enjoy a repast of roots. After this comfortless supper was ended, he wrapped himself in his skins and thought that he would lie down and enjoy a little sleep. He did so, and the only sounds which broke the stillness of the air were caused by the falling of the dew from the leaves and the whistling of the whippoorwill. It was now past midnight, and the Winnebago was yet undisturbed. A whoop is heard in the forest so remote from his grassy couch as not to be heard by the unconscious sleeper. But what can this shouting mean? A party of the Iroquois warriors have fallen upon the trail of their enemy, and are in hot pursuit. But still the Winnebago warrior is in the midst of a pleasant dream. On come his enemies, and his death is inevitable. The shouting of the Iroquois is now distinct and clear, but in the twinkling of an eye it is swallowed up in a much louder and more dismal shriek, which startled the Winnebago to his feet. He is astonished, and wonders whence comes the noise. He looks upwards, and lo! perched upon one of the branches of the tree under which he had been resting, the form of a large white owl. It rolls its large yellow eyes upon him, and tells him that an enemy is on his trail, and that he must flee for his life. And this is the way in which the white owl manifested its gratitude to the Winnebago hunter for his kindness in sparing its own life many years before. And since that time the owl has ever been considered a very good and a wise bird, and when it perches above the wigwam of the red man it is always safe from harm.

DEATH OF THE GIANT CANNIBAL.

The following story was obtained from the lips of a Chippewa warrior named *Maw-gun-nub*, or Setting-ahead. He told it with as serious an air as if it had been a matter of actual and important history, and was evidently a firm believer in the wonders therein contained.

An Indian village stood upon the borders of the Lake of the Woods. It was a summer day, and a heavy rain storm had passed over the country, when a large Giant or Cannibal suddenly made his appearance in the village. He was as tall as the tallest hemlock, and carried a club in his hand which was longer than the longest canoe. He told the Indians that he had come from a far country in the North; that he was tired and hungry; and that all the wild rice and game in the village must be immediately brought to his feet that he might satisfy his appetite. His orders were obeyed, and when the food was brought, and the inhabitants of the village were collected together to see him enjoy his feast, the Giant told them he was not yet satisfied; whereupon, with one blow of his huge club, he destroyed, with one exception, all the people who had treated him so kindly. The only person who escaped the dreadful blow was a little boy, who happened to be sick in one of the wigwams.

After the Giant had committed his cruel deed, he devoured a number of the dead bodies, and during the night disappeared without discovering the boy. In a few days the boy was well enough to move about, and as he went from one wigwam to another, he thought of his friends who had been so suddenly killed, and was very unhappy. For many seasons did he live alone. While very young his food consisted of such birds as the partridge, but as he grew up to the estate of manhood, he became a successful hunter, and often feasted upon the deer and the buffalo. He became a strong man, but was very lonely, and every time he thought of the Giant who had destroyed his relatives and friends he thirsted for revenge.

Time passed on, and the Chippewa hunter became uneasy and discontented. He fasted for many days, and called upon the Great Spirit to give him power to discover and destroy the Giant who had done him so much harm. The Great Spirit took pity upon him, heard his prayer, and sent to his assistance a troop of a hundred men, from whose backs grew the most beautiful of wings. They told the hunter that they knew all about the Giant, and would help him to take his life. They said that the Giant was very fond of the meat of the white bear, and that if the hunter would give a bear feast they were certain that the Giant would make his appearance and ask for a portion of the choice food. The time for giving the feast was appointed, and it was to take place in a large natural wigwam, formed by the locked branches of many trees; whereupon the strange people disappeared and the hunter started towards the north after a bear.

The hunter was successful; the appointed time arrived, the feast was ready, and the strange people were on the ground. The dancing and the singing were all over, and the hot bear soup filled the wigwam with a pleasant odor. A heavy tramp was heard in the woods, and in a little time the Giant made his appearance, attracted to the place by the smell of the soup. He came rushing to the wigwam like one who knew not what it was to fear; but when he saw the array of people with wings he became very quiet, and asked the hunter if he might participate in the feast. The hunter told him that he might, on condition that he would go to the mouth of a certain stream that emptied into the lake, and bring therefrom to the wigwam a large rock which he would find there. The Giant was angry at this request, but as he was afraid of the people with wings he dared not disobey. He did as he was bidden, and the thong which he used to hold the rock on his back cut a deep gash in his forehead.

The hunter was not yet satisfied, and he told the Giant that before he could be admitted to the feast he must bring to the wigwam a gill-net that would reach across the widest stream. The Giant departed, and, having obtained a beautiful net from a *mammoth spider* that lived in a cave, he brought it to the hunter. The hunter was well pleased, but not yet fully satisfied. One more thing did he demand from the Giant before he could be admitted to the feast, which was this, that he must make his appearance at the feast wearing a robe made of weasel skins, with the teeth and claws all on. This robe was obtained, the Giant was admitted, and the feast proceeded.

It lasted for several days and nights, and the hunter, the strange people, and the Giant danced and caroused together as if they had been the best of friends. The Giant was delighted with the singing of his entertainers, and while he praised them to the skies he did not know that in his bowl of soup the Chippewa hunter, who had not forgotten the death of his friends, had placed a bitter root, which would deprive him of his strength. But such was, indeed, the case. On the last night of the feast the Giant became very tired and stupid, and asked permission to enjoy some sleep. Permission was granted, and in the centre of the great lodge was spread for his accommodation his weasel-skin robe. Upon the stone which he brought from the river did he rest his head, and over him was spread the net he had obtained from the mammoth spider. He then fell into a deep sleep, and the men with wings and the hunter continued the revelry. Each man supplied himself with a war club, and they performed the dance of revenge. They formed a ring around the sleeping Giant, and at a signal made by the hunter they all gave him a severe blow, when the spirit-men disappeared into the air, and the weasel-skin robe suddenly became alive. The little animals feasted upon the Giant with evident satisfaction, and by morning there was nothing left of him but his bones. These did the hunter gather into a heap, and having burnt them to ashes, he threw them into the air, and immediately there came into existence all the beautiful birds which now fill the world. And in this manner was the great Giant of the Chippewas destroyed, and instead of his living to feast upon the flesh of man, his own body, by the wisdom of the Great Spirit, was turned into the birds, which are the animal food of man.

THE CHIPPEWA MAGICIAN.

THIS legend, with at least a score of variations, was related to me by a Chippewa hunter named *Ka-zhe-osh*, or the *Fleet Flyer*. It is excessively romantic, but will most certainly enlist the sympathies of the ladies.

Near the head of the Mississippi is Sandy Lake. In the centre of this lake there is an island, and on this island, in the olden times, stood a Chippewa village. The chief of this village had a daughter, and that daughter had a lover, who was the greatest warrior of his tribe, and a magician. He had the power of turning himself into any kind of animal he pleased, and for this reason he was looked upon with suspicion by the females of his acquaintance. He lived in a secluded lodge on the outskirts of the village, and none ever disturbed him in his seclusion without express permission; and a greater number of scalps hung from the poles of his lodge than from those of any other in the tribe. The chief's daughter admired him for his noble bearing and his exploits, but she could not reconcile herself to become his wife. She was afraid of the strange power that he possessed, but she loved her father, and had promised him that she would never disobey his commands in regard to choosing her husband, though she trusted that the magician would never be mentioned in that connection.

In view of this state of things the magician made interest with the entire brotherhood of warriors and hunters, and proclaimed his intention of leading them upon the war-path to a distant country. He was unhappy, and hoped to find peace of mind by wandering into strange lands. At an appointed time the party assembled upon a neighboring plain, and they went through the ceremonies of the war-dance. They also shouted a loud war song, with the following burden :—

"We love the whoop of our enemies;
We are going to war,
We are going to war, on the other side of the world."

On witnessing these preparations, the chief of the village became troubled. He well knew that if the old men and the women and children under his charge should be abandoned by the fighting men and hunters of the tribe, they would be visited by much suffering, and he determined to avoid the calamity. But how could this be done? He thought of only one method, which was to give the magician his daughter. He told the daughter, and she promised to obey. He made the proposition to the magician, and it was accepted. It was on certain conditions, however, and these were as follows :—

The magician was first to capture the largest white-fish in the lake, then kill a white deer, and finally win a foot-race of fifteen miles against the swiftest runner in the tribe. All these things the magician promised to do, and he did them all. He turned himself into an otter, and by the assistance of the chief of the otters secured the largest fish that had ever been seen, and appearing in his own form again, deposited it in the lodge of the chief. He also turned himself into a black wolf, and having ranged the forest for a white deer he caught it, and again resuming his natural form carried it to the lodge where lived his betrothed. In running the race that had been proposed he had one hundred competitors, and at the end of the fifteen miles was stationed the chief's daughter, with a belt of wampum in her hand to crown the victor. The magician started upon the race in the form of a man, but before he had run a mile he turned himself into a hawk, and swooping to the side of the maiden, demanded that she should now become an inmate of his lodge. She consented, and the chief gave her to the magician. Before he took her away he called together the men of his tribe who had competed with him for the prize, and complimented them for their great activity in running the race, and condoled with them in their disappointment. He then told the chief that he did not thank him for what he had done, and turning to the daughter he said that as she had cost him so much trouble, she must enter his camp and do all his work for him, even to the end of her days. And ever since that time has it been the lot of all Indian women to act as the servants of their husbands.

THE LOVER STAR.

I obtained the following legend from the lips of an Indian trader, whom I met at the island of La Pointe, in Lake Superior. He said it was related to him by a hunter of the Chippewyan nation, and that he had heard a similar story among the Chippewas.

THERE was once a quarrel among the stars, when one of them was driven away from its home in the heavens and descended to the earth. It wandered from one tribe of Indians to another, and had been seen hovering over the camp-fires of a thousand Indians, when they were preparing themselves for sleep. It always attracted attention and inspired wonder and admiration. It often lighted upon the heads of little children, as if for the purpose of playing with them, but they were invariably frightened and drove it away by their loud crying. Among all the people in the world, only one could be found who was not afraid of this beautiful star; and this was a little girl, the daughter of a Chippewyan warrior. She was not afraid of the star, but rather than this, she loved it with her whole heart, and was very happy in her love. That she was loved by the star in return there could be no doubt, for wherever she traveled with her father through the wilderness there, as the night came on did the star follow, but it was never seen in the day time. When the girl awoke at night, the star floated just above her head; and, when she was asleep, it was so constant in its watchfulness, that she never opened her eyes, even at midnight, without beholding its brilliant light. People wondered at this strange condition of things, but how much more did they wonder, when they found that the father of the girl never returned from the hunt without an abundance of game. They therefore concluded that the star must be the son of the Good Spirit, and they ever after spoke of it with veneration.

Time passed on, and it was midsummer. The Indian girl had gone into the woods for the purpose of gathering berries. Those of the wintergreen were nearly all eaten up by the pigeons and the deer, and, as the cranberries were beginning to ripen, she wandered into a large marsh with a view of filling her willow basket with them. She did so, and in the tangled thickets of the swamp she lost her way. She became frightened and cried aloud for her father to come to her assistance. The only creatures that answered her cries were the frogs and the lonely bittern. The night was rapidly coming, and the farther she wandered the more intricate became her path. At one time she was compelled to wade into the water even to her knees, and then again would she fall into a deep hole and almost become drowned among the poisonous slime and weeds. Night came, and the poor girl looked up at the sky, hoping that she might see the star that she loved. A storm had arisen, and the rain fell so rapidly that a star could not live in it, and therefore was there none to be seen. The storm continued, the waters of the country rose, and in rushing into the deeper lakes, they destroyed the Indian girl, and washed her body away so that it never could be found.

Many seasons passed away and the star continued to be seen above the watch-fires of the Chippewyans; but it would never remain long in one place, and its light appeared to have become dimmed. It ever seemed to be looking for something that it could not find, and people knew that it was unhappy on account of the untimely death of the girl it had loved. Additional years passed on, and with the leaves of autumn, it finally disappeared. A cold and long winter soon followed, and then the hottest summer that had ever been known. During this season it so happened that a hunter chanced at night to follow a bear into one of the largest swamps of the land, when to his astonishment he discovered a small light hanging over the water. It was so beautiful that he followed it for a long distance, but it led into such dangerous places that he gave up the pursuit, and returned to tell his people what he had seen. And then it was that the oldest men of the tribe told him that the light he had seen was the star that had been driven from heaven, and that it was now wandering over the earth for the purpose of finding the beautiful girl it had loved. And that same star is still upon the earth, and is often seen by the hunters as they journey at night through the wilderness.

ORIGIN OF THE POTTOWATOMIES.

According to the belief of the Pottowatomies, there once lived on the western shore of Lake Michigan two great spirits. Their names were *Kit-che-mo-ne-to*, or the Good Spirit, and *Mat-che-mo-me-to*, the Evil Spirit. They were equally powerful, but the creation of the world was attributed to the former. When he had piled up the mountains, and filled the valleys with running streams, he proceeded to people the world with living creatures, and allotted to each variety its peculiar sphere. He then endeavored to create a being that should resemble himself, but in this attempt he did not succeed. The animal that he made looked and acted more like a wolf than any other creature. Disappointed at this failure the Good Spirit became angry, and seizing the strange creature he had made he threw it into a great lake, and it was drowned. A storm arose, and the waters of the lake made a terrible noise as they beat upon its rocky shores. Among the shells and pebbles washed upon the sands were the bones of the strange animal that the Good Spirit had made, and when the storm had abated the bones were turned into a being who bore a strong likeness to the present race of Pottowatomies, and that being was the first woman. So well pleased with this creation was the Good Spirit that he made five other beings resembling her in form, but only more rugged, who were to help her in all her employments; and these were the first men. One of them was named *U-sa-me*, or Smoking Weed; another *Wa-pa-ho*, or Pumpkin; another *Esh-kos-sim-in*, or the Melon; another *Ko-kees*, or the Bean; and the other *Mon-ta-min*, or Yellow Maize. The business of these several beings was to protect and gather the various productions of the earth after which they were named, and in doing this they continued to be employed from the time that the acorn fell to the ground until it became one of the largest trees of the forest.

The world had now become very beautiful, and the few men who had the care of it very proud. They became the friends of the Evil Spirit. They quarreled among themselves, and in process of time with the woman, whom they had for a long time obeyed. They looked upon her as the queen of the world, and coveted her power and happiness. They tried to take her life, but without success. She became acquainted with the wickedness of their hearts, and regretted that she had ever been created. So unhappy did she become that she prayed to the Good Spirit to take her to the sky; and when the following evening came she was transformed into a star, and ever since that time has been the first to take her station in the horizon after the sun has disappeared behind the distant hills. And it is thought that so long as this star remains unchanged no misfortune can happen to the world.

When the five young men found themselves alone they were sorry for the unkind feelings they had manifested towards the woman, and were constantly missing the brightness of her smiles and the music of her voice, which they now remembered with mingled feelings of pleasure and pain. They were in great tribulation, and expected to perish from the face of the earth for their wickedness. They called upon the Evil Spirit for comfort and power, but he heard them not; he had abandoned them to their fate. They then thought that they would implore the assistance of the Good Spirit. They did so, and told him that they only wanted each the companionship of a woman, like the one that had been taken away. Their prayer was answered, and thus did they become the husbands of affectionate wives, from whom are descended the nation of Pottowatomies, or *the people who make their own fires.*

ORIGIN OF THE CHOCTAWS.

The *sea* alluded to in this legend is supposed to be the *Gulf of Mexico*, and the *mighty river* the *Mississippi*. So said the educated Choctaw *Pitchlyn*, from whom it was obtained. The idea that the Choctaws were the original mound builders, will strike the reader as something new.

ACCORDING to the traditions of the Choctaws, the first of their race came from the bosom of a magnificent sea. Even when they first made their appearance upon the earth they were so numerous as to cover the sloping and sandy shore of the ocean, far as the eye could reach, and for a long time did they follow the margin of the sea before they could find a place suited to their wants. The name of their principal chief has long since been forgotten, but it is well remembered that he was a prophet of great age and wisdom. For many moons did they travel without fatigue, and all the time were their bodies strengthened by pleasant breezes, and their hearts, on the other hand gladdened by the luxuriance of a perpetual summer. In process of time, however, the multitude was visited by sickness, and one after another were left upon the shore the dead bodies of old women and little children. The heart of the Prophet became troubled, and, planting a long staff that he carried in his hand, and which was endowed with the miraculous power of an oracle, he told his people that from the spot designated they must turn their faces towards the unknown wilderness. But before entering upon this portion of their journey he specified a certain day for starting, and told them that they were at liberty, in the meantime, to enjoy themselves by feasting and dancing, and performing their national rights.

It was now early morning, and the hour appointed for starting. Heavy clouds and flying mists rested upon the sea, but the beautiful waves melted upon the shore as joyfully as ever before. The staff which the Prophet had planted was found leaning towards the north, and in that direction did the multitude take up their line of march. Their journey lay across streams, over hills and mountains, through tangled forests, and over immense prairies. They were now in an entirely strange country, and as they trusted in their magic staff they planted it every night with the utmost care, and arose in the morning with great eagerness to ascertain the direction towards which it leaned. And thus had they traveled for many days when they found themselves upon the margin of an *O-kee-na-chitto*, or great highway of water. Here did they pitch their tents, and having planted the staff, retired to repose. When morning ing came the oracle told them that they must cross the mighty river before them. They built themselves a thousand rafts, and reached the opposite shore in safety. They now found themselves in a country of surpassing loveliness, where the trees were so high as almost to touch the clouds, and where game of every variety and the sweetest of fruits were found in the greatest abundance. The flowers of this land were more brilliant than any they had ever before seen, and so large as often to shield them from the sunlight of noon. With the climate of the land they were delighted, and the air they breathed seemed to fill their bodies with a new vigor. So pleased were they with all that they saw that they built mounds in all the more beautiful valleys they passed through, so that the Master of Life might know that they were not an ungrateful people. In this new country did they conclude to remain, and here did they establish their national government with its benign laws.

Time passed on, and the Choctaw nation became so powerful that its hunting grounds extended even to the sky. Troubles now arose among the younger warriors and hunters of the nation, until it came to pass that they abandoned the cabins of their forefathers, and settled in distant regions of the earth.

Thus from the very body of the Choctaw nation have sprung those other nations which are known as the Chickasaws, the Cherokees, the Creeks or Muskogees, the Shawnees and the Delawares. And in process of time the Choctaws founded a great city, wherein their more aged men might spend their days in peace; and, because they loved those of their people who had long before departed into distant regions, they called this city *Yazoo*, the meaning of which is, *home of the people who are gone.*

THE DANCING GHOSTS.

THAT beautiful phenomenon known to the white man as the Aurora Borealis, or Northern Lights, is called by the Chippewa Indians *Je-bi-ne-me-id-de-wand*, or the Dancing Ghosts. The legends accounting for it are numerous, and the following, which was related to the translator by a Chippewa hunter, named *Kehes-Chock*, or Precipice Leaper, is quite as fantastic as the phenomenon itself. That it is a very ancient tradition is evident from the fact that the sacrifice to which it alludes has not been practised by the Chippewas for at least a century.

There was a time when all the inhabitants of the far North were afflicted by a famine. It was in the depth of winter, and the weather had for a long time been so cold that even the white bear was afraid to leave his hiding place. The prairies were so deeply covered with snow that the deer and the buffalo were compelled to wander to a warmer climate, and the lakes and rivers were so closely packed with ice that it was only once in a while that even a fish could be obtained. Such sorrow as reigned throughout the land had never before been known. The magicians and wise men kept themselves hidden in their cabins. The warriors and hunters, instead of boasting of their exploits, crowded around their camp-fires, and in silence meditated upon their unhappy doom. Mothers abandoned their children to seek for berries in the desolate forests, and the fingers of the young women had become stiff from idleness, for they had not any skins out of which to make the comfortable moccasin. From one end of the Chippewa country to the other was heard the cry of hunger and distress. That the Great Spirit was angry with his people was universally believed, but for what reason none of the magicians could tell. The chief of the Chippewas was the oldest man in the nation, and he was consulted in regard to the impending calamity. He could give no reason for the famine, but stated that he had been informed in a dream that the anger of the Great Spirit could be appeased by a human sacrifice. How this should come to pass, however, he could not tell, and therefore concluded to summon to his lodge all the medicine-men who lived within a day's journey, for the purpose of consulting with them. He did so, and when the council was ended it was proclaimed that three Chippewas should be immediately bound to the stake and consumed. They were to be selected by lot from among the warriors of the tribe; and, when this sad intelligence was promulgated, a national assembly was ordered to convene.

The appointed time arrived, and, in the presence of a large multitude, the fatal lots were cast, and three of the bravest men of the tribe were thus appointed to the sacrifice. They submitted to their fate without a murmur. Whilst their friends gathered around them with wild lamentations, and decked them with the costliest robes and ornaments to be found in all the tribe, the youthful warriors uttered not a word about their untimely departure, but only spoke in the most poetical language of the happy hunting grounds upon which they were about to enter. The spot selected for the sacrifice was the summit of a neighboring hill which was covered with woods. Upon this spot had three stakes been closely erected, around which there had been collected a large pile of dry branches and other combustible materials. To the stakes, at the hour of midnight, and by the hands of the magicians, unattended by spectators, were the three warriors securely fastened. They performed their cruel duty in silence, and the only sounds that broke the stillness of that winter night were the songs and the shoutings of the multitude assembled in the neighboring village. The incantations of the priests being ended, they applied a torch to the faggots, and, returning to their village, spent the remainder of the night in performing a variety of strange and heart-sickening ceremonies.

Morning dawned, and upon the hill of sacrifice was to be seen only a pile of smouldering ashes. On that day the weather moderated, and an unusual number of hunters went forth in pursuit of game. They were all more successful than they had been for many seasons, and there was an abundance of sweet game, such as the buffalo, the bear, and the deer in every wigwam. A council was called, and the patriarch chief proclaimed the glad tidings that the Great Spirit had accepted their sacrifice, and that it was now the duty of his children to express their gratitude by a feast—the feast of *bitter roots.*

The appointed night arrived, and the bitterest roots which could be found in the lodges of the magicians were collected together and made into a soup. The company assembled to partake of this feast, was the largest that had ever been known, and, as they were to conclude their ceremony of thankfulness by dancing, they had cleared the snow from the centre of their village, and on this spot were they duly congregated. It was a cold and remarkably clear night, and their watchfires burnt with uncommon brilliancy. It was now the hour of midnight, and the bitter soup was all gone. The flutes and the drums had just been brought out, and the dancers, decked in their most uncouth dresses, were about to enter the charmed ring, when a series of loud shoutings were heard, and the eyes of the entire multitude were intently fixed upon the northern sky, which was illuminated by a most brilliant and unearthly light. It was a light of many colors, and as changeable as the reflections upon a summer sea at the sunset hour. Across this light were constantly dancing three huge figures of a crimson hue, and these did the magicians proclaim to be the ghosts of the three warriors who had given up their bodies for the benefit of their people, and who had thus become great chiefs in the spirit-land. The fire by which their bodies had been consumed had also consumed every feeling of revenge; and ever since that remote period it has been their greatest pleasure to illume by their appearance on winter nights the pathway of the hunters over the snowy plains of the north.

THE STRANGE WOMAN.

It was in olden times, and two Choctaw hunters were spending the night by their watch-fire in a bend of the river Alabama. The game and the fish of their country were with every new moon becoming less abundant, and all that they had to satisfy their hunger on the night in question, was the tough flesh of a black hawk. They were very tired, and as they mused upon their unfortunate condition, and thought of their hungry children, they were very unhappy, and talked despondingly. But they roasted the bird before the fire, and proceeded to enjoy as comfortable a meal as they could. Hardly had they commenced eating, however, before they were startled by a singular noise, resembling the cooing of a dove. They jumped up and looked around them to ascertain the cause. In one direction they saw nothing but the moon just rising above the forest trees on the opposite side of the river. They looked up and down the river, but could see nothing but the sandy shores and the dark waters. They listened, and nothing could they hear but the murmur of the flowing stream. They turned their eyes in that direction opposite the moon, and to their astonishment, they discovered standing upon the summit of a grassy mound, the form of a beautiful woman. They hastened to her side, when she told them she was very hungry, whereupon they ran after their roasted hawk, and gave it all into the hands of the strange woman. She barely tasted of the proffered food, but told the hunters that their kindness had preserved her from death, and that she would not forget them when she returned to the happy grounds of her father, who was the *Hosh-tal-li*, or Great Spirit of the Choctaws. She had one request to make, and this was, that when the next moon of midsummer should arrive, they should visit the spot where she then stood. A pleasant breeze swept among the forest leaves, and the strange woman suddenly disappeared.

The hunters were astonished, but they returned to their families, and kept all that they had seen and heard, hidden in their hearts. Summer came, and they once more visited the mound on the banks of the Alabama. They found it covered with a new plant, whose leaves were like the knives of the white man. It yielded a delicious food, which has since been known among the Choctaws as the sweet toncha or Indian maize.

THE VAGABOND BACHELOR.

In the great wilderness of the north, midway between Hudson's Bay and Lake Ontario, lies a beautiful sheet of water called Stone Lake. It is surrounded with hills, which are covered with a dense forest, and the length thereof is about twelve miles. On the shore of this lake there stood, in the olden time, an Ottawa village, and the most notorious vagabond in said village was an old bachelor. He was a kind-hearted rogue, and though he pretended to have a cabin of his own, he spent the most of his time lounging about the wigwams of his friends, where he was treated with the attention usually bestowed upon the oldest dog of an Indian village. The low cunning for which he was distinguished made him the laughing-stock of all who knew him, and his proverbial cowardice had won for him the contempt of all the hunters and warriors. Whenever a war party was convened for the purpose of pursuing an enemy, Wis-ka-go-twa, or the White Liver, always happened to be in the woods; but when they returned, singing their songs of victory, the vagabond bachelor generally mingled conspicuously with the victors.

But, in process of time, Wis-ka-go-twa took it into his head to get married, and from that moment began the troubles of his life. As soon as his resolution had become known among the young women of the village, they came together in secret council, and unanimously agreed that not one of them would ever listen to the expected proposals of the bachelor, for they thought him too great a coward to enjoy the pleasures of matrimony. Years elapsed, and the vagabond was still in the enjoyment of his bachelorhood.

In the meanwhile a beautiful maiden, named Muck-o-wiss, or the Whippoorwill, had budded into the full maturity of life. She was the chief attraction of the village, and the heart of many a brave warrior and expert hunter had been humbled beneath her influence. Among those who had entered her lodge in the quiet night, and whispered the story of his love, was Wis-ka-go-twa. She deigned not to reply to his avowals, and he became unhappy. He asked the consent of her father to their union, and he said that he had no objections provided his daughter was willing. It so happened, however, that the maiden was not willing, for she was a member of that female confederacy which had doomed the vagabond lover to the miseries of single life. Time passed on, and he was the victim of a settled melancholy.

The sunny days of autumn were nearly numbered, and an occasional blast from the far north had brought a shudder to the breast of Wis-ka-go-twa, for they reminded him of the long winter which he was likely to spend in his wigwam alone. He pondered upon the gloomy prospect before him, and in his frenzy made the desperate resolution that he would, by any means in his power, obtain the love of his soft-eyed charmer. He consequently began to exert himself in his daily hunts, and whenever he obtained an uncommonly fat beaver, or large bear, he carefully deposited it before the lodge of Muck-o-wiss, and he now mingled, more frequently than ever before, in the various games of the village, and was not behind his more youthful rivals in jumping and playing ball. In a variety of ways did he obtain renown, but it was at the expense of efforts which nearly deprived him of life. Again did he sue for the smiles of Muck-o-wiss, but she told him he was an old man, and that he did not wear in his hair a single plume of the eagle, to show that he had ever taken a scalp.

The disappointed vagabond now turned his attention to war. It so happened, however, that a permanent peace had been established between the Ottawas and the neighboring tribes, so that our hero was baffled on this score also. But he had heard it reported in the village that a party of Iroquois warriors had been seen on that side of the Great Lake, and as they were heartily hated by his own tribe, he conceived the idea of absenting himself for a few days, for the purpose of playing a deceptive game upon the maiden of his love and the entire population of the village where he lived. Having formed this determination, he kept it entirely to himself, and on a certain morning he launched his canoe upon the lake and disappeared, as if going upon a hunting expedition.

Four or five days had elapsed, and the vagabond bachelor was not yet returned. On the afternoon of the sixth day, a couple of Indian boys, who had been frolicking away the morning in the woods, returned to the village in an uncommonly excited mood. They visited almost every wigwam, and related a grand discovery which they had made. While chasing a deer into a secluded bay, about ten miles down the lake, they announced that they had seen Wis-ka-go-twa engaged in a most singular employment. They were aware of his peculiar reputation, and when they saw him in this out-of-the-way place, they watched him in silence from behind a fallen tree. The first act which they saw him perform was, to shoot into the side of his little canoe some twenty of his flint-headed arrows, which mutilated the canoe in a most disgraceful manner. He next took some unknown instrument, and inflicted a number of severe wounds upon his arms and legs. But the deepest incision which he made was on his leg, just above the knee, into which they were astonished to see him place, with a small stick, a kind of white material, which resembled the dry shell of a turtle. All this being accomplished, they saw the vagabond embark in his leaky canoe, as if about to return to the village. They suspected the game that was being played, so they made the shortest cut home and related the foregoing particulars.

An hour or two passed on, and, as the sun was setting, the villagers were attracted by a canoe upon the lake. They watched it with peculiar interest, and found that it was steadily approaching. Presently it made its appearance within hailing distance, when it was discovered to be occupied by the vagabond bachelor. Every man, woman, and child immediately made their appearance on the shore, apparently for the purpose of welcoming the returning hunter, but in reality with a view of enjoying what they supposed would turn out a good joke. The hunter looked upon the crowd with evident satisfaction, but he manifested his feelings in a very novel manner, for he was momentarily uttering a long-drawn groan, as if suffering from a severe wound. As the canoe touched the sand it was found to be half full of bloody water, and one of the sides had evidently been fired into by the arrows of an enemy. A murmur ran through the crowd that Wis-ka-go-twa must have had a dreadful time, and he was called upon to give the particulars, when he did so in a few words. He had been overtaken, he said, by a party of Iroquois, consisting of some twenty men, who attacked him while he was pursuing a bear, and though he succeeded in killing four of his rascally pursuers, his canoe had been sadly mutilated, and he had received a wound which he feared would be the cause of his death. In due time the wound was revealed to the public eye, and the young women turned away with a shudder; and then the vagabond bachelor was conveyed to his lodge, and the medicine-man sent for to administer relief.

A day or two elapsed, and the poor hunter was evidently in a bad way. They asked him what individual in the village he would have to attend him. He expressed a preference for the father of Muck-o-wiss, who came and faithfully attended to his duties as a nurse; but the sick was not yet satisfied. "Whom will you have now?" asked the old man, and the name of Muck-o-wiss trembled on the lips of the sick lover. His chief desire was granted, and for three days did the maiden attend to the little wants of her unfortunate lover. Another day and he was rapidly mending. He was now so nearly restored that the maiden began to talk of returning to her mother's wigwam. This intelligence roused the hunter from his bed of furs, and he once more avowed his undying attachment to the charming maiden. She repulsed him with a frown, and retired from the lodge; so the hunter was again sadly disappointed. The maiden hastened to tell the news to all the women of the village, and after they had enjoyed themselves for upwards of an hour, Muck-o-wiss returned to the wigwam of her lover, and told him that she would become his wife on one condition, which was, that on the day he should succeed in killing five bears, on that day would she enter his lodge and make it her permanent home. For an Indian to kill five bears on one day was considered a remarkable feat, and the roguish Muck-o-wiss thought herself secure.

Days passed on, and the vagabond bachelor was again restored to sound health and devoting himself to the chase. It was just the season when the black bear takes up its annual journey for the south, and the hunter had discovered a narrow place in the lake, where the animals were in the habit of coming. It was the last day of autumn, and early in the morning he had stationed himself in a good ambush. By the time the sun cast a short shadow, he had killed three fine specimens, and placed them before the lodge of his intended wife. The middle of the afternoon arrived, and he had deposited the fourth animal at the same place. The sunset hour was nigh at hand, and the hunter had killed and placed in his canoe the fifth and largest bear he had ever seen. The happiest hour of the poor man's life was now surely nigh at hand. Impatiently did he paddle his way home. The villagers saw that the vagabond bachelor had been successful, and Muck-o-wiss and all her female companions were filled with consternation. But the truly heroic warriors, who had striven in vain to win the love of the village beauty, were not only astonished, but indignant, for they could not bear the idea of losing, in such a manner, the prize which had urged them on in the more noble deeds of war. But now has the canoe once more reached the shore. Upon his back has the hunter lifted his prize, and up the bank is he toiling and staggering along with the immense load, and now has he fixed his eye upon the lodge where he is hoping to receive his promised bride. His heart flutters with tumultuous joy—his knees tremble from fatigue—a strange faintness passes over his brain—he reels from his upright position—the bear falls to the ground—and the vagabond bachelor is—dead.

ORIGIN OF THE WATER LILY.

Many, many moons ago, an old and very celebrated hunter of the Pottowattomie nation was at the point of death, in a remote forest. He was alone on his bed of leaves, for he had been stricken with the hand of disease while returning from a hunting expedition. Among the treasures that he was to leave behind him was a beautiful hickory arrow, with which he had killed a great number of animals. The head thereof was made of a pure white flint, and the feathers which adorned it had been plucked from the wings of the scarlet bird. It had been the means of saving his life on many occasions, and its virtues were so peculiar, that it could pass entire through a buffalo without being tinged with the life-blood of the animal.

The greatest weight which rested upon the mind of the dying Indian, arose from the idea that he could not bequeath his arrow to his oldest son. He was alone in the wilderness, and it made him very unhappy to think that the treasure of his family might yet become the property of an enemy, who would be likely to cross his trail after the ravens or wolves had eaten his flesh. But this was a thought that he could not possibly endure, and as the pall of night settled upon the world, he fixed his eyes upon the northern star, which had guided him through many dangers, and prayed to the Master of Life that he would take his arrow and carry it safely to the smiling planet. A moment more and the unknown hunter buried his head among the dry leaves, and—died.

On the following night, a terrible gale of wind swept over the land, which took the arrow from the ground and hurled it into the upper air. A strange silence immediately followed, when the northern star was seen to tremble in the sky: another brief period elapsed, and there was a deafening noise heard in the firmament, when the evening star left its own quiet home, and fell upon the northern star for the purpose of winning, by single combat, the arrow of the great hunter. The conflict was a desperate one, and as the two stars fought for the earthly prize, sparks of white light shot from their sides, and in unnumbered particles fell upon the country now known as Michigan. A long rain storm soon followed, by which the particles of light were taken to the river, and by a decree of the Master of Life, were changed into the beautiful white lilies which adorn the numerous streams of the western country.

THE FAITHFUL COUSINS.

I NOW speak of two Chippewa hunters, who lived among the Porcupine mountains, near Lake Superior. They were the oldest sons of two brothers, and noted in their village for the warm friendship existing between them, and for their prowess in hunting. They were very famous throughout the land, and into whatever village they happened to enter, the old men asked them to remain and marry their handsome women, but the hunters laughed at all such proposals, for they had pledged their words to each other that they would ever remain single and free.

It was when the leaves were fading, that the young cousins heard of a great hunt which was to take place in a distant village. It was got up by an old warrior, who was the father of a beautiful daughter, and he had determined that the most successful hunter should become his son-in-law. This intelligence had been conveyed to the cousins in a secret manner, and on departing from their own village, they spoke not a word of their determination. In due time the hunt took place, and an immense quantity of game was taken. Some of the hunters brought home two bears, some three and four deer, but the two cousins captured each five bears. As no one man had eclipsed his fellows, it was resolved by the warrior that the man who should bring to his lodge the scalps of ten bears, should be the successful candidate for the hand of his daughter. Another hunt took place, and each of the cousins brought in, not only the scalps of ten full-grown bears, but also a large quantity of choice meats, which they deposited at the tent-door of the chief. The difficulty of making a selection was now even greater than before, but the truth was, the young friends had no desire to marry the beautiful girl, but were only anxious to manifest their bravery, or rather wonderful expertness in killing wild animals. Their singular conduct astonished everybody, but mostly the venerable warrior and his favorite daughter.

The important question must be decided, however, and the old man resorted to a number of expedients to decide upon a future son-in-law. The first was that the two cousins should enter upon a wrestling match—they did so, and the twain fell to the ground at the same moment. The next was that they should try their agility in leaping over a suspended stick, but in this trial they also came out exactly even. The third was, that they should shoot their arrows at a pair of humming birds, and the maker of the best shot to be the lady's husband; the arrows were thrown, and the right wing of each bird broken. The fourth expedient was that they should go upon a squirrel hunt—they did so, and each one returned with just exactly one hundred of those sprightly creatures. It now came to pass, and was whispered about the village, that one of the cousins had really become interested in the girl who was the innocent cause of so much contention, and when her father found this out, he resolved to make one more experiment. He therefore commanded the young men to kill each a specimen of the *ke necoh* or war-eagle, and the one who should present her with the greatest number of perfectly formed feathers, would be welcomed as a relative. The trial was made and the whole number of feathers obtained was twenty-one, the odd feather having been gained by the enamored cousin. The girl was of course awarded to him in due time, but what was the surprise of all the villagers, when it was proclaimed that he would not receive the prize unless the young men of the tribe should first build him a handsome lodge and furnish it with the choicest of meats and skins. At this suggestion the young men were greatly enraged, but they concluded, in consideration of their admiration of the Indian girl, to change their minds, and forthwith proceeded to erect the new lodge.

In the meanwhile, it was ascertained that the unlucky cousin had become somewhat offended at his companion, whereupon the accepted lover joined the other in a bear hunt for the purpose of effecting a reconciliation. It so happened, however, that the existing coldness between them could not be removed, and while the twain were toiling up a remote hill with the view of encamping for the night, the disappointed cousin was suddenly transformed into a large fire-fly, and having ascended into the air, immediately experienced another change, and became what is known as the Northern Star. The remaining cousin felt himself severely punished by this abandonment for having broken his vow, and therefore became an exile from his native land and led a comfortless and solitary life; while the maiden whom he was to wed, it is said, is still waiting patiently, but in vain, for the return of her long lost lover.

THE OSAGE DAMSEL.

THERE once lived in the Osage country an Indian whose name was *Koo-zhe-ge-ne-cah*, or *The Distant Man.* He had been a famous warrior and hunter, but time had weakened his arm and lifted a mist before his eye. His wives were all dead, and the only one of his kindred left upon earth to minister to his wants was a little damsel, his grandchild, and the joy of his old age. The twain were much beloved by all their tribe, and when journeying across the broad prairies they were always supplied with the gentlest horses, and they never had to ask the second time for their favorite food. Whenever the tribe came to a halt on the bank of a river, in a country abounding in game, the first tent-poles planted in the ground were those belonging to the Distant Man and his child, and their tent always stood next to that of the chief.

It was midsummer, and the entire Osage nation was encamped upon a plain at the foot of a mountain, covered to the very summit with rich grass and brilliant flowers. The last hunts had been successful, and in every lodge was to be found an abundance of buffalo and deer meat. Feasting and merry-making, dancing and playing ball, were the chief employments of the hour throughout the entire village, while in every direction upon the prairies the horses, with their feet hobbled, were cropping their sweet food. The children and the dogs sported upon the green together, and many a laugh resounded long and loud. The sun was near his setting, when suddenly an unusual stillness pervaded the air. The people gathered together in haste and wondered what it could all mean. The strange silence caused them to listen with increased attention, when a distant whoop came stealing along the air. It seemed to come from the neighboring mountain, and as the multitude cast their eyes in that direction, they saw a single horseman coming towards their encampment with the speed of the wind. They waited in breathless expectation, and were astonished at the boldness of the stranger in riding with such fury directly into their midst.

He was mounted upon a black horse of gigantic size, with splendidly flowing mane and tail, and an eye of intense brilliancy, and was caparisoned in a most gorgeous manner. The stranger was clad from head to foot in a dress of many colors, and from his hair hung a great variety of the most curious plumes. He carried a lance, and to his side were fastened a bow and a quiver of arrows. He was in the prime of life, and his bearing was that of a warrior chief. He avowed himself the son of the Master of Life, and his home to be in the Spirit Land. He said that there was a woman in that land who had told him that the most beautiful maiden in the Osage nation was her daughter. From other lips also had he heard that she was good as well as beautiful, and that her only protector and friend was an old man named *Koo-ze-ghe-ne-cah.* He had asked for a dream that he might see this being of the earth. Having seen her, and being in want of a wife, he was now come to demand her of her venerable parent, and forthwith rode to the door of his tent to make a bargain. The stranger dismounted not from his horse, but talked with the old man leaning upon the neck of his noble animal, the maiden meanwhile sitting in pensive quietness within her tent-door, working a pair of moccasins. The old man doubted the stranger's words, and desired him to prove that he was the son of the Master of Life. "What sign of my nature and power would you witness?" inquired the stranger. "That you would cover the heavens with thick darkness, picture it with lightning, and fill the air with loud thunder," replied the old man. "Do this, and my daughter shall be your bride." Suddenly a storm arose, and the sign was fulfilled to the utmost extent, so that the entire nation were stricken with fear. Night came on, the sky was without a cloud, but spangled with stars, and the air was perfectly serene, and when the stranger and his steed were sought for, it was found that they had disappeared. Peace rested upon the Osage village, and the oldest men of that tribe never enjoyed a more refreshing sleep than on that memorable night.

On the following day everything about the Osage encampment wore its ordinary aspect, and the events of the previous day were talked over as people talk of their dreams. The old man and the maiden made an offering to the Master of Life, and while the former, before the assembled nation, promised to give up his child, she, in her turn, expressed her entire willingness to become the bride of the stranger, should he ever return. Not only was she prompted to do this by the honor conferred upon her, and also by the nobleness of the stranger, but she thought it would make her so happy to rejoin her long departed mother in the Spirit Land. She was only troubled about the feeble old man, whom she dearly loved; but when the whole nation promised, as with one voice, to make him the object of their peculiar care, she was satisfied.

Again was the sun in the western horizon. Again did the stranger appear mounted as before. But as he entered the village, there trotted by his side a white horse of exceeding beauty, decked from forelock to tail with the richest and rarest of ornaments. He had come for his bride, and was impatient to be gone. He led the white horse to the tent of the girl he loved, and throwing at her feet a dress of scarlet feathers, he motioned her to prepare for a long journey. When she was ready, he motioned to the white horse to fall upon his knees, and the maiden leaped upon his back. The twain then walked their horses to the outskirts of the village, and as they passed along, the stranger took from his quiver and tossed into the hands of the Osage chief and each of his warriors and hunters, a charmed arrow, which, he said, would enable them not only to subdue their enemies, but also supply them with an abundance of game, as long as they roamed the prairies. The stranger now gave a whoop and the horses started upon the run. Their path lay over the mountain, where the stranger had been first seen. They flew more swiftly than the evening breeze, and just as the sun disappeared, they reached the summit of the mountain and also disappeared, as if received into the bosom of a golden cloud.

THE SPECTRE AND HUNTER.

The following legend was originally translated into English by an educated Choctaw, named *J. L. McDonald*, and subsequently embodied in a private letter to another Choctaw, named *Peter P. Pitchlyn*. The former of these very worthy Indian gentlemen has long been dead, and it is therefore with very great pleasure that I avail myself of the opportunity, kindly afforded me by the latter gentleman, of associating the legendary relic with my own. I have ventured, by the permission and advice of Mr. Pitchlyn, to alter an occasional expression in the text, but have not trespassed upon the spirit of the story.

KO-WAY-HOOM-MAH, or the Red Panther, once started out on a hunting expedition. He had an excellent bow, and carried with him some jerked venison. His only companion was a large white dog, which attended him in all his rambles. This dog was a cherished favorite, and shared in all his master's privations and successes. He was the social companion of the hunter by day, and his watchful guardian by night.

The hunter had travelled far, and as the evening approached, he encamped upon a spot that bore every indication of an excellent hunting-ground. Deer-tracks were seen in abundance, and turkeys were heard clucking in various directions, as they retired to their roosting places. Ko-way-hoom-mah kindled a fire, and having shared a portion of his provision with his dog, he spread his deer-skin and his blanket by the crackling fire, and mused on the adventures of the day already past, and on the probable success of the ensuing one. It was a bright starlight night; the air was calm, and a slight frost which was falling, rendered the fire comfortable and cheering. His dog lay crouched and slumbering at his feet, and from his stifled cries, seemed dreaming of the chase. Everything tended to soothe the feelings of our hunter, and to prolong that pleasant train of associations, which the beauty of the night and the anticipations of the morrow were calculated to inspire. At length, when his musings were assuming that indefinite and dreamy state which precedes a sound slumber, he was startled by a distant cry, which thrilled on his ear, and roused him into instant watchfulness. He listened with breathless attention, and in a few minutes again heard the cry, keen, long, and piercing. The dog gave a plaintive and ominous howl. Ko-way-hoom-mah felt uneasy. Can it be a lost hunter? was the inquiry which suggested itself. Surely not, for a true hunter feels lost nowhere. What then can it be? With these reflections our hunter stepped forth, gathered more fuel, and again replenished his fire. Again came a cry, keen, long, and painfully thrilling, as before. The voice was evidently approaching, and again the dog raised a low and mournful howl. Ko-way-hoom-mah then felt the blood curdling near his heart, and folding his blanket around him, he seated himself by the fire and fixed his eyes intently in the direction from which he expected the approach of his startling visitor. In a few moments he heard the approach of his footsteps. In another minute a ghastly shape made its appearance, and advanced towards the fire. It seemed to be the figure of a hunter, like himself. Its form was tall and gaunt, its features livid and unearthly. A tattered robe was girded round his waist, and covered his shoulders, and he bore an unstrung bow and a few broken arrows.

The spectre advanced to the fire, and seemed to shiver with cold. He stretched forth one hand, then the other to the fire, and as he did so, he fixed his hollow and ghastly eye on Ko-way-hoom-mah, and a slight smile lighted up his livid countenance, but not a word did he utter. Ko-way-hoom-mah felt his flesh and hair creep, and the blood freezing in his veins, yet with instinctive Indian courtesy he presented his deer-skin as a seat for his grim visitor. The spectre waved his hand, and shook his head in refusal. He stepped aside, plucked up a parcel of briers from an adjacent thicket, spread them by the fire, and on his thorny couch he stretched himself and seemed to court repose.

Our hunter was petrified with mingled fear and astonishment. His eyes continued long riveted on the strange and ghastly being stretched before him, and he was only awakened from his trance of horror by the voice of his faithful dog. "Arise," said the dog, suddenly and supernaturally gifted with speech, "Arise, and flee for your life! The spectre now slumbers: should you also slumber, you are lost. Arise and flee while I stay and watch!" Ko-way-hoom-mah arose, and stole softly from the fire. Having advanced a few hundred paces, he stopped to listen; all was silent, and with a beating heart he continued his stealthy and rapid flight. Again he listened, and again with renewed confidence, he pursued his rapid course, until he had gained several miles on his route homeward. Feeling at length a sense of safety, he paused to recover breath, on the brow of a lofty hill. The night was calm and serene, the stars shone with steady lustre, and as Ko-way-hoom-mah gazed upwards, he breathed freely and felt every apprehension vanish. Alas! on the instant, the distant baying of his dog struck on his ear; with a thrill of renewed apprehension, he bent his ear to listen, and the appalling cry of his dog, now more distinctly audible, convinced him that the spectre was in full pursuit. Again he fled with accelerated speed over hill, over plain, through swamps and thickets, till once more he paused by the side of a deep and rapid river. The heavy baying of his dog told him too truly, that his fearful pursuer was close at hand. One minute he stood for breath, and he then plunged into the stream. But scarcely had he gained the centre, when the spectre appeared on the bank, and plunged in after him, closely followed by the panting dog. Ko-way-hoom-mah's apprehensions now amounted to agony. He fancied he saw the hollow and glassy eyeballs of his pursuer glaring above the water, and that his skeleton hand was already outstretched to grapple with him. With a cry of horror he was about to give up the struggle for life and sink beneath the waves, when his faithful dog, with a fierce yell seized upon his master's enemy. After a short but severe struggle they both sunk; the waters settled over them forever. He became an altered man. He shunned the dance and the ball play, and his former hilarity gave place to a settled melancholy. In about a year after this strange adventure he joined a war party against a distant enemy and never returned.

APPENDIX.

After completing the history of my adventures in pursuit of scenery and sport in the United States, Canada, and New Brunswick, I could not but regret that I had no experiences to record in regard to Nova Scotia. I had heard of its salmon and its moose, and my heart had been drawn towards this "Acadia" by the beautiful history of "Evangeline," yet I had only looked upon its hills from the Bay of Fundy. Just at that moment, however, the work of a brother angler came to my relief, and I have to thank him for helping me to complete my own. The work in question is entitled "*Sporting Adventures in the New World*," and was written by Leut. Campbell Hardy of the Royal Artillery. His materials, though highly interesting and valuable, are put together in a somewhat desultory manner, but as angling and moose hunting are his leading themes, I shall confine my quotations chiefly to these.

The peninsula of Nova Scotia including Cape Breton is about three hundred miles long and seventy wide, and the isthmus connecting it with New Brunswick is only ten miles wide. Halifax is its principal city and the seat of Government, and on the Bay of Fundy coast are a number of flourishing towns, flanked by beautiful rural scenery: as a general thing however, the Province is still a country of gentle hills, of numerous lakes and rivers, of vast pine forests, and of mossy plains or barrens. Like New Brunswick the population is composed of English, Scotch and Irish, but it claims to be the home of only one tribe of Indians, a remnant of the Micmacs, only numbering about one thousand souls.

But let us turn to sporting matters, and listen to the pleasant words of Leut. Hardy:

The forest tracks of Nova Scotia, remote from roads or settlements, still harbor large herds of the moose. It is even strange that this animal, so adverse to the most distant sound of an axe, or other sounds foreign to the natural forest music, and which cause him to fly precipitately for long distances, should still be found in such numbers as he is in Nova Scotia. The probable number of these noble animals in this Province is difficult to be ascertained, even approximately. It must consist of several thousand head.

The carriboo is so seldom met with now in Nova Scotia, that it may be considered as on the verge of extinction in that province. This may be the cause of the extreme wariness and timidity of the animal. He is still more liable to be scared than the moose, and, when once started, will travel for days, seldom revisiting the country where he was first alarmed.

The carriboo, or rein-deer of North America, is identical with the rein-deer of northern Europe. The animal generally stands from three to four feet in height at the shoulder.

The horns are long, branching, and partly palmated. The brow antlers stretch forward over the forehead, almost in contact with each other, and resembling human hands placed vertically side by side, with the fingers extended. The color of the antlers, which decorate the head of the female as well those of the male, is deep reddish brown.

The coat of the carriboo is close and shining. In the summer, it is of a dirty fawn color, changing in winter to a tawny white. The hoof of this animal is broad and spreading, and enables him, by its expansive elasticity, to travel over deep snow and on ice with great facility. When lifted from the ground, the divisions of the hoof contract, coming in contact with each other with a sharp clicking sound, which some naturalists have attributed to the crackling of the knee joint.

The carriboo browses exclusively on succulent lichens—either those found on barrens, or on the trunks of hard-wood trees.

The flesh is like venison, and more esteemed than that of the moose. The carriboo is a gregarious animal. Though the Indians assert, that vast herds, containing nearly a hundred of these animals, once roamed over Nova Scotia, more than four or five together are now seldom met with. They are generally hunted in open country, thickly interspersed with barrens, and the sport partakes of the nature of deer-stalking; the hunter crawling along, taking advantage of sheltering masses of rock, tall patches of ground laurels, or moss-grown mounds, to within range of the herd. Great attention must be paid to the direction of the wind, as the carriboo is possessed of the most delicate sense of smell; and, when once it has got wind of a human being, farewell to all hopes of getting a shot on the part of the sportsman.

The lowing of the carriboo is a short, hoarse bellow, more like the bark of a large dog, than the voice of one of the deer tribe.

In the western parts of Nova Scotia, and in the neighborhood of the Cobequid Mountains, near its junction with New Brunswick, carriboo are still tolerably plentiful. No attempt has ever been made to use these animals in America, as is done in Northern Europe, for the purpose of draught. The docility of the Laplander's rein-deer is the result of ages of domestication; and it was first attempted by him, as his only resource.

The black bear of America is found everywhere in Nova Scotia. Unlike the former animals, he appears to prefer the neighborhood, not of large towns certainly, but of small farms and settlements. He grows to the length of five feet, standing, sometimes, more than three feet in height. The coat of this animal is thick, glossy, when in good condition, and jet black. On each side of the muzzle, appears a patch of tawny color. The head is sharper and longer than that of the European bear. The eye is set low down in the head, black and twinkling, and strongly indicative of his ferocious disposition.

In the neighborhood of Halifax, bears often appear, and cause great uneasiness to the small farmers and settlers living by the side of bush roads, between Halifax and St. Margaret's Bay, by predatory excursions on the sheep folds. When stopping at one of these log houses in the neighborhood of some small lakes, on which I had been trout-fishing, I have seen the cattle come rushing from the bush, panting and evidently in great terror, up to the door of the house. They had evidently been pursued by a bear.

These animals seldom molest a man, unless assaulted by him first; and then, be it ever so slight a blow or wound, they will immediately turn on him, and the conflict, if he has not a bullet wherewith to drop the animal at once, becomes exceedingly doubtful. The bear will parry the strongest blow of an axe, with the greatest dexterity and ease, with his powerful arms; and, when once he has embraced the individual in his vice-like grasp, the knife becomes the man's last chance. I have seen Indians exhibiting frightful scars received during a combat with a bear.

On the approach of winter, the bear, who is now prodigiously fat after revelling on the numerous berries which ripen in the fall, crawls to his den, generally under the roots of some dead giant of the forest, or between overhanging masses of rock. Here he quickly falls asleep, and passes the long winter in one uninterrupted snooze.

Sometimes, when the first snows of winter have fallen, the Indian visits the various dens in a large forest district, and discovers whether Bruin has gone to roost or not, by the tracks on the snow outside. A few pokes on the ribs, with a long stick; or, if very obstinate and sleepy, the rousing effects of the thick smoke of a birch bark torch, will bring out the bear, who is at once shot in the head. The skin of the black bear forms a handsome ornament, either for the decoration of a sleigh, or as a rug. It may generally be purchased for from five to eight dollars.

Young bears, to which the female gives birth two at a time, in the month of April, are frequently brought into Halifax, by the Indians, for sale. They may be easily tamed, though, when they grow up, their friendship can never be relied on.

Bears are often trapped, in the summer, in the dead-falls. A small semi-circular enclosure is made, by driving stakes firmly into the ground, between two trees, the trunks of which are a few feet apart. Over the entrance to the enclosure, and slightly attached to the trunks of the trees, is suspended a cross-beam, heavily loaded at either end by immense logs of timber. A bait of flesh, or dead game, is placed inside the enclosure, and the surrounding trees are smeared with honey, of which the animal is inordinately fond. A bar is placed across the entrance of the enclosure, and so connected with the cross-beam, that, upon Bruin's attempting to force his way to the bait, the beam and its weight of superincumbent timber, come down by the run on the back of the unlucky glutton, and make him a hopeless prisoner.

The gray wolf has but lately made his appearance in Nova Scotia, not as in other Provinces, however, in company with his prey, the Canadian deer (*Cervus virginianus.*) The gray wolf is a large, fierce, and powerful animal. In Maine and New Brunswick, several instances have been known of his attacking singly and destroying a human being. This animal sometimes grows to the length of six feet. The hair is long, fine, and of a silver gray. A broad band of black, here and there, showing shining silvery hairs, extend from the head down the back. The tail is long and bushy, as the brush of a fox. A wolf skin forms a frequent decoration for the back of a sleigh.

They are seldom seen, as they are very vigilant, and constantly travelling. In their present numbers, they can earn but a precarious livelihood in this Province, as they are too few to venture an attack on the moose, or even the carriboo. A single blow from the powerful fore-leg of a moose would astonish a bear, and would tell much more on the lean ribs of a starving wolf.

The American fox is a larger and more darkly-colored animal than his European relative. This animal is common in the woods of Nova Scotia, and his short, sharp bark may often be heard echoing through the trees on a clear, calm night. He subsists on rabbits and small game.

The black fox, generally supposed to be an accidental variety of the common fox, is rarely met with in this Province.

Its skin is a small fortune to the lucky Indian who shoots one of these animals, as it is worth from twenty or thirty pounds sterling.

The loup cervier, commonly called the "lucifee" by the settlers, is abundant in the woods of Nova Scotia. Its fur is long and glossy, of a brownish-gray on the back, becoming nearly white below. A few irregular dusky spots and markings cover the skin. Tufts of stiff black hair grow on the tips of the ears. The tail is very short, seldom exceeding three inches in length. The length of the animal is about three feet. It is a timid creature, flying from the presence of man, and subsisting on rabbits and partridges.

The wild cat is more abundant than the former animal, is nearly of the same size, but of a lighter and more tawny color. It is a powerful animal, its fore-arms being very thick and muscular, and is a match for a very large dog. Its tail is longer than that of the lucifee, and is tipped with black.

The beaver once was found on every lake, brook, and river in Nova Scotia. Pursued for the sake of his beautiful coat, more relentlessly than any living creature except the buffalo, the beaver is nearly exterminated in the Provinces of Nova Scotia and New Brunswick. A few, however, are still to be met with on the banks of the shady brooks which join that beautiful chain of lakes and rivers running across the Province of Nova Scotia, between Liverpool and Annapolis. Here, in consequence of the decreasing demand for their skins in the European market, they are said to be on the increase.

The discovery and destruction of this interesting quadruped has been greatly facilitated by the conspicuity of his aquatic tenement, and its accompanying defensive structure—the "dam." The dam is constructed of brush-wood, or even logs of small timbers, several inches in diameter, gnawed through by the powerful incisor teeth of this animal, and conveyed to the destination on its back. Wherever the brook or river is too shallow to admit of the building of its semi-submerged mud-house, the water is deepened by the beaver throwing up a substantial dam, sometimes entirely across the channel. The house itself is of mud, conical in shape, and its chamber, to which there is a slanting entrance from above the surface, is situated below the level of the water.

The beaver is easily domesticated, and will evince the affection of a dog for its master. In the spring of 1853, an Indian brought me a tame beaver, which he had captured when quite young, in the neighborhood of Lake Rossignol, in the western end of Nova Scotia; when he wished to leave it, the little animal shuffled after him, whining piteously, and having reached him, scrambled up his clothes to his neck. The Indian afterwards sold it to a zealous naturalist residing about two miles from Halifax, at the head of the North-West Arm. Nothing would satisfy it for days afterwards, but nestling in the Indian's blanket, which he was obliged to leave for that purpose. Its owner fed it on bred and milk, with a few cabbage leaves and other esculent vegetables. The animal was perfectly tame, appeared pleased at being noticed, and answered to the name of "Cobeetch," the Indian for beaver.

I have frequently seen in brooks, pieces of timber which showed marks of the beaver's teeth; and not long since were to be seen the remains of a beaver-dam, in a small brook, which trickles into the North-West Arm of the sea, near Halifax.

The otter is larger than the European variety, and is of a uniform dark-brown color. It is numerous in the lakes of Nova Scotia, where it revels on the plentiful trout. Their paths often appear among the sedges and grasses, on the low swamps, in the neighborhood of lakes. In these they are often caught by steel traps attached to a large log. The American otter is sometimes three feet in length and its fur is valuable, a good skin often fetching five dollars. Otters leave curious trails on the snow which covers the lakes in winter. The track is broad, and conveys the idea of having been formed by a large cart-wheel.

The mink and the muskrat abound in the Nova Scotian lakes. The fur of the former is valuable, and of a dark reddish-brown color. Considerably smaller than the otter, the mink, like him, subsists on fish, and is often captured in miniature dead-falls for the sake of the skin. The muskrat, called "muskquash" by the Indians, is a beaver in miniature. Its hind feet are webbed like those of that animal, and it lives in mud-houses, partially submerged in sedgy swamps.

The Indians can call muskrats by squeaking into their closed hands; the animal, coming out from the reeds, is immediately shot for its skin, which is worth fourpence or sixpence in the market. Many of these skins were formerly used for the purpose of mixing the fur with that of the beaver in the manufacture of hats. When dead, the muskquash smells strongly of musk. They are easily tamed, but must be kept in a tin cage, on account of their propensities for gnawing wood.

The Canadian porcupine is abundant in the forests of the Provinces. The Indian name is "Madwiss." This animal is about two feet in length, and closely covered with long, coarse brown hair, intermixed with sharp spines three inches long. These spines grow most numerously on the lower part of the back. They are extremely sharp, and on very close examination, their points will be found to be armed with minute barbs, pointing downwards, thus rendering the quill, when once it has entered the flesh of a man or animal, difficult of extraction.

The quills are of a dusky white color, tipped with black. They are extensively used by the squaws in ornamenting sheets of birch bark with curious and gaudy designs. The squaws stain them of the brightest and most durable colors. Some of the dyes are procured at the chemists; while others, are extracted from flowers or bark. They preserve the secrets of obtaining these dyes with great caution.

The porcupine proves good eating in the fall, when in good condition, from feeding on blueberries and beech-nuts. In the winter, they may constantly be seen on the branches, inaccessible to climbers, of the hemlock; on the bark and foliage of which they feed at this season. They are dull creatures, slow of motion, and, when surprised in a tree, will take no pains to escape, until knocked over by a shot or stone. They live in dens under collected masses of rock, or roots of trees. In summer time they peel the bark of young spruces, betraying, by the conspicuous denuded stem, their whereabouts to the prowling Indian.

Among the game birds found in Nova Scotia, the American woodcock is entitled to the first place, and notice. It is smaller than the European woodcock. The upper parts of the plumage are dark reddish-brown, barred with black, the breast being very light, almost tawny. Its flavor is equally good with that of the European bird. The woodcock arrives in Nova Scotia in April, sometimes earlier, if the spring be forward, breeds in this country, and does not leave it till the sharp frosts set in at the beginning of November.

Excellent sport may be had with these birds in clumps of thick alder bushes standing in meadows by the roadside, in the months of September and October. Well-timed and necessary laws lately have imposed a fine upon shooting this bird in the summer, as was formerly the case, the young birds being destroyed wholesale, before they were full-grown and able to fly. It requires a quick eye to kill three out of four woodcocks, put up in the dense and tall alder copses in which they are found. The sportsmen sometimes, however, when they have a number of good dogs or beaters, surround the covers. The woodcock seems to travel late in the evening, and at night, for, unless disturbed, they are never seen on the wing during the day.

Large bags are annually made by sportsmen from Halifax, in the covers, which are tolerably numerous within a circuit of twenty miles from that city. Many can boast of having shot two hundred couple of these birds in a season, going out for a day at a time, twice or three times a week, perhaps.

By far the best grounds for cock in Nova Scotia, and perhaps in North America, are in the neighborhood of the picturesque village of Kentville, situated on the Annapolis road, at a distance of about sixty miles from Halifax. The country is here composed of low copses of alder and hazel, for some distance on either side of the road, and the ground interspersed with ferns, heaths, and moist mosses. The flights of woodcock, which arrive in these covers annually, are surprising. The sport can only be surpassed by that to be enjoyed in Albania.

The woodcock does not appear to have been found in Nova Scotia at its first settlement. He is never seen far from clearings in the forest, though here and there likely-looking covers may be met with.

A drive on a fresh autumnal morning through the gorgeous scenery of the fall, and then a day in cover, watching the motions and working of the lively little "cockers," returning in the evening with a bag containing eight or ten couple of plump cock, and the good dogs reposing in the wagon between your knees, conduce to render a day's sport, with these delicious birds, a delightful change to the monotony of town life.

The snipe arrives in Nova Scotia, and leaves the country, later than the woodcock. They are very plentiful in the marshes around Kentville. Perhaps, the best snipe ground in the world is the Great Tantemara marsh, in the south-eastern part of New Brunswick. The American snipe is nearly identical with the European.

Two kinds of partridges, or rather grouse, are found in the woods of Nova Scotia. The best, most lively, and handsomest bird of the two, is the ruffed grouse. This bird is called, in Nova Scotia, the "birch partridge," from its being generally found in hills covered by groves of birch, on the young buds of which they feed. This bird is wilder, and not so stupid as the spruce partridge, which is described elsewhere.

The birch partridge is a very handsome bird, its general plumage being reddish brown, mottled everywhere with shades of light fawn and dusky color. When irate, it struts about in the fashion of the male turkey, drooping its wings, expanding its broad tail, and elevating its ruff, which extends from the back of the head down the sides of the neck.

These birds are very good eating in the autumn and winter, though not to be compared with the English partridge in this respect.

Amongst the earliest migratory birds which arrive in this province in the spring, is the American robin. This bird is one of the thrushes, rather larger than the common English thrush, and much more gaudily colored. The bill is yellow; the head, wings, and tail, black. The back is of a bluish slate color, and the breast bright red, the color of brick dust.

By all, the arrival of the robin is hailed with pleasure. They arrive in great numbers, frequenting the barrens in search of berries, and pasture-meadows for worms.

Groups of these birds may be seen hopping about in the green meadows in the neighborhood of settlements, while, perched on the top rail of a snake fence, or on a branch of a solitary tree, may be noticed the watchful male, ready to announce to the feeding birds the approach of danger.

The song of the robin is melodious, and very similar, in some of its strains, to that of the English thrush. Their being good eating, numerous, and easily shot, extinguishes, however, all the romantic feelings of regard, with which the arrival of this early, pretty, and sociable songster, should be attended, on the part of many of the lower class of Nova Scotia sportsmen, who go out on the barrens between the North-West Arm and the Three-mile House, or along hedge-rows in green meadows, in quest of robins.

After the expenditure of a great amount of powder and shot, a couple, perhaps, of robins are brought to town in triumph, held by the tail.

For several days towards the end of summer, Halifax common, and the open fields towards the North-West Arm, are the scene of great excitement from the arrival of large flights of plover, which birds stop here to rest before proceeding farther southward. Every man or boy, who can muster up a "shooting iron," goes out to blaze away at the plover as they pass.

Some of the sportsmen kneel down, with powder and shot lying loosely beside them, ready for quick and indiscriminate loading. "Here's another lot comin'," is the cry, and bang go dozens of guns, pointed at the dense flight of plover. Then there is a general scramble for the slain. Some of the more knowing ones only load with a little loose powder, and claim as many of the dead birds as they ought to have put shot into their barrel.

Of all the British provinces of North America, Nova Scotia

offers the greatest facilities and opportunities to the orthodox sportsman, whether resident or visitor, civil or military, who may wish to pass a week or so in the wild old woods, or by the side of her numerous and picturesque rivers and lakes.

There are five methods by which moose may be hunted or killed in Nova Scotia, viz., creeping on them in the fall and winter, calling the bull-moose in the fall, running them down on snow-shoes in February and March, bringing to bay with dogs, and snaring. The first three are orthodox; the last two practices arrant poaching.

The fall is the most enjoyable time for hunting the moose. The bull is, at this season, in his full vigor, and is truly a noble animal to behold. Adorned with massive antlers, and evincing a roaming, wild, and sometimes fierce disposition, there is more excitement attendant on shooting a bull-moose in the fall, than at any other time of the year.

The delicious days and mild nights, particularly during the Indian summer, are much preferable to the cold variable weather of the winter; while the science and woodcraft displayed by the Indian hunter in discovering and following a moose track, in places where, even by the closest scrutiny, the eye of the white man cannot distinguish the foot print; and the delightful ease of walking in moccasins over the elastic carpeting of moss in the fir forests, and on the soft, moist, newly-fallen leaves in the hard woods, give to this season undeniable precedence.

In the fall, too, additional sport may be obtained at night, and sometimes even during the day, by calling the bull moose. Most of the Indians, who make it their business to accompany the sportsman into the woods, are good hands at calling. The moose "call" is a trumpet, made by rolling a sheet of birch-bark into a cone. No material has been found to equal birch-bark for this purpose. Metal will not answer, producing a sound too shrill and ringing. The Indian commences to call at sun-down, ceasing when it becomes dark, till moon-rise; as a moose coming up, when there was not sufficient light to see along the barrels, would almost certainly escape.

The very best time to call is towards morning—for an hour before dawn, and for a short time after daybreak. At this time, moose appear to be less cautious, and more eager to answer the call than they are in the early part of the night. In calling, the Indian and sportsman conceal themselves behind a rock, or a clump of dwarf evergreens, on the edge of a barren, the Indian standing on the top of a rock, or sometimes climbing a tree, so as to give the sound of his call every advantage for diffusing itself through the surrounding forest.

When an answer is obtained, and the moose appears to be bent on coming up, the Indian either recedes, or sends the sportsman some hundred yards or so in advance; or, should the animal hesitate on arriving in the neighborhood of the caller, the Indian has a better chance of allaying the animal's suspicions, by the apparent distance of the cow. The moose, hearing the call at a greater distance than he had expected, again advances, and, at a few paces, probably receives the fire of the sportsman.

Nothing can be more productive of feelings of excitement than sitting, wrapped in blankets, on the edge of a forest-girt plain, the moon peering through mists of gently-falling dew, and faintly illuminating the wild scene, now flashing on the white surface of a granite boulder, and then sparkling in the water of the swamp, and on the bedewed mounds of moss, and clumps of ground-laurels; nothing can be more exciting, when the wild notes of the Indian's call, rending the calm air, have dispersed over the echoing forest, than the succeeding moments of listening for an answer.

You scarcely believed your ears to have been capable of such exertion, if so it may be termed.

And then, when, far away from over the hills, and through the dense fir-forests, comes the booming answer of a bull moose; when you hear the distant crashing of branches, and the rattling the massive antlers against the trees; and when, at length the monarch of the American forest emerges from the woods, and stands snorting and bellowing on the open barren, his proportions looming gigantic through the hazy atmosphere—then does the blood course through your veins as it never did before; and, scarcely knowing what is about to happen, you grasp the ready rifle, and crouch in the protecting bushes. It is hard to take precise aim by moonlight. Unless the bead on the barrel be of polished silver, it is advisable to chalk the end of the gun.

Some hunters draw a line with a piece of chalk from the bead to the eye. However, in calling, one has seldom occasion for a long shot; indeed, I have heard of the hair of a moose's coat having been singed by the flash, so close has he advanced to the ambush.

Calling is seldom attempted, either at night or by day, if there is anything like a breeze stirring through the woods. Moose are more cautious in windy weather, are longer in coming up, and generally endeavor to get round to leeward of the caller. The Indians will seldom call when it is windy; they say it only makes confusion amongst the moose, and spoils the country; and they are very averse to starting a moose without getting a shot at him.

I have never heard two Indians call exactly alike, and the settlers assert that they can call as well as an Indian on this account. They say that any loud noise at night will make a moose come up to the spot. This idea is erroneous. The difference of note does not signify, for the cow moose differ widely in their call; but it is in giving vent to the sound, making it appear to come from the lungs of a moose, and not from those of a man, that the Indian excels. Apropos of notes: I once went out to call moose in the neighborhood of Halifax with a white settler, for one night. He had a cockney reputation of being a good hand at calling moose. He represented his calling as "fust chop. He had a most grand note, larned from the best Ingin hunter in Novy Scoshy."

At his first call, I scarcely knew whether to laugh, or to be angry with him for disturbing the country. I asked him whether he had ever heard the bray of an English jackass.

He "guessed not."

"Well then," said I, "the noise you have just made is it to

a T," and if you can get an answer from any other living creature, I'm a Dutchman!"

In the fall of 1853, a white settler, who thought he would try his hand at calling, as moose were numerous in the woods at the back of his clearing, got, as he expressed it, "A'most a horrid scarin'" from a bull moose.

To his surprise he obtained an answer to his first call, and the moose came, in broad daylight, right up to the man, who was so taken "aback," that he did not fire till the animal was nearly upon him. He then discharged his gun without taking aim, and of course missed the moose, who attacked him at once, knocking him over. He said that for some minutes he did not know whether he was on his head or his heels, and that when he came to his senses again, he found, no doubt to his great relief, his persecutor gone. He was badly bruised, but by good luck escaped having his skull fractured by a blow from the foreleg of the powerful animal.

The calling season lasts from the beginning of September to the end of October; the best time to make an expedition for this purpose being for a week before and a week after the full moon, in October. It is a curious fact, that a bull moose, if he be five miles distant when he first hears the call, will, even should it not be repeated, come in a perfectly straight course, through dense forests, and over rocky barrens and brooks, to within a few yards of the very spot where the call had been made.

Creeping moose, when the snow is on the ground, is a sport not appreciated by all. Heathful, manly, and exciting, though it be, it is attended with so much "roughing it," and by so many disappointments, owing to the state of the weather, that it is not every one who will care to repeat the experiment, particularly if a shot has not been obtained in the first attempt. Still, for a person who can stand, and derive benefit from a hard day's work, and who likes a life in the woods at all seasons, it is enticing enough.

Moose, as has been before observed, herd together in winter, forming what is termed a "yard;" their movements being more or less restricted, according to the inclemency of the weather, the depth of the snow, and their wildness occasioned by proximity to settlements.

In the winter of 1852–53, I was hunting in the neighborhood of Petite, Nova Scotia, in company with an Indian, named Joe Cope, the best hunter in the Province, although his sight and hearing are beginning to fail him. During the whole fortnight I was out, the weather was clear, calm, and frosty, and there was only a foot of snow in the woods. From these reasons, and from frequently being started by parties who were taking advantage of the good sledding on the bush-paths, for the purpose of hauling timber, the moose did not yard at all. They were always on the move, feeding as they went.

They never lay down without making a *detour*, and coming back to leeward of their tracks; and then they were constantly on the *qui vive*, lying with their heads down the wind, so as to have a clear view of the country to leeward, whilst their keen sense of smell would detect the scent of any creature passing to the windward of their position.

Moose, however, were in great abundance, and we looked forward to a favorable change of weather as bringing certain sport. One afternoon returning to camp, after an unsuccessful trudge on the barrens, in hopes of seeing carriboo or moose, enjoying the sun by the edge of the woods, we saw the Shubenacadie mountains, distant about fifteen miles, become gradually enveloped in what appeared to be a thick mist.

"Yes—no—yes. My sake! I am very glad—he snow fast on mountains—plenty snow to-night—moose steak for dinner to-morrow," said old Joe in great glee.

In half an hour the flakes which drifted up with a gradually increasing breeze, fell thickly, and the iron crust which had formed on the surface of the old snow during the late continuance of frost, relaxed.

As there was an hour's daylight still to be calculated upon, we went to look after tracks in a swampy valley covered with thick evergreens, distant about half a mile from camp.

Here we at once hit off the tracks of two moose. They were quite fresh. "Gone by, only two, tree minute," said Joe. Just as our excitement was at its pitch, expecting to see the moose every instant, it suddenly fell quite calm again. However, we continued to creep with great caution; and presently old Joe, after bobbing his head about as he tried to make out some object in the distant forest, beckoned me to come cautiously behind him.

"Moose—there—fire," whispered he, his rugged features enlivened by a savage grin of exultation.

For some seconds I could not discover the moose. At length seeing a dark patch looming through some thick bushes, at the distance of at least one hundred yards, I let drive with both barrels. On rushing up, we found that both moose had gone off; a few drops of blood on the snow, however, showed that one was wounded.

"I very sorry, but I sure if I try take you more handy, moose start before you get shot," said the Indian.

"Oh, I know it was not your fault Joe," answered I, "but I think we shall get him yet."

"Sartain," said Joe. "Moose-steak for dinner to-morrow, too dark to get him to-night, he stiff in mornin."

We followed the track of the wounded moose for a short distance, and returned to camp with the expectation of killing him in an hour after breakfast next morning. But our hopes were doomed to disappointment; when on waking next morning, we found that the snow, before so long wanted, had fallen most inopportunely, completely covering up the tracks of our moose. Tracking him by the blood marks on the trees, against which he had brushed in his course for a short distance, we found to our chagrin, that he had taken to the open barrens, and we were obliged to leave the poor brute to perish, most probably from his wound.

Wind is indispensable in winter hunting. On a calm day, however soft the snow might be, the tread of the hunter will in nine cases out of ten start these wary animals, particularly should they be lying down. Unless there is a good breeze stirring the branches of the forest, it is only by chance that a shot may be obtained at moose, however numerous they may be. When a moose is started, he quickly gains his legs and plunges forward for about fifty yards. Then he invariably stops for a second or two to ascertain the cause of alarm, and make up his mind in what direction to shape his flight.

This momentary pause often leads to his destruction, for the hunter on hearing him start, will often be able to obtain a glimpse of if not a shot at the moose, by rushing on in the direction of the sound.

A started moose will alarm all the moose which may be yarded in the country through which he flies. Conseqently, it is useless to attempt hunting in the direction he has gone.

The snapping of the boughs where moose are feeding, often makes the Indian hunter aware of their proximity. Although every Indian can creep on and shoot moose when by himself, few can officiate as good hunters to accompany the white sportsman.

Much additional caution is necessary from the comparatively clumsy manner in which the white man will travel through the woods, and the whole affair is connected with so much more labor and contracted resources on the part of the Indian, that it requires an old and experienced hunter—one who has made it his business to accompany parties of sportsmen into the bush—to ensure them a chance of success.

The Indian Joe Cope, is one of the best of this class. He is, though getting old, still a very good hunter, and understands perfectly all the necessaries for a camp, and ways of making it comfortable. He is a merry old fellow withal, having at his command an unlimited number of sporting anecdotes wherewith to enliven the camp in the long evenings.

His son "Jem," commonly called by his father, "the boy Jeem," usually accompanies old Joe in the capacity of camp-keeper; and a capital one he makes too. He will guess the exact moment of your return to camp, after the day's hunting, and will have prepared a kettle of delicious soup—a sort of "*omnium gatherum*" of partridges, hares, peas, onions, &c. He takes care that the camp larder shall never be short of game; for he is a good shot at partridge, and is "great" at snaring hares.

The "boy Jeem" promises to turn out as good a hunter as his father. I have often been out with them together, when old Joe has appealed to his son for his judgment as to the age of a track, or of a bitten bough, or concerning the manœuvres of a yard of moose.

"I b'lieve Jeem right," he would say, looking at me with a grin of satisfaction. One of Joe's recommending points is, that though he has shot nearly as many moose as he has hairs on his head, he hunts with the excitement and enthusiasm of a young hand. Joe, as well as several other Indians, entertains a firm belief that moose originally came from the sea; and that, in a case of extreme emergency, they will again betake themselves to that element.

"'Bout thirty year ago," says Joe, "there warn't not a single moose in whole province. They bin so hunted and destroyed for 'bout ten year, they all go to sea. Ingin go all over woods, everywhere, and never see single sign or track of moose anywhere—only carriboo—plenty carriboo then. Well, Capting, my father, he find first moose-track, when they begin to come back agen. I was leetle boy, then, and I never seen moose. We live in wigwam, away on Beaver-bank road; and, one day, my father came back to camp, and say, 'Joe, I seen fresh moose-track. Come along with me.' Well, we went; and father crept, and shot big cow moose. I never seen moose, and I 'most 'fraid to go near the poor brute.

"Well, we hauled it out whole to camp; and all the Ingin, from all parts of province, come to see carciss; and the old Ingin, they all clap their hands, and say, 'Good time come agen—the moose come back.'

"Well, Capting, after that, moose was seen almost every where; and one man see two moose swim ashore on Basin of Minas; and, since then, plenty moose all over province. I 'most 'fraid, though, these rascals settlers, snarin, and runnin 'em down with their brutes of dogs, will drive the poor brutes away to sea agen."

Joe is a most honest and straightforward Indian, when in the woods, in the capacity of hunter; but if once overruled, or badly-treated, will never accompany the same person again.

His hatred of all white men, who are not of the class of his employers, particularly the settlers in the interior, is intense, and is often productive of much amusement. In the winter of 1852, I was proceeding along a bush-path, with Joe and Jim, dragging a hand sled, loaded with our camping apparatus, when we met a party of settlers, and their teams. One of them calling Joe aside, asked him whether he had not cut some moose snares in that neighborhood, the fall previous.

"Sure I did, always when I see them."

"Well, Joe," replied the settler, who, as I afterwards heard, had set them himself; "they belonged to a friend of mine, and I guess if you stop about here, you'll get your camp set a-fire."

Joe flared up immediately.

"I tell you what it is, you rascal. I know you. If you, or any other same sort, come near camp, and try do anything, I shoot you, 'pon me soul, all same as one moose. There now, you mind, I take my oate I do it, you villain!"

I should not have been surprised at old Joe carrying his threat into execution. The previous fall, his son Jim had fired at some animal, I believe a bear, which had crept up to him and his father while calling moose at night.

"What was it, Jeem?" asked old Joe, as the creature went crashing off through the bushes.

"Man," said Jim; "he creep on us. What business he come to meddle with us? I seen him standin' when I fire."

When Joe has occasion to enter the bar-room of a roadside inn, as is sometimes the case in travelling to and from the hunting-country, he sits down in a corner, very sulky, and seldom vouchsafes an answer to the numerous questions put to him by inquisitive Blue-noses.

On one occasion he was returning with me to Halifax, after an unsuccessful moose hunt, and was particularly short to the settlers, and teamsters in the bar-room of the twenty-seven mile house.

"Well, now, tell how you'd act when you got fixed in a snow-storm, and couldn't find camp?" asked one of his persecutors.

No answer from Joe, who drew volumes from his pipe, and spat with great emphasis on the floor.

"I guess you couldn't fix a moose with that are shootin-iron of yourn, at a hundred yards—could you now?"

It was too much for poor Joe, who said:

"Wat you want know for? You mind your own business, and I do mine. Spose I ask question 'bout hay, and all that sort, wat fool I look. And now you want know 'bout my business, you look like fool. You people always 'quiring and askin' foolish question which don't consarn you." And with that, he stalked out of the room.

From his frequent employment, and being paid a dollar a day, Joe should be well off. He is, however, always hard up. One day, in the early spring, when salmŏn was very scarce, and selling at a dollar per pound in the market, a friend of mine met him returning to camp with the head and shoulders of a fine salmon.

"Hallo! Joe, what on earth are you going to do with that salmon?"

"Why, Capting, Mrs. Cope he say this morning, 'Mr. Cope, I very fond of salmon, 'spose you try and get a leetle bit for dinner to-day.' I tell him yes, and I see this very fine piece very cheap."

He had paid a pound currency for it.

Mrs. Cope makes a little money by working designs on birch bark with porcupine quills. Quill work, as it is termed, fetches a high price in Halifax, where it is bought by travellers to Europe or the States.

Joe said in my room one day, "Mrs. Cope he make a hundred a year by his work, and I make good deal by huntin'. 'Spose 'bout a hundred a-year too."

Before he departed, however, he said:

"Capting, I most shockin hard up just now. You got dollar handy! Pon my word I pay you in few days."

There are many other good Indians who can hunt with "the

gentlemen," besides Joe Cope. Ned Nolan, Williams, the Pauls of Ship Harbor, the Glodes of Annapolis, and Joe Penaul of Chester, are all capital hands in the woods. They all ask the regular charge of one dollar per diem. In this Province, the Indians do not claim the moose shot by the sportsmen—a much more satisfactory arrangement than that which prevails in Canada, where, for every moose that is shot, the Indians charge the sportsman one pound extra, claiming the whole carcass into the bargain.

To return from this digression, to the sport of creeping moose in winter. Creeping may commence in November, when the first snow has fallen. At this time, the bull moose is adorned with antlers, and the snow not falling very deep does not necessitate the use of snow-shoes. However, as the snow may all disappear in one night at this time of year, and as the ground is constantly frozen, and thereby rendered callous to the impression of a moose's foot, sport cannot always be reckoned upon.

The very best time to go out after moose in the winter is, about the middle of January. If it be a hard season, with plenty of snow on the ground; and if he be favored with a fair amount of windy weather, and occasional snow storms, the sportsman who goes into the woods, accompanied by good Indians, and has fixed upon a good hunting country, may make sure of success.

In the month of March, the snow generally lies very deep in the woods, and its surface is covered by a crust, caused by the alternate influence of the sun and frost. The hunter can travel easily on snow-shoes, while the unfortunate moose breaks through the crust at every step, sometimes sinking up to his body and grazing his legs against the sharp edges of the broken surface.

Running moose down is rather a murderous practice; as, when a fresh track is found, and the moose started, the persevering hunter is certain to come up with the animal, after a chase more or less protracted. The moose is then shot, defenceless, and in a state of complete exhaustion.

Sometimes, when the snow is very deep, moose may be run down in a quarter of an hour, while at others he may be pursued for days, the hunter giving up the chase at dusk, camping primitively on the spot, and recommencing the pursuit at daybreak next morning. At all events, from the certainty of shooting the animal, then in a state of utter helplessness, I consider the sport as inferior to creeping.

It is so destructive in a hard winter, that it should be prohibited by law, as well as the practice of running moose down with dogs. Chasing moose with dogs is such an unsportsmanlike proceeding, that it is seldom practised, except by the settlers, who love to hear the yelping of their own brutes of curs, and to destroy a moose from mere wantonness, when they ought to be attending to their unprogressing farms and clearings.

The plan adopted is this: a party of these people go out into the woods with a pack of all the big long-legged curs that can be mustered in the neighborhood. Surrounding some hardwood hill, in which they know moose are yarded, they turn in the dogs. The moose are at once started, and should they get past the "gunners," are quickly brought to bay by the dogs, and shot.

A dog will make more noise when after moose, than after any other game. Nothing scares moose so much as the voice of a dog; and a pack of curs yelping through the woods will so alarm the moose in the surrounding country that they will immediately leave it never to return.

Snaring moose is still practised in Nova Scotia by the settlers, in spite of a heavy fine. The most common way of constructing the snare is as follows. The trees are felled in a line for about one hundred yards in the woods. Falling on one another, they form a fence some five or six feet high. Several gaps are made in this fence wide enough to admit of the passage of the moose. A young tree is bent down by the united exertions of several men over the gap, and is fastened by a catch attached to a false platform. A noosed rope is fastened to the end of the tree, and suspended round the opening. The unfortunate moose, after walking along the fence till he arrives at the gap, attempts to pass through; but, stepping on the platform, the tree flies back, drawing the noose tightly round his head or legs. From the disposition to roam, evinced by moose in the fall, snares are generally set at this season.

The carcass of a snared moose is generally comparatively worthless, from the bruising it has received during the struggles of the animal in endeavoring to escape, particularly if he be only entangled by the legs. Sometimes the settler, not visiting his snares regularly, finds a moose in one, weighing perhaps twelve hundred pounds, in a state of decomposition.

It is from these snares being placed in haunts only known to themselves, and from the difficulty of tracing the original setter of the snare when it is found, that one of these infamous cases seldom meets with punishment. In fact, law is of little value in the backwoods.

Sometimes a simple rope with a running noose is fastened to a tree, and suspended round an opening in the bushes, leading to a barren—for moose often form regular paths, like those of rabbits, only on a larger scale—by which they enter and depart from small barrens.

A society has lately been organized in Halifax for the preservation of the game and fish of Nova Scotia. Its exertions have at present, been confined to the removal of dams and other obstructions to the progress of salmon up the provincial rivers to their spawning grounds. This society is under the direction of an able and active gentleman, through whose exertions much has been done for the preservation of salmon, Captain C—.

May we not hope that this society, aided by the ability and well directed efforts of its president, who is a thorough sportsman, will shortly do something towards preventing the extinction of the much persecuted moose of Nova Scotia? The forests through which he ranges will probably remain uncleared for ages, but cannot long continue to be the resort of this noble animal, whose extinction, not far distant, unless the wholesale destruction by the poaching practices above alluded to, be put a stop to by energetic and well directed efforts, would be a subject of regret both to naturalists and sportsmen, and—when too late—to the Nova Scotians themselves.

I do not believe that more than one species of moose-deer is to be found in North America, though the moose of Canada are said to be larger than those of Nova Scotia and New Brunswick; and I have heard the distinguishing appellation of the black bell moose applied to those of Nova Scotia. I think that the difference in size, if any, is to be accounted for by difference of climate and food.

A bull moose, when at his full-growth, which he attains in his sixth year, will stand seventeen or eighteen hands at the shoulder, and will weigh from one thousand to twelve hundred pounds. His food consists of the leaves and tender branches of maples, birches, moosewood, (of which he is particularly fond, and will travel long distances in search of,) mountain ash, dogwood, witherod, and a variety of other shrubs.

In the winter months, when the leaves have fallen, the tops of young shoots are pulled down by his long muscular upper lip, called the mouffle, resembling the short prehensile proboscis of the tapir, and are bitten off; and, at this season, when overtaken by hunger, on his way through green woods, he will often feed on the boughs of young evergreens, eschewing, however, those of the spruces.

His short neck will not allow him to graze, or pick up anything from the ground without a very wide separation of the fore-legs, or by kneeling, which position, however, he often assumes to crop the fresh grass in some swampy meadow in the spring.

The coat of the moose is composed of long stiff bristles of a light ash color near their roots, and is of a dark russet brown color, which in the bull in winter changes to a glossy black. From behind the ears down the short neck and part of the back runs a hog mane composed of bristles nearly a foot in length. Under the body and on the legs, the hair is of a fawn, or, more properly, sandy color. The eye is black, large, and very expressive.

The flesh of the cow moose in winter is excellent, bearing

the same comparison to beef that venison does to mutton. The mouffle is considered a delicacy; and soup made of it has a strong resemblance to that made of turtle.

Not the least curious feature about this extraordinary animal is the bell, as it is termed, which is a pendant piece of skin, covered with long black hair, growing from the junction of his disproportionately long head with the short neck. The antlers, which adorn the bull only, are massive and palmated, fringed with short spikes or tines, the number of which, as some assert, though erroneously, indicates the age of the animal. The lowest tine extends forwards over the forehead, and supplies the place of the brow antler.

In travelling, the moose, slightly elevating his head, rests his antlers on his shoulders, in which position they do not offer so much obstruction to the progress of the animal through the dense covers of his wooded haunts. Towards the end of January, bull moose shed their horns, which, beginning to shoot again in April, have attained their full growth by September.

These antlers, which often measure four feet from tip to tip, and weigh sometimes as much as sixty pounds, would, if used as such, prove formidable weapons of offence to any adversary; but the moose, unless in the calling season, between the beginning of September and the end of October, and then, only when wounded, seldom uses them against his pursuers. In the calling season, bull moose, animated by the spirit of jealousy, have dreadful conflicts.

An Indian told me that, often when calling moose, in the fall, which is effected by imitating the plaintive cry of the female, upon a trumpet of birch bark, and not succeeding in luring the suspicious animal in their range, he had changed his tactics, and, by imitating the note of the bull moose, had at once induced the bull, whose rage at finding a rival, got the better of his prudence, to come crashing madly through the bushes to destruction.

The same Indian said he had killed a moose, in the fall, a great part of whose flesh was literally worthless, from the wounds he had received in a recent joust. The fore-leg is the most common weapon used by the moose, when attacking a man or dog. Rearing up on his hind-legs, he strikes downwards with the fore-legs with amazing force and velocity. A blow given by a full-grown moose would, if delivered on the head of a man, fracture his skull; and I have seen a dog disabled by a blow from a young one in my possession, then scarcely able to stand, being only a week old. The cow moose gives birth to two calves in April.

As soon as the ground is covered with deep snow, in winter, moose, discontinuing their wandering habits, herd together, and form what is termed a moose-yard, by treading down the snow in some part of the forest covered with hard wood, as all timber and brushwood of a deciduous nature is called, which will afford them good browsing. In one of these yards, they will remain as long as the supply of provender lasts, or until they are disturbed, trampling down the snow in large circles, concentric with, and gradually increasing as they feed outwards from the original starting point.

In Canada, where the snow falls to a much greater depth than in Nova Scotia and New Brunswick, these yards are more regularly defined, and the moose more reluctant to leave them; consequently, the Indians, having discovered a yard, (called *ravagé* by the French Canadians,) taking a favorable opportunity, can return, days or weeks afterwards, with a party of sportsmen, and shoot nearly every moose in the yard.

In the summer months, the moose, partly from being tormented by the hosts of musquitoes and black flies which swarm in the woods at this season, and partly for the sake of feeding on the leaves and tendrils of water-lilies, and other aquatic plants, passes the hottest part of the day nearly submerged in the water of the little ponds and lakes which occur at such frequent intervals in the forests of Nova Scotia and New Brunswick.

He is a fast swimmer, and is difficult to be overtaken, even by the fleet canoe of the Indian, by whom, however, he is often surprised and shot in the long chain of lakes and rivers which, running across Nova Scotia, between Annapolis and Liverpool, is continually traversed by Indians on furring and trapping expeditions.

Although so thoroughly wild, and averse to the approach even of the common animals of the forest, it is a singular circumstance, that the moose when taken young can be easily domesticated, and becomes at once perfectly tame and audaciously familiar.

Having reared and kept for upwards of eight months a young moose, I noticed several curious facts concerning the habits and actions of these animals.

The calf moose in question was brought to me with another of the same age, which could not have been more than a few days old, in the end of April. They were bull and cow, and had been surprised in the woods by some black men who were searching for partridges. Their mother forsaking them on the approach of the men, they were easily caught, and brought into Halifax next day in a bullock-cart with legs bound. The cow died in a few days from the effects of a fall, which as I afterwards found she had received from the cart. The young bull, by great attention and repeated visiting, lived, and appeared to thrive. Few people have succeeded in bringing up young moose; for they have generally sickened and died from want of suitable and natural food.

I was advised to procure a domestic cow to suckle my moose calf—knowing, however, that, from the food of the moose being principally leaves, branches, and bark, its milk could not be so rich as that of the common cow, I diluted it with an equal quantity of water, which I gave to the young moose from a bottle, thickening it gradually with a little Indian meal.

When I found that he would mouth and swallow leaves and tender boughs, I sent into the woods every morning for a fresh supply of the young shoots of maples, moose-wood, dogwood, and witherod, of the leaves and berries of which last two shrubs, moose are especially fond from their extreme bitterness. A lump of rock-salt appeared to afford him great satisfaction, and might have been conducive to his health.

In November, he being at the time eight months old, and in

perfectly excellent health and condition, I adopted by mischance an expedient which caused his untimely, and, by me, much regretted death. The winter having set in, and it being inconvenient to send into the woods for a supply of boughs, I resolved to try a substitute. I fixed upon turnips, of which a pailful was given to him one evening, and which he appeared to relish greatly. Next morning, to my dismay, I found the poor creature dead, his body dreadfully distended, so much so as to have caused death by suffocation, if it had not been brought on by any other internal derangement. On inquiring as to the probable cause of his death, I learnt too late that turnips, when given too suddenly and in too great quantities to domestic cattle, will often cause death.

I regretted losing him the more, as I intended in the following spring to have sent him to England, as a present to the Zoological Society, which at present I believe, does not possess a living specimen of the *Cerves alces*, either of Europe or America.

So tame was my young moose, that he would come into a room and jump several times over chairs, backwards and forwards, for a piece of bread. He had a great *penchant* for tobacco-smoke, which, if puffed in his face, would cause him to rub his head with great satisfaction against the individual.

His gambols were sometimes very amusing. Throwing back his ears, and dropping the under jaw, he would gallop madly up and down on a grass plot, now and then rearing up on his hind legs, and striking ferociously with his fore feet at the trunks of trees, or anything within reach, varying the amusement by an occasional shy and kick behind at some imaginary object. No palings could keep him from gardens, in which, when not watched he would constantly be found, reveling on the boughs of currant and lilac bushes; in fact, tasting fruit and flowers most indiscriminately. On being approached for the purpose of being turned out, the cunning little brute would immediately lie down, from which position, his hide being as callous as that of a jackass, he could be got up with difficulty.

In the very hot days of summer, when he appeared to miss

the cool plunge in the lake, which these animals, in their wild condition, always indulge in at this time of year, I continually caused buckets of water to be thrown over him.

At the Agricultural show at Halifax, in the fall of 1853, a young moose was exhibited in company with a domestic cow which suckled it. It appeared from the owner's account, that the cow had in the spring strayed into the woods, as cattle often will do, causing the owner a long and weary trudge through the bush, till guided by the sound of their tinkling bells, he finds them.

A few weeks afterwards, she found her way back to the farm, in company with a young moose, towards whom she manifested the same affection as if it had been her own offspring. It is probable that her milk agreed with the young moose, owing to her having been forced during her residence in the woods, to feed on the same description of food as these animals.

Some years ago, a tame moose, full-grown, was in the possession of a person named Schultz, who keeps the eighteen mile house from Halifax, on the Truro road, by the side of the Grand Lake. This animal had been, by great trouble, broken in to draw a sledge, which he did with great ease and at a surprising pace. Being allowed to roam about at large during the day, he would often swim across the Grand Lake to the opposite shore, about two miles distant, whence he would return at the sound of the conk, which is generally used in the interior of Nova Scotia to recall laborers from the woods. I believe he was finally sent to the States, where these animals in a domesticated state, fetch high prices, exciting almost as great curiosity, though they are still occasionally found in the highlands of New York, as they would in England.

The moose is as strictly an inhabitant of the forests of Eastern North America, as the American elk or wapiti is of the prairies of Western America, the domains of one beginning nearly where those of the other leave off.

Commencing with Nova Scotia, which, I believe, contains a greater number of these animals than any district of its size in North America, we find him abundant in the wild forests of the State of Maine, and, though now only occasionally met with, still farther west in the same latitude, in the mountainous district called the Adirondack, or the highlands of New York.

Throughout his whole book Lieut. Hardy proves himself to be a devoted lover of nature; but as he throws a capital fly, his piscatorial facts and incidents possess a peculiar value. After commenting upon the general mildness of the Acadian climate, and especially upon the delights of spring he thus proceeds:

To the disciple of old Isaak, too, this glorious season is hailed with delight, as it entices the trout from his wintry retreats, and causes the noble salmon to ascend his favorite rivers, and revel in the cool fresh water. No country can offer greater inducements to the fly fisherman—particularly him who seeks combat with the 'king of fishes'—than British North America.

Unhindered by bailiffs, trespassing notices or other obstructions to the enjoyment of fishing in the Old World (where even Norway has loosened the angler's purse-strings, before allowing him a cast over the waters of her salmon rivers,) the orthodox sportsman may here roam from stream to stream, casting his fly, at almost every throw, with a certainty of success, over pools by the side of which many a Cis-Atlantic angler would envy him his position.

Salmon ascend the rivers of the provinces at different times of the spring and summer. They first appear in the rivers of the southern and south-eastern coasts of Nova Scotia. In Gold River, which flows into Chester Bay, about forty miles from Halifax, salmon will take a fly in the first week in April, even before the snow-water has been all discharged from the river.

The rivers to the north-east of Halifax are not favored by their visits till the end of May and the beginning of June, while they do not ascend the Atlantic rivers of New Brunswick till late in June.

After spawning, which is completed by the middle of November in all the provincial streams, the salmon, aided by the fall floods, or freshets, as they are termed, return to the sea. Sometimes, however, they will pass the winter in a torpid and emaciated state under the ice in the lakes.

In the beginning of April, I have seen two spent salmon, evidently having been under the ice all the winter, taken with the worm by a trout-fisherman, in a small stream about seven miles distant from Halifax, called Salmon River.

About a month after the arrival of the older fish in the river, the grilse revisit their native fresh water. From their beauty, liveliness, and delicate flavor, when caught, they afford great sport to the fly fisherman, and may be taken with an occasional older and heavier salmon, from the middle of July till the end of August, in the northern rivers of New Brunswick.

The size of the salmon which frequent the different rivers of these provinces varies considerably. In the rivers to the westward of Nova Scotia, the fish are large, twelve or fifteen pounds being the common weights.

The sea trout ascends for a short distance only, and with the tide, those rivers of New Brunswick which flow into the Gulf of St. Lawrence, the streams of Prince Edward's Island, and the river Philip in Nova Scotia.

A fish, generally known by the settlers under the name of sea trout, white trout, or tide trout, is very numerous in all the rivers of the provinces which it ascends in company with the salmon.

This fish is in reality the common river trout, which acquiring habits like those of the salmon, and spending the winter months in salt water, returns to the river a much livelier and prettier fish than its relatives, which have not attempted the voyage.

The true sea trout has no pink spots, and is of a dark bluish green on the back; the tide trout is marked in precisely the same way as the river trout, only its markings have become fainter.

Tide trout are very bright and silvery; their flesh is firm and pink, like that of the salmon. I have caught these fish in all stages of their migration to and from the sea, and am satisfied that they are no other than the common river trout, which have found their way to the salt water, and have certainly benefited by it.

They are lively fish when caught as they ascend their native rivers, and show determined play, sometimes salmon-like, attempting a jump. They often attain a weight of four or five pounds, though they average from one to three pounds. When they are numerous, a day's sport with these silvery fish by the side of a fine rapid river is inferior only to salmon fishing.

In every river, lake, and mountain streamlet throughout the Northern States, and the British possessions of the northern continent of America, is found the fresh water trout.

Though of many shades of color, sizes and conformations in different rivers and lakes, it has been determined that only one description of the fresh water or river trout is found in this continent.

The trout does not appear to love the larger and rougher rivers, and is not often taken in them of a large size. I have, however, caught trout of four pounds weight when fishing for salmon in the Nepisiguit.

Small clear streams, which have a sandy or shingly bottom, appear to be their favorite resorts. For instance, the Tabusintac, one of the prettiest streamlets of New Brunswick, running through thirty miles of most romantic scenery, is literally alive with trout. In summer time the bed of this river is, where the stream is broad and shallow, almost dried up.

On these occasions, the settlers residing near the mouth of the river net them in the deep holes, and barrel down large quantities annually.

The river trout of America is one of the most beautiful fresh-water fishes in the world. Its back is of a glossy olive green, fading towards the belly into delicate primrose. On the back and sides are fantastic markings of deep yellow. The sides are dotted with spangles of the most vivid azure and crimson.

The lake trout, which is found abundantly in every sheet of fresh water, whether having communication with the sea or not, in the Provinces, is not colored with such richness or purity of tint as the river trout. Neither is he generally such a well shaped fish.

In lakes with high rocky shores, in which the water is deep and dark colored, the trout are almost black on their backs, their spots and markings dull, and the belly of a dirty orange color. The head and jaws of these fish are disproportionately large, and their flesh comparatively unpalatable.

In others, trout are found of a light color, well-proportioned, with small heads and thick shoulders, and as game and well flavored as the river trout.

In some lakes, trout will only rise at the artificial fly during one month in the year, while in others they will take the fly readily at any time of the year that the surface of the water is free from ice.

As a general rule, however, trout will not rise in the lakes during several weeks of the extremely hot weather, which comes in the months of July and August, unless very early in the morning before the sun is fairly on the water.

Trout may readily be taken in the winter by cutting a hole through the ice on a lake, and by fishing for them with bait. They at once flock round the opening in the ice in great numbers, and are pulled out and thrown on the ice, where, in a minute or two, they freeze perfectly stiff.

I have taken them in the depth of winter with bait, in a run out of a large lake, where, from the rapidity of the water, ice had not formed.

Several of the New Brunswick lakes contain trout of a large size, sometimes attaining a weight of six or seven pounds. This fish, I believe, is the *Salmo ferox*, known in Scotland by the name of the Loch Awe trout. He is a comparatively worthless fish, though, from his size and vigor, he affords good sport to the troller.

Many other fish inhabit the rivers and lakes of New Brunswick and Nova Scotia which, as never pursued for the sake of sport, shall be noticed briefly here.

The most frequent of this class are shad, gaspereaux, smelts, eels, white fish, perch, sturgeon, bass, cat-fish and suckers. There are also others which at present have not even a scientific name.

The shad and the gaspereaux are both similar to the herring in habits and appearance. The gaspereaux, known to the settlers by the name of alewives, ascend the rivers of New

Boston and Nova Scotia in vast shoals from the middle of April to the end of June. They are rather larger than the common herring. They form one of the principal items of exportation in Nova Scotia, in whose rivers they are taken in scoop nets attached to long poles. They look very pretty and tempting to the fly fisherman, when sporting in the cool fresh water near the mouths of rivers, their silvery sides gleaming in the sunbeams. Unfortunately, however, they will rarely take a fly; so much so as to make it quite useless to throw over them.

Perch may be taken in great numbers in the lakes, with bait. They are insipid in flavor and seldom exceed eight inches in length.

Nearly every river in these Provinces contains eels in abundance. The settlers, who smoke and use them as an article of food in winter, take them in hoop baskets with a narrow mouth, and baited with offal. As soon as a sufficient number of eels have entered the basket or bag, it is quickly drawn ashore, where the eels are killed with sticks after a long contest, for these fish are most tenacious of life.

The sucker is a disagreeable-looking fish with a long cartilaginous mouth opening underneath the head. They swim near the bottom of rivers, and of the runs between lakes. Their flesh is unpalatable.

After giving his readers a whole chapter of advice in regard to fishing tackle and flies, Lieut. Hardy proceeds as follows:

The Yankees have invented a spring gaff, and a very ingenious contrivance it is. At the end of the handle are two jaws, each similar to the iron of the common gaff. These bend back on the principle of a steel trap. When bent back at right angles to the handle, they catch and are released, flying back to their original position with great strength by virtue of a powerful spring, on the instrument coming in contact with any part of a fish. It is said that a salmon is completely paralyzed, when he is caught by the strong jaws of this instrument. However, from the danger resulting to one's own legs in using this powerful weapon, in the hurry and excitement attendant on landing a salmon, I prefer the old gaff.

Many sportsmen think it necessary to go out for a fishing excursion with their legs encased in high, cumbrous waterproof boots or leggings. It is a great mistake. They are the worst possible things for slipping on the stones and rocks in brooks or rivers, and encumber the general motions of the body. One must make up one's mind to get wet—possibly, regularly ducked, which would be a worse case if the boots were on at the time, as they would fill with water, and prevent the possibility of getting dry so long as they were on.

A good pair of dry worsted socks, taken in the pocket, to put on when the day's sport is concluded, will prevent the chance of a cold, catarrh, or rheumatism. When on a fishing expedition of several days, the sportsman, living constantly in the open air, need not fear any of these maladies. It is the change from a house to a camp, or *vice versâ*, which is to be dreaded on this account. An Indian will tell you, that if he goes into a house, and sits by a fire, he is sure to catch cold; so do you generally in your first night in camp, but by the next night it is all gone. The secret is that you are breathing the same atmosphere.

The best description of cloth of which the sportman's clothes, whether he be hunting or fishing, in winter and summer, should be made, is the homespun cloth of the country.

It is a mixture of wool and cotton, the less cotton the better. It is strong, warm, and light, and when saturated with water, will dry sooner than any other description.

Flannel shirts form an indispensable item in a wardrobe for the bush, whether in summer or winter. Scarlet is a bad color for any part of the fishing costume. In a clear river, the appearance of a red shirt will scare salmon from a pool as effectually as a passing canoe.

The angler in British North America must at all times of the summer expect great annoyance from the attacks of the insect tribe, such as mosquitos, black flies, and sand flies. They literally swarm in the woods, by the lake, or river side, and are all equally venomous. Even the Indians suffer from their attacks. The settlers daub every exposed part with grease, or sometimes even tar. Compositions called Mosquito Repellant, and Angler's Defence, are sold in all the provincial towns. They are used as lotions, and remain efficacious for about half an hour after application.

One of the best means of keeping off the flies, is by wearing a veil of the finest gauze fastened round the cap, and drawn in round the neck under the chin. It forms a bag round the head; and even the diminutive sand-fly cannot penetrate its meshes, if the gauze be fine. Old kid gloves, with the ends of fingers cut off, will be found useful in protecting the hands.

As Lieut. Hardy's publication was intended chiefly for the edification of English readers, he has found it necessary to consider at some length a variety of matters quite familiar to sportsmen and others on this side of the Atlantic. The substance of his general information bearing upon Nova Scotia has already been given in the foregoing pages; and if I were not afraid of having the wind taken out of my own sail, and had the necessary space at my command, I should take pleasure in reproducing some of his exploits, not only in Nova Scotia, but also in New Brunswick. It is due to myself, however, to state that, notwithstanding the acknowledged skill of Lieut. Hardy, my name was one of terror, or perhaps of affection, to the salmon of the British American Provinces, for at least half a dozen years before the music of American waterfalls had gratified his ear. As truth compels me to yield the palm to him in regard to all matters appertaining to moose-hunting, I cannot but believe that he will award to me the wreath of artificial flies, and a genius for fish stories if not for angling. While he may occasionally take pleasure in "drawing a long bow," I hope he will not object to my throwing a long line, when the peerless salmon has started upon his annual summer tour.

THE END.

A PARTING PARAGRAPH.

As the author could not make it convenient to read the proofs of this publication while it was going through the press, he asks the indulgence of his readers for occasional errors, some of which may be corrected as follows:

VOLUME I.

Page 1, line 4, for pilgrimagés, read *pilgrimage.*
" 12, in title, for Legends, read *Legend.*
" 13, " 23, for was seen, read *were seen.*
" 14, " 33, for little, read *lithe.*
" 14, " 35, for the, read *ten.*
" 20, " 15, after down, add *to.*
" 424, " 1, for the Hickory-nut Gap, read *Ashville.*
" 449, " 7, for with, read *if on a.*

VOLUME II.

Page 19, line 13, for Bolestown, read *Boiestown.*
" 70, " 14, for whereat, read *whereupon.*
" 72, " 18, after swamp, insert *and it.*
" 111, " 34, for one, read *our.*
" 137, " 32, for break of day, read *breakfast.*
" 160, " 15, for regious, read *regions.*
" 161, " 33, for larks, read *lark.*
" 173, " 35, for Toumey, read *Tuomey.*
" 205, " 22, for vassa, read *vassc.*
" 216, " 1, for the journey, read *my journey.*
" 329, " 6, for streams, read *stream.*
" 332, " 11, for Miramacha, read *Miramachi.*
" 352, " 34, insert *fish* after game.

When he comes to the article on Pike Fishing, the reader will be pleased to settle the difficulty which exists there between the pronouns.

Volume VI.

No.
41. The Microscope and its Marvels.
42. Pre-Columbian Discovery of America.
43. Herman—A Tale.
44. Public Libraries.
45. Australia and Van Dieman's Land.
46. The Lone Star—A Tale.
47. Religion of the Greeks.
48. Heyne—A Biography.

Volume VII.

49. Water Supply of Towns.
50. Ancient Scandinavia.
51. The Lost Letter—The Somnambule.
52. Life in an Indiaman.
53. The Law of Storms.
54. Santilian's Choice—A Tale.
55. The Isthmus of Panama.
56. Daniel de Foe.

Volume VIII.

57. Ocean Routes.
58. Cromwell and his Contemporaries.
59. Life at Græfenberg.
60. Life at Græfenberg—Concluded.
61. The Black Gondola—A Tale.
62. Ancient Philosophic Sects.
63. The Wonders of Human Folly.
64. Lady Mary Wortley Montagu.

Volume IX.

65. Recent Decorative Art.
66. Alchemy and the Alchemists.
67. The Lost Laird—A Tale of '45.
68. German Poets and Poetry.

No.
69. The Deserts of Africa.
70. Sigismund Temple.
71. Electric Communications.
72. Fichte—A Biography.

Volume X.

73. Ancient Rites and Mysteries.
74. Siberia and the Russian Penal Settlements.
75. Harriette; or, The Rash Reply.
76. Childhood; or, Experimental Philosophy.
77. Confucius.
78. The Temptation.
79. Siam and the Siamese.
80. Thomas Moore.

Volume XI.

81. The Isthmus of Suez.
82. Animal Instincts and Intelligence.
83. Realized Wishes—A Tale.
84. Troubadors and Trouveres.
85. New Zealand.
86. Tower of Fontenay, and the Heiress of the Vaughans.
87. Industrial Investments and Associations.
88. Lord Brougham.

Volume XII.

89. Railway Communications.
90. The Incas of Peru.
91. Marfreda; or, The Icelanders.
92. What is Philosophy.
93. European Intercourse with Japan.
94. The Half-Caste—A Tale.
95. The Progress of America.
96. The Duke of Wellington.

NOTICES OF THE PRESS.

One of the cheapest and best of the useful knowledge Publications of the day.—*Literary World.*

Every family in the land should possess a set of these books.—*Saturday Evening Post.*

We commend this series of Fireside Books with no grudging tone of praise. They are unexceptionable in their moral tone, and of varied interest.—*Southern Lit. Gazette.*

Every choice Library should possess these "Papers."—*Penna. Inquirer.*

A good book for Family Fireside Reading, and conveys a great deal of instruction in an agreeable and popular manner.—*N. American and U. S. Gazette.*

TAILOR'S STATISTICS OF COAL: Including Mineral Bituminous Substances employed in Arts and Manufactures; with their Geographical, Geological, and Commercial Distribution, and Amount of Production and Consumption on the American Continent; with Incidental Statistics of the Iron Manufacture. By R. C. Taylor, F. G. S. L., &c., &c. Second Edition, revised and brought down to 1854, by S. S. Haldeman, Prof. of Natural Science, &c. 1 vol. 8vo., colored maps and plates, $5.00

[*From the Scientific American.*]

A new edition of Taylor's Statistics of Coal is published by J. W. Moore, of Philadelphia. When the first edition was published a few years ago, its thorough scientific character and accurate information at once brought new laurels to its able author. The *Edinburg Review* passed a high eulogium upon it, and with no part of it have we ever heard a fault mentioned. This edition is revised and brought down to 1854, by Professor S. S. Haldeman, the venerable author having departed this life in 1851. It is chiefly devoted to the Coal and Iron natural resources of America; and no American, we assert, can have a proper idea, of the vast internal resources of his country and be ignorant of the contents of this book. No library, public or private, can be complete without a copy of it. The publisher has spared no pains in making this an attractive work, it being embellished with numerous wood cuts and colored maps, printed on fine paper, 640 pages 8vo.

BURTON'S ANATOMY OF MELANCHOLY. What it is, with all the Kinds, Causes, Symptoms, Prognostics, and Several Cures of it. In Three Partitions; with their several Sections, Members, and Sub-sections, Philosophically, Medically, and Historically opened and cut up. A new edition, corrected and enriched by translations of the numerous classical extracts. To which is prefixed an account of the author. From the last London edition. 1 vol. 8vo., cloth, $2.50.

[*City Item.*]

The book is an inexhaustible fountain, where every mind, no matter what may be its peculiar organization, or the nature of its momentary needs, can draw at will nourishment and strength; such perfect mingling of immense erudition, profound thought, sparkling humor, and exuberant fancy, exists no where else out of Shakspeare.

THE WORKS OF MICHAEL DE MONTAIGNE, comprising his Essays, Letters, a Journey through Germany and Italy; with notes from all the Commentators, Biographical and Bibliographical Notices, &c., &c., &c. By William Hazlett. 1 vol. 8vo., pp. 686, cloth, $2.50.

[*Inquirer.*]

This is a truly valuable publication, and embodies much that may be read with profit.

[*North American.*]

This work is too well known, and too highly appreciated by the literary world to require eulogy.

[*Hallam.*]

So long as an unaffected style and good nature shall charm—so long as the lovers of desultory and cheerful conversation shall be more numerous than those who prefer a lecture or a sermon—so long as reading is sought by the many as an amusement in idleness, or a resource in pain—so long will Montaigne be among the favorite authors of mankind.

THE KORAN, commonly called the Alcoran of Mahommed; translated into English immediately from the original Arabic, with Explanatory Notes, taken from the most approved Commentators. To which is prefixed a preliminary discourse by George Sale, gent. A new edition, with a Memoir of the Translator, and with various readings and illustrative notes from Savary's Version of the Koran. 1 vol. 8vo., cloth. Numerous maps and plates, $2.50.

[*Louisville Journal.*]

This work is too well known to require a lengthy eulogy, and no library, public or private, is complete without this celebrated and interesting work. The publisher has spared no pains to make this an attractive work, being the sixth edition, printed on fine paper with numerous maps.

WALKER'S MANLY EXERCISES. Containing Rowing, Sailing, Riding, Driving, Racing, Hunting, Shooting, and other Manly Sports, the whole carefully revised or written by "CRAVEN," from the Ninth London Edition, embellished with 44 beautiful engravings. 12mo. neatly bound.

[*From the Boston Daily Journal.*]

This is an American edition of an English work, and is an excellent and valuable treatise, illustrated by numerous engravings upon various manly exercises, mentioned in the title. So far as these exercises can be taught by rote, this manual is just the work to do it. There are few huntsmen, gymnasts, or yachters, &c., who will not derive many valuable hints from this volume.

[*From the N. Y. Evening Times.*]

In the present completeness is the best work of its class.

There can be no doubt of its being a very valuable book, both as a manual of instruction in many useful acquirements, as well as a very important manual for the development of the body, and thus securing a healthy and vigorous system. It is one of the best books parents can place in the hands of their boys.

KNAPP'S LECTURES ON CHRISTIAN THEOLOGY. Translated by Leonard Wood, Jun., D. D., President of Bowdoin College, Brunswick, Maine. Sixth American Edition, $2.50.

This work is used as a Text Book in many of the Theological Schools in the United States.

THE COMPLETE PROSE WORKS OF JOHN MILTON, with a Biographical Introduction by Rufus W. Griswold. Bound in 2 vols. 8vo., and also one thick 8vo. vol.

This is the only edition of the complete prose works of that highly celebrated author, John Milton, that is published in this country, and it is needless to add that a copy should be found in every gentleman's library, and no public institution should be without a copy.

THE THEORY OF EFFECT, embracing the contrast of Light and Shade, of Color and Harmony. By an Artist. With fifteen illustrations by Hinckley. 18mo. cloth, 75 cents.

[*From the Baltimore Advertiser.*]

This work is by an artist of Philadelphia, and is an elementary treatise which will be found very useful to those who desire to learn the principles of the art of drawing. The work, though brief, contains many useful hints and suggestions of a practical character, together with simple and efficient rules.

THE CALCULATOR'S CONSTANT COMPANION for Practical Men, Machinists, Mechanics, and Engineers. By Oliver Byrne. $1.00.

[*From the Boston Daily Atlas.*]

This little volume is well adapted to its object, which is to be a labor-saving machine to practical men in making the necessary calculations of their daily business avocations, and will be found highly useful for all kinds of mechanics and engineers.

A MANUAL FOR PRACTICAL SURVEYORS, containing methods indispensably necessary for Actual Field Operations. By E. W. Beans, Norristown, Montgomery Co., Pa. 18mo. cloth, 75 cents; 18mo. sheep, 75 cents; 18mo. tucks, $1.25

[*From the London Artisan.*]

The author of this work is perfectly right when he says in his Preface, that "many of the publications in general use appear to have been written by those who were engaged in the instruction of youth, and who were unacquainted with the practical part of surveying." "There seems to be wanted a more minute detail of expedients employed in the field." This little work, which is not too bulky for the pocket, is just the sort of thing which a young surveyor ought to study before commencing practice; or he will find that all his fine problems, learned at school, will be thrown at his head by his impatient "chief." We therefore take pleasure in recommending this work.

THE INSTRUCTIVE GIFT; or, Narratives for the Young. Translated from the German. Illustrated by 8 beautiful colored plates. Cloth, $1.00; cloth, gilt, $1.25.

MY PLAY IS STUDY: A book for Children. Translated from the German by L. Lermont. Illustrated by 4 beautiful colored plates. Cloth, 62 cents; cloth, gilt, 75 cents.

EXAMPLES OF GOODNESS. Narrated for the Young. Translated from the German. Illustrated by 4 beautiful colored plates. Cloth, 62 cents; cloth, gilt, 75 cents.

CHAMBERS' INFORMATION FOR THE PEOPLE. A popular Cyclopedia, Tenth American Edition, with numerous additions, and more than five hundred Engravings. 2 vols. Royal 8vo. half morocco, $5.00.

CHAMBERS' REPOSITORY of Instructive and Amusing Tracts, a Collection of choice Miscellaneous matter. Vols. 1 and 2 now ready. Fancy boards, 38 cents; cloth, 50 cents.

CHAMBERS' MISCELLANY of useful and entertaining Tracts, complete in 20 vols. Fancy boards, 38 cents; 10 vols. cloth, $7.50. 10 vols. half calf and morocco, $12.00.

AN EXPOSITION OF THE PROPHECIES OF THE APOCALYPSE, by the Rev. James De Pui, A. M., Chaplain in the U. S. Army. (Just published.) 12mo. cloth, 75 cents.

SMITH'S JUVENILE DRAWING BOOK, containing the rudiments of the Art, in a series of Progressive Lessons, 24 plates of subjects, easily copied. Small 4to. cloth, 16th edition, 75 cents.

HOUSEHOLD VERSES, by Bernard Barton. Embellished with a Vignette Title-Page and Frontispiece. 12mo. Illuminated covers. New edition, 50 cents. Cloth, gilt, 75 cents.

SCENES AND INCIDENTS ON THE WESTERN PRAIRIES, during Eight Expeditions, and including a residence of nearly nine years in Northern Mexico. Illustrated with Maps and Engravings. By Josiah Gregg.

[*Inquirer*]

The author's motives in the above work is to convey as much information on the subjects treated on as he could compass. His descriptions are, therefore, real descriptions, and his anecdotes real anecdotes.

MYSTERIES OF CITY LIFE; or, Stray Leaves from the World's Book. By James Rees, author of the "Philadelphia Locksmith," "The Night-Hawk Papers," &c. 12mo. Paper, 75 cents. Cloth, $1.00

BIBLIA HEBRAICA. Secundom Epitiones. Jos. Athiae, Joannis, Leusden, Jo. Simonis, Alirumque, inprimis, Everardi VanDer Hooght, D. Henrici Opitii, et Wolfii Heidin heim, cum additionibus Clavique Masoretica et Rabbinica Augusti Hahn. Mune denuo recognita et emendata ab Isaaco Leeser, V. D. M., et Josepho Jaquett, V. B. M. The above is stereotyped from the last Leipsic edition, and beautifully bound in the German style, thick 8vo. $3. New edition.

www.ingramcontent.com/pod-product-compliance
Lightning Source LLC
LaVergne TN
LVHW021300110826
845150LV00003B/438

* 9 7 8 1 4 2 5 5 5 9 7 9 3 *